WARWICK THE KINGMAKER

Warwick the Kingmaker
Politics, Power and Fame

A. J. POLLARD

hambledon
continuum

For Sandra, Richard and Edward

Hambledon Continuum is an imprint of Continuum Books
Continuum UK, The Tower Building, 11 York Road, London SE1 7NX
Continuum US, 80 Maiden Lane, Suite 704, New York, NY 10038

www.continuumbooks.com

First published 2007

British Library Cataloguing-in-Publication Data
A catalogue record for this book is available from the British Library.

ISBN 978 1 84725 182 4

Typeset by Egan Reid, Auckland, New Zealand

Contents

Illustrations

Plates

Map

BEAUCHAMP

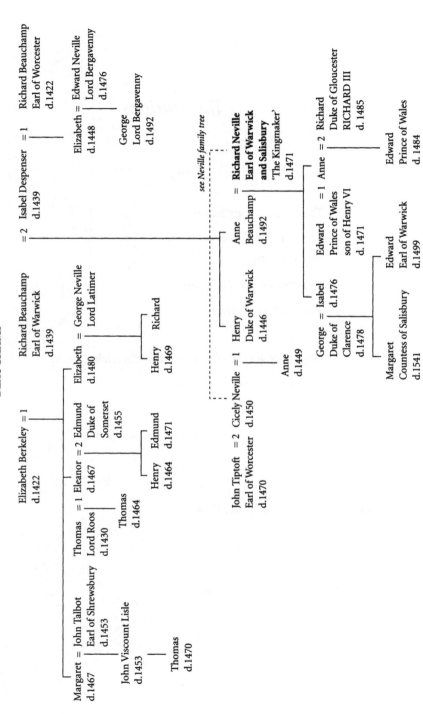

Richard Beauchamp
Earl of Warwick
d.1439

= 2   Isabel Despenser
d.1439

= 1   Richard Beauchamp
Earl of Worcester
d.1422

Elizabeth = Edward Neville
d.1448   Lord Bergavenny
d.1476

George
Lord Bergavenny
d.1492

Elizabeth Berkeley = 1
d.1422

Elizabeth = George Neville
d.1480   Lord Latimer

Henry   Richard
d.1469

Margaret = John Talbot
d.1467   Earl of Shrewsbury
d.1453

Thomas = 1 Eleanor = 2 Edmund
Lord Roos   d.1467   Duke of
d.1430   Somerset
             d.1455

John Viscount Lisle
d.1453

Thomas
d.1464

Henry   Edmund
d.1464   d.1471

Thomas
d.1470

see Neville family tree

John Tiptoft = 2 Cicely Neville = 1 Henry
Earl of Worcester   d.1450   Duke of Warwick
d.1470   d.1446

Anne
d.1449

Anne
Beauchamp
d.1492

= **Richard Neville
Earl of Warwick
and Salisbury**
'The Kingmaker'
d.1471

George = Isabel
Duke of   d.1476
Clarence
d.1478

Edward
Prince of Wales
son of Henry VI
d.1471

Anne =2 Richard
Duke of Gloucester
RICHARD III
d.1485

Margaret
Countess of Salisbury
d.1541

Edward
Earl of Warwick
d.1499

Edward
Prince of Wales
d.1484

NEVILLE

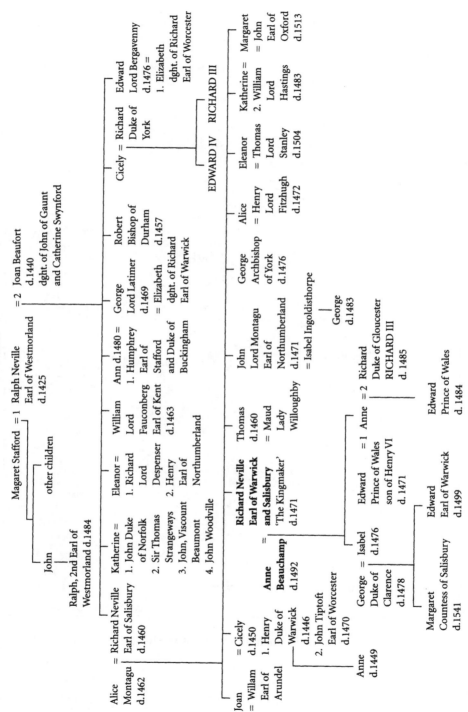

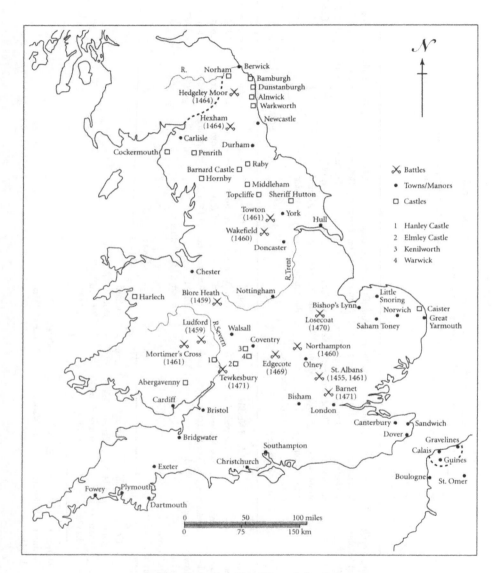

England during the War of the Roses

Preface

When I became a postgraduate student at Bristol University in 1964, Charles Ross proposed that I should undertake a study of Warwick the Kingmaker. After a month or two of preliminary exploration we decided that there was not enough material for a doctoral thesis and that I should move on to a study of the Talbot family in the fifteenth century. I became embroiled in the affairs of the Neville family later, after I had moved to northern England. Researching the history of the north-east, especially northern Yorkshire and County Durham in the later fifteenth century, it was impossible not to run into Warwick and his father, another Richard Neville, earl of Salisbury. My return to where I almost began lay in the study of Warwick as a northerner. This full study of his career, however, derives from the contribution I made on Warwick the Kingmaker for the *Oxford DNB*, which I completed several years ago. My knowledge has deepened and my thoughts moved on since then, in some respects significantly. This work thus offers a modified interpretation of the earl's career, but I am grateful to both Henry Summerson and Christine Carpenter for helping me shape my perception and putting me right on several matters then.

Readers will also become aware that I owe an immense debt to other scholars who have gone before me. I wish to acknowledge in particular David Grummitt's work on Calais, Edward Meek's research on diplomacy in the 1460s, Livia Visser-Fuchs' important analysis of Burgundian chroniclers, especially Waurin, Peter Booth's consideration of Cumbria, and Christine Carpenter's study of Warwickshire society.[1] Above all, I owe a great deal to the work of Michael Hicks. It has been particularly difficult writing this book in the shadow of his own *Warwick the Kingmaker*, published in 1998. I cannot possibly match the depth of his scholarship and knowledge of the record sources. I readily, and gratefully, record my debt to his research on the Warwick inheritance and on Warwick's naval power.[2] And I make no apology for following his meticulous reconstruction of the earl's itinerary. I have, however, placed a different emphasis on aspects of the earl's career and interpreted several moments in it differently. Moreover, in contrast to Professor Hicks' account, the focus here is on Warwick as he was at the height of his power in the 1460s.[3] The reader will find, too, that I have not written at length on the general political history of 1449–71. I have consciously avoided being drawn into the debates and controversies about the last years of

Henry VI's reign and the first decade of Edward IV's. The 1450s, in particular, is a complex and difficult decade on which to write, and several historians have offered their own interpretation of it. To some extent Hicks' study of Warwick is also his study of the politics of the last decade of the reign of that unfortunate monarch, Henry VI.[4] I myself have written elsewhere on this and the Wars of the Roses.[5] This is about Warwick the Kingmaker's role in the politics of his time, not about the politics themselves in detail.

I have incurred many other debts of gratitude. First I must thank Tony Morris for asking me to write this book. He knows how long it has taken to travel from first suggestion to final publication. I would like also like to thank those who attended lectures and seminars at Cardiff, Durham, London, the University of Illinois and the International Medieval Congress at Kalamazoo for patiently hearing my versions of various chapters and making helpful suggestions. My colleagues at Teesside allowed me to have a sabbatical term at a critical moment, for which I am most grateful. The library staff, too, handled a stream of inter-library loan requests with unfailing patience. Melanie Devine and Janette Garrett have been generous in making their research material available to me. Alexandra Elam helped out with some finer points of Italian; Geoff Watkins with subtleties of French. Rob Liddiard, who shares my penchant for the Purnell Partwork of Churchill's *History of the English Speaking People*, came to my rescue with a copy of Charles Ross's essay on Warwick; John Ramsden tipped me off about I. D. Colvin's work; and Jim Bolton was a source of wisdom about London and the collection of customs. David Grummitt was exceptionally generous in allowing me to read draft chapters of his work on Calais, without which that chapter could not have been written. I'm also grateful to him for reading it in draft. Above all, I am indebted to Linda Clark who not only made draft copies of the biographies of members of parliament between 1422 and 1461 available to me, but also read the complete typescript, helping me to clarify the text and saving me from many errors. Nigel Saul, who read the typescript for Hambledon Continuum, had valuable advice to offer as well as picking up more errors. Other mistakes, for which I am entirely responsible, no doubt remain. I would also like to thank Ben Hayes, Barbara Ball, Eva Osborne, Slav Todorov and David White for taking the work from typescript to published book. Last, as is always the case, I thank my wife Sandra for putting up with long periods of withdrawal, both literal and metaphorical (and not for the first time), as I grappled with the mighty earl. To her this book is dedicated with love.

A. J. Pollard
St Valentine's Day, 2007

Abbreviations

Annales	'Annales Rerum Anglicarum', in *The Wars of the English in France*, ed. J. Stevenson (RS, 2 vols in 3, 1864), ii (2)
Arrivall	*The Historie of the Arrivall of King Edward IV*, ed. J. Bruce (Camden Society, 1838)
Bale's Chronicle	'Bale's Chronicle', in *Six Town Chronicles*, ed. R. Flenley (Oxford, 1911)
BIHR	*Bulletin of the Institute of Historical Research*
CFR	*Calendar of Fine Rolls*
Chastellain, *Oeuvres*	G. de Chastellain, *Oeuvres*, ed. K. Letenhove (Bruxelles, 6 vols, 1863–5)
Chronicle of the Rebellion in Lincolnshire	*The Chronicle of the Rebellion in Lincolnshire, 1470*, ed. J. G. Nichols (Camden Society, 1847)
Commynes, *Memoirs*	Philippe de Commynes, *Memoirs: the Reign of Louis XI, 1461–83*, trans. Michael Jones (Harmondsworth,1972)
CPR	*Calendar of Patent Rolls*
CSPM	*Calendar of State Papers and Manuscripts … of Milan*, vol. 1, ed. A. B. Hinds (1912)
EETS	Early English Text Society
EHR	*English Historical Review*
Eng. Chron.	*An English Chronicle 1377–1461*, ed. W. Marx (Woodbridge, 2003)
Great Chronicle	*The Great Chronicle of London*, eds A. H. Thomas and I. D Thornley (1938)
Gregory's Chronicle	*The Historical Collections of London Citizens in the Fifteenth Century*, ed. J. Gairdner (Camden, new series, xvii, 1876)
Hicks, *Warwick*	Michael Hicks, *Warwick the Kingmaker* (Oxford: Blackwell, 1998)
HR	*Historical Research*
John Vale's Book	*The Politics of Fifteenth Century England: John Vale's Book*, eds M. L. Kekewich and others

	(Stroud: Sutton for the Richard III and Yorkist History Trust, 1995)
NH	Northern History
Oxford DNB	The Oxford Dictionary of National Biography: From the earliest times to the year 2000, eds H. C. G. Mathew and B. Harrison, 61 vols (Oxford, 2004)
PL	The Paston Letters, ed. J. Gairdner, 6 vols (1904)
PROME	The Parliament Rolls of Medieval England, ed. C. Given-Wilson, 16 vols (Woodbridge, 2005)
RS	Rolls Series
Short English Chronicle	'The Short English Chronicle', in Three Fifteenth Century Chronicles, ed. J. Gairdner (Camden, 3rd series, xxvii, 1880)
TCWAAS	Transactions of the Cumberland and Westmorland Archaeological and Architectural Society
Warkworth, Chronicle	A Chronicle of the First Thirteen Years of the Reign of Edward the Fourth, by John Warkworth, ed. J. O. Halliwell (Camden Society, 1839)
Waurin, Recueil des Croniques	Recueil des Croniques et Anchiennes Istories de la Grant Bretaigne, ed. W. Hardy, 5 vols (RS, 1864–91)

In the text Middle English prose has been modernized; verse has been left in the original language.

Introduction

On 9 February 1456 the House of Lords debated Halley's Comet. We know that because John Bocking told Sir John Fastolf. Writing from London to Sir John at Caister, he reported that the Lords had that very day spoken 'of a greet gleaming star that but late hath been seen divers times, marvellous in appearance'. 'This day', Bocking also reported, 'my Lords York and Warwick came to Parliament in a good array, to the number of 400 men, all jacked and in brigantines [wearing body armour], and no lord else, whereof many men marvelld'.[1] There was much marvelling that day. But the Lords had reason to be taken aback by an inept attempt, based on unreliable information, to forestall a supposed plot to arrest the duke. The rumour had circulated two days earlier, Bocking added, that York was about to be discharged as protector of the realm and that if he had not come strong, he would have been distressed (seized by force). It all seemed a bit unlikely to Bocking, for he had been informed by a reliable source ('a great man') close to the king, that York was to be named chief councillor. The chat was, anyway, that no one could think of anyone who was in a position to carry out such an enterprise against York. Who knew what was going on? Even so he concluded, 'men speak and divine much matter of the coming this day in such array to Westminster'.[2]

What did they divine of Halley's Comet? Did anyone put two and two together and conclude that it portended the emergence of another glittering star, marvellous in appearance, Richard Neville, earl of Warwick? Did anyone realize that they were witnessing that day the confirmation of his rise to dominance in English politics? Did anyone predict that he would bestride the English political scene for the next fifteen years? Did anyone foresee that he would put the house of York on the throne in five years' time and then put it down again nine years later? For it was Warwick and *no lord else* who backed York in this armed demonstration. Not even his father, the other member of the triumvirate who had been ruling England for the last few months, was prepared to put his head above the parapet on this occasion. On this day, the day the Lords debated Halley's Comet, it became absolutely clear that Warwick was now the principal lieutenant of the house of York, a role he was to play for the next decade.

Richard Neville, earl of Warwick, made a deep and lasting impression on contemporaries. His role as the arbiter of English politics at the height of the

Wars of the Roses, has never ceased to capture the imagination. His sobriquet, 'Kingmaker', has entered the political language for the man behind the scenes who fixes the succession of party leaders, though Warwick himself was always front stage. Modern historians have not on the whole been kind to Richard Neville. The dominant view, summed up by Charles Ross in 1969, is that he was avaricious, unscrupulous, factious, arrogant, self-aggrandizing and overweeningly ambitious. He was a man who had no cause to offer except his own self-advancement, and whose only consistency lay in sacrificing principle to expediency. A typical politician, one might suppose.[3] J. R. Lander, who was even more enamoured of Edward IV than Ross, emphasized Warwick's bitter resentment against the king, his inability to tolerate anything but a dominant position, his inordinate avariciousness and rampant acquisitiveness. A generation later, in 1997, Christine Carpenter, another whose admiration for Edward IV appears to have no bounds, referred to 'his (Warwick's) grandiose view of himself as the arbiter of England's destinies at home and abroad', and saw his personal ambitions alone as responsible for the upheavals of 1469–71.[4] These historians, pitching Warwick against Edward IV, are but the most recent articulators of a long line of opinion, stretching back to David Hume in the eighteenth century, that has condemned Warwick as 'the greatest as well as the last of those mighty barons that formerly overawed the crown and rendered the people incapable of any regular system of civil government'.[5]

There have been exceptions, notably Charles Oman in 1893 and Paul Murray Kendall in 1957, but they have been considered quixotic by mainstream historians.[6] Recently, however, an awareness emerged that a more thorough reappraisal of the earl's career was long overdue. Colin Richmond, writing in 1995, called for a fresh look, though in his view Warwick's amorality as the first of the serial killers of the Wars of the Roses stood in the way of a favourable rehabilitation.[7] That rehabilitation was then undertaken by Michael Hicks in his *Warwick the Kingmaker*, the first major scholarly study of his career, published in 1998. Hicks found much to admire: Warwick's energy, his daring, his political flare, his strength of will and determination, and the very way he stamped himself on his times. Yet, there is a deep-seated ambiguity running through the portrayal. He is also seen as greedy, grossly enriching himself at the king's expense. While one Yorkist poem written shortly after Barnet chose to stress that he died, not as a power-hungry and turbulent baron seeking his own advancement, but as a representative of public opinion, in reality he peddled public grievances as the cloak for his own private ends. Thus, even though Professor Hicks saw much to admire in the earl, it ultimately appears that he found it difficult to break completely free from the received view of the twentieth century.[8] This work continues this reappraisal of Warwick's career.

Contemporary narrative accounts and other sources shape the history of the Kingmaker. It is the information that contemporaries recorded about him and the gloss that they gave it that determine how historians view Richard Neville. There were, in fact, two quite different contemporary perceptions: one profoundly hostile; the other highly favourable. The hostile view is to be found in the official and quasi-official reports, newsletters and verses generated as Edward IV fought for his survival on the throne in 1470–71 and reasserted his authority on his kingdom thereafter. These were cautious in language, more regretful than vengeful, being designed as they were to persuade others to the justice of Edward's cause and the unreasonable and treasonable behaviour of the earl.[9] Comment was more extreme in the outpouring of Burgundian and pro-Burgundian texts, written by authors at the time, and subsequently, who were incensed by the earl's alliance with Louis XI and declaration of war against the duke in 1470–71. These contemporary texts, not generally known in England until the nineteenth century, which characterized the earl as a perfidious traitor, have provided persuasive evidence to underpin the modern perception.[10] But English texts written between 1471 and 1485 were largely silent; the second continuation of Crowland Chronicle, the most authoritative, if reticent, account of Yorkist England, completed in 1486, was circumspect. By the time that the author, a well-placed civil servant, came to write his memoir, Richard Neville, who had died a loyal Lancastrian, had been rehabilitated.[11]

Rarely does the unrestrained post-1471 Yorkist perception of the earl appear in England after 1485. It is to be found most dramatically in the pages of the mid-sixteenth century *Mirrour for Magistrates*. This was a work inspired by the medieval tradition of the mirrors for princes, showing by exemplars how rulers and great men should or should not conduct themselves. A series of famous men, in a literary pageant, speak from the past. A decidedly unflattering verdict on the earl is put into the mouth of Anthony, Earl Rivers. He 'was a praunsing courser/That hauty hart of hys could beare no mate'. He hated Rivers' kin and spited them.

> He troubled oft the kynges unstedy state
> And that because he would not be hys warde.

He was a traitor, who suborned the duke of Clarence, stirred up the people in rebellion against the king, who nevertheless nobly

> assayed by fayre meanes to asswage
> His enemyes yre, reveled by rebels rage.

But Warwick was not pacified, thus,

> Hys constant rancor causeles was extreme.
> No meane could he serve the quarell to discus,

Tyl he had driuen the king out of the realme.
Neither would he then be waked from his dream.
For whan my brother [in law] was cum and placed again,
He stynted not tyll he was stoutly slayne.[12]

This passage in the *Mirrour* is all the more remarkable when set beside the alternative, and more frequently quoted, portrait, put into the earl's own mouth which reflects the dominant view of the mid-sixteenth century. It may well be that the author had access to Flemish sources, but it stands out as an unusual reiteration of the post-1471 Yorkist version of his career.[13]

In marked contrast, contemporary sources, both English and Burgundian, that were written before Neville's rebellion against Edward IV, are highly favourable and sympathetic to the earl. He was the hero of the Yorkist accounts produced shortly after Edward IV came to the throne, in London and other English chronicles, in the outpouring of political verses justifying the Yorkist succession, and also in Burgundian chronicles composed in the early 1460s.[14] This is not in itself surprising, given the context in which they were written and the manner, also recorded in these sources, by which contemporaries were bombarded with Yorkist propaganda from 1459. There are, however, two accounts, which are particularly favourable, which warrant more detailed consideration.

One is to be found incorporated in Jehan de Waurin's *Recueil des Croniques*. This recounts in detail English affairs from 1456 until 1461, before the second battle of St Albans. Dr Visser Fuchs has convincingly demonstrated that Waurin incorporated an account emanating from the earl's immediate circle which was most likely composed in January/February 1461 to reassure the duke of Burgundy that it was not then the intent of the Yorkists, even after the death of Richard of York and Warwick's own father at Wakefield, to depose Henry VI. This account gave a particular gloss on the events of 1456–60. It stressed Warwick's popularity in Calais, his statesmanship in governing the town and his principled opposition to York's claim to the throne.[15] A further passage, a lengthy report of the insulting reception by Edward IV of a French embassy in 1467, is also sympathetic to the earl. It may be that this passage was drawn from an account given by one of the ambassadors which came into Waurin's hands. It has been rather crudely set into the narrative for it leads into a very short and ill-informed summary of Warwick's estrangement with Edward IV which jumps from 1467 to 1469, for which clearly the author had no reliable source.[16] On the events of 1469–71, Waurin is both far better informed and clearly less sympathetic to the earl, since he draws heavily on accounts favourable to Edward IV to which he later had access.[17]

Secondly, the fragment of a London Chronicle known as Bale's Chronicle also carries an account which has all the signs of being influenced by Warwick's own 'spin'.[18] It too develops a line that is not only favourable to, but also focuses on, the earl's role in events after 1456. The document has particular knowledge about the Neville family as a whole. Thus, it gives unusual prominence in 1448 to the war on the Scottish border, in which, it claims, Richard Neville, earl of Salisbury excelled; it is the only London Chronicle to note that William Neville, Lord Fauconberg, was taken prisoner at Pont de l'Arche ('pount large') in 1450. York and Salisbury, as protector and chancellor together 'worshipfully ruled and governed' England in 1454. The author noted, for no apparent reason, that Salisbury did not attend the second sitting of the commission of oyer and terminer that sat in London in May 1456 to try those accused of rioting against the Lombards. Individually, perhaps, the inclusion of each item does not betoken much, but taken together they suggest a particular source of information. And so too with Warwick himself. He is picked out for special mention in 1450: on 24 November, at the height of tension between the dukes of Somerset and York, 'came the Earl of Warwick through the city with a mighty people arrayed for war'. It is his presence that dominates the text after 1456. Apart from an account of riots between the lawyers at the Inns of Court and the inhabitants of Fleet Street and a discussion of how the city rejected the crown's attempt to place Lord Scales in command over it, the last pages of this fragment are taken up almost entirely with Warwick's deeds.[19] For the calendar year of 1458 the author has made but three entries, all concerning Warwick.

In particular, there are the two passages, one of 10 lines concerning an attempt on Warwick's life in 1456 and the other of 14, describing his attack on Spanish shipping in the Channel in 1458, which go to inordinate and duplicating length in his praise. The two passages bear quoting in full, for, although the final comments have been cited many times as evidence of the earl's esteem and fame, the significance of the passages is somewhat diminished by being edited. The first is as follows:

> This year the Friday the 5 November came the earl of Warwick unto London. And the same day after his coming rode against him to have distressed him the dukes of Exeter and Somerset, the duke's son of Somerset and the Earl of Shrewsbury, Treasurer and the lords Roos and other with 400 people and more as was reported. But thanked be God the said Earl was therof warned ['ware'] and purveyed a remedy against their malice and came in safety to the city of London and they durst not counter [countre] with him for he was named and taken in all places for the most courageous and manliest knight living.[20]

The second is:

> The earl of Warwick being in Kent had gathered a great fellowship and a navy of ships intending to keep the sea and to meet with the fleet of Spain and do some enterprise upon the sea in resisting the malice of the king and the lord's adversaries wherein that no lord of the land took the jeopardy nor laboured for the honour and profit of the king and the land but only he, for the which manhood and his great policy and deeds doing of worship in fortifying of Calais and other feats of arms [that] all the commonalty of

this land had him in great laud and charity ... and so reputed and taken for as famous a knight as was living.[21]

Both these passages could have emanated from sources close to Warwick. Thanked be God, the author repeats, he was aware of the plot on his life and was able to take steps to protect himself from the malice of his enemies. Only he and he alone stood up for the honour and profit of king and country. But, above all, it is the representation of the earl in chivalric terms which suggests that the author was familiar with the earl's representation of himself. The very repetition of virtually the same praise at the end of both passages hints at the possibility that the author forgot that he had already used it once, and might reflect the use of another text which had come into his hands. Even so, the sheer weight given, out of all proportion to the rest of the text, to Warwick's renown, to the fear he struck into his opponents, and to the manner in which he alone stood up for the defence of English interests, suggests that he was being fed a line by Warwick's own people.

Given the favourable weighting of the sources for the earlier stages of Warwick's career, it is perhaps remarkable that modern interpretation has so persistently cut against the grain of contemporary views expressed before 1470. Professor Hicks has written wisely that we should not judge Warwick's career by the *bouleversement* of his last year.[22] One could equally add that we should not base our judgement of him on texts written immediately after the *bouleversement*. This is, in effect, what most of his modern historians have done. The challenge is to probe beneath the partisanship so apparent in all the contemporary writings about him, both earlier in his career and after the last year of his life, both those highly favourable and those highly hostile towards him. One can do so by reference to other more incidental and more neutral sources, such as letters in the surviving collections of private correspondence or in diplomatic correspondence (although these themselves had their own agendas), and to record evidence. Ultimately, however, one has to work with the grain of contemporary opinion, however partisan, to seek to find the man and assess his career.

The materials do not exist, however, to write a biography of the Kingmaker. Such materials rarely exist for any medieval figure, however prominent. We lack the direct personal insights provided by correspondence and memoirs. Most of the few letters that survive are business or political correspondence. We thus see the man almost entirely through his actions and public persona. For this reason this work is a political study, exploring not just what happened on the national, and international, stage, but giving significant attention to the provincial roots of Warwick's power, the exercise of his lordship and the degree of loyalty he commanded. It also offers a reinterpretation of Richard Neville's engagement with popular politics, which was such a distinctive and controversial aspect of his life, as well as a revaluation of his chivalric standing, which has been too readily dismissed by modern historians. Thus, the first four chapters tell the story of the earl's extraordinary political career. This narrative establishes a framework for subsequent more analytical chapters. The first of these is an assessment of his wealth and finances and the administration of his estates; the following two consider in detail the exercise of his lordship in several parts of England; the eighth chapter examines his relationship with Calais; the ninth explores his appeal to popular support; and the last discusses his chivalric reputation. The work concludes by revisiting his historical reputation and considers the reasons for the low regard in which he has been held by most historians from the mid-eighteenth to the end of the twentieth century.

The work, therefore, seeks to place Warwick the Kingmaker in his political world and to understand him within the political culture of fifteenth-century England. It seeks to view his controversial career as contemporaries and near contemporaries might have perceived it. This is, of course, ultimately only an aspiration, for the historian can only see the past from the perspective of his or her own age. It is a reconsideration of what one might call the Warwick phenomenon in the mid-fifteenth century; it is a study of a man who became a celebrity, 'a great gleaming star … marvellous in appearance'.

PART ONE

Politics

Premier Earl, 1428–55

Richard Neville, the future earl of Warwick, was born on 22 November 1428, the eldest son of Sir Richard Neville and Alice, daughter and heiress of Thomas Montagu, fourth earl of Salisbury, who was killed at the siege of Orleans just a year after his grandson's birth.[1] His father, who was born in 1400, was the eldest son of the second marriage of Ralph Neville, earl of Westmorland to Joan Beaufort, daughter of John of Gaunt. He took the title of his deceased father-in-law in 1429. Little is known of Richard the younger's childhood and youth. It is to be supposed that he spent most of his first seven years, as was customary, in the care of his mother and a team of nurses, but where is not known. It is possible that it was principally in castles and manor houses held by her from the Montagu inheritance, rather than in Neville palaces in the north. His grandmother, Joan, still held Middleham, and although she had made a lease of it to the earl of Salisbury during her life, it was traditionally one of the 'ladies" residences under earlier Nevilles, and had been extensively 'modernized' by her and Earl Ralph after their marriage. She did not die until 1440,and so if the child Richard spent any time at Middleham, or even Sheriff Hutton, it would probably have been in the household of his paternal grandmother.[2] If the customary practice of aristocratic child-rearing were followed in his case he would at the age of seven, in 1435, have moved into a male-dominated household for his education and training in courtesy, hunting, and eventually the military arts. John Hardyng, a hardy Northumbrian soldier, writing two decades later on the education of boys, said that at fourteen they should learn to hunt, and then at sixteen, 'to werray and to wage, to jouste and ryde, and castels to assayle.[3] Who might have been responsible for such a programme in young Richard's case in the early 1440s we do not know. However, he was by that time married.

When he was seven Richard married Anne Beauchamp, two years his elder, the daughter of Richard Beauchamp, earl of Warwick, and his second countess, Isabel Despenser, as part of a double contract in which his sister Cicely married Anne's brother, Henry, the heir to the earldom. The agreement between the two fathers was reached at Leicester in March 1436 and the wedding itself celebrated at Abergavenny, one of the lordships of the bride's father, two or three months later. At the time of the marriage there was no expectation that Richard would inherit his new father-in-law's earldom. Salisbury, it seems, was keen to make the match for his daughter to Henry. He was prepared to pay a marriage portion of over £3,000, a substantial amount, so as to secure it, the down payment on the day of the espousal being provided by the crown from arrears of wages owed to him. The marriage of his son to Warwick's daughter at the same time was possibly a further part of the bargain required by Beauchamp, for Salisbury might have preferred to find a bride who was an heiress. At the time of the betrothal, young Richard Neville's prospect was that he would have to wait for his father to die before he could enter into any significant property of his own, other than that set aside by his father and father-in-law to provide an adequate income to support him and Anne when they, some seven years later, began to cohabit and established an independent household. It was not a particularly good match at the time. It was also, quite clearly, not a love match; although the law did allow for them to terminate the contract before consummation if both parties agreed. However, as they grew up, they clearly accepted each other and their parents' decision. It is not known when the marriage was consummated, though conventionally it would have been at around the age of fourteen, in 1443 or thereabouts.[4]

It was customary for betrothed children to be maintained by the parents of the girl. Nothing would have been more appropriate, therefore, than for Richard Neville to have received his education from 1436 in the household of the great Richard Beauchamp, alongside others of his henchmen (as gentle children sent to school in an aristocratic household were called) until the earl's death three years later, when young Richard was eleven. None less than the king himself, six years older than Richard, shared the same experience. After the earl's death his executors might have taken over the responsibility. In 1443 or thereabouts, if the custom were followed, the couple would have moved into their own household establishment, albeit still under the tutelage and guidance of trusted adults. Richard was knighted by Henry VI in or before 1445, slightly before his eighteenth birthday. The coronation of Queen Margaret might have been the occasion. This almost certainly marked the coming of adulthood. As the son of a courtier high in favour he appears to have joined, with his brother-in-law Henry Beauchamp (d. 1446), the group of young noblemen in personal attendance on the king, for in the letters patent first conferring the title of earl of Warwick on him in 1449, specific reference is made to his service about the king's person. The same letters refer to his service in Scotland. It is possible that from 1446, when his father renegotiated an extended contract as warden of the west march in order to include Sir Richard as joint warden for twenty years from 1453, he was already acting as his father's lieutenant. He may have seen military service in the war of 1448–9.[5]

Richard Neville not only enjoyed a conventional aristocratic upbringing, but did so at the heart of the Lancastrian regime. He was at birth marked out for an illustrious career, following his father and grandfather in the service of the dynasty. The key moment in the emergence of the Neville family had been the marriage of Ralph to Joan Beaufort, the daughter of John of Gaunt by Katherine Swynford. This lineage was the foundation of his spectacular career. He was an exceptionally privileged child born into the inner circle of the Lancastrian elite ruling England in the early years of the reign of Henry IV. His father was the first cousin of Henry V; he was the cousin once removed of Henry VI. He himself was born to play a prominent role in English affairs.

The Nevilles were a long established county Durham family seated at Raby and Brancepeth, who had risen to prominence in the Scottish wars of the fourteenth century. Warwick's great grandfather, John Lord Neville, who died in 1388, had been high in the service of John of Gaunt and had been part of the court circle which aroused considerable hostility towards the end of Edward III's reign. His son and successor, Ralph, had not initially been inclined to a high-profile political career. Although he continued in the duke of Lancaster's service, being one of his generously rewarded retainers, he initially seems to have been more interested in a sporting life, for he accumulated a series of foresterships in the north of England. This changed after the death of Lady Neville and his rapid marriage in 1396 to Joan Beaufort, herself newly widowed, which brought him even closer to the duke. A year later he was created earl of Westmorland. The family's fortunes were transformed, however, by the events of 1399 and the usurpation of the throne by Gaunt's son, Henry of Bolingbroke, the half-brother of Westmorland's countess. From the very moment of Henry IV's landing at Ravenspur in the summer of 1399 to reclaim his inheritance, until Westmorland's own death in 1425, he never wavered in his loyalty and commitment to the regime. Amply rewarded from the beginning, his greatest service was in resisting Percy risings in 1403 and 1405. He was never as close to Henry V as he had been to Henry IV, yet nevertheless performed valuable service on the borders with Scotland, especially as warden of the west march. In 1422 he was one of the elder statesmen who ensured the smooth succession of the infant Henry VI to the throne and the establishment of a stable government in his minority.[6]

Ralph Neville was also responsible for ensuring that his family by Joan Beaufort took precedence over his eldest son and his siblings. From the time of his marriage to Joan Beaufort, and it may have been part of the marriage settlement, he began the process of partitioning his estates. By a series of enfeoffments he transferred his Yorkshire properties, Middleham and Sheriff Hutton, to himself and his countess jointly, with remainder to the heirs of their bodies. Penrith in Westmorland had been granted to him and Joan by the king on their marriage and was likewise entailed in heir male. Ralph even attempted to settle his principal seat in Durham, Raby, on his second family. At first his heir, John Lord Neville, seems to have acquiesced. John predeceased his father, but his son Ralph, who inherited the title, contested the settlement after he came of age in

1427. It was not, however, until after the death of the countess Joan in 1440 that a settlement was reached which left Raby, as well as Brancepeth and a handful of properties elsewhere in England, in the hands of the senior line. It was an unequal division, which ensured the domination of the junior branch of the family for the immediate future. The odds had been heavily stacked in Salisbury's favour. Cardinal Beaufort, his uncle and mother's brother; Thomas Langley, bishop of Durham until his death in 1437; and Prior John Wessington of Durham cathedral priory had all acted on his behalf.[7]

At the heart of the junior Neville patrimony lay the lordship of Middleham in Richmondshire. It became the family's principal residence. Before 1399 the Nevilles had not played a prominent role in the affairs of this liberty, equal in size to the county palatine of Durham immediately to its north: the family had focused on Durham. But the Nevilles had always been an important Richmondshire family, not only in terms of landholding but also as one of the three feeholders of the honour of Richmond. In the late fourteenth century, however, John Lord Neville, and then Ralph, had been content to play second fiddle to Richard, Lord Scrope, the builder of Bolton Castle. The revolution of 1399 was a revolution in Richmondshire too, for the Scropes of Bolton, especially latterly Lord Scrope's son William, earl of Wiltshire, had been prominent in the service of Richard II. In 1399 Ralph Neville displaced Lord Scrope. He was immediately granted the lordship of Richmond for life. John of Gaunt had been earl of Richmond for thirty years before surrendering the earldom to the duke of Brittany in 1372. He had, however, never accepted the finality of this loss and had continued to exercise influence in Richmondshire itself, both directly and through his retainers, including both Scrope and Neville. The marriage between Joan and Ralph, and the settlement of Middleham on the heirs of their bodies, was in part an aspect of Gaunt's continuing interest in the lordship. In 1399 Henry IV recovered the earldom of Richmond for the house of Lancaster; his grant of the lordship to Neville for life was a logical extension of the family alliance. It is even possible that Ralph wished to extend the grant from life to heir male, and thus provide the title of earl of Richmond for his son, Richard, born in 1400. If so, neither Henry IV nor Henry V would accede to this. However, possession of the lordship of Richmond remained a matter of great importance to Ralph's descendants. After ten years in the hands of John, duke of Bedford between 1425 and 1435, it was eventually restored to Richard Neville, earl of Salisbury, who by grants dated 1445 and 1449 finally secured in tail male all the mesne property, administration of justice and feudal dues within the 'liberty, honour and lordship of Richmondshire', including the reversion of the dower portion of Jacquetta, duchess of Bedford.[8] The title still eluded Richard Neville, but he had secured for the time being the hereditary rights of the earl in the lordship of Richmond.

Other sons of Ralph Neville by Joan Beaufort prospered because of the dynastic connection. The second son, William, born in 1401, was married to Joan, the mentally handicapped heiress of Sir Thomas Fauconberg of Skelton and heiress to her grandfather's title which William inherited; George was married to the heiress of Lord Latimer; Robert, born in 1404 and destined for the church, became bishop of Durham in 1437; and the youngest son, Edward, married Elizabeth, heiress of Richard Beauchamp, earl of Worcester, and was to become Lord Bergavenny. The daughters were married into the greater aristocracy too. Katherine, who may have been the first born, married John Mowbray, fifth duke of Norfolk (he died in 1432). She subsequently married Sir Thomas Strangways; then, John, Viscount Beaumont, killed at Northampton in 1460; and lastly, in 1467, Sir John Woodville. Eleanor was married twice: to Richard, Lord Despenser and then Henry Percy, second earl of Northumberland. Anne was also married twice: to Humphrey Stafford, duke of Buckingham (another prominent casualty of Northampton), and then to Sir Walter Blount. Ralph Neville's youngest daughter, Cicely, married Richard, duke of York. This network of marriage alliances, further consolidated the junior Neville family's position at the heart of the Lancastrian regime. The sons, through their advantageous marriages and ecclesiastical preferment, greatly extended the power and influence of the family, in the north of England in particular; the daughters extended the connections with the greater aristocracy. It does not follow that family ties ensured future political alliance. Against the closeness of the future relationship with the house of York and the support of John Mowbray, fourth duke of Norfolk, should be set the later enmity with the houses of Percy, Stafford and Beaumont. Richard Neville the younger, if not his father, was responsible for the deaths of three of his uncles by marriage: Henry, earl of Northumberland at the first battle of St Albans, Humphrey, duke of Buckingham at Northampton and John, Viscount Beaumont also at Northampton. Civil war was subsequently to divide the extended Neville family, but before 1450 marriage alliances enhanced the Nevilles' place in the Lancastrian ruling elite.[9]

The marriages and careers of Richard Neville's own siblings were not as significant of those of his uncles and aunts. There were no great heiresses available for his younger brothers Thomas and John. Thomas married Maud Stanhope, the niece and joint heiress of Ralph, Lord Cromwell; John wed Isabel Ingoldisthorpe, a niece of John Tiptoft, earl of Worcester, both as adults. His youngest and able brother, George, enjoyed a more spectacular career first as bishop of Exeter and then as archbishop of York. Not only Cicely (wife of the duke of Warwick), but all his sisters fared rather better in the marriage market: Joan married William, eighth earl of Arundel; Alice married Henry, Lord FitzHugh; Eleanor married Thomas, second Lord Stanley; Katherine was first married to William Bonville, Lord Harrington, and then to William, Lord Hastings;

and Margaret married John de Vere, thirteenth earl of Oxford. These marriage alliances strengthened his network, especially after 1461, but did not necessarily ensure full political support. FitzHugh proved to be a staunch ally, but Stanley stood aside in Richard Neville's final crisis and Hastings was unquestionably Edward IV's man. The marriage of Margaret, by the earl's own arrangement, to John de Vere in about 1463, which secured de Vere's succession to the earldom of Oxford following the treason of his father and brother, was more overtly political. This was to be a significant factor at the end of Neville's career when he returned to the Lancastrian fold. On the field of Barnet two of Warwick's brothers-in-law faced each other: Oxford alongside him, Hastings on the opposing side. Marriage alliances did not create lasting political alliances. In this Warwick was typical of members of the greater peerage, all of whom were linked to some degree by blood.[10] Warwick grew up as a highly privileged Lancastrian nobleman's son, with a conventional education, prestigious early marriage, extensive familial links within the Lancastrian establishment and the prospect of succeeding his father as the head of his house, comprising a great northern family. His life was transformed, however, by his unexpected succession to the earldom of Warwick in the summer of 1449, when he had not yet reached his twenty-first birthday.

Two lives had stood between him and this dignity: those of his brother-in-law Henry, who died in 1446, and the latter's infant daughter and sole heir, Anne, who herself died in 1449. Henry's next heir was his full sister, Anne, Neville's wife. In her right he became earl. For all but one year between 1439 and 1449 there had been no adult Beauchamp. The minority of Henry lasted until 1445; that of his daughter for a further three years after his death. Between 1439 and 1445, the bulk of the estates were in the hands of custodians, initially chosen by Isabel, the dowager countess of Warwick. After 1446 they were put again in the hands of custodians. The earl of Salisbury was one both before 1445 and after 1446, with Sir John Beauchamp of Powicke, the only other person to hold the post in both minorities. The other two custodians after 1446 were the duke of Suffolk, who had secured the wardship and marriage of the infant Anne Beauchamp and Lord Sudeley, who with Sir John Beauchamp, was a feoffee of the Despenser estates of Isabel Beauchamp, held in trust. Salisbury's interests were plain: those of his daughter as countess, then duchess, and lastly dowager countess of Warwick, and of his son Richard, after 1446, as the husband of the heir.[11]

As custodian Salisbury was assiduous in protecting his son's reversionary interest. All four were granted the farm of Anne Beauchamp's estates in 1446. The custodians conducted a thorough search and analysis of the title deeds. They had to act quickly to prevent the estates and offices being used to reward importunate courtiers. Salisbury himself, who had been granted the office of steward and chief forester of Barnard Castle by Duke Henry (and in all probability had held it since the death of Earl Richard) promptly overturned a grant to Sir William

Beauchamp. The biggest threat came from his fellow custodian, Sir John Beauchamp, who himself entered a claim to the earldom as heir male. He was persuaded to withdraw, and, possibly in compensation, was granted a barony. At the same time, it seems, Salisbury's own brother Edward, Lord Bergavenny, claimed the lordship of Abergavenny from which his title derived. He may have attempted to occupy it. The custodians, in order to protect their interest, retained a significant number of gentry in the lordship. Inquisitions post mortem confirmed that Anne was the sole heir and identified the lands to which she should succeed. Because of assignment of dower to Duchess Cicely (Salisbury's daughter) and to Eleanor, countess of Northumberland (Salisbury's sister), the widow of Richard Lord Despenser who had died in 1414, and lands held in trust, only one quarter of the income was available to the custodians, a significant proportion of which was assigned to the maintenance of Anne Beauchamp.

When Anne Beauchamp died at the age of 3 on 3 June 1449, Salisbury was thus on hand to oversee the succession to his son, and knew what was due to him. He was assisted by the fact that possible rival claimants, especially the husbands of Richard Beauchamp's daughters by his first countess, the earl of Shrewsbury (married to the eldest, Margaret), the duke of Somerset (married to Eleanor) and Lord Latimer (married to Elizabeth) were not on the scene. Somerset and Shrewsbury were defending Normandy, which was assaulted by Charles VII of France in the very same month, and were detained there for at least a year. On account of the mental illness of George Neville, Lord Latimer, the earl of Salisbury gained control of his brother's lands by December 1449, and no doubt stood in him for him personally, even though he was not given formal custody until June 1451. Salisbury himself, as well as Suffolk, was free to attend court and the parliament that was in session at Winchester. He could not have been better placed. Richard Neville was created earl of Warwick within a fortnight.[12] The process by which he was vested in the vast Beauchamp inheritance was quickly set in motion.

Securing the inheritance, however, proved to be far more difficult. In strict law, since Duke Henry had received livery of his estates, the whole should have passed without dispute to his only surviving sister, on the grounds of the exclusion of the half-blood. That is to say that at the moment Duke Henry had been granted seisin, his half-sisters had lost the rights they had enjoyed while their father was alive and he had been a minor: the only heir after his daughter's death was his full sister, the new countess of Warwick. There were three constituent elements to this inheritance: the Beauchamp estates that Countess Anne inherited from her brother; the lordship of Abergavenny in which she was also sole heir of her brother; and the Despenser estates, in which she was the joint heir of her mother. The Countess Anne's right to the properties pertaining to all three was contested in the following years. Not in dispute, however, was a body of estates, originally from the Beauchamp element, which had been put in trust by Richard Beauchamp. At the core of this trust were manors which had been settled by his father, Earl Thomas Beauchamp (d. 1401) on his brother William and his wife Joan, the lady of Abergavenny, and which had reverted to Earl Richard on her death in 1435.

The new Countess Anne's half-sisters, the daughters of their father's first marriage to Elizabeth Berkeley, who had been the joint heirs before the second marriage, did not hesitate to claim a quarter share each of the Beauchamp estates that were not in trust. John Talbot, earl of Shrewsbury, as husband of the eldest daughter, Margaret, as his will drawn up in 1452 indicated, even had hopes for the title himself. It was probably as well for the Nevilles that Talbot, never hesitant to use force, was later preoccupied with his conflict with Lord Berkeley over the rights of his son John by Margaret Beauchamp in the Lisle inheritance.[13] The elder sisters claimed that a joint enfeoffment of twenty-two manors to Earl Richard and Countess Isabel in 1423, with reversion to all his heirs in default of male heirs entitled each of them to a quarter share of these. At first it appears that Richard Neville, newly earl, was prepared to compromise. A final concord drafted on 22 June 1449 with his attorneys, Thomas Colt and Henry Sotehill, recognized their claims. On 5 July the three elder sisters petitioned for a licence to enter their parts. However, Warwick subsequently hardened his line, and entered all the properties himself, both those included in the settlement of 1423 and those excluded to which he had a clearer claim. The inquisitions post mortem on these estates, when they were finally held between March and December 1450, unanimously concluded in every county that Warwick's countess was the sole heir by reason of the exclusion of the half blood.

The sisters continued to contest these decisions. At the end of 1450 they were granted the custody of those of the late Duchess Cicely's dower lands to which they were deemed in the grant to be heiresses. These were her portion of the Beauchamp estates that she had held, which they appear to have successfully occupied for a while. Margaret, countess of Shrewsbury, it is known, secured possession of Drayton Bassett, which she held for the rest of her life. In February 1454, however, Warwick who had now allied himself with the duke of York at the time of the king's first illness, was confirmed as the sole heir in right of his wife. Not surprisingly the sisters reasserted their claim after the earl's attainder in 1459. And although Edward IV confirmed the Countess Anne's status as the sole heir once more in the first parliament of his reign, the elder women continued to hold until their deaths nine manors between them, somewhat less than they had originally claimed. A settlement was reached in 1466 when the earl conceded the loss of these to the Countess Margaret and her sisters and recognized that in the event of the failure of his line, the title and possession of Warwick should revert to her descendants (as it did in 1547 with the succession of John Dudley as earl of Warwick). Nevertheless, Richard Neville had succeeded in securing the bulk of the Beauchamp estates, including the core properties of Warwick itself and Elmley in Worcestershire.[14]

Another property, part of the Beauchamp element of the inheritance which was disputed by the coheirs, was the hereditary Warwick chamberlainship of the exchequer. John Brome of Baddesley Clinton had been granted the office by Duke Henry on 3 June 1446, eight days before the duke's death. His grant was confirmed on 4 July and again by Henry VI in November 1449. He continued to hold the office during the life of the dowager Duchess Cicely. Several months after her death, on 5 December 1450, his hold on the office was confirmed. Warwick, however, was able to expel him and have his own man, Thomas Colt, installed two days later. In an attempt to resolve the issue, the office was put into commission pending a settlement. Early in 1451 the king ruled that the office belonged to all four sisters. Attacks by Warwick's men on Brome's property in the summer of 1451 were probably designed to force him to surrender the office, which he did not. The case was referred to the exchequer court, but not determined before the king fell ill in 1453. It was not until February 1454 that Warwick was able to recover it.[15]

Warwick also took up a claim inherited by his wife from Duke Henry to the reversion to the lordship of the Channel Islands after the death of Humphrey of Gloucester, which had been granted to Beauchamp in 1445. Since Duke Henry predeceased Duke Humphrey, this grant had not been realized. But in 1449 both Richard Neville and the husbands of his wife's half-sisters claimed it. Neville's claim in right of his wife, as Duke Henry's heir, was the stronger and, despite confusing grants by the crown in 1449, he was in occupation by January 1452. However, the lordship was resumed to the crown under the act of resumption later in that year. On 24 September John Nanfan was appointed warden and governor. While Warwick was unwilling to surrender the title, which he used in a letter to Nanfan in 1455, Nanfan remained in post as warden, confirmed and extended in 1457 and 1460, until his death in 1463. This arrangement seems to have been a compromise acceptable to Warwick, for Nanfan, a one-time servant of Earl Richard Beauchamp, had entered his service. In 1458 Nanfan was one of those commissioned to fit out the *Grace Dieu* for Warwick, and in 1459 he was to provide welcome shelter for the earl and his fellow lords in their flight from England.[16]

The half-sisters did not have an interest in the other elements of the Warwick inheritance: the lordship of Abergavenny and the Despenser lands. The descent of these was complex and interconnected because Isabel Despenser, Richard Beauchamp's second countess, had previously been married to his cousin, another Richard, earl of Worcester and Lord Bergavenny, who had died in 1422. She had two daughters, one by each husband: the elder, Elizabeth, the heiress to the barony of Bergavenny and the younger, Anne, from 1449 countess of Warwick. Elizabeth had died in 1448, having married Warwick's uncle, Edward. Their son George was now the heir to this barony and to a half-share of his mother's Despenser inheritance. But Abergavenny itself, from which the barony took its title, had reverted to Richard Beauchamp, earl of Warwick in 1435. Edward Neville had contested this several times, and did so again in 1449 when he was granted licence to enter the lordship. However, the first inquisition post mortem on the deceased infant countess of Warwick, for Herefordshire, found in September 1449 that her sole heir in Abergavenny, Pain's Castle (a Beauchamp lordship) and Ewyas Lacy (a Despenser lordship) was her aunt Anne, the new countess of Warwick. It may well have been that the jury was overawed: Warwick had been at Abergavenny securing possession the preceding day. And he retained possession of the lordship even though his uncle challenged the findings of the inquisition and managed to secure one more favourable to him in the following year. [17]

The new earl and countess were initially prepared to accept, as in law they ought, the division of the third element, the Despenser estates, the other half passing to Warwick's cousin, George Neville, who was still a minor. A week after the death of the infant Anne Beauchamp in June 1449, John Tiptoft and his new wife, Cicely Neville, the dowager duchess of Warwick, had been granted custody of George Neville's Despenser lands and John was created earl of Worcester. Just as the inquisitions post mortem held in 1450 found the Countess Anne to be the sole heir to the Beauchamp estates, so they rightly found her to be coheir with George in those Despenser estates that were not held in trust by the late countess Isabel's feoffees. In a new inquisition in Herefordshire, the jury reversed its decision over Ewyas Lacy, ruling that that too should be divided. A similar judgement followed on the dower lands held by the Duchess Cicely after her death in July 1450. The Despenser lands were thus partitioned according to law. [18]

Nine-tenths of the law, however, is possession. Regardless of inquisitions and royal licences, Warwick set about occupying as much of the Bergavenny and Despenser property as he could. We have seen that he entered Abergavenny in September 1449. At the same time he also took possession of the whole of Glamorgan, part of the Despenser inheritance, probably with the connivance of his sister and the earl of Worcester who were the guardians of George Neville's moiety. He appointed his men as steward (William Herbert) and sheriff (his brother Sir Thomas Neville). All the revenues were subsequently delivered to him; writs were issued in Cardiff in his name only as Lord Despenser. On May 1450 the earl of Worcester formally surrendered the custody of George Neville's share of the Despenser inheritance to him. The act of resumption of January 1451, however, removed his custody. It seems nevertheless, that he never surrendered it. He, and he alone, issued a new charter to Cardiff borough on 12 March following. His custody was formally restored on 26 February 1452. George Neville came of age in 1457, but Warwick blithely ignored his rights and retained possession of his Despenser inheritance. George himself seems to have acquiesced, for he and his father adhered to the Yorkists, and their Neville kinsmen in 1459–61. He was, however, formally dispossessed by an act of the first Yorkist parliament in 1461 which declared the Countess of Warwick to be the sole heir of their mother to the Despenser inheritance. Thus what had been de facto since 1449, became *de jure*. Tewkesbury, and other properties, which had been in the hands of the late Countess Isabel's feoffees, had also passed into Warwick's possession by then.[19] The earl annexed the whole of the Despenser inheritance, of which only a half was his countess's by right.

The earl's possession of almost all the estates enjoyed by Earl Richard Beauchamp was endorsed by the full support of key Beauchamp councillors, administrators and retainers, who had been managing the estates since 1439. They, in effect, determined the issue. Prominent among its members were Thomas Hugford, who had served Earl Richard Beauchamp since 1417, and was one of his executors and was appointed constable of Warwick Castle by Duke Henry; Nicholas Rody, who had served Earl Richard even longer, was another executor and had been appointed steward of Warwick by Duke Henry; and William Berkeswell, one-time chaplain of Guy's Cliffe and treasurer to the earl, as well as dean of St Mary's Warwick. All three were the trustees of the Beauchamp Trust, the principal purpose of which was the building of the Beauchamp chapel at St Mary's Collegiate church in Warwick. They all continued in the earl's service until their deaths (1469, 1458 and 1470 respectively). Two others who had long-standing family and personal connections with the Beauchamps, John Throckmorton and John Nanfan, moved into the earl's service, as perhaps did Ralph Butler, Lord Sudeley and John, Lord Beauchamp of Powick. Particularly significant is the fact that these men, as feoffees of either the Beauchamp Trust, or of the Despenser Trust set up by the Countess Isabel, accepted the Countess Anne as the sole heir and Warwick as the new lord from the start.[20] For his part the earl, who spent much of his time in 1449–50 residing at Warwick, and visiting neighbouring lordships, enthusiastically adopted the traditions of the earldom, in relationship to the famous badge of the bear and ragged staff, the legend of Guy of Warwick, as the founder of several monasteries, especially Tewkesbury Abbey, and as patron of Guy's Cliffe chantry and the collegiate church of St Mary in Warwick.[21]

Through these early years in which he was consolidating his hold on the earldom of Warwick, the fluctuations of court politics were critical to Richard Neville. His initial entry into the inheritance owed much to the advantageous position his family held and the good fortune that so many of his potential rivals were absent. But the twists and turns in the manner in which his claim was treated by the crown, closely matched the rise and fall of favour at court. Henry VI was a king who had little inclination or capacity to rule. Particularly germane to Warwick's situation in 1449–53, were the king's willingness to put almost all decision-making in the hands of his principal courtiers, and his fecklessness in the exercise of his grace, whether by grants or pardons. He conceded requests to almost everyone who could gain access to him, even beyond the capacity of his favoured ministers to control.[22] When Warwick entered the earldom, the duke of Suffolk was in the ascendant; his father, though not as assiduous an attender of council, was still, because of his Beaufort blood, high in favour. Richard Neville the younger himself, as the patent creating him earl noted, had been in private attendance on the king. The very grant of the earldom, as an act of royal grace, was itself a consequence of the access to the king enjoyed by the Nevilles.[23]

This closeness to the court stood Warwick in good stead until the end of 1450. He had attended the meeting of parliament at Westminster in January to March which impeached Suffolk, and was one of those present when the king pardoned the duke and sent him into exile. During this session he was recognized as premier earl of England. Several times later in the year he drew upon the manpower of his new earldom to demonstrate his total commitment to the regime: he attended the meeting of parliament in Leicester, so John Paston was informed, with 400 men or more, and received exemptions in his favour in the act of resumption passed during the session as well as the grant of the custody of the lands of George Neville, heir to Lord Bergavenny. Warwick and his men, with reinforcements hastily raised, accompanied the king in June to counter Cade's revolt.[24] It would appear that he distanced himself from the duke of York's bid to prevent the duke of Somerset, who had returned from presiding over the loss of Normandy, taking Suffolk's place as the king's chief minister. York appeared dramatically at the new parliament on 23 November, after it had already assembled, with a substantial retinue behind him and his sword borne in state before him. Although at this time it was not declared, it seems that he staked his claim for pre-eminence on his status as putative heir presumptive. His own man, Sir William Oldhall, had been elected speaker. A bill for resumption was introduced, and proceedings were begun against named traitors. York had backing in parliament and on the streets. When, late in November, rioting broke out in London, and Somerset's life was threatened, Warwick and Salisbury were among those who stepped in to restore order. Shortly afterwards Warwick's claim to the chamberlainship of the Exchequer was recognized.[25] During the Christmas recess, partly as a result of Neville support, Somerset consolidated his power.

Warwick had helped thwart York, but in so doing had accelerated Somerset's rise to pre-eminence. He seems to have been over-confident of his family standing and to have underestimated Edmund Beaufort, for, no sooner had the duke secured his position at court than he turned on the earl. Now that he and his brother-in-law the earl of Shrewsbury were back in England and high in favour, they set about recovering what they believed to be their inheritance. The lands which Warwick's deceased sister, the dowager Duchess Cicely, had held in dower were granted to all four Beauchamp sisters as joint heirs; the earl was expelled from the chamberlainship of the Exchequer, and lost the custody of George Neville. Yet Warwick did not waver in his loyalty to the crown. To a large extent Somerset and Shrewsbury were too late. Neville had had eighteen months to secure the inheritance and it seems that physically dislodging him from George Neville's lands or from occupying most of his sister's dower proved impossible. The earl played no part at court and did not attend council. He spent most of 1451 in the West Midlands and South Wales, presumably strengthening his control of the disputed inheritance. In February 1452 he once more turned out in strength for the crown to help face down York at Dartford, for which his most significant reward was the renewal of the custody of George Neville, in effect confirmation of the status quo. Most of 1452 was spent again in the West Midlands and Glamorgan. The creation of Edmund Tudor as earl of Richmond was a blow to his longer-term prospects, more immediately for his father, and the granting of precedence over him to the new earl and his brother Jasper as earl of Pembroke, a slight.[26] But it seems that throughout 1452 and into the summer of 1453 Warwick was content to keep a low profile while doing all he could to make his position as the heir to his father-in-law impregnable.

But, in the summer of 1453, Richard Neville's position was directly challenged by an increasingly confident duke of Somerset. Guided by Edmund Beaufort, Henry VI seemed at last to have grown into his kingship. Over the preceding two years financial retrenchment had been begun, law and order had been more effectively enforced, and the king had been persuaded to show himself more on judicial progresses. Gascony had been recovered the previous year. And the queen was at last pregnant. This was the optimistic context in which parliament was summoned to meet at Reading in March 1453 and subsequently sat at Westminster until July. For the first time Warwick was a trier of petitions. He began to attend council. A compliant House of Commons enrolled a formal condemnation of all criticism that had been made of the court since 1450; tunnage and poundage was granted to the king for life, as they had been to his father after Agincourt; and the Commons granted the king the provision to raise 20,000 archers for the defence of the realm. With this demonstration of support Somerset turned on York. He was deprived of offices and his retainer Sir William Oldhall, the speaker of the parliament that had met at the end of 1450, was attainted.[27]

But York was not the only target. Edward Neville, Lord Bergavenny was once more granted licence to enter Abergavenny and, in the middle of June, Somerset himself was granted the custody of George Neville's lands. It was immediately apparent that Somerset meant to take possession, especially of his share of Glamorgan, by force if necessary. Warwick resisted. On 19 July William Herbert,

Warwick's appointed sheriff of the county, was summoned to Westminster. By the end of the month the council had been informed that there was a virtual state of war over Cardiff and Cowbridge. Warwick, who was there in person on more than one occasion in July and August, was ordered to submit and to surrender the castles to Lord Dudley. He refused, strengthened his garrisons and denied him entry.[28]

At the same time a violent quarrel had blown up between Warwick's father and younger brothers and the Percy family in Yorkshire. Tension had been rising between the two families both in Cumberland and Yorkshire, especially through growing Percy resentment of the Neville hegemony. What seems to have triggered violence was the marriage between Sir Thomas Neville and Maud Stanhope, the niece and co-heiress of Ralph, Lord Cromwell, and perhaps a plan by Cromwell to settle Wressle on the couple. Wressle was one of the Percy properties confiscated by the crown in 1405 which had never been returned. It had been granted to Cromwell for life in 1438. A settlement benefiting the Nevilles would have added insult to injury. Its prospect may have been particularly provocative since the earl of Northumberland appears to have promised the lordship, if he were able to recover it, to his volatile younger son Thomas, Lord Egremont. A royal licence was issued for the marriage on 1 May 1453. Within two weeks Egremont was recruiting followers. He ignored summons to court and an order to serve in Gascony. In July there was tit-for-tat raiding of property, in which Warwick's young brother, John, was active. All attempts to impose order from Westminster failed. Finally, in August, Egremont and his younger brother Sir Richard Percy ambushed and attacked the wedding party, including Salisbury and his countess, and the groom and bride, travelling north from the ceremony at Tattershall in Lincolnshire as they passed through Heworth near York. This was but the prelude to a major confrontation of the massed forces of both families, led by the earls, outside Topcliffe on 20 October. Warwick was summoned to support his family. Having secured possession of Glamorgan, he was on his way north in September. This was the first time he had returned since he inherited his earldom in 1449. No fighting took place: the mediation of the archbishop of York prevented bloodshed and allowed the two sides to disperse.[29] But the lines had been drawn. Neville was now irrevocably opposed to Percy, and Warwick himself knew that Somerset was his enemy.

While these events were unfolding, the king fell seriously ill. He had been travelling west, with Somerset, perhaps to deal with disturbances in the West Country, or even Glamorgan. He was at the royal hunting lodge of Clarendon in Wiltshire in the middle of August when he collapsed. He fell into a catatonic state in which he would not, or could not, talk. He remained in this condition for sixteen months. The king's collapse, and the extended crisis that ensued, transformed the course of events and Warwick's life. At first the royal councillors assumed that the king would recover quickly. Government, beyond the routine operation of chancery, Exchequer and the courts, was paralysed. It may have been the birth of Edward, Prince of Wales, on 13 October that spurred the lords to action. Parliament, which was due to reassemble on 13 November, was prorogued. A series of great councils was convened. At first Somerset tried to exclude York, but he was overruled. On 21 November the duke of Norfolk accused Somerset of treason. Somerset was sent to the Tower. By this time Warwick, as well as his father, was regularly attending routine council meetings. It became clear that a group of peers, all with grievances against Somerset and his allies, had attached themselves to York. They included, as well as the earls of Salisbury and Warwick, the earl of Devon and Lord Cromwell, who was deeply involved in a dispute over the manor of Ampthill with the duke of Exeter.[30]

For several months the kingdom remained in conciliar government under the presidency of the chancellor, the aged Cardinal Kemp, archbishop of Canterbury. Both Salisbury and Warwick served on this governing council. In January the queen proposed that she be made regent. This was rejected. Tensions were running so high that the king and the chancellor were protected by armed men. As the delayed session of parliament, due to meet on 14 February, approached, the Lords, it was reported, were all arming themselves. Warwick, John Stodeley reported (probably to the duke of Norfolk), was arranging to have a thousand men in London in addition to the fellowship he would bring with him. On the day before the assembly, York was appointed the king's lieutenant in its deliberations. Even before it met Warwick was restored to the chamberlainship of the Exchequer. But not much progress could be made in public business. The death of the chancellor, Cardinal Kemp, on 22 March forced the issue. Without a chancellor, the administration of the kingdom would come to a halt. Only the king or his conciliarly selected deputy could appoint a new chancellor. The king was still comatose. The council nominated York as protector of the realm, on the model of 1422, on 28 March. On 3 April he was formally installed by act of parliament and a continual council appointed to rule the kingdom with him. The day before, Salisbury had been appointed chancellor, the first lay chancellor for fifty years.[31] Warwick had also been nominated to the continual council, which was also sworn into office on 2 April. Like his fellow councillors, and in the tradition of the speaker of the House of Commons, he claimed he was unfit to serve, in his case because he was 'young of age' and 'younger of discretion and wisdom' (he was 25).[32] To some extent the excuse was valid: he had had, unlike his father who swore him in, very little experience in public office or as a councillor. Not that this was in the event to deter him.

In some respects, the Neville commitment to York, which was to have such a dramatic impact on the affairs of the kingdom, was not what might have been expected. It is true that the earl of Salisbury was the duke's brother-in-law, as the husband of his youngest sister Cicely. He had served in France under York's command; he might once have been something of a mentor. But, as Cardinal Beaufort's nephew, the earl had always been close to the court, and had benefited substantially from the favour he enjoyed. Neither he nor Warwick had shown any inclination to support York since 1450. The Nevilles, as close kinsmen to the king through their Beaufort blood, would, one might have predicted, taken the side of Edmund Beaufort. It is true that in the last year or two Salisbury had suffered one or two minor reverses, but not sufficient, one would have thought, to have driven him into political alliance with his dissident brother-in-law. The recent quarrel with the Percys, in itself, provided no compelling reason to cause the family to change. Although the Percys had recently allied themselves with the duke of Exeter, the earl of Northumberland had not as yet shown any inclination to take the duke of Somerset's part. He had largely absented himself from council in recent months. As events were to show he was more inclined to take matters into his own hands in the country.

The deciding issue seems, therefore, to have been Richard Neville the younger's recent conflict with Somerset and the determination of the Nevilles, both father and son, to ensure that Warwick held on to all that he had secured in the last four years. The priority was to remove and keep Somerset from court. In this they were at one with York. There was nothing as yet to suggest that either Salisbury or Warwick shared York's avowed concern for the common weal and frequently reiterated promise to reform the government of the kingdom. It was a short-term response to a recent threat to the house of Neville's acquisition of the earldom of Warwick and the grasping of an opportunity to proceed against the Percys. Given that the king could recover his senses at any time, it was a high-risk strategy and probably demanded a degree of ruthlessness in execution which neither York nor Salisbury possessed.

In the summer, the duke of Exeter, who, having his own claims on the protectorship, resented York's appointment, rose in rebellion in Yorkshire with Thomas Percy, Lord Egremont. The duke of York acted decisively, marched north and dispersed them, probably with Warwick in his company, for on 15 and 16 June 1454 the two presided over judicial proceedings in York, which condemned them. Egremont had escaped, but Exeter was seized from sanctuary and imprisoned at Pontefract. From York, the duke and earl moved to Derby where early in July they held hearings over the sacking of Sir Walter Blount's manor of Elvaston. The proceedings in York continued, but were suspended in August without any final judgement. Two months later Egremont appeared on the scene again. He was captured in a skirmish with Warwick's younger brothers at Stamford Bridge outside York. Condemned for trespass and required to pay damages, which he could not meet, he was imprisoned in Newgate as a debtor. Warwick had been back in the city of York to close the hearings against Egremont in August. His father, who had remained at Westminster during the summer, travelled down to Yorkshire with the great seal and the two were to be found at Middleham, Sheriff Hutton and Barnard Castle (Warwick's own castle) through to the end of September.[33]

The two earls were back in Westminster by November, where at a council meeting a last attempt was made to bring Somerset to trial; the council, which had persistently prevaricated in acting on the duke of Norfolk's accusations, refused to proceed. By then the king was showing signs of recovery. Shortly after Christmas he had fully regained his senses. Early in the new year York stood down as protector. Somerset had not been removed permanently from the scene. He was released from the Tower, giving assurances that he would stay away from the court until he had answered the charges against him. But at a council meeting on 4 March, over which the king presided, the constraint was removed, he was absolved of all blame and restored to the captaincy of Calais. Somerset and York entered into bonds to accept arbitration. Three days later Salisbury resigned as chancellor, and Exeter too was released. Warwick had ceased to be a councillor by 5 February.[34]

Warwick's role during York's first protectorate was secondary. It was his father, as chancellor, who was the dominant Neville partner. His rewards too were slight: a promise of the Channel Islands, which had been resumed by the crown under the act of resumption of 1452 that was not fulfilled. He and his father renewed their joint wardenship of the west march for twenty years with an improved rate of pay.[35] Although he had been active in council and had given his full support, it was his father who was York's right-hand man. His own priority had remained the full control of his countess's inheritance, which he had now secured. Yet, having secured the inheritance he was then poised to assert himself as an independent political figure. He did so in the immediate aftermath of the end of the protectorate, and within a year he had supplanted his father as York's lieutenant.

2

York's Lieutenant, 1455–60

York and Salisbury withdrew from the court early in March 1455; Warwick may well have decamped earlier. A great council was summoned early in April to meet at Leicester on 21 May. The crown's intention is not clear. The Yorkists subsequently claimed that Somerset was planning to deal with them once and for all: the Leicester council was to arraign and condemn them for treason. It is possible, however, that Somerset was not in full control, and that the majority of the lords in attendance at court were seeking a reconciliation, the king himself perhaps wishing it. Nevertheless, it is clear that York and his allies either did not believe that that was the intent, or had already decided that they would seize power by force come what may. Theirs was a pre-emptive strike to recover the control of the kingdom they had recently lost.[1]

As soon as the council was summoned, York and the Neville earls began to call up their retainers and to prepare for armed confrontation. A significant contingent of borderers was raised by Sir Robert Ogle, one of Salisbury's men. They mobilized rapidly, and apparently without the court being aware of their intentions until it was too late, for, when the royal household set out from London, a day or two late, it travelled with no more than the customary light escort. It may be that it had warning of the approaching Yorkist forces when it reached Watford, for it was decided then that the more neutral duke of Buckingham rather than Somerset should take command. Nevertheless, the entourage carried on to St Albans on the following morning (22 May). It arrived at 7.00 a.m. to find the road running north out of the town blocked by York's men. There they stopped, strung out down St Peter's Street, in the marketplace and back into Holywell Street, where, towards the rear of the cavalcade, the king and the lords in attendance waited. Lord Clifford, with the advance guard, rapidly put up what defences they could across St Peter's Street. In the meantime, as all waited, the duke of Buckingham went forward to negotiate for three hours with York. York's demands – the removal of Somerset and others from the king's presence – were unacceptable. Buckingham may not have believed that York would actually attack. But, probably before all attempts by him to find a peaceful solution were exhausted, the Nevilles launched an assault. They had moved their men round to the west of the unfortified town. Sir Robert Ogle broke through to the marketplace, and Warwick, further to the south, came through the gardens and houses onto Holywell Street. Shortly afterwards Clifford's men in St Peter's Street were attacked. Clifford was probably killed defending the barricades; Warwick's men surrounded the royal party, and cut down and killed the duke of Somerset and the earl of Northumberland. The king withdrew into the abbey. There the lords presented themselves to him, took him into their protective custody and ordered an end to the fighting (probably still continuing in St Peter's Street).[2]

In a flurry of surviving accounts justifying their action, the victors claimed that they had acted in self-defence, and stressed that they were the king's true liegemen, who had removed traitors from his presence. That done, they would now, they stated, in the king's name restore unity to the kingdom. To remove all doubt about their loyalty, a crown-wearing ceremony, ritually renewing Henry's monarchy, was staged at St Paul's on Whit Sunday, 25 May. Parliament was summoned to assemble on 9 July. The parliament itself had as its declared objective the restoration of perfect love and rest among the lords, and the politic and restful rule of the land, but its principal acts were to exonerate the victors and to lay the blame for the battle firmly on the shoulders of the dead and a quartet of the king's household men, especially Sir Thomas Thorpe, who had been the speaker in the parliament of 1453–4, whom they particularly distrusted. A general pardon was offered to everyone else, although subsequently the duke of Exeter was arrested and returned to captivity. A new start was to be made: a series of committees were set up to deal with reform, including the finances of the household and the defence of the realm.[3]

Notwithstanding their confident rhetoric, York and the Nevilles were more edgy. The king was separated from his household; the young Henry, earl of Dorset, heir to Edmund Beaufort, was placed under Warwick's custody; the lords maintained armed escorts; and an extraordinary row broke out between Warwick and Lord Cromwell in which the earl accused Cromwell of being 'the beginner of all that journey at St Albans'.[4] What lay behind this no one knows. The show of unity and introduction of reforms barely disguised the reality of a government that had come to power by force and force alone and was not itself united. The lengths to which York and the Nevilles went to justify their actions, suggest that they were fully aware that they had taken a step beyond what had hitherto been accepted as justifiable action. In the end, York was no more able afterwards to secure his claimed right to be the king's principal minister than he had been before.

The second session of parliament began on 11 November. The day before, York was appointed lieutenant to open it in the absence of the king who was reported to be ill again. Almost as soon as proceedings began the speaker, York's retainer William Burley, proposed that York be made protector again; which he duly was. The grounds were renewed disturbances in the West Country between the earl of Devon and Lord Bonville. York did not go down there until after the worst of the disorders were over. He was also obliged to abandon his old ally, the earl, and favour Lord Bonville, who had come to an understanding with the earl of Salisbury and had supported the nomination of his 24-year-old son George to the bishopric of Exeter, vacant since September. George was provided only after the king's nominee had been removed on 4 February 1456.[5]

The main business was the introduction of a new and far more thorough bill of resumption, which would, if implemented, have significantly reduced the crown's freedom of action and made it more answerable to conciliar control. It received little support from the body of the lords, who had much to lose by its implementation, and who stayed away from the last sessions. The duke's reluctance to purge the royal household and install his own men, which would have been seen as an unwarranted invasion of the king's personal prerogative, meant that others close to him, especially the queen, who emerged as the alternative focus of power at court, undermined his position. It was probably the clauses seeking to reduce significantly the incomes of the queen and the prince of Wales that galvanized her into direct political action. York himself was conscious of the mounting opposition: he and Warwick came with an armed retinue to the opening of the third session in January 1456 on the basis of false reports that he would be forcibly removed from the protectorate. He was determined to see the bill through.[6] It was the bill, however, that brought the protectorate down two weeks later. The king's health was sufficiently recovered by 25 February for him to relieve York of the office with the assent of the Lords. Parliament was then dissolved after the passage of a severely emasculated act, and not before Salisbury had been granted the stewardship of the north parts of the duchy of Lancaster in succession to the recently deceased Lord Cromwell.

Warwick was fully engaged in council and parliament throughout this period, but initially no more so than his father and uncle Lord Fauconberg. He was himself particularly preoccupied with establishing himself as the captain of Calais. One of the first acts immediately after St Albans was Warwick's appointment as Somerset's successor (as reported by John Crane to John Paston on 25 May).[7] But before Warwick could take up the post, agreement had to be reached with the garrison for the settlement of arrears and with the Company of the Staple to make further financial provision. It took a year for a deal to be reached that was satisfactory to all parties. Lord Fauconberg and York's man, Sir Edmund Mulso, undertook lengthy initial negotiations with the garrison and the Staplers. By 4 August 1455, they were sufficiently advanced for Warwick to indent. Proposed terms for a settlement were put to a meeting of council on 27 October. The Staplers, however, were unwilling to underwrite the significant sums needed to pay the garrison without further concessions, and the garrison needed a copper-bottomed guarantee that their arrears would be paid and future salaries met. The garrison also wanted to be assured that Warwick would not replace

them with his own men and that they would not in any way be victimized for
their previous allegiance. Because the negotiations had stalled, Warwick sought,
before the end of the parliamentary session on 13 December, to be absolved from
all responsibility for the safety of Calais. A settlement was finally reached in the
last session of the parliament. The Staplers agreed to underwrite a complete
settlement of the garrison's demands. Although York was removed from the
protectorate on 25 February 1456, on 16 March a final agreement was drawn up
and 20 April was set as the date for Neville to take command. Fauconberg was
commissioned to take possession on his behalf.[8]

The successful installation of Warwick in Calais was the major long-term
Yorkist gain from the victory at St Albans, even though it took nearly a year to
secure. But St Albans led to an arguably more significant shift in the relative
political roles of the Nevilles, father and son. During the first protectorate there is
no doubt that Salisbury was the more important of the two. By February 1456 it
was apparent that Warwick had begun to take the lead. There were several signs of
Warwick's emergence as the dominant, and more headstrong, of the two. He had
been the first to abandon the court after the restoration of the duke of Somerset
in 1455. He personally led part of the assault at St Albans. He seems to have
been first on the scene in the marketplace when Somerset and Northumberland
were surrounded and killed. Salisbury is not mentioned in any of the accounts
of the battle. His brother Fauconberg was in the king's entourage. One suspects
that he was more willing to come to a peaceful solution than Warwick. Indeed,
it is not impossible that Warwick himself launched the attack. We have seen that
it was Warwick who quarrelled with Cromwell about the responsibility for the
fighting, perhaps in retaliation for an accusation levied at him. Finally, it was
he, and he alone, who accompanied York with an armed retinue to the opening
of the third session of the parliament on 9 February 1456. There was 'no lord
else', not even the earl of Salisbury. He was no longer the inexperienced young
man of 1453, though some might have felt that he still lacked discretion and
wisdom. A picture emerges of a man less cautious than York and less prudent
than his father; a man more ready to act first and ask questions afterwards; and
a man not as bound by ties of kinship and loyalty to the king as his father, or
even the duke. The 28-year-old Warwick was of a new generation. He wore his
commitment to the house of Lancaster more lightly than his father. Salisbury
may always have been a reluctant rebel: he was steeped in the collective conciliar
approach characteristic of his earlier years at court. Not so his son. Warwick and
his father, one may therefore suppose, had different views on the course of action
they should follow. If one can detect a new ruthlessness and single-mindedness in
the Yorkist camp in 1455–6, from St Albans to the armed descent on parliament
in February the following year, it probably came from Warwick. It is possibly the
case that from the moment that Somerset was restored to favour, Warwick had

taken the initiative in arguing that the time had come to deal with him once and for all. He emerged in this year as the dynamic force in the Yorkist camp.

The historian remains somewhat in the position of John Bocking in February 1456 of not knowing what was really going on in the next three years or so. The evidence is patchy, ambiguous and contradictory. The result is that not only do modern interpretations differ, but also the very chronology is, on occasion, in dispute. This is as true of Warwick as it is of the other major players. For a few months during the spring and summer of 1456 York continued in favour with the king. Conciliar government continued; Salisbury remained one of the most frequent attenders. He sat on the first session of the judicial proceedings held at the Guildhall in London on 1 May to try those responsible for recent rioting in London. Warwick was preoccupied with the transfer of power in Calais. He was resident at Warwick Castle during May. All three attended a special council meeting early in June. Thereafter York, and possibly Salisbury, travelled north to confront James II of Scotland, who had renounced the truce, besieged Roxburgh and raided into Northumberland. Warwick may have made his first visit to Calais then.[9]

The apparent political harmony broke down in the autumn. The queen and her household, including the infant prince of Wales, had moved to the West Midlands, residing for much of the time at Kenilworth. It would appear that, after the threat represented by the failed bill of resumption, she was determined to assert the implicit authority of the infant prince in the West Midlands and Wales. Particularly at issue was possession of Carmarthen and Aberystwyth, which York had taken into his custody before the prince of Wales was invested in April 1454. Edmund Tudor, whom she had appointed the prince's lieutenant, quickly came into conflict with York's deputies, Sir Walter Devereux and Sir William Herbert. There were serious disturbances, to the extent that the king and his household were also brought down to the midlands in August. By September it had been decided, to what extent on the initiative of the queen is uncertain, to change the major offices of state. Laurence Booth, the queen's chancellor, became keeper of the privy seal in September.

Another great council was summoned, this time to Coventry later in the month, and Richard Neville almost certainly attended it. Devereux and Herbert were called to account and submitted themselves. Thomas Bourgchier, archbishop of Canterbury and Henry, Viscount Bourgchier, who had held the posts of chancellor and treasurer since St Albans, were removed from office. Their replacements, William Wayneflete, bishop of Winchester and John Talbot, earl of Shrewsbury were closer to the court. It was reported by James Gresham to John Paston on 16 October that York was still in favour with the king, but not the queen; and indeed had it not been for the intervention of the duke of Buckingham, who was not pleased at the dismissal of his own kinsmen from office, he would have been set upon when he left. The young duke of Somerset, Gresham also reported, was involved in a brawl in the city in which several men were killed, to which a later chronicler added the gloss that he had purposed to have attacked York.[10] It is also possible that an attempt was made on the earl's life, the first of several, after the end of the council meeting.[11]

As far as one can determine from cursory and imprecise evidence relating to a further great council held at Coventry from 15 February until early March 1457, by the spring of that year hostility to York and Warwick at court had hardened. The attainder of 1459 referred to the occasion at a council at Coventry in which the duke of Buckingham and all other lords, begged the king on bended knee not to show any more leniency to the duke of York if he continued to act contrary to his royal estate. All lords agreed not to use force to settle their disputes, but the duke and Warwick were required to make a solemn oath to the same effect. York was compensated for surrendering the custody of the Welsh castles and reappointed lieutenant of Ireland, perhaps in the hope that he would go there in person.[12] By April 1457 it was clear that the Queen and the court party coalescing around her were in the driving seat. She herself as yet was not overtly hostile to Warwick. Indeed she countenanced the marriage of her ward, Isabel Ingoldisthorpe, who through her mother was in line of succession to a portion of the earldom of Worcester, to the earl's brother, Sir John Neville. The marriage was brokered by her uncle Worcester. It was celebrated on 25 April at Canterbury. Warwick was present.[13]

Shortly afterwards, the earl, his countess and Lord Fauconberg crossed to Calais where he took up residence for an extended stay. The earl had been there briefly in December 1456,[14] but this marks the real beginning of his personal association with the town. There are several reasons why in the spring of 1457 he should have decided to devote his energies to the captaincy. Over the last year he and his father, as well as York, had increasingly been marginalized by the resurgent court party at the head of which the queen had placed herself. His father had withdrawn to his northern estates. It may have become apparent to him that they were going to have to bide their time before they could make a further bid for power. He probably felt himself to be in physical danger from the heirs of the dead of St Albans, especially the young Henry, duke of Somerset. The queen had established herself on the basis of the prince of Wales' patrimony in the West Midlands, with serious consequences for Warwick's lordship there. The court was frequently at Coventry or Kenilworth, and attached to it those hostile to him. Discretion in this respect may have been the better part of valour.[15] On the other hand, Calais had its positive attractions. It offered him an independent command, an opportunity to act freely away from the court, and a chance to make a name for himself as a significant figure on the European stage. He seized the moment. His actions as captain of Calais were to make him the most important man in England and the most renowned Englishman on the continent.

Warwick spent the most part of the next three years in Calais. Professor Hicks has calculated that he received wages for being in residence for 267 days from midsummer 1457 to midsummer 1458.[16] His visits to England were few and far between, the longest being in the spring and early summer of 1458. The earl at first busied himself establishing his personal authority over the garrison, pacifying the marches, which were seriously disturbed, negotiating with representatives of the duke of Burgundy to secure the truce between the two, and securing the enclave against an anticipated French assault. The French attack, when it came, was not on Calais (it was surrounded by the Burgundian-held territory of Flanders and Picardy) but on Sandwich, which was the principal supply point for the garrison and link to England. At dawn on 28 August 1457 Pierre de Brézé, seneschal of Normandy attacked, sacked and looted the town from the sea. He was driven off by Sir Thomas Kyriell, but not before he had done considerable damage, not only to the town, but also to confidence that the crown could defend the coast effectively.[17] The attack also seems to have stimulated an attempt to heal the divisions between the lords. A council, about which little is known, met in October and November. Warwick probably attended, as did the duke of York, for it was during its meeting that he was appointed keeper of the seas. The appointment was first agreed on 3 October; the earl sealed his indenture on 26 November and the letters patent were issued at the end of December. He need not have been present at any of these moments, but it is apparent that the council, including his many enemies on it, accepted that he was the only man for the job. It was logical, since he was already established at Calais, and already had his own ships, and close relationships with the men of the Cinque Ports.[18] The effect of de Brézé's raid was to give even more military responsibility to the earl.

It is also apparent that, at the meetings held at Westminster in the autumn, a major effort was launched at reconciliation between the rival parties of St Albans.[19] A further council was summoned to Westminster for 26 January 1458. The lords all attended in armed strength. Somerset, Northumberland, Clifford and their allies were reported to have over 2,000 men; York, Salisbury and Warwick were said to have 1,500. Such was the fear of violence that the mayor of London raised a force of 500 men to police the city. The Yorkists were accommodated within the walls, possibly because they were fewer in number or because they enjoyed greater favour with the citizens. Warwick, with his reported 600 men, resplendent in their livery of red jackets embroidered with white ragged staffs, was the last to arrive – not until 14 February, after he had been delayed by contrary winds.[20] Only then did full negotiations begin. It took a month for the arbitrators, a panel of bishops and lords going to and fro between the parties on behalf of the king, to shape an agreement acceptable to both. The Yorkists accepted that they would pay compensation to the heirs of the victims and establish a chantry for their souls: Warwick agreed to pay 1,000 marks to Lord Clifford (not necessarily because he was responsible for his death). All parties sealed bonds, Warwick and his father for £8,000 each, to abide by the award. On 25 March, the feast of the Annunciation of the Virgin Mary, a solemn Loveday was enacted, with a mass and procession whereby the agreement was blessed and the parties were all once more ritually reconciled. In the procession Warwick walked with the duke of Exeter, possibly because he was admiral.[21]

The Love Day was a major effort at reconciliation and for a while, superficially, it succeeded. Feasting and jousting in celebration continued until May. Warwick was confirmed as keeper of the seas and received a commission to deal with piracy. A certain degree of fudging was permitted as he was also appointed in April with Buckingham to a commission to enquire into accusations against Fauconberg for piracy (presumable as his uncle's lieutenant at Calais during his absence) from which he was subsequently and not surprisingly exonerated.[22] But the arbitration was not a satisfactory long-term solution. The Yorkists had made the greater concession and accepted blame they had denied immediately after the battle, but it was not enough to satisfy their enemies who, it soon became apparent, still wanted revenge. The courtiers' feasting and jousting reported by chroniclers may have been as much in celebration of a perceived victory as a show of general joy. Warwick withdrew to Calais again in May. The author of Bale's Chronicle noted that on 9 May, by the king's commandment, Warwick rode through London 'in embassy with a goodly fellowship'; he spent the night of 11 May at Canterbury and crossed to Calais the following day.[23] This was an embassy for which formal letters were issued on 14 May to discuss further infringements of the truce with Burgundy and included Warwick's brothers and Richard Beauchamp, the bishop of Salisbury. They met with a substantial embassy from the duke of Burgundy in June, but it is likely that discussion of breaches of the truce were a mask for negotiations on some other, more substantial, issue. What was actually being negotiated by this and by another embassy formally commissioned in August, which included Sir John Wenlock and Louis Galet, to negotiate with both France and Burgundy, remains particularly murky. Wenlock and Galet were both linked to Calais as well as being *persona grata* at court. The second embassy was charged with negotiating marriage agreements with either France or Burgundy between the infant prince of Wales, York's son the earl of March, and Henry, duke of Somerset, himself as yet unmarried, and French princesses. There were suspicions that York, through Warwick, was negotiating on his own behalf. It is not clear, however, what the English diplomatic purpose was, or who in fact was determining it. Charles VII certainly came to this conclusion and pulled out early in 1459.[24]

But, by then, English politics had once more become polarized. Yet again Warwick's precipitate actions led to confrontation and brought the uneasy truce agreed at St Paul's on Lady Day to an end. During the summer of 1458, even while these negotiations were going on, he launched a series of attacks on neutral shipping in the Channel. The first, dramatically reported by John Jerningham to John Paston, was an attack on Spanish ships on 28 May; a second attack was made a few weeks later on the Hanseatic bay fleet, in flagrant violation of a truce concluded two years earlier; and a third took on Genoese ships. There may well have been others not reported. There were several reasons for these attacks. By the summer of 1458, payment of the Calais garrison was again deeply in arrears; the Staplers were continuing to suffer from the loss of revenue through licences issued to foreign merchants, especially Italians, to ship wool independently; customs revenues from which the earl was meant to receive his wages as keeper of the seas were meagre; and Warwick probably wanted to assert English control of the Channel over all shipping. The Hanse complained officially to the crown and an enquiry was established on 31 July.[25]

By the autumn of 1458 the government was seriously concerned about Warwick's conduct, which might have been perceived as undermining the concurrent diplomatic initiatives and to have increased, rather than decreased, the risk of attack on England's coasts. Warwick's actions were all the more flagrant in their contempt for authority in that he had been commissioned to eradicate piracy, not to perpetuate it. Chancellor Waynflete wrote to Southampton on 7 September revealing that fear of another French attack, suspected collusion, and the recent attacks on Genoese and Hanseatic ships were causes of government concern.[26] It was therefore determined to call Warwick to account at yet another general council summoned to meet at Westminster on 11 October. He was reluctant to attend, for he suspected that its intention was to deprive him of the captaincy and discipline him. Although he crossed the Channel at the end of September, he at first kept away from London. He was at Collyweston on 7 October, and in Yorkshire at the end of the month and early in November, where letters were delivered to him by royal messengers, repeatedly demanding his attendance at the council. He finally went up to Westminster, but no sooner had he arrived than a brawl developed between some of his men and household men in the palace. It quickly escalated into a confrontation between him and senior household officers (perhaps as a result of an attempt to arrest him), from which he either fought his way out or was bundled to safety by his supporters. He made good his escape eventually, back to Calais.[27]

What exactly happened is unclear. Warwick claimed a year later that there had been a plot to assassinate him.[28] In his report on recent English affairs to Charles VII early in 1459 Maine herald remarked that it was well known that a 'great parliament' had been planned to remove him from office. This was well known ('et est ce tout notoire') and Warwick, he said, was well aware of it. Warwick was reported to have declared publicly and melodramatically that he would give up all his lands in England rather than surrender Calais. The *English Chronicle* reports that soon after the brawl he was indeed removed by privy seal and Somerset appointed in his place, but that Warwick, claiming (disingenuously) that he had been appointed by parliament, would not obey the privy seal.[29] The fracas may even have started accidentally: in one report it was said to have begun when one of Warwick's men trod on the foot of a household man. In the tense atmosphere, tempers flared and weapons were drawn.[30] The favourably inclined author of Bale's Chronicle conceded that because of his men's violence actually within the verge of the royal household, the earl should have been committed to the Tower, but that 'he wisely purveyed a remedy therefore' implying that an attempt was made to arrest him, *after* the brawl, as being responsible for it, but that he then resisted arrest and escaped.[31] One will never know, but it is probably the case that the government, which in October had been reshaped on more partisan lines to the liking of the queen, with the earl of Wiltshire replacing Shrewsbury as treasurer and Sir Thomas Tuddenham becoming treasurer of the household, was already preparing to take a firmer line towards him. It might be significant that, two years later, Friar Brackley advised John Paston to remind the earl of the role of Tuddenham in the fight at Westminster wharf.[32] Warwick was probably lucky to escape and justified in believing that there was a plan to remove him from office by one means or another.

Certainly this incident marks a point of no return. Gregory's Chronicle recalled that, after 1458, the lords never came all together to any parliament or council 'but it were in field with spear and shield'. It is at about this time, after 1 November, that Salisbury called his council together at Middleham and resolved to take full part with the duke of York. Whether this resolution preceded or followed the fracas at Westminster cannot be known. It might have proceeded independently, and Warwick's presence in Yorkshire at the end of October suggests that father and son might already have come to some understanding. Lord Fauconberg was removed from his post as joint custodian of Windsor Castle later in November and new moves were made against Sir William Oldhall.[33] At the same time, a loan was negotiated by the new treasurer with the Staplers to cover the expenses of the household in return for customs concessions, an agreement was made not to issue more licences to Italians, and permission was given to negotiate independently with the duke of Burgundy to ban all wool imports to his territories that did not pass through the Staple. This agreement, while primarily of financial benefit to the court, might also have been designed to drive a wedge between Warwick and the Staplers and thus undermine his position in Calais.[34] By the end of 1458, all parties seemed to be set on course for a renewal of civil war: the lines were more firmly drawn than they had been in 1455; there was now more at stake; and it was more likely that a resolution would not be found until one side had achieved a decisive victory over the other.

Yet the evidence remains opaque. It is impossible to be certain about the precise course of events. There can be little doubt that there was an air of crisis in the first half of 1459. It is not clear, however, whether the court was more concerned about a possible French attack than a possible Yorkist rebellion. The court itself might not have been too sure where the greater threat lay. After Warwick's return to Calais it appears that the embassy under Wenlock and Galet acted on his behalf to prevent a rapprochement between Burgundy and France. Wenlock, whom the court still trusted, reported that France was preparing another attack on England.[35] It might be that the issue of commissions of array, especially in the south east in February, which omitted York and his allies, was a response to this, rather than against a precautionary move against Warwick. Other steps towards defensive readiness might also have been designed to protect the realm against a feared French or Scottish attack than a descent on England by Warwick and rebellion by York and Salisbury. Castles were to be repaired; bows and arrows were to be stockpiled; the queen began to recruit in Cheshire; and the royal household was armed 'against certain misruled and seditious persons'. Warwick was authorized to arrest ships to strengthen his navy; Salisbury was paid for the defence of the west march. All this was done, as the order to stockpile weapons in the Tower put it on 7 May, because of 'the enemies on every side approaching upon us as well upon the sea as on land'.[36] Were they domestic enemies or foreign enemies?

The hostile author of the *English Chronicle* writing after Edward IV's accession to the throne, had no doubts: they were domestic enemies, the realm was out of all good government, and the queen and her affinity ruled the kingdom as she liked. The return of the court to Coventry in May 1459 might endorse his view. In June, according to Benet, the Yorkists were indicted, on the advice of the queen, at a Coventry council meeting held in their absence. It might have been intended to call a parliament in which to condemn them. Subsequently the Yorkists claimed that this was the case. Whether indictments were made or not, as in May 1455, they decided to get their retaliation in first. The subsequent act of attainder (passed at the end of the year) implied that, in July, Warwick was in treasonable correspondence with York through Thomas Vaughan and Sir William Oldhall. York, Salisbury and Warwick perhaps also used Warwick's mother, who was condemned for an act of treason on 1 August, as a go-between.[37]

Salisbury was the first to act.[38] According to the subsequent indictment he set off from Middleham with his retainers and their contingents early in September. He was joined by supporters from the north west. He either took that route to gather more support, or was forced to go that way because the court had moved to Nottingham. The intention was to meet up with York and Warwick in the West Midlands, perhaps to come before the king at Kenilworth, but he was intercepted by a Lancastrian force at Blore Heath on 23 September. Although he was victorious and able to march on, he was severely weakened and his two sons, Sir Thomas and Sir John Neville, were captured and imprisoned at Chester. Warwick set off at a similar time from Calais with 600 men from the garrison. He was in London by 20 September and narrowly escaped being intercepted himself by a Lancastrian force under the duke of Somerset at Coleshill in Warwickshire a few days later. If he had hoped to raise his own men in the West Midlands it proved impossible because of the presence there of royalists in strength. The two earls finally joined York at Ludlow. They were much weaker than they had hoped. Not only had Salisbury suffered losses and Warwick not been able to raise men in the midlands, it also seems that almost all their potential sympathizers among the peerage (Stanley, the Bourgchiers, Norfolk, even Arundel) had not stirred. Moreover, the court seems to have had advance knowledge of their plans, for forces had been raised and sent to intercept them. Unlike in 1455, the court was not taken by surprise.

The combined forces of the three lords advanced from Ludlow to face the king's host at Worcester. They were outnumbered and withdrew back to Ludlow, where they prepared to defend themselves below the town at Ludford. All the time they were in communication with the king through Garter King of Arms, protesting their loyalty, peaceful intent and just cause, and requesting an audience with him to put their case. Their true intent was, they insisted, 'to the prosperity and augmentation of your high estate, and to the common weal of this realm'.[39] This declaration links in with the manifesto that Warwick issued on his landing. Their only concern, they stated, was better government. The common weal and rule of law had been overturned by the covetous councillors serving the king, who were robbing him of his livelihood and impoverishing the realm. All they wished to do was to present themselves to the king, 'as lowly as we can' to reform the state of affairs and punish the evil ministers. They were prepared to employ their persons and labours to assist the king, if it pleased him, without private interest or personal grudge so as to put everything right.[40] They were not believed; and it is hard to suppose that they were sincere in their protestations of a peaceful intent. Pardons were offered, but were rejected. The abbot of St Albans, John Whethamstede, in recalling these events from the court perspective, put a speech into the earl of Warwick's mouth explaining why the lords would not accept them. It may be that Warwick did reply on behalf of the three; if not, it is revealing of his perceived status, anyway, that Whethamstede characterized him as their spokesman. His supposed response, presented in a highly literary manner as reported speech in the text, probably captures the essence. Pardons were valueless: they had been pardoned before, even by confirmation of parliament for actions at St Albans, but this fact had been ignored. Furthermore, those about the king were not his true and obedient subjects and would not respect a royal pardon, and he (Warwick) himself had experience of their untrustworthiness when attending a great council at Westminster.[41] Behind these reasons for rejecting the king's grace lies the real purpose of their action: a determination to seize power, by force if necessary, in the king's name.

Desertion by elements of the Calais garrison, led by Andrew Trollope, who claimed that they had been misled by Warwick into thinking that they would not be confronting the king, gives the lie to their public utterances, even those sworn solemnly in Worcester Cathedral. The desertion itself, either at Ludford or earlier, further weakened the Yorkist lords. Facing an impossible position, on the night of 12/13 October, the three lords and their closest servants abandoned camp. York with his second son Edmund, earl of Rutland, and Thomas Colt crossed Wales and took ship to Ireland; Warwick, Salisbury and York's heir, Edward earl of March, accompanied by Wenlock, Sir Walter Blount, York's man Sir James Pickering and the loyal remnant of the Calais garrison made their way to north Devon and eventually by boat to Calais.[42] The attempt to repeat the action of St Albans had failed utterly: fundamentally because they were isolated politically. The nation as a whole was not prepared to take up arms against a king to whom it was still loyal and perceived them, however much they attempted to present themselves otherwise, as pursuing private interests and personal resentments.

Parliament had been summoned to Coventry even before the lords broke camp and fled. The assembly which met on 20 November was packed with royal supporters and had but one purpose: to complete the condemnation and ruin of the Yorkist lords. The process of attainder was adopted; a committee of lawyers prepared the bill with great care. At the same time the royalist position was justified in the *Somnium Vigilantis*, which set out to demolish the Yorkist propaganda and to demonstrate that no cause, not even the cause of reform, could justify the raising of arms against the king. It took a month to pass the act, which stripped twenty seven rebels and their heirs of gentle status and confiscated their estates. Wenlock was among the condemned. The threat of wider proscription and the requirement that all lords present should take an oath of loyalty persuaded others to take out pardons, including many who had ridden with Salisbury, and Sir Walter Blount and Louis Galet who had crossed from Calais.[43] Their offices were distributed to their enemies: Lord Clifford becoming warden of the west march. Bishop Booth of Durham himself seized Barnard Castle, to which the bishops of Durham had a long-standing claim of the rights of forfeiture, and his right was acknowledged by a proviso to the act of attainder. Others of Warwick's estates from the Beauchamp inheritance were seized and redistributed to Richard Beauchamp's elder daughters in recognition of their long-standing claim. The rest were placed in the custody of loyal servants of the crown.[44]

Even before parliament met, action had been taken to dislodge Warwick from Calais. On 9 October he had been replaced as captain by Henry, duke of Somerset.

By the end of the month Somerset had raised troops and crossed the Channel, but the Yorkist earls had entered Calais already and he was forced to withdraw to Guînes, which he took and occupied. Skirmishing continued throughout the winter. Despite all their efforts, the government could not dislodge the earl. A government embargo on trading through Calais probably proved counter-productive, because it drove the Staplers into Warwick's arms. The attempt to take Calais was further hindered by support Warwick received from the people of Kent, and the garrison's own vigorous counter-attacks, including a bold raid on Sandwich in January 1460, which seized a fleet being gathered to reinforce Somerset, and captured Lord Rivers and other Lancastrian captains. Warwick himself boldly sailed to Dublin in March 1460 to confer with York, evading royal fleets in both directions. Following his return, having established a safe haven by a second raid on Sandwich led by Lord Fauconberg, and having flooded Kent with reformist propaganda, the Calais lords landed at Sandwich at the end of June.[45]

The Yorkist lords entered London on 2 July. Warwick and the earls swore a solemn oath in St Paul's that they were true subjects of the king, come only to reform the government of the kingdom and remove the evil persons from about his person. This time the evil persons were named: they were Buckingham, Shrewsbury, Wiltshire and Beaumont. Wiltshire had in fact fled the kingdom. These men were probably picked out precisely because York and the Nevilles did not have long-standing personal grudges against them. They were those who were then about the king, and had been particularly active at court in the last year. Identifying them as evil and covetous ministers was consistent with the repeated claim of the earls that they acted only for the common good and the king's true interest. Leaving Salisbury to blockade the Tower, where Lord Scales, Lord Hungerford and other councillors had taken refuge, Warwick set off with the earl of March and Lord Fauconberg to face Henry VI at Northampton on 10 July. He had gathered more support than he had in September 1459. Not only was there a significant force of Kentish levies at his back, but he had also been joined by Viscount Bourgchier, Lords Audley, Bergavenny, Clinton and Say. Lesser peers they may have been, but their presence reveals that the Yorkists had gained some sympathy in the intervening months. The battle, fought in pouring rain, was brief, its outcome aided by desertion in the king's camp by Lord Grey of Ruthin. Warwick gave orders to spare the commons. His men made straight for the king's tent, where the duke of Buckingham, the earl of Shrewsbury, Viscount Beaumont, and Lord Egremont were killed defending him. The king, once more, became a guest of the Yorkists. The queen and her son, who had probably remained in Coventry, escaped. Warwick was now, for the first time, in command of the kingdom. He was to remain at the helm for several years to come.[46]

3

England's Caesar, 1460–65

The victors of Northampton returned to London with the levers of power in their hands. The chief officers of state were replaced. The most significant appointment was of Warwick's brother George, bishop of Exeter, as chancellor. Bourgchier became treasurer. But additionally, for the first time, the king's household was purged, with Salisbury as chamberlain taking charge. Warwick himself made a brief visit to Calais where he came to terms with Somerset, who was allowed to march out of Guînes on the understanding that he would not take arms against him again. Parliament was summoned to meet at Westminster on 7 October. York as yet had shown no urgency to return to England. If a joint invasion had been planned, it had not been acted upon. The victory was Warwick's; the new government was Warwick's. The duke landed in the Wirral on 8 September. Warwick rode to meet him at Shrewsbury in mid-September, but returned to London in time for the opening of the assembly. York, after a circuitous and stately progress to rally support, arrived at Westminster three days later. He strode into the Lords' house and walked straight to the chair of state as if to occupy it by right. But, instead of acclamation, as he appeared to expect, he was challenged by Archbishop Bourgchier and faced a stony silence.[1]

Something had not gone to plan, but it is not at all clear what. The later account in the Waurin Relation, compiled early in 1461 when Warwick was endeavouring to convince his ally the duke of Burgundy that Henry VI was secure on the throne, stressed that the earls, all three of them including March, had been surprised by York's actions and had brokered the compromise which led to the duke being recognised as heir to the throne. This account, which takes the story back to Warwick's appointment as captain of Calais, continually reiterates how he and his father always maintained that they would assist the duke as long as he did not challenge the king himself. They never made war on the king, only against his disloyal subjects and internal enemies. Their own loyalty to the house of Lancaster was absolute. This accurately reflects the stand repeatedly taken by him in all public utterances right through to the victory at Northampton. In this narrative York revealed his ambition to take the throne only *after* Warwick had met him at Shrewsbury. He there received a petition urging him to claim it. When parliament opened, the earl was still not aware of the duke's claim. Only when the duke actually occupied the royal chambers at Westminster did

Warwick realize what he had in mind. He had to be told by his father, who, as chamberlain, delivered the news that the king had been put out of his lodgings. Warwick remonstrated with York. He called a council at Blackfriars. The young Edward of March was persuaded to support Warwick and the council in resisting the duke: both earls reiterated that they had promised to protect the king while he was alive. A delegation was sent to York led by the bishops of Rochester and Ely. York insisted on his intention to be crowned on St Edward's day. Finally, having been persuaded by Sir Thomas Neville, York relented and accepted a compromise by which he would be made the king's heir. York was then commissioned as the king's lieutenant to bring order to the realm and on 1 November a crown-wearing ceremony was conducted at St Paul's followed by a feast at which Sir John Neville acted as chamberlain of the household. The people cried out, 'Vive le roy henry et le comte de Warewic'.[2]

Apart from the gloss given on the prominent and loyal role of the earl in persuading York to step back from the throne itself, the account in the Waurin Relation is substantially in agreement with the official record of a series of meetings in parliament which arrived at the compromise solution of York being made heir apparent. This was enacted by statute modelled on the Treaty of Troyes of 1421, by which Henry V had become the heir to the throne of France and regent during Charles VI's lifetime.[3] To some extent the Waurin Relation gloss is corroborated by a letter to the earl of Worcester, at the time in Venice, written before the final Accord was enacted. It described the dramatic moment in which York laid claim to the throne. The lords, the unknown correspondent reported, withdrew into council at Blackfriars and 'some time sent and some time wrote to my lord of York till at the last it was agreed to take such direction as they would advise him'. 'Wherein', he added, 'my lord of Warwick be had him so that his fame is like to be of great memory'. The outcome was that the king would keep his throne. The informant did not know, or it had not yet been agreed, that York would become heir apparent. It is nevertheless clear that he believed that Warwick led the resistance to the duke and had been instrumental in preserving Henry VI on the throne. We cannot be sure that this is an independent source. The sentence about Warwick suggests that it too came from his circle. Worcester was an ally of Neville; for all we know, the author of the letter could have been the earl's secretary.[4]

However, one thing is clear: In October 1460 Warwick claimed to be no part of York's attempted coup and publicly aligned himself, with his father and uncle and the other lords, in opposition to it. It is, nevertheless, incredible that he was taken completely by surprise when York entered parliament to claim the throne. York had undertaken a circuitous progress through the marches, recruiting new retainers as he went. In the contracts no reference was made to the regnal year or allegiance to the king. Before he reached London he adopted and displayed the full arms of England and as he travelled he had a sword carried upright before him as if it were the sword of state. Warwick could not but have known. It would also be surprising if Warwick and March, if no one else, had not been privy to York's plans, probably since the spring when Warwick took such a great risk to go by sea to confer with the duke in Dublin. What they there decided has ever since remained controversial. That they discussed plans for an invasion is likely. But was that all? Later, Edward IV remembered that voyage as being of great significance to his future, for Warwick brought back with him 'the greatest joy and consolation earthly'. What, in retrospect, could have been of greater joy to the young king than that on this occasion his right-hand man had agreed with his father to support his dynasty's claim to the throne? There is thus reason to suspect that Warwick and York not only agreed an invasion plan, but also determined that York would claim the throne.[5] If so, it is equally apparent that Warwick deliberately maintained the pretence that the collective aim of the Yorkists remained, as it always had been, removal of evil ministers and reform. Perhaps they hoped to orchestrate a 'popular' election, overriding the likely opposition of men like Warwick's own father and uncle, the earl of Salisbury and Lord Fauconberg. One can be fairly certain that Salisbury and Fauconberg would have balked at the deposition of Henry VI. One element of truth in the Waurin Relation might be that Salisbury, as new chamberlain, was surprised and taken aback by York's intrusion into the palace. It is noticeable in this account, too, that his son Sir John acted as chamberlain of the household, and thus his deputy, in the feast celebrating the Accord. In so far as Warwick, and possibly March, had dissembled, it might well be that they knew that they would not have been able to carry Warwick's father and uncle with them. But they also seem to have failed to orchestrate support in the House of Lords, in the commons, or popular support in London. Indeed the Waurin Relation specifically refers to popular opposition to York.

There is another possibility: that the intention from the beginning was to secure York's adoption as heir apparent. This might seem too far-fetched, but a rumour from London was reported in July to Francesco Coppini, which he passed on to the duke of Milan, that the lords would make a son of the duke of York king, that they would pass over the king's son and that they were already saying that he was not the king's son. The author of the *English Chronicle* actually inserted in his account for 1459 the fact that a slander was circulating then that 'the queen was defamed and slandered that he that was called prince was not her son but a bastard gotten in adultery'.[6] This is a much employed slur, that was going to surface again in relation to Edward IV, but the report of its circulation is, to say the least, thought-provoking. If York, March and Warwick had schemed to make York heir apparent, not only their dissembling, but also their manipulation of their peers, had been remarkable. Either way, it is quite possible that Warwick had for some months been party to an elaborate charade, concealing his and the duke's true intentions from his kinsmen, until York finally made public his claim to the throne.

All accounts agree that Warwick was in command. From the moment the earls landed in July, all contemporary sources take it for granted that the kingdom was under his rule. Francesco Coppini, papal legate instructed by Pius II to raise support for a crusade, had attached himself to the Yorkist earls at Calais in the winter of 1459–60. He came with them in July and gave full papal backing to the Yorkist cause. In return, he hoped to secure their commitment to his master's dream, as well as the English bishopric he was promised. He too was not an impartial witness: but his, and his servants', correspondence with the duke of Milan leaves no doubt that Warwick was the man with whom he treated and the person who decided policy. Coppini himself wrote from Bruges as early as 22 March 1460 that Warwick would perform miracles. A newsletter recounting the battle of Northampton and its aftermath presents Warwick as the only man who mattered: fortune favoured him at the battle; he took the king into his power; the government of the realm would remain in his hands. 'Thus one may say that today everything is in Warwick's power.' He had indeed 'done marvellous things'.[7] And so it remained until York was made protector of the realm and king's lieutenant for a third time at the end of October. But within two months York and Salisbury were dead.

The Act of Accord of 31 October 1460, which left Henry VI on the throne, but recognized York as his heir and protector of the realm, was an expedient that could only be imposed by the sword. The queen and her supporters were never going to accept the disinheritance of her son without a fight. Warwick had already been commissioned to restore order in the midlands (and thereby regain control of his estates) on 8 September,[8] though there is no evidence that he made more than a cursory visit. Fresh dispositions were made after 31 October. York and Salisbury were commissioned immediately after the proroguing of parliament on 1 December to enforce their authority in the north where Margaret of Anjou was mustering her forces. Finding, perhaps to their surprise, that they were outnumbered, they took refuge in Sandal Castle. On 30 December, perhaps lured out by a Lancastrian detachment, or foraging for supplies, or even seeking to make a break-out, according to friendly accounts after a truce had been negotiated, they were overwhelmed. York and his son the earl of Rutland, Sir Thomas Neville and others were killed on the field. Salisbury was taken alive, brought to Pontefract and there lynched.[9]

The victorious Lancastrian army swept south. Warwick, who had remained in control of the government in London and had opened the second session of parliament which convened in January 1461, frantically raised troops in the south east and East Anglia, painting an alarming picture of the rapacious intent of the northerners who were then descending on the southern counties. With these levies, and with the dukes of Norfolk and Suffolk at his side, on 12 February he marched out of London to face his enemies. The battle that followed near St Albans on 17 February was by all accounts more confused than most. More than one London contemporary remarked that the Yorkist army, in which there were many inexperienced militia men, lacked effective leadership. The Lancastrians, who had the more experienced soldiers, enjoyed more effective leadership and benefited from desertions in the Yorkist ranks, won the day. The king, who had been brought to the field but was stationed away from danger, was rescued by the Queen's men. The royal army marched on towards London.[10]

Fleeing westward, Warwick and the remnants of his army met up with Edward of March, the new duke of York, at Burford, fresh from victory at Mortimer's Cross earlier in the month. There they decided to march immediately on London, arriving in time to prevent the city falling to the hesitant Queen Margaret, who, on hearing of their approach, withdrew. Warwick and Edward, already styling himself true heir to the throne, entered the city on 27 February. Five days later, having been 'elected' by a hastily gathered assembly, Edward took possession of the throne.[11] There was no time to relax. The Lancastrian army withdrawing northwards was still a potent threat. Edward IV immediately set about the task of pursuit. The duke of Norfolk raised further forces in East Anglia. Warwick rode down to the West Midlands in strength on 7 March. For the first time since the invasion in July he was able to recover effective control and recruit significant numbers in the region. He then marched through Lichfield, raising more levies as he went, to join Fauconberg, who had left London on 11 March with the vanguard, and Edward IV who had set out two days later, at Doncaster on about 27 March.[12]

The Yorkists were now able to raise a significant number of men and bring out a more impressive number of peers. Support had begun to swing their way after the Accord, and apparently increased after Edward assumed the crown. The Yorkist cause may have been perceived to have greater legitimacy, as they claimed, under the terms of the November Accord. The popular support evidently enjoyed by Warwick in the south-eastern counties might additionally have encouraged more peers to have thrown in their lot. It is noticeable, for instance, that the earl of Arundel, Sir Thomas Kyriel, and Edward Neville, Lord Bergavenny, with interests in Kent and Sussex, who had either been neutral or hostile, now rallied to him. Did they find it politic to follow where popular opinion led? But perhaps more decisive in January and February had been the fear that had been engendered by the Lancastrian army as it moved south. It may well be that the tales of rape and pillage, which had grown in the telling and had been effectively stoked by Warwick, had the effect of rallying southern and midland support. At the same time, the Lancastrians consolidated their support. Some peers, such as Anthony Woodville, Lord Scales, who had attended the second session of the Westminster parliament, made their way to join Henry VI. The political nation had become polarized as it had never been before. There were few who did not now take one side or another. The two parties had gathered the largest armies that had as yet taken the field, and were ever to do so again in the civil wars, for the long-awaited decisive encounter.

Edward IV's pursuing army finally caught up with the retreating Lancastrian host in southern Yorkshire. It turned to fight north of the River Aire. On the 28 March, only a day after Warwick had come into the camp, and not waiting for the duke of Norfolk to arrive with his reinforcements, Fauconberg's vanguard and Warwick's men pushed north and forced a crossing at Ferrybridge. They took casualties, including the death of John Radcliffe, Lord Fitzwater. Warwick was reported to have been wounded in the leg. The main army immediately followed up, and on the next day it faced the Lancastrians on the field of Towton. Victory was won after a titanic struggle by the divisions under the command of the new king and Lord Fauconberg. Warwick himself may have been less to the fore in the battle as a result of his wound. The day was finally decided in the afternoon by the arrival of the duke of Norfolk who immediately threw his men into the fray. The casualties were huge, if not the 28,000 reported by the heralds and then circulated around Europe, partly because the fleeing Lancastrians found themselves trapped trying to cross the Cock Beck, to their rear. The earls of Devon and Northumberland and Lord Clifford were among the dead. The army was destroyed. Henry VI, his queen and son escaped first to Newcastle and then to Scotland; those peers who had not been hacked to death, holed out where they could. The victory was complete. Edward IV and Warwick were the rulers of the realm.[13]

The rapidly changing events and violent swings in fortune over the three months between the end of December and the end of March had been brought to a bloody end on the field of Towton. The escalating tensions and conflicts of the previous decade were relieved and resolved, for the time being at least, by the change of dynasty and the verdict of battle. Word quickly spread that Warwick had made Edward IV king. Coppini, who was undoubtedly under the earl's spell, had no doubts. On 17 April he wrote to Francesco Sforza that, after several fluctuations, 'my lord of Warwick has come off best and made a new king of the son of York, the earl of March, who together with Warwick returned with me to England [in July 1460]'. Things were looking up, he added, for this new king is 'young, prudent and magnanimous'. As seen from Flanders, the victory was Warwick's. The French ambassador to Milan, writing from Bruges on 12 April, remarked of Towton that King Edward and Warwick came off victors, but added that on *Warwick's* side 8,000 were killed, on King Henry's 20,000. A confused letter of 9 April from Ghent to Milan remarked that Calais was in fête over Warwick's victory over the king. These views were picked up and set down years later by Commynes, who repeated that Edward was made king by the earl.[14] Was this so?

Warwick continually insisted, until after the defeat at the second battle of St Albans, that the intention was not to depose Henry VI. Was it he, then, who persuaded Edward of York to seize the throne, or was it Edward of York who insisted that that was what would now happen? Whose initiative was it? There can be absolutely no doubt that Warwick was the ruler of England after York's death until the assumption of the throne by Edward IV in March. Antonio della Torre, who had it is true entered the earl's service, wrote to Sforza on 9 January 1461 to report the defeat at Wakefield and the preparations being made by Warwick to resist the queen's army. Because of his valour and popularity he was confident Warwick would prevail. Two weeks later he wrote to Sforza again, remarking in passing that the earl was 'like another Caesar in these parts'. The earl himself was negotiating with the pope, the duke of Burgundy and the dauphin of France. The Milanese ambassador to France, Prospero de Camulio, remarked in April that the duke, who attached great importance to England, kept in with the earl of Warwick.[15]

What we cannot deduce is who made the decision after the defeat at St Albans when Edward and Neville met in the Cotswolds. Was it really true that Warwick put Edward on the throne? One source asserts that the earl persuaded the young duke of York to march immediately on London because of his popularity there.[16] In reality, Edward was already en route. It is perfectly possible that it was Edward, flush from his victory at Mortimer's Cross, who rallied Warwick and insisted that the moment was right to take the throne that his father had been prevented from occupying by the concerted opposition of the peers. He could do so on the grounds that the Lancastrians had violated the accord that had made his father heir to the throne, and that he, as his heir, now had the right. Warwick, who had been at pains in the last month or two to assure Burgundy and others that, while he was in his care, Henry VI was safe on the throne, no doubt recognized that his own survival now demanded a bolder course. His brother George, the chancellor, revealed their true attitude to Henry VI when, in a later letter to Coppini, he twice dismissed Henry VI as 'our puppet', and as a statue of a king, whom they lost at St Albans.[17] The Nevilles perhaps recognized that, for their immediate survival, the time had come to depose him. Warwick had made such decisions before, and was to make them again.

Edward IV was only eighteen, and untried in war, but he had already revealed his mettle. Moreover, the decisiveness with which the Yorkists acted after he assumed the throne, the speed with which they pursued the retreating Lancastrian army, and the manner in which they threw themselves into action as soon as they had overhauled them, have all the hallmarks of Edward's generalship as shown a decade later, and little of Warwick's more defensive approach. Some commentators were sure that Towton was *his* victory. Richard Beauchamp, bishop of Salisbury, who was one of those who had thrown in his lot with the new regime, wrote in his letter to Coppini that they had been saved from destruction by the retreat of the queen's army, which might have been prompted by their hearing of Edward, duke of York's approach. After his assumption of the throne 'our most glorious King Edward' set out in pursuit. The battle on Palm Sunday might not have been won had not 'the prince single-handedly cast himself into the fray as he did so notably with the greatest of human courage'. But Beauchamp himself was no more neutral than Coppini. He had already been promoted to the council by the king. This may be a telling reason why he described the young Edward as a saviour sent by God, in whose sight, he acknowledged, he had found such grace and favour.[18] Between two partisan views it is impossible to judge.

But most commentators stressed the partnership between the vigorous new king and the more experienced earl. Speculation in the despatches sent to Milan after the battle referred consistently to what King Edward and Warwick would do. As Camulio, the Milanese ambassador to France, wrote on 18 April, 'the reputation of Edward and Warwick is great owing to their good conduct'. If the fugitive Henry VI and his queen were captured, as was rumoured, the kingdom could be considered settled and quiet under king Edward and the earl of Warwick. Both king and earl wrote to the duke of Milan in letters carried by Antonio della Torre. The duke replied to both on the same day, 14 June, stating that Messer Antonio was returning to England with his replies. To the king he wrote that he had heard from Camulio of his memorable victory gained through his consummate military skill and personal valour; to Warwick he referred to his deep affection for him, his hope that Coppini would be acceptable to his majesty and Warwick's lordship (for an English see) and indicated, cryptically, that he had instructed Camulio to gratify his lordship.[19] It was indeed Edward IV and Warwick who ruled England for the next three or four years.

Edward IV acknowledged the debt he owed to Warwick and his kinsmen in the rewards heaped upon them in the first weeks of the reign, many granted when the king was a guest of the earl at Middleham in the first week of May. The earl was confirmed as great chamberlain of England and made master of the king's mews, warden of the Cinque Ports, and constable of Dover Castle, all for life. His captaincy of Calais was renewed as was the keepership of the seas. In the north, his wardenship of the west march was confirmed, to which was added the wardenship of the east march until 1463, when his brother, John Neville, Lord and later Marquess Montagu, succeeded him. He was made steward of the duchy of Lancaster in both the north and south parts, and granted all the stewardships of the duchy in Yorkshire. He received liberal grants of the confiscated estates of his defeated enemies, including parts of the Percy estates in Yorkshire, and later, the honour of Cockermouth in Cumberland, as well as the Clifford lordship of Skipton. Several of these grants were confirmations of offices he already held, or which had been held by his father. Two points stand out: he was given virtual control of the north of England and of all the standing military resources of the crown, on land and sea. One region eluded him. He was initially granted offices of the Staffords and Talbots in Wales, but these were soon redirected to Sir William Herbert, now Lord Herbert, who had served Richard of York loyally in his last years. Warwick may have been offended (his actions a decade later suggest so), but in reality he could not at one and the same time defend the north of England and regain control of Wales.[20]

In the immediate aftermath of Towton, the victorious Yorkists quickly secured the control of Yorkshire and Durham, receiving the submission of Bishop Booth on 12 April. At Durham both bishop and earl petitioned the king regarding possession of Barnard Castle. Not surprisingly, he ruled in favour of the earl. King and earl then pressed on to Newcastle. They went no further. Lancastrians garrisoned the principal strongholds of northern Northumberland (Bamburgh, Alnwick and Dunstanburgh), and Margaret of Anjou had ceded Berwick to the Scots. Having dealt with the earl of Wiltshire and other fugitives who had been captured, the king then returned to London and Westminster for his coronation on 28 June. The Nevilles stayed on. Fauconberg, now earl of Kent, was appointed captain of Newcastle. Warwick remained in overall command. His hands were full. There were disturbances in Yorkshire which he was commissioned to suppress on 13 May. A week or so later a joint Lancastrian and Scottish force laid siege to Carlise. It took six weeks for John Neville to relieve the city. In addition, also in June, Sir Thomas Neville of Brancepeth, of the rival family, led a sortie into county Durham which Bishop Booth's levies dispersed. All this detracted from the need to retake the Northumberland castles and Naworth where Sir Humphrey Dacre was holding out. Alnwick and Dunstanburgh were taken by the end of September, but Alnwick was soon retaken by Sir William Tailboys; Bamburgh was still in Lancastrian hands in December; and Naworth did not finally fall until the following year.[21]

It was difficult to secure control of the far north. Nevertheless, by the time Edward IV's first parliament met at Westminster on 4 November, the north appeared to be sufficiently settled for Warwick, Kent and John Neville to attend. The assembly selected Warwick's retainer, Sir James Strangways, as speaker. In its first session, an act of parliament was passed disinheriting George Neville of Bergavenny and settling the whole of the Dispenser inheritance on Countess Anne. Warwick had occupied George's share for several years: possession was now made legal. By this act Warwick finally secured in law the whole of his countess's inheritance. He played a full role in parliamentary proceedings. He remained in London after the session ended in December, probably visiting Calais as well as the Cinque Ports in February and March, before preparing to go to sea to resist the French, who were threatening to raid the south coast.[22] In the event, however, Kent was commissioned to command the fleet and Warwick returned north to deal with the borders with Scotland. Scotland continued, under the regency of Mary of Guelders, the widow of James II, to shelter and assist Margaret of Anjou and the Lancastrian exiles. In April, Queen Margaret had sailed to France to seek the support of the new king, Louis XI, leaving Henry VI and the prince of Wales in Scotland. The threat of the Auld Alliance being reactivated was real. In the same month, Warwick travelled to Dumfries to negotiate with the Scots, but without success. He withdrew to Middleham and prepared to raid the west march. This, coordinated with a raid from the Highlands by dissident Scottish lords, was sufficient to bring the Scots back to the negotiating table, first at Carlisle and then at Lincluden to agree a short truce. Alnwick was subsequently recovered by Lord Hastings and Sir Ralph Grey.[23]

In October 1462, however, Margaret of Anjou landed at Bamburgh with a small French force commanded by Pierre de Brézé. Dunstanburgh and Alnwick soon fell into their hands. The Scots renewed their support for Lancaster. Edward IV responded by calling out his household and marching north to face them. He arrived at Durham on 30 November where he fell ill with measles. It was left to Warwick to coordinate the investment of the three castles and fight off the anticipated Scottish invasion, expected, so John Paston III wrote on 11 December from the field, within a week. The Scots did not appear when anticipated. They were still expected on 28 December when Edward IV wrote to Chancellor Neville that the invasion was imminent. By the time they did appear before Alnwick, early in January 1463, Bamburgh and Dunstanburgh had surrendered. Warwick drew his forces together in defensive array, but the Scots were unwilling to attack. They rescued the garrison and withdrew, leaving the castle to the earl.[24]

Edward IV and Warwick offered generous terms to the garrisons. The duke of Somerset, Sir Ralph Percy, brother of the dead third earl and head of the family, and Sir Humphrey Neville, acting head of the senior line of the Nevilles because of the incapacity of the second earl of Westmorland, were granted pardons, received back into favour and their estates restored. This was a calculated risk, but it is likely that king and earl believed that they could make peace with the kinsmen of their old enemies and that they would be prepared to forget old enmities in the face of the threat from Scotland. Accordingly, Percy was installed as captain of Bamburgh and Dunstanburgh, with Neville as his second in command; Sir John Astley was given command of Alnwick. Warwick, who was still warden of the east march, must surely have been party to this policy of clemency. And indeed, one can understand, how, after his recent experience he could have been convinced that Northumberland could only be held securely against future attack if the castles were captained by men who had the confidence of the local gentry and their tenants, who traditionally defended the border. In overlooking the good service of another Northumbrian, Sir Ralph Grey, however, who had been in command of Alnwick, he and the king made a serious mistake.[25]

The Scots having been outfaced, and the castles having been recovered and garrisoned, king and earl returned south. The earl was at Middleham in the second half of January. He perhaps attended the funeral and burial in Guisborough Priory of his uncle, William, Lord Fauconberg and earl of Kent, who had died at Durham on 9 January, possibly of illness contracted during his last campaign. He was also, no doubt, planning the interment of his father, brother and mother at Bisham which took place on 14/15 February. From there he went up to council meetings and the opening of a new parliament at Westminster on 29 April. He now surrendered command of the east march to his brother John.[26] Any celebration of peace in the north was short-lived for news soon arrived that Percy had declared again for Lancaster and, what was probably worse, the disgruntled Grey had seized Alnwick, turned his coat and admitted a group of Lancastrians under the command of Lord Hungerford. The Scots at once took to arms. Fortunately, Montagu was on the spot and, according to a report sent to the duke of Burgundy on 19 June, prevented a raid on Newcastle and intercepted French ships seeking to supply Bamburgh. Warwick, with his brother-in-law, Lord Stanley, set out from London on 3 June. By the time they had reached the north, an army in which both queens, Mary of Guelders and Margaret of Anjou, with their charges (James III of Scotland and Henry VI) had invested Norham, defended by Lord Ogle. Neville was raising troops from Middleham on 11 July and Durham four days later, including the clergy of the province of York, and no doubt bringing out St Cuthbert's banner to protect his men. Marching rapidly north, he relieved the garrison before the end of the month. He followed up with a raid deep into Scotland, laying everything waste as he went. His prompt and decisive action had prevented Norham as well as Berwick falling into Scottish hands.[27]

In the meantime, Edward IV declared his intention to mount a major expedition against Scotland and persuaded parliament, assembled on 29 April 1463, and convocation to vote taxes to pay for it. Parliament was prorogued on 17 June. A fleet was fitted out to support an invasion by land and the king himself began to move north. At Northampton, however, Somerset slipped away from his entourage, eventually making his way north to rejoin the Lancastrians. At some point, however, probably after hearing of Warwick's success at the end of July, the king turned back. While at Fotheringhay, relaxing and hunting, Edward issued letters calling troops to muster at Newcastle on 13 September.

At some point plans were changed. Rather than recovering the castles immediately by force, it was decided to seek to restore the truces with Scotland and France and thus isolate the Lancastrians. A powerful delegation under the chancellor, George Neville, was already on its way to negotiate with the king of France and duke of Burgundy at the end of August. These negotiations led to a year-long truce between England and France sealed on 8 October, in which, importantly, both agreed not to support the other's enemies. This done, the way was open for negotiations to be held with the Scots. Warwick himself was commissioned to treat with Scottish ambassadors at York for a renewal of the truce in December. The king himself came north to participate in the negotiations and early that month a truce was agreed, to extend until the following October, while negotiations for a permanent peace were scheduled to take place at Newcastle in March.

Early in the new year the earl was back in the south, participating in judicial hearings dealing with a rash of disorder and popular disturbances in several counties. He was at Coventry in January, and Gloucester early in February. He then travelled up to London to engage in further negotiations with French envoys. All through the winter Northumberland was left in the hands of the exiled Lancastrians, most of whom congregated there, with Henry VI himself. Montagu was left holding the line of the Tyne.

It was Montagu who finally restored Yorkist control in the early summer of 1464. On or about 25 April, while he was marching to Norham to meet the delayed Scottish embassy to escort them to York (to which the second round of negotiations had been relocated for security reasons), he overwhelmed a party of Lancastrians that sought to intercept him. Sir Ralph Percy was killed in this action at Hedgeley Moor. Edward had been making preparations to return in strength to recover Northumberland, but he, and Warwick travelling before him, who was at York on 5 May, concluded a fifteen-year truce with the Scots early in June. By the time that he arrived in York, the king knew that the Lancastrians had already been decisively defeated by Lord Montagu at Hexham on 15 May and the Neville brothers had taken a fearful revenge. All the leaders were captured. In the succeeding days they were executed in sequence, four including Somerset immediately after the battle, others at Newcastle, Middleham and York. Only those executed at York had the benefit of even a show trial, under the constable, the earl of Worcester. Over thirty men were beheaded between 15 and 28 May. It is likely that Warwick was party to these acts and may well have overseen the executions at Middleham on 18 May.[28]

Warwick and Montagu were commissioned to complete the reduction of the Northumberland castles, agreeing terms with the defenders if possible. Dunstanburgh and Alnwick surrendered without a fight. Grey and Neville in Bamburgh, who had been excluded from an amnesty, resisted. For the first time artillery was used to beat down the walls. All three castles were in Yorkist hands by the end of June. As his reward, Montagu was created earl of Northumberland and granted the forfeited Percy estates in the county. Warwick then proceeded to Lochmaben stone near Dumfries to hold a March Day under the terms of the new truce. It had taken more than three years after Towton to pacify the far north. With the exception of Harlech, the kingdom was finally under Yorkist control.

It is not at all surprising that contemporaries regarded Warwick, in the opening years of Edward's reign, as the real ruler of England. Bishop Kennedy of St Andrews, who had negotiated with him, wrote a year or two later that he was the 'governor of the realm of England under King Edward'. 'They have but two rulers', joked the governor of Abbeville in a letter to Louis XI, 'M de Warwick and another whose name I have forgotten'. He was, Commynes considered, like a father to Edward IV: he 'governed King Edward in his youth and directed his affairs'.[29] But it was largely to foreign observers that Warwick appeared all powerful. In reality, the relationship between the two was more of a partnership between mighty subject and insecure king, and it would be entirely wrong to suppose that Warwick was the sole author of royal policy during these early years. Nevertheless, the relationship between king and great subject was unusually, and unprecedentedly, weighted towards the subject. For these three years the earl had been largely engaged in the defence of the throne in the north, although this had not prevented him from playing, when he could, a leading role in council and parliament. In addition, his brother George, as chancellor, had presided over the council seated in Westminster and carried the burden of central administration and diplomacy. While the king had other important servants such as Lords Hastings and Herbert, there is no doubt that the Neville brothers, all three of them, had been indispensable to him. Warwick now looked forward to playing a more prominent role on the international stage. Neville had maintained his diplomatic contacts with Burgundy and France while engaged in the defence of the north. Although, at a conference at St Omer in the autumn of 1463, the opening of negotiations for a tripartite settlement with Burgundy and France was left in the hands of his brother, the chancellor George Neville, and his lieutenant of Calais, John, Lord Wenlock, in late March 1464, Warwick was in London to open negotiations with French ambassadors, led by Jean de Lannoy. The truce was confirmed and extended to the seas on 14 April, a proposal for Edward IV to marry Louis XI's sister-in-law, Bona, daughter of the duke of Savoy, was discussed, and an agreement was reached for further talks at St Omer in May. Warwick himself wrote to Louis XI encouraging the king to believe that Edward IV was sympathetic to the marriage proposal. But the talks never materialized. Lord Wenlock was eventually sent to sue for a postponement to October.[30] By then the earl had discovered the reason for the lack of urgency during the summer.

On 1 May 1464 Edward IV had secretly married Elizabeth Woodville. She was the daughter of Richard, Lord Rivers, he whom the earl and Edward IV had berated at Calais in 1460 as an upstart. He had made his peace with the new regime. The story is that the widowed Elizabeth had met the king when pressing a suit for the restoration of property forfeited by her late husband, John Grey, Lord Ferrers of Groby. She was older than the king. He was smitten. The secrecy of Edward's marriage, and the fact that it was not revealed until Warwick pressed at a council meeting in late September for instructions for his forthcoming embassy, make it clear that Edward feared the reaction of Warwick and others to his precipitate act. He knew that his choice of bride would not meet with approval, because of her not being a virgin, her relatively inferior social background (although her mother, Jacquetta of Luxemburg was a great French princess), and the political and diplomatic implications of the match. By choosing to marry in secret he risked adding insult to injury, for he clearly continued to allow Warwick to believe that he was eligible.[31] The manner, as much as the fact, of the marriage, while it reveals the extent to which the king was in awe of Warwick, was also a declaration of independence, marking a turning point in the relationship between the two. Rumour reached Milan that most of the lords were very much dissatisfied and were seeking to find a means of annulling the marriage at the council held at Reading in which Edward announced the news. This may reflect Warwick and George Neville's initial reaction, as probably did the resentment of the lords that they were not consulted, which Lord Wenlock reported to Lannoy on 3 October. Wenlock tellingly added that the lords recognized that the marriage was a fait accompli and that they had to move on. In February 1465 the Milanese ambassador to France reported that Margaret of Anjou, begging for French support, had written to Louis XI that Edward IV and Warwick had come to very great division. Louis XI was dismissive and unbelieving: 'look how proudly she writes', he sneered. Whatever his true feelings, Warwick himself put on a brave face. He had gallantly escorted the new queen on her first ceremonial public appearance at Reading Abbey on 29 September.[32]

Richard Neville swallowed his pride. He was, no doubt, to some extent mollified in the following spring by the grants of Cockermouth, Egremont, and the shrievalty of Westmorland, as well as by the promotion of his brother George to be archbishop of York. There was no visible rift. Business continued as usual. In November 1464 he had visited the Cinque Ports. Then he was back in York on the king's behalf to prorogue for the second time a session of parliament called to meet in the city. Having been in Coventry on 10 January 1465, he attended the parliamentary session that finally started at Westminster on 21 January. Two months after the parliament's dissolution, in May, he went to Calais, his first visit since 1460. He returned to London in July, where he spent most of that and the following month. He was at hand to escort the recently captured Henry VI from Islington through London to his imprisonment in the Tower. He visited Warwick, with the king's young brother, the duke of Gloucester, in his entourage at the end of August. Then he travelled north again for the enthronement of his brother George at the end of September. December found him negotiating with the Scots at Newcastle.[33]

It is notable, however, that Warwick had not been present at the queen's coronation on 26 May 1465. He had taken no part in the grand tournament held on the following day. The sumptuous installation at York of George Neville as archbishop of York on 22 September might be seen as a riposte to the other coronation in the south. The enthronement was marked by up to a week of feasting and celebration, on a scale greater, it has been suggested, than even a sovereign customarily enjoyed at his coronation. It was attended by the archbishop's brothers-in-law (the earl of Oxford, Lords FitzHugh, Hastings and Stanley) and 22 other peers, including all the lords of the north and the king's 13-year-old brother, Richard, duke of Gloucester then residing in the earl's household, 8 bishops, 18 abbots, 60 knights and 79 esquires, most of whom were wearing the king's livery. The mayor and prominent citizens of York, as well as the mayor of the Calais Staple, were also present. Warwick, Northumberland and Lord Hastings performed the ritual offices of steward, treasurer and controller. The great hall and four other chambers in the archbishop's palace were used. The ladies sat separately from the gentlemen. This was a spectacular celebration of Neville power at its zenith. It impact was such that the order of the day was recorded for posterity and used subsequently as a model of the etiquette for such an event. The king and queen were not present.[34]

The earl distanced himself, or was distanced from, the new courtly society with which the king surrounded himself in the years immediately following his marriage. This was dominated by the queen's family, especially her father and brother Anthony, Lord Scales, their associates, and the group known as the new Yorkists – Lords Ferrers, Hastings, Herbert, and Stafford. Warwick may have had little desire to participate in the jousting, courtly shows and revelling which now characterized the king's court. These were the years in which Edward's lavish and highly chivalric court style was forged. In April 1465 Scales had accepted the commission of the ladies of the court to perform a feat of arms with a figure worthy of his status. And so was set in train the plans for the great tournament between him and the Bastard of Burgundy, which, after much delay, finally took place at Smithfield in June 1467. Richard Neville had little time for the new Camelot. And perhaps the new Camelot had little time for him.[35]

There was more to it than style. The round of marriages of the queen's five sisters, brother and son, Sir Thomas Grey, in these years into the ranks of the established peerage bound the new first family more firmly into the political elite. Warwick was not excluded. He acted as godfather to the king's first child, Elizabeth at her christening in February 1466. He presumably did not object to the marriage of his 65-year-old aunt Katherine, the dowager duchess of Norfolk, to the queen's 20-year old brother John. But the marriage of the young Henry

Stafford, duke of Buckingham to Katherine Woodville in 1465 was said to be at his great displeasure, probably because he had hoped for this marriage for his daughter Isabel, then fourteen. The marriage in October 1466 of Sir Thomas Grey, the queen's elder son by her first marriage, to the king's niece, Anne Holland, daughter and heiress of the duke of Exeter, who was already betrothed to his nephew, George Neville, son of John, added insult to injury.[36]

These, however, were but the symptoms of a profound change in the relationship between king and earl. After 1464, Warwick found himself no longer at the very centre of court and politics. An alternative focus emerged, one in which the king was his own man and could shake off what he might have come to see as the overbearing tutelage of the man who had made him king. And moreover he found an alternative father figure and elder statesman in Richard Woodville, Earl Rivers. Within five years Rivers, who was promoted Treasurer in 1466, had completely displaced Warwick as the king's right-hand man. In briefings, which appear to have come from those close to Warwick himself after he had seized power in the summer of 1469, and were duly sent back to Milan, it was put out that since her coronation the queen had always exerted herself to aggrandize her relations to the point that they had control of the entire government of the realm.[37] The queen's role was exaggerated and the chronology extended, but in substance the charge was true from 1467. The marriage to Elizabeth Woodville may not in itself have caused the breach between Warwick and the king, but its political consequences were profound.

4

The Third King, 1465–71

The occasion of the open estrangement between Warwick and Edward was disagreement over foreign policy. By 1465 the king found himself being courted not only by Louis XI but also by the great princes of France, including the dukes of Burgundy and Brittany, who rebelled against Louis that summer. While the existing truces were regularly renewed, the choice facing England lay between the king and the dukes. National sentiment and tradition favoured a triple alliance against France, but there were reasons for considering a break with tradition. England had become engaged in a damaging trade war with the duke of Burgundy. Commercial relationships between the Netherlands and England had deteriorated as a result of steps taken to protect English trade in 1463. A devaluation of the currency ordered by Edward IV in September 1464 (at the same council meeting at which he had announced his marriage) had made matters worse for the Flemish and had led immediately to a ban on the sale of all English cloth in the duke of Burgundy's territories.[1]

In May 1465 Warwick headed an embassy empowered to treat at will with Burgundy and France, but the outbreak of civil war in France prevented any progress being made, and the delegation returned empty handed to London early in June. It was not until the spring of 1466 that the commission was reissued and Warwick was instructed to treat, first with Burgundy and then with France, to discover what was on offer. By then, Burgundy had become stronger, both by the treaty of Conflans, which had restored the Somme towns to the duke, and by the diplomatic possibilities extended by the death of Isabella, countess of Charolais, freeing the duke's heir, Charles, for an advantageous marriage. This time the ambassadors were to discuss with Burgundy possible ways of ending the trade war then raging, and also a proposed marriage between Charles and Edward's sister Margaret. It is likely that it was at this meeting in April that a personal antipathy between Warwick and Charles, remembered by both Commynes and Crowland, was born.[2] Negotiations with France the following month were more amicable, but led only to a renewal of the truce and a proposal that a similar marriage alliance should be concluded between Margaret and a Valois prince.

Throughout 1466 a stream of envoys passed between England, France, and Burgundy. It soon became apparent that Warwick, with Lord Wenlock, Richard

Whetehill, Louis Galet, based in Calais, and his secretary, Robert Neville, doing most of the detailed negotiation, was moving towards a French alliance, while the king, encouraged by Earl Rivers, moved towards a Burgundian alliance. Warwick was not entrusted again with negotiations with Charles. It was Rivers, with his links with the court of Burgundy through his countess, who took over. By October Edward IV and Charles had put their signatures to a secret non-aggression pact and agreed to continue negotiations for a marriage alliance. These as yet made little progress because Duke Philip would not make concessions on the trade dispute. All this was opposed by Warwick. Nevertheless, Edward, to increase the pressure on Burgundy, was keen to encourage rival French negotiations. Thus, while one embassy was sent to Bruges to discuss further a Burgundian alliance, Warwick was sent on a separate embassy to France in May 1467. He arrived at Rouen on 6 or 7 June and was lavishly, almost regally, entertained by Louis XI. On offer were a marriage, perhaps of Richard of Gloucester with the king's second daughter, a pension of 4,000 crowns, generous commercial concessions to offset lost markets in Flanders, and, in exchange for an alliance against Burgundy, a promise to discuss English claims in France. With these terms carried by French envoys, Warwick returned to England, landing at Dover on 24 June.[3] He discovered that, in his absence, his brother George had been dismissed as chancellor on 8 June, the king himself riding down to his mansion of The More to collect the Great Seal. (A few months later George discovered that Thomas Bourgchier, archbishop of Canterbury, not himself as he had hoped, had been, on the king's recommendation, granted a cardinal's hat.)[4] In Earl Richard's absence, too, further negotiations between England and Burgundy had been conducted behind the scenes of the great sporting event of the long-planned Smithfield tournament between Lord Scales and the Bastard of Burgundy. These had been cut short by news of the death of Philip the Good. The French envoys, when they arrived, were largely ignored by the king, and the day they left empty-handed the king announced the renewal of his pact with Charolais, now Duke Charles of Burgundy. On 28 September the Burgundian trade embargo was lifted, and two days later Princess Margaret came before the council to declare formally her willingness to marry Duke Charles.

By midsummer 1467 Warwick knew that he had lost the argument over the direction of foreign policy. He cannot have been deceived by the king. He knew that the French and Burgundians were being played against each other to achieve the best terms. But, in effect, the king had played Rivers against Warwick in a competition over these terms. It had probably been unwise of Neville to have become so committed to a Francophile policy, or swayed by a personal antipathy to Charles, count of Charolais. He might not have realized how much the odds had been stacked against him. But the *manner* in which the final deal with Burgundy had been struck while he was in France, possibly when he was boasting that he could deliver a treaty, was deeply humiliating, as was the subsequent treatment of the French ambassadors. He had lost face. Not surprisingly, Louis XI was reported to have complained bitterly that he had made promises without achieving anything.[5] He had also lost a place at the heart of the council. The dismissal of George Neville, also while he was in France, additionally brought home to him the extent to which his position had been undermined, and he was now marginalized at court. As the star of Earl Rivers waxed, so Earl Richard's waned. He had been slighted. In effect, he too had been dismissed. In a fury he withdrew to his estates in the north of England.

John Warkworth later wrote that, after the announcement of the king's marriage, there 'rose great dissension ever more and more between the King and him, for that and other, etc'; and that after the dismissal of George Neville the earl did all that he could to make himself strong; the king all that he could to undermine him. 'And yet they were accorded divers times: but they never loved together after'.[6] It took time for Warwick and Edward to fall out irrevocably. As Warkworth said, 'they were accorded divers times'. Over the winter of 1467–8 Warwick stayed away from court. He was embarrassed by the revelation that he had been secretly negotiating with the papacy for a dispensation for his daughter Isabel to marry the king's brother, George, duke of Clarence. More damagingly, a messenger from Margaret of Anjou, captured in the autumn on his way to her supporters in Harlech, reported that it was widely said in France that the earl's sympathies now lay with the house of Lancaster. He was summoned to court to answer the charge, but refused to come. Edward conceded that he would accept his denial from Yorkshire.[7]

Yet it was true that there was talk of that kind in France, whether well founded or not. The despatches of the Milanese ambassador to the French court were full of gossip that the earl was contemplating rebellion. As early as 19 May 1467, even before Warwick's embassy to Rouen, the duke of Milan was told that if the English in the end entered into a treaty with Burgundy, the French were talking of treating with Warwick to restore King Henry. On 12 September he was told that Edward and Warwick were constantly at strife and that Warwick was raising troops. Louis was also being lobbied by Margaret of Anjou's representative, Sir John Fortescue, who was already doing his utmost to promote the Lancastrian cause. In February 1468 the ambassador reported that the earl had won over a brother of the king (Clarence), but that they were nevertheless treating for an accommodation, and that the earl had sent word to France.[8]

There is no doubt that Warwick had been in personal communication with Louis XI for several years (as he had been with other European rulers, including Philip of Burgundy and the duke of Milan). His secretary, Robert Neville, was paid for undertaking missions to the French court four times between 1464 and 1466, as had, on at least one occasion, Warwick herald. He was sent there again at the end of 1467, returning on Christmas Eve with William Moneypenny who became the principal intermediary between Warwick and Louis. Neville travelled straight north; Moneypenny stayed in London to discuss matters with Warwick's council there. Hopes were high that a dispensation would not be forthcoming for the Anglo-Burgundian marriage. A later letter from Moneypenny reported that Warwick would send Robert Neville to France again, and that in the meantime he was consulting his brother John Neville. Moneypenny's reports to Louis XI encouraged him to think that Warwick was already plotting rebellion. They assured him that none loved him as much as Warwick, and that England loved none as much as Warwick.[9]

Yet the Milanese ambassador gave a different impression. In February 1468 he reported a lively dinner conversation in which Louis provoked Margaret of Anjou's brother John of Calabria by praising Warwick as a great friend of France. On this occasion, as reported, Louis did not appear to be favourable to any idea of helping Margaret of Anjou, let alone persuading Warwick to change sides.[10] In all these communications it is impossible to tell what was wishful thinking, deliberate misinformation, or accurate reportage. It is not inconceivable that Loius XI and John of Calabria put on a show for the benefit of the ambassador, confident that it would be spread around the courts of Europe, so as to conceal their real purpose. There is no doubt, however, that speculation about a reconciliation between Margaret of Anjou and Warwick, brokered by Louis XI, was rife in late 1467.

However, by January 1468, Warwick had decided to end his stand-off with Edward IV, and to return to court and council. Moneypenny duly reported to Louis that the earl, having initially refused, had decided to attend a council meeting called in his own country at Coventry. He had been persuaded, it was said by the author of the *Annales*, by the more emollient George Neville. At the council meeting, according to Moneypenny, Warwick and the king each tried to persuade the other to change their foreign policy preferences. The king was anxious to secure Warwick's support for a planned triple alliance and invasion of France; Warwick argued against it. At least, however, the king and Warwick were talking again. Warwick, the author of the *Annales* noted, was reconciled with Lords Herbert and Stafford, but not, significantly, with those who were now the authors of the king's policy and closest to him at court, Rivers and Lord Scales.[11] It seems that he outwardly acceded and began attending council more regularly. It may be that, in the late autumn of 1467, Warwick had seriously contemplated rebellion, and even been receptive to the idea of a rapprochement with Margaret of Anjou. If so, in the end more cautious counsel prevailed, probably that of his brothers, and he returned, if grudgingly, to court.[12]

For the next few months all seemed to be well once more between king and his resentful premier earl. Warwick was sweetened by the grant of the profitable wardship of Francis, Lord Lovell. Besides, the earl still had in his charge Edward's youngest brother, Richard, duke of Gloucester. The earl appointed Lord Hastings as his steward in the east midlands at this time. Back at court and council, in June he participated in the ceremonial departure of Margaret of York for her wedding to the duke of Burgundy, escorting her from London to Dover. His influence probably helped determine the declaration of war against the Hanse in the same month. Plans by now were well under way for a renewal of war with France to which Warwick was opposed. The king had announced his intention at the opening of the second session of the current parliament on 12 May. He was willingly voted two fifteenths and tenths. An expeditionary force was sent to Brittany under Lord Mountjoy and conveyed by a fleet commanded by Anthony Woodville, Lord Scales. It recovered Jersey, but achieved little else. To add injury to insult, on 23 September, Scales was made warden of the Channel Islands, the title to which Warwick had continued to lay claim since 1452.[13]

Louis XI's response was to stir up trouble in England. In June he sponsored the landing in Wales of Jasper Tudor, who reinforced the garrison holding out in Harlech, and in July 1468 a Lancastrian agent named John Cornelius revealed under torture a network of plots and plotters that reached very close to Warwick himself. Among those accused was John Hawkins, a servant of Lord Wenlock. Hawkins implicated the London draper Sir Thomas Cook. Because of the account given in sympathetic London chronicles it was long supposed that Cook, who was found guilty of misprision of treason and heavily fined, was innocent and the victim of Woodville greed, but recent research has concluded that he had indeed known about the conspiracy and had not reported it. A considerable number of people were named by Cornelius, several of whom were tried and hanged.[14] But it did not stop there. In the autumn another of Margaret of Anjou's emissaries to her friends in England, Richard Stairs, was apprehended. This time an altogether more significant coven of plotters was revealed. They included Henry Courtenay, heir to the earldom of Devon, Thomas Hungerford, son of the Lord Hungerford executed after Hexham, and John de Vere, earl of Oxford, whose father had also been executed as a traitor in 1462. Oxford turned king's evidence, and through him several others were implicated. In January, Courtenay and Hungerford were tried, found guilty and executed.[15]

Very little evidence was produced and consequently it has proved difficult to establish the extent and seriousness of these plots. Warwick was not implicated, but one plotter was a servant of his deputy in Calais, Lord Wenlock, and it is hard not to believe that Wenlock knew something of what was afoot. Moreover, Oxford had not long before married Warwick's sister, Margaret. His succession to his earldom after the trial and execution for treason of both his father and elder brother in 1462, and his entry into his inheritance in January 1464, may well have been brokered by Neville, who also arranged his marriage to his remaining unmarried sister at the same time. Oxford occupied a seat of honour at the high table on the left hand of George Neville at the archbishop's enthronement in September 1465, while Margaret Neville, his countess, sat with her sister-in-law at the top table in the ladies' chamber.[16] The earl was surely aware of de Vere's continued contacts with the Lancastrian court in exile. He was not naïve. His brother-in-law and a servant of his lieutenant in Calais were involved. It is hard not to suppose that he had some knowledge of what was afoot. And if he had not himself been engaged, or had directly condoned it, knowledge nevertheless, as with Cook, constituted misprision of treason. Edward IV may well have had his suspicions, albeit that Warwick was appointed to the commissions to try the traitors. He did, however, take the precaution of recalling his youngest brother, Richard of Gloucester, then 16, to court. Yet it is likely that when these plots came to light the earl, having possibly flirted with the idea of a Lancastrian solution to his problems in the autumn of 1467, had already put it to one side.

Warwick benefited in 1468 from growing disillusion with Edward IV's regime. Any hopes that Edward had held that a more aggressive stance towards France might unite his fragmenting kingdom were dashed. Disorder and lawlessness seem to have increased during the year. There were disturbances in Yorkshire and in the north midlands. By the end of the year, the general level of disillusion and dissatisfaction with Edward's IV's regime was becoming apparent. The king had not, John Warkworth commented, brought the promised peace and prosperity, rather, there had been continued unrest, further taxation and disruption of trade. As satisfaction with the regime waned, so the popularity of the estranged earl grew. It was of this year that Robert Fabyan wrote that he was ever held in favour of the commons; it was in this year that William Moneypenny noted that he had never been so popular and that he attracted crowds as he passed who cried out, 'A Warwick! A Warwick!' At the same time there were riots in Kent against the rule of Earl Rivers. The court jester offended the king but won sympathy in London for his quickly leaked quip that the rivers of the kingdom were so swollen that they had become impassable.[17]

Throughout the autumn and winter of 1468 and spring of 1469 Warwick nevertheless continued to give a convincing impression that he was reconciled with the king and content with his circumstances. It was reported to Sir John Paston that he was engaged in discussion with the duke of Norfolk over the matter of Caister 'in the king's chamber' at Westminster in October. In the spring he was once more commissioned to command a fleet for the safe-custody of the sea, perhaps against the Hanse, although when his ships did put to sea they were reported to have harassed the west coast of France. In April he crossed to Calais, ostensibly to deal with local security, but also to represent the king in meetings with Duke Charles of Burgundy and the Emperor at Ardres and St Omer. In May he was back in England to attend the ceremony at Windsor in which Duke Charles was invested in the Order of the Garter. When Edward IV set out on pilgrimage to Walsingham in early June, on holiday in effect, he believed himself to be completely secure. Warwick rode down to Sandwich for the innocuous-seeming relaunch of his refitted flagship, the *Trinity*.[18] It was then that he struck.

There had been further disturbances in the north that spring, with which John Neville had dealt. A rising under a captain who took the name of Robin of Redesdale had been put down. A second, under Robert Hillyard, taking the name of Robin of Holderness, seeking the restoration of Henry Percy, had been even more ruthlessly suppressed. When Robin of Redesdale appeared again later in June it appeared at first that this was just another popular rising. This Robin of Redesdale, however, was no commoner, but probably a member of the Conyers family, a son or brother of Warwick's steward of Middleham, Sir John Conyers. It rapidly became apparent that this was a rebellion of Warwick's northern retainers and that its intention was to rid the realm of the evil ministers about the king, especially Earl Rivers. The rebels marched south to confront them, gathering popular support as they advanced.[19]

Warwick meanwhile crossed to Calais with his daughter Isabel, the duke of Clarence and his brother George, archbishop of York.[20] They were armed with a dispensation for the marriage of Isabel and Clarence, which Archbishop Neville had secretly negotiated with the Papacy. By the time the Neville party reached Calais on 6 July, the king was fully alert to the danger. He called up troops from Wales and the West Country under William Herbert, earl of Pembroke and Humphrey Stafford, earl of Devon and recruited what men he could in East Anglia. He sent Earl Rivers and his sons away for their own protection. On 9 July he wrote to Warwick and Clarence, calling upon them to deny the rumours circulating about their actions. Two days later Clarence and Isabel were married. On 12 July the duke and earl issued a manifesto condemning the covetous rule of those about the king, likening Edward IV to previous kings who had been deposed, and announcing that they would lay their plans for remedy before the king. They summoned their friends in the South East to join them at Canterbury on 16 July. From there they marched up to London, gathering more support before setting off to Coventry, repeating the plan of campaign of 1459.

However, by the time they were on their way, the king had already been defeated. The troops raised by Pembroke and Devon had been overwhelmed by Robin of Redesdale's men at a hard-fought and bloody engagement at Edgecote, near Banbury, on 26 July. Pembroke and his brother were captured, taken to Northampton and there executed on Warwick's orders. Devon fled, but was captured by a mob in Bridgwater and lynched. A few days later Earl Rivers and his son Sir John Woodville were hunted down in the Forest of Dean and murdered. The king, with only a small escort, and unaware of the danger he was in, was intercepted by Archbishop Neville at Olney and taken into custody. He was first held at Warwick, where no doubt the earl confronted him, and then in mid-August moved for greater security to Middleham.

Warwick's intentions now that he had the king and the kingdom under his control are not clear. Public statements maintained that the earl intended to rule in King Edward's name. Luchino Dallaghiexia wrote to Milan from London on 16 August that the earl was at the king's side and that Edward IV was not at liberty to go where he wished. A parliament was to be called, and in that the government of the realm would be arranged. On 18 September, the Milanese ambassador to France wrote home that Clarence and Warwick were still in arms, were persecuting Edward IV and 'keep making a great gathering of troops to constrain him and deprive him of the crown'. It is quite possible that this was what was intended to happen at a parliament. As early as February 1468 it had been said in France that the earl had won over Clarence against the king himself, which implies rather more than to help him rid the realm of evil ministers. The Calais manifesto clearly threatened deposition. Rumours circulated that Edward IV was not a legitimate son of the duke of York.[21] Moreover, Warwick must surely have known from his own experience that if it had proved impossible for Richard of York to rule the kingdom in the name of Henry VI, it would be even less likely that he could do so through a captive Edward IV.

If a parliamentary deposition were being planned, at an assembly summoned to meet at York on 22 September, events moved too fast for Clarence and the earl. The kingdom proved rapidly to be ungovernable: there were riots in London; the duke of Norfolk took advantage of the situation to lay siege to Caister; and most damaging of all at the end of August Sir Humphrey Neville of Brancepeth raised Hexhamshire in the Lancastrian cause. Neville was the earl of Westmorland's kinsman and Warwick's cousin. A rebellion by him threatened not only the house of York, but also Warwick's own possession of his northern estates. It had to be suppressed. The earl, however, found that he could not call out the county levies without royal authorization. Edward IV, understandably, refused to cooperate unless he was given freedom of action. Some form of agreement was reached between the king and earl, which enabled Warwick to release him but remain in a position of favour and authority. Accordingly, Neville and his brother were captured and executed by royal command at York on 29 September. Parliament was cancelled; instead, the king called a council to York, and subsequently, with Warwick in his company, returned in state to Westminster. Sir John Paston reported in October that 'the king himself hath good language of the Lords of Clarence, of Warwick, and of my lords of York [Archbishop Neville] and Oxford, saying they be his best friends'. But, he added ominously, 'his household men have other language'.[22] Clarence and Warwick had held back from any plan to depose Edward; but they had rid him of his evil ministers and, in the apparent reconciliation with the king, had achieved the ends they had ostensibly sought.

It would seem that over the winter of 1469–70, in a series of great councils, an attempt was made to structure a new regime agreeable both to the king and to Warwick. It was a precarious entente. The appointment of William Grey, bishop of Ely, to replace Earl Rivers as treasurer was uncontentious. The promotion of Warwick's erstwhile charge, the young duke of Gloucester to be constable of England might have been acceptable too, but less so the surrender to him of the justiciarship of South Wales, taken in August after the overthrow of William Herbert. The earl refused to surrender the castles in Carmarthen and Cardigan. Edward IV also began the process of restoring Henry Percy as fourth earl of Northumberland. In October he was granted his estates in Cumberland, Northumberland and Yorkshire. The Percy restoration was a delicate matter because John Neville, earl of Northumberland, had remained loyal to Edward IV. In compensation, he was given the hand of the king's eldest daughter, Elizabeth, for his own son George, created duke of Bedford at the time of the betrothal in January 1470, and a month later he was granted the forfeited estates of the Courtenays in the West Country. But Warwick and Clarence were not compensated for the loss of their forfeitures in Cumberland and Yorkshire. On the restoration of Henry Percy to his title in March, John Neville was promoted to Marquess Montagu.[23]

By then, however, Warwick and Clarence were in revolt again, this time, it soon became apparent, with the definite aim of deposing Edward.[24] Disturbances in Lincolnshire provided the opportunity. Richard, Lord Welles, and his son Sir Robert attacked Sir Thomas Burgh, the master of the king's horse. The king could not allow such an assault on one of his senior servants to pass unpunished (perhaps as intended). Lord Welles obeyed a summons to appear before him, but Sir Robert raised a general insurrection. By 12 March Edward IV had learnt that Warwick and Clarence were behind it. The plan seems to have been to lure the king north to be entrapped between a rising in Yorkshire of the earl's men and an army raised by Warwick and Clarence in the midlands following on his heels. However, the recklessness of Sir Robert Welles, who foolishly attempted to rescue his father, undermined it. Welles was routed near Empingham on what became known as Losecoat Field and, before his execution, implicated Warwick and Clarence. Knowing what was afoot, Edward IV marched north to York to confront the Richmondshire rebels under the command of Lord Scrope of Bolton. Warwick and Clarence shadowed him, and Montagu, still loyal to the king, raised the marches. In this game of cat and mouse, Warwick's nerve broke first. From Doncaster he crossed the Pennines hoping to secure the support of his brother-in-law, Lord Stanley. Edward IV marched on to York where he received the submission of Scrope and his captains. He thereupon declared Warwick and Clarence traitors (and at this moment restored Percy to the earldom of Northumberland and promoted Montagu), and then turned to confront the remaining rebels.

But Warwick and Clarence, finding that Stanley would not come out for them and hearing of the submission of the earl's Richmondshire men, turned and fled with their closest followers. Passing through the midlands, where they were joined by Warwick's countess, his daughter the duchess of Clarence and his younger daughter Anne, they continued south to Devon. And although Edward gave chase, the party managed to take boats at Dartmouth early in April and escape. They first sailed to Southampton, where they tried to seize some of the earl's fleet, including the *Trinity*. But they were beaten off with the loss of several men, some of whom were later tried and executed in the constable's court. They moved on to Calais where they were denied access, possibly despite the sympathy of Lord Wenlock. Fortunately, the flotilla was reinforced by a squadron of ships under the command of Thomas Neville, the Bastard of Fauconberg, who deserted the fleet that had been commissioned to defend the seas against the Hanse. For a while they held station in the straits of Dover where they preyed on shipping, including a convoy of Flemish merchantmen. They put into the Seine estuary on 1 May, where they were granted refuge by Louis XI.[25]

In England Edward IV took steps further to diminish Warwick's power in the north by removing him and his lieutenant, Lord FitzHugh, from the wardenship of the west march and restoring Barnard Castle to Bishop Booth of Durham.[26] In France Warwick and Louis XI entered into complex negotiations. For two months Warwick's ships continued to prey on shipping, especially Flemish and Dutch vessels in the Channel from the Seine and later Barfleur. The duke of Burgundy finally raised a powerful fleet himself, which was joined by English ships under Anthony, Lord Rivers and, according to the Chronicle of Flanders, drove the earl ashore on 2 July. Thereafter this fleet was able to maintain an effective blockade. On 17 May the Milanese ambassador to France, Sforza de' Bettini, reported home that Louis XI had urged Warwick to descend on England as soon as possible, ideally with the Lancastrian exiles in his company; he was at this stage reluctant to be drawn into conflict again with Burgundy. Warwick, however, held out for more substantial logistical and diplomatic support.[27]

Earl and king did not meet until 8 June when Clarence and Warwick rode down to Amboise, where, according to Bettini, they were cordially received. They stayed for four days in negotiation. Bettini reported that Warwick did not want to be present when the queen arrived, but wished Louis to induce her to agree to a reconciliation and marriage alliance between his daughter Anne and the Lancastrian prince of Wales. When that was done, Warwick would return to the Loire, but the rest of the party remain in Normandy. The countess and her daughters then returned to Valognes in the Cotentin. Queen Margaret, Bettini later reported, arrived at Amboise on 25 June and proved intractable. Finally, he wrote again from Angers on 20 July, that she had relented and that she and Warwick were now expected to formalize the agreement. It had already been decided that the prince would follow Warwick after he had restored Henry VI. They both arrived, he next reported, on 22 July. Warwick, with great reverence and on his knees asked and was granted forgiveness, and he did homage and fealty there and then to Henry VI.[28]

The principal English source for the agreement, which provides only a summary, gives a different chronology and a slightly different gloss. It is entitled 'the Manner and Guiding between the queen Margaret, and of her son and the earl of Warwick' (known as the *Manner and Guiding*) and begins 'Here followeth the guiding of the earl of Warwick from 15 July to 4 August, which day he departed.'[29] It recounts how, by the means of the king of France, Warwick 'purchased' a pardon of the queen and her son, how the marriage was treated and how his passage across the sea with an armed force was appointed. It concentrates on the first. The queen, it confirms, was 'right difficult' over the matter of the pardon. She would not bend until after 'many entreaties and meetings'. Warwick was required to confess his fault and to excuse himself. This, one assumes, is a summary of the terms which Margaret had insisted upon *before* agreeing to meet Warwick. At Angers he is described as abasing himself and begging her forgiveness, indeed 'purchasing' a pardon. Once again the words of the queen and responses by the earl may well have been uttered before they finally met. Indeed the text giving the queen's demands, reads as though it was delivered without Warwick being present, and thus what she had argued earlier at Amboise. Warwick's response may well have been a separate written communication, although he is represented as having spoken to the queen. When the two actually met, all that was left was the public ritual reported by Bettini. According to the *Manner and Guiding*, she was scarcely less difficult over the marriage, it taking 15 days for her to agree. This too must surely refer to the preliminaries. Finally, solemn oaths were sworn upon the true cross in the cathedral church of St Mary, by Warwick to hold always to the cause of King Henry and the prince and serve them truly and faithfully, by King Louis to assist in the recovery of the English throne, and by Queen Margaret to accept Warwick as a true subject of King Henry. The duke of Guienne, the king's brother, also took an oath as a guarantor, dated 30 July, which fixes the date of the ceremony in the cathedral formalizing the agreement.[30]

The *Manner and Guiding* is cursory on practical details. It confirms that Warwick was to go on ahead and secure the kingdom; it records that he was to be regent and governor of the realm after he had recovered it (but leaves unanswered the question of what would happen after the prince returned); and it confirms that Clarence would enjoy the duchy of York. Many other points were spoken of, however, which were, to our loss, 'over long to put in writing'. It ends with a note concerning the aid that Louis was to give Warwick and the earl's promise to sail without delay.[31] According to Bettini, Warwick and the queen left Angers for Normandy on 31 July; the *Manner and Guiding*, which, judging from a passing remark that Warwick was still in France, was compiled within a month, gives 4 August as the earl's date of departure. Bettini also reported that the marriage between Anne Neville and Edward, Prince of Wales was to be celebrated, on Warwick's insistence, as soon as possible. The *Manner and Guiding*, on the contrary, categorically states that Anne Neville would be in the keeping of the queen and that the 'said marriage shall not be perfected until the earl of Warwick had been with an army over the sea into England and that he had recovered the realm of England'. And this is what seems to have been the case. Bettini added on 7 August that the earl had decided not to lose time waiting for his daughter's marriage.[32] In the event, too, Warwick was prevented by adverse winds and the Anglo-Burgundian blockade of la Hogue, where his fleet was gathering, from setting sail until a month later, in early September, when a gale dispersed the blockading fleet. His men disembarked at various Devon ports on 13 September.[33]

Warwick's plan, yet again, was to mount a decoy to draw Edward IV north, while he himself slipped the blockade. The stratagem may originally have been planned to take place in July. The Chronicle of Flanders tells of how on 2 July Warwick set sail from Normandy 'to go to the north of England, where he had many friends' but was intercepted by the Burgundian fleet which drove his fleet ashore. The account is precise in its details, including the date, *before* the rapprochement with Margaret of Anjou. A rising led by Lord FitzHugh did take place in the north a month later, and its timing implies that it was planned and begun before the alliance between Warwick and Margaret of Anjou was solemnized and proclaimed at Angers on 30 July. On 5 August Sir John Paston reported from London to his brother John that 'There be many folks up in the north so that Percy is not able to resist them'. If one allows for the time it would have taken for Warwick's emissaries to travel to northern England from Normandy, for the rebels to raise their men, and for the news of the rising to reach London, it must have been planned well in advance of the negotiations at Angers. Additionally, the *Manner and Guiding* reveals that Warwick was in correspondence with supporters in England while at Angers, and before then. Paston added that 'the king hath sent for his feedmen to come to him, for he will go to put them down'. Edward IV reached Ripon on 14 August and the rebellion melted away before him. The rebels sued for pardons, which were granted on 10 September. Certainly the rising in Yorkshire and Cumberland proved premature: it was extremely difficult to coordinate a naval expedition with an uprising behind the lines. But, in the event, Edward IV lingered in Yorkshire in September and was caught off-guard when Warwick and Clarence, with Jasper Tudor, earl of Pembroke, and John de Vere, earl of Oxford, landed in Devon on 13 September. The rising at the end of July is thus unlikely to have been a deliberate feint, even if in the event this is what fortuitously it turned out to be.[34]

Warwick appealed to the country in the name of Henry VI. Whereas the earl's rebellions in 1469 and earlier in 1470 had received only lukewarm support, now thousands flocked to the Lancastrian colours as the army marched first to Bristol, where the earl recovered his artillery train, and thence to Coventry, where the earl of Shrewsbury and Lord Stanley, both of whom had pointedly refused to support him in March, now came in. There was also a rising in Kent, which Warwick's agents might have stimulated. Edward IV, returning from Yorkshire to confront his enemies, learnt that Montagu to his rear was planning not to join him, as he expected, but rather to attack him. The king was now caught in the very trap he had avoided six months earlier; he and a small party of faithful followers hurriedly abandoned their troops, took to the sea at Bishop's Lynn on 2 October, and fled to the Netherlands. England lay at Warwick's feet. London was in uproar. The pregnant queen fled to sanctuary in Westminster Abbey.[35] The contrast with the events of September 1470 and the preceding spring and the autumn of 1469 is marked. When Warwick's quarrel with Edward IV had been but an internal dispute within the house of York, a matter essentially of court factionalism, the majority of the political nation stood aside. The widespread support the earl received when he returned in the name of the house of Lancaster and the speed with which Edward IV's position collapsed, revealed the extent of his failure and the scale of Warwick's continued popularity. Crowds were out again lining the roads crying 'Warwick! Warwick!' Multitudes thronged to him.[36]

Warwick entered London in triumph on 6 October and presented himself on bended knee to his true sovereign. Henry VI had already been released from the Tower and was in the care of Bishop Waynflete of Winchester. He was a pitiful figure, incapable of ruling. The earl assumed the position of the lieutenant of the realm, leading an interim government pending the return of Margaret of Anjou and the prince of Wales. The Readeption of Henry VI, dated from 29 September, had begun. It was an interim government that the earl led. George Neville, archbishop of York, returned as chancellor; John Langstrother, the prior of the hospital of St John became treasurer, and John Hales, bishop of Coventry, keeper of the Privy Seal. Otherwise the personnel of government remained much the same. The outgoing chancellor, Robert Stillington, and Privy Seal, Thomas Rotherham joined Queen Elizabeth in sanctuary. John Tiptoft, earl of Worcester, did not. He was captured, tried by his enemy and replacement as constable, the earl of Oxford, and condemned to death. He was not forgiven for his treatment of Warwick's men captured at Southampton earlier in the year, whose bodies had been impaled in addition to the customary indignities of execution for treason. Others had escaped with the king – including the duke of Gloucester, Earl Rivers and Lord Hastings. Some Yorkists lords, such as Lords Dinham and Dudley, were able to make their peace. Few rewards were distributed. Restoration was reward enough for Oxford and Pembroke. Warwick made himself chamberlain and

admiral and recovered the captaincy of Calais. Clarence became lieutenant of
Ireland; Montagu was restored to the wardenship of the east march. Parliament
was summoned to Westminster on 26 November, the principal purpose of which
was to attaint the rebel duke of York, 'calling himself Edward IV', and grant the
duchy to Clarence. This was an interim government pending the full restoration
of Lancastrian rule.[37]

The distrustful Louis XI and Margaret of Anjou were unwilling finally to
commit themselves until they had received confirmation from a French embassy
that Warwick was indeed in full command of the kingdom. On 5 December
Bettini wrote to Milan from Amboise that Queen Margaret and her party were
still there, for the king would not give them permission to leave until he had a
reply from his ambassadors. Their reassurance was delivered before 19 December
when he wrote to the duke again. They had reported, too, that the earl was ready
to declare war on Burgundy. The Queen and her party had already left. He did
not report that Edward Prince of Wales and Anne Neville had been married at
Amboise on 13 December.[38] Louis himself had not waited to invade Burgundian
territory. The formal alliance with Henry VI was sealed by early February. In
essence it reproduced the terms discussed in 1467: they encompassed a ten-year
truce, a trade agreement, and, a novelty, the promise of Holland and Zeeland for
Warwick from a dismembered Burgundy. By February Louis had recovered the
two Somme towns of St Quentin and Amiens; Warwick was preparing to come
to his assistance.[39]

The precipitate attack on Burgundy in December 1470 led Duke Charles to
look more favourably on the cause of his brother-in-law who was in exile in
Holland. The dukes of Somerset and Exeter, still resident in his court, were able
to maintain his neutrality for several months, but once Louis declared war he
became more sympathetic. He received Edward IV early in January and agreed
to fit out an expedition. By the end of February the exiled king had a small force
and flotilla gathered at Veere. Queen Margaret had still not sailed and she found
that, at the end of the month, the winds that rendered her port-bound carried
Edward and his small expeditionary force over to the east coast of England. It was
characteristic that whereas Warwick had spent months in the summer strengthening his forces and securing substantial military and diplomatic support before
he launched his invasion, Edward IV risked all to return as soon as he possibly
could, however small his band of supporters were. And his gamble paid off.[40]

Edward IV sailed on 11 March. He landed at Ravenspur at the mouth of the
Humber on 14 March.[41] He found a cautious welcome. Claiming, as Henry IV
had before him, to have returned only to recover his duchy, he was allowed to
pass York and through to his lordship of Wakefield. If few rallied to him, none
opposed him. Northumberland could not persuade his retainers to fight for
Edward IV because they still hated him for the deaths at Towton; Montagu, at

Pontefract, and equally hated locally, could not raise men in south Yorkshire in the cause of Lancaster without Percy backing. Thus Edward was able to pass through hostile territory. At Nottingham he was joined by 600 men raised by Sir William Parr and Sir James Harrington. An army raised by the earl of Oxford and the duke of Exeter who had recently returned to England, failed to intercept him at Retford. At Leicester, Lord Hastings called up 3,000 men. Although still only about 5,000 strong, Edward pressed on to confront Warwick at Coventry. Warwick, as cautious as ever, was waiting until he had overwhelming force – not only the troops of Oxford and Exeter tracking Edward, but also a large army led by the duke of Clarence approaching from the West Country. He confidently expected that when he had brought all these troops together he could march out and crush his enemy. He was, however, outmanoeuvred. Just as Montagu had returned to the family fold in the autumn of 1470, so now Clarence abandoned Warwick. Edward IV had been in communication with him since the summer of 1470 and had exploited his essential vulnerability in the new regime. Where once he had been indispensable to Warwick, now under a restored Lancastrian monarchy his situation was precarious.

On 3 April, three miles from the town of Warwick, on the Banbury road, Edward and Clarence met and joined forces. Now the forces were more equal. It was now Edward who challenged Warwick. The earl, however, declined. Upon this, Edward marched straight to London. The city gates were opened to him on 11 April. Archbishop Neville submitted before he arrived. Henry VI, who had been paraded around the street in a mockery of a royal entry, in an effort to restore confidence, surrendered to his 'cousin of York', declaring naively that he knew that he was safe in his hands. Having been reunited with his queen and met for the first time his first son, born in November, Edward marched out again to face Warwick who had been shadowing him with Oxford and Exeter. On the night of 13 April the two armies drew up lines opposite each other near Barnet. On the following morning, Easter Sunday, in thick fog, they finally engaged. In the bad visibility the battle lines became unaligned and confused. The earl of Oxford routed Hastings's men opposite him, but on regrouping and returning to the field attacked not the rear of Edward IV's army as he believed, but Montagu's flank, which fought back. Cries of treason were heard. Montagu fell and the Lancastrian line broke. Warwick took to his horse and fled, but was caught and killed. After all was over, the bodies of the Neville brothers, stripped of their armour, were brought back to London and there displayed for three days in St Paul's, so that all could see that the mighty earl of Warwick was dead. The bodies were then handed over to Archbishop Neville for burial in the family vault at Bisham.

In the end Warwick was 'out-generalled' by Edward IV. It was his additional misfortune that Queen Margaret and her troops did not land in England in time to reinforce him. With great irony they finally landed on the very day of Barnet, and this force too was overwhelmed by Edward IV at Tewkesbury on 4 May. Edward IV still had some mopping up to do. A tardy rising in Richmondshire collapsed on news of the victory at Tewkesbury. Kent rose again in May, led by the Bastard of Fauconberg and elements from Calais, who made an attempt on London. The garrison in Calais did not surrender, on terms, until later in the summer. The continued resistance came from the remnants of Warwick's followers, prepared even after his death to carry on in his name.[42] The Lancastrian dynasty, which the earl had briefly restored, ended with the death of Edward, Prince of Wales on or after the field of Tewkesbury. Anne Neville had not been carrying a child; Henry VI's days were numbered for all his touching faith in his cousin of York. He died, the duke of Gloucester being at the Tower that night, on 21 May.[43] It may have been that residual distrust of Warwick had contributed to a lack of vigour in the Lancastrian camp. It is noticeable that the duke of Somerset, who had returned to England with the duke of Exeter, could not bring himself to fight alongside Warwick and had taken himself off to await the Lancastrian landing in the West Country. Louis XI's extreme caution in not allowing Queen Margaret to travel earlier, coupled with the speed with which he went to war, so driving Burgundy into Edward IV's hands, acted against the longer-term prospects of the Lancastrian restoration, but then he probably had a shrewd idea that, once fully established in power, the Lancastrians might renege on the treaty. Misfortune played its part, but in the last resort it was Warwick's customary caution which lost him the war and his life. He who had dared had ultimately won.

The Readeption of Henry VI could well have succeeded. It was supported by a majority of the political nation and commanded considerable popular backing. Its failure was ultimately military. Warwick's career went full circle. The man who had been a loyal servant of the house of Lancaster in 1451 died its loyal servant in 1471. While he was a cautious general, he was a daring politician. He was, remarked a Milanese ambassador in 1469, as astute a man as ever was Ulysses.[44] From the moment he seized the initiative in Calais in 1457 he dominated English politics. He was its arbiter for over a decade. While he served mightily in the cause of York for several years, being indispensable to Edward IV in his usurpation of the throne, he revealed a capacity to set all that at nought when it no longer benefited him. He may have been thwarted in his ambition to become a duke; lacking a male heir, he certainly had ambitions for a daughter to be married to a king of England and for his descendants to enjoy the crown. In the manner in which he was prepared to set himself up above kings in the pursuit of his interests and ambitions, he was unique among English magnates in the fifteenth century. Not without reason did the Flemish chronicler, de But, liken him because of his deeds and reputation to a third king of England.[45] And it is no wonder that not only did he amaze his contemporaries but also divided opinion both then and since by his temerity.

PART TWO

Power

5

Estates and Finances

Warwick was the greatest lord in England between 1461 and 1471. The foundation of his greatness lay in his landed wealth. He held a dozen lordships and associated estates drawn from four great inheritances in twenty-eight English counties, Glamorgan and Powys. The significant exceptions seem to be Lancashire, Cheshire, Shropshire, Derbyshire and Lincolnshire. His estates in Nottinghamshire, near Bawtry, were close to the boundary of Yorkshire. There was a gap running across North Wales and the north west and east midlands that divided his northern from his southern landed interests. Even in this gap, especially Lancashire, through the exercise of royal office such as the chief stewardship of the north parts of the duchy of Lancaster, he was not without influence. Warwick was a national presence during the 1460s. The later recollection of John Rous that he was

> by his father's and mother's inheritance earl of Salisbury and lord of Middleham and many other great manors in the north and, by his lady and wife Dame Anne Beauchamp, earl of Warwick and lord of many other great lordships in every coast [part] of the land

was only a slight exaggeration.[1] Perhaps no other nobleman, with the exception of John of Gaunt in the late fourteenth century, certainly no other non-royal magnate, had ever enjoyed, or was ever again to enjoy, such a presence throughout the realm.

What disposable income did Warwick enjoy at the height of his power? What was there to spend after local overheads, such as payment of estate officials, repairs and maintenance? Ideally, this is calculated most accurately from receivers and receiver-general accounts. Manorial records such as reeves', bailiffs' and farmers' accounts give more detail, and reveal the deduction of more local costs. Alternative sources, such as *valors*, summaries by accounting officials of what was expected after all deductions in a year, are valuable summaries, but they do not record what was actually rendered. Nevertheless, they do probably indicate what was most important to accountants and, indirectly, creditors. Unfortunately there is a general dearth of Neville estate material for 1449–71. There is a receiver's account for Middleham of 1465–6, and some accounts for other properties held by Warwick in the north, and occasional bailiffs' accounts

for particular manors.[2] The historian has, therefore, to resort to a reconstruction
from surviving financial records outside these years, particularly from before
1449. There is an obvious drawback in that it cannot be certain whether what
was rendered twenty years before Richard Neville entered his inheritance was
still being generated afterwards. There was a general fall in incomes from land
in England of some ten per cent, higher in the north, between 1420 and 1450.
Landed income did not begin to recover in most parts of the country until after
1471. In Wales there was a catastrophic decline in income after 1440 as tenants
withheld payments on a massive scale.[3] Allowances need to be made, therefore,
for a downward movement of income, the precise scale of which is not known.
Notwithstanding all these caveats, a 'guesstimate' can be essayed for 1465, the year
at which Warwick was at the zenith of his fortune, after he had acquired the full
Montagu inheritance, and when he held the largest number of forfeited estates.

In one important respect Neville was fortunate: his estates were not extensively
encumbered with dower for any extended period. When he entered the earldom
of Warwick in 1449, his sister Cicely, dowager duchess of Warwick, was still alive.
She died, however, in July 1450. His mother, too, did not long outlive his father;
she died towards the end of 1462. Having successfully secured his rights to the
full Beauchamp inheritance, and having recovered by parliamentary enactment
the tail male portion of the Montagu inheritance that had escheated to the crown
in 1429 (and been subsequently sold to Cardinal Beaufort to endow St Cross
Hospital, Winchester), he enjoyed, after his mother's death in 1462, all the estates
to which he had a claim. The only estate in his hands burdened with dower was
the honour of Richmond proportion of the combined Middleham/Richmond
lordship held by Jacquetta, duchess of Bedford, Countess Rivers, costing
him approximately £150 per annum, and a dower of 500 marks a year from
Glamorgan enjoyed by his sister Eleanor, widow of Henry Percy, second earl of
Northumberland from 1455.[4]

The Beauchamp properties rendered £2,600–700 per annum to Richard
Beauchamp, earl of Warwick in 1420–22. After the death of his first countess in
1422 he married Isabel Despenser, whose estates, it has been calculated, were
worth a further £2,000. A *valor* of 1432–3 calculated the combined English and
Welsh estates of the Beauchamp and Despenser inheritances to be £5,471 clear,
including the Lisle estates which did not descend to the Kingmaker.[5] Richard
Beauchamp did not inherit the Beauchamp of Bergavenny estates until 1436;
one can suppose that all his landed inheritance was yielding him almost £6,000
per annum when he died in 1439. Not all of this came to Warwick. Property to
the anticipated value of £325 was set aside by Earl Richard in the Beauchamp
Trust to pay for the building of the Beauchamp chapel and other pious works.
Evidence suggests that it was producing no more than £270 yearly by the time of
Richard Neville's death. In 1466 a further handful of properties were conceded

by the earl, particularly Drayton Bassett, in settlement of his dispute with the dowager countess of Shrewsbury.[6]

We do not know precisely what contribution the Welsh marcher lordships of Abergavenny, Elwell, Ewyas Lacy and Glamorgan made to the total income enjoyed by Richard Beauchamp at his death. It was probably well over £1,000. Revenues from marcher lordships held by the dukes of Buckingham (Brecon and Newport) collapsed between 1448 and 1457, being reduced to barely one quarter from Brecon, and two-thirds from Newport. The duke of York's revenues from his South Wales lordships fell by approximately a half in the same period; the yield of Denbigh by two-thirds between 1443 and 1469.[7] One might expect, therefore, that Warwick's income from his Welsh lordships by 1465 was in the region of a half that enjoyed at the end of his life by his father-in-law. If one applies a fall of 10% for English estates and 50% for Welsh, one arrives at a disposable income from the Beauchamp/Despenser inheritances of the countess of approximately £3,000 per annum in the mid-1460s.

The calculations for the Neville/Montagu estates, the inheritance from his father and mother which Warwick entered in 1461/2, are more straightforward. Estate records from the last four decades of the fifteenth century suggest an income of approximately £1,850 from Middleham, Sheriff Hutton and Penrith. In 1465–6 Middleham produced nearly £1,000.[8] The Montagu properties, worth some £1,100 in the early 1440s, perhaps yielded rather less a decade or two later because of a recession in the cloth industry in Wiltshire and neighbouring counties.[9] Thus the value of Warwick's own inheritance was not far short of his countess's. To this we should add something in the order of £300 from the Neville of Latimer estate, of which he was custodian,[10] and something in the order of £1,000 from the forfeited Percy and Clifford estates in Cumberland, Westmorland and Yorkshire.[11] Bearing in mind that there were other acquisitions (for example in Norfolk, Erdington in Warwickshire and Collyweston in Northamptonshire), as well as other scattered properties that had been granted to him after 1461 (such as Newport Pagnell confiscated from the earl of Wiltshire), and other gaps in this calculation, his total disposable annual income from land was probably not far short of £7,000.[12] He did not always have this at hand as money to be spent. His father, for instance, saw only £594 of the paper value of £818 of his southern estates in 1455–6.[13] Estates could run into arrears in particular years, some of which were never recovered; debts were settled from source. It was the anticipated revenue which mattered.

£7,000 a year anticipated disposable income in the mid-1460s placed Warwick far above his contemporaries. Some magnates whose wealth was significant, though none would have approached this level, were in eclipse either by forfeiture or minority. In this category for most of, if not all of the decade, were the Beauforts, Butlers, Courtenays, Hollands, Percys, Staffords and Talbots. The estates of the dukes of Norfolk were heavily encumbered with dower; the dukes of Suffolk were poorly endowed.[14] Thus in 1465, in terms of landed wealth alone, the earl was at least five times wealthier than any other subject of the crown. Until the duke of Clarence entered the estate carved out for him by his brother the king in 1467, he stood alone among his contemporaries. Arguably, in real terms, taking account of falling landed income in mid-century, Warwick was the wealthiest single magnate of the fifteenth century. Richard of York, whose income has been estimated at £6–7,000 in 1443, enjoyed considerably less in the 1450s when the revenues of Welsh estates collapsed. John of Gaunt's income in 1399–1400, at over £10,000, was higher, but, allowing for falling landed incomes since then, the difference between the two in real terms was not significant. Clarence after 1471, may have had £6,000 to dispose of; Gloucester perhaps a little less.[15] But all these were royal dukes, close in line to the throne; Warwick was but the premier earl.

Income from offices is almost impossible to calculate. Commynes heard that Warwick's income from office alone was £8,000 a year.[16] We do not know the basis of this claim: whether he had heard what the total sums notionally paid to Warwick were, whether he had information concerning the amount he actually received, or whether someone had told him what profit Warwick took, or whether it was just a wild guess. If it was the profit of office, it was undoubtedly an exaggeration. The offices which involved the earl handling the largest sums of money were the captaincy of Calais, the keepership of the seas (1457–65) and wardenship of the west march. For Calais he should have received almost £20,000 per annum at war-time rates. But we know he did not, and we cannot be certain that he was even able to draw down his personal salary of over £180 a year. As keeper of the seas between 1457 and 1465 he was to receive revenue from tunnage and poundage from all ports, initially with the exception of Sandwich and Southampton, as well as £1,000 yearly from the duchy of Lancaster, and the spoils of war. The income from tunnage and poundage had been just over £6,000 in 1432–3, considerably less at the beginning of Edward IV's reign.[17] Being a time of peace, the salary for the wardenship of the west march in 1465 was £1,250, to which could be added profits from the warden's courts. Much of this was consumed in wages and other costs. The constableship of Dover and wardenship of the Cinque Ports produced the castleward, herbage and advowsons pertaining to the castle and forfeitures, 'shares' and wrecks pertaining to the wardenship over and above £300 for his sustenance and the payment of priests, servants, watchmen and other officers, £146 of which came from the fee farm of Southampton.[18]

But with these major offices, it all depended on whether the earl could in fact secure payment from the Exchequer. Almost all was assigned to other sources, especially customs. The treasurer of Calais continued to find it difficult to secure payment of the garrison's wages in the early 1460s. Various hand-to-mouth expedients were tried, including the assignment of most of the revenue from parliamentary taxation for an invasion of Scotland in 1463 which did not take place. Eventually, by the Act of Retainer in 1466, the Company of the Staple undertook to pay the garrison's wages itself from the custom and subsidy on wool, which from henceforward they would collect themselves.[19] Being a chamberlain of the Exchequer no doubt helped. However, there was always competition between assignees, some sources being allocated several times over.

For the keepership of the seas the earl was entitled to nominate his own collectors of tunnage and poundage without being answerable to the Exchequer, an arrangement that should have ensured prompt payment. Between 15 January and 30 August 1458 his nominees in eleven ports from Newcastle upon Tyne to Plymouth and Fowey were appointed by the crown. Several were removed between October 1459 and January 1460, only in their turn to be replaced once more by Warwick's nominees in August 1460. More of the earl's nominees were appointed a year after Edward IV came to the throne, between 24 March 1462 and the end of that year. These last collectors, the letters of commission stated, were nominated by Warwick 'according to the form and ordinance lately published by the king and his council for the said earl for the keeping of the sea'; in other words, in accordance with the terms of the renewed indenture, sealed on 13 February 1462. A copy of this indenture has not survived, but it may be significant that one of his nominees was to Southampton, just as one in August 1460 had been to Sandwich, the two ports excluded from the original terms of payment in 1457.[20] It is possible, therefore, that after the seizure of power in 1460 Warwick drew on all the revenues of tunnage and poundage. If he did so, he still continued to receive the additional £1,000 from the duchy of Lancaster, for a warrant for issue to the Exchequer on 25 February 1462 ordered the payment of this money for three years from November 1461, also under the terms of the indenture recently made.[21]

Several of those nominated were prominent local men not known to have been connected with the earl. Such were John Richardson of Newcastle, mayor in 1460, and frequent Tyne commissioner, and Thomas Gale, gentleman and merchant, at Dartmouth, who became deputy butler in the port and was from time to time on commissions to inquire into local disorders.[22] Others, however, are known to have been Warwick's servants. John Otter was nominated by him to London on 15 January 1458. He was removed on 13 November 1459, but subsequently nominated to Southampton on 18 March 1462. Daniel Sheldon, Warwick's one-time feodary of Barton Hundred in Gloucestershire, was his nominee to Bristol in August 1460, and then to Bridgwater in Somerset on 18 May 1462. He was one of the servants of the earl, with Thomas Otter and others, who had been commanded in August 1461 to fit out the *Grace Dieu* at the earl's expense. Henry Auger, his nominee to London on 31 December 1462 (replacing an earlier nominee of 1 August 1460), had previously been nominated by the earl to Chichester in the summer of 1459. He too was employed from time to time fitting out and victualling Warwick's ships.[23] Other collectors nominated by Warwick were trusted by him, as their record of service shows, even if not initially his servants. Vincent Pittlesden moved from Plymouth and Fowey in 1458 to Southampton in August 1460. John Bulstrode, his man at Lynn in 1458, moved to Yarmouth in 1462.[24]

We have no way of knowing, however, how much these men might have been able to collect and deliver to Warwick, since he was not required to account to the Exchequer. Matters were made worse by a general trade depression and a commercial war with the duke of Burgundy, which made the value of customs even lower. It would appear that Warwick had to borrow from John Tiptoft, earl of Worcester, the treasurer, and Robert Stillington, keeper of the Privy Seal, to pay for his fleet. This seems the likely explanation of the grant in the summer of 1463 of two-thirds of the revenue of tunnage and poundage from London, Southampton and Sandwich to Tiptoft and one third to Stillington in repayment of nearly £2,000 to Tiptoft and a little short of £1,000 to Stillington 'for certain causes touching the keeping of the sea' until repayment was complete. Warwick also had difficulty in realizing the duchy of Lancaster payments additionally set aside for the keepership of the seas.[25] Profits of war at sea would not have been sufficient to compensate for any shortfall. It is difficult, in the end, to see how the earl can have been anything but out of pocket in respect of these major military commands.

Many offices were sinecures, most lucratively the Warwick chamberlainship of the Exchequer, exercised by deputy, for which there should have been no difficulty in securing regular payment.[26] All offices had the potential for profit, over and above the fee paid in the form of perquisites and sweeteners that flowed with them. The mastership of the king's mews, for instance, had attached to it the right to take the king's prises of falcon, goshawks and others birds sold within the realm ranging from 20s. to 6s. 8d. per bird.[27] Warwick will have managed to squeeze a profit out of many of his offices, but how much one can only guess. More important probably was the authority, power and opportunity to exercise lordship they conferred. As warden of the Cinque Ports, for instance, he held Shepway courts (in person in February 1462). The status and authority conferred by the wardenship was a major factor in his popular standing in Kent after 1460.[28] And the captaincy of Calais, wardenship of the west march and keepership of seas conferred direct military power. There were other sources of income. Warwick built up a significant fleet of ships. They had a dual role: in war they provided the core of his navy; in peacetime he traded with them. He and his agents received licences to trade with Spain, Bordeaux and Normandy.[29] In addition to all this there was the stream of sweeteners, gifts and bribes that flowed his way, which by their very nature are unquantifiable.

If it is impossible to calculate Neville's total net income, it is even more difficult to grasp the scale of his expenditure. The principal outlay was on his household: both the permanent establishment, which perhaps moved from seat to seat, and the itinerant, or riding household which accompanied the earl wherever he went. No evidence has survived on the size and cost of the household. There can be little doubt, however, that it was staffed with the usual dignitaries – steward, butler, controller, and treasurer – and that there was a significant number of wardrobe, chamber, kitchen and stable staff, as well as a hunting establishment and a troupe of entertainers. On St George's Day 1464, six of the earl's minstrels provided the entertainment at a feast held by John, Lord Howard.[30] The size of the household varied, as councillors, administrators and retainers moved in and out, and it was greatly expanded at meal times by the customs of hospitality (effectively open house) and the giving of doles to the poor. It has been calculated, in line with declining incomes, that the size of aristocratic households generally fell in the fourteenth and fifteenth centuries, expanding again in the early sixteenth. It is conceivable that Warwick spent considerably more than his contemporaries, and possibly reverted to an earlier, more flamboyant, lifestyle. Robert Fabyan, the author of the *Great Chronicle* of London, remembered from his youth 'the exceeding household which he daily kept in all countries wherever he sojourned or lay'. Moreover, he recalled specifically that 'when he came to London he held such a house that 6 oxen were eaten at a breakfast, and every tavern was full of his meat, for who had any acquaintance in that house, he should have had as much sodden and roast [boiled and roasted meat] as he might carry upon a long dagger'.[31] His was a display of aristocratic hospitality on an unforgettable scale. Even the Burgundians were impressed by the lavishness of his style. Chastellain noted that the Bastard of Burgundy was spectacularly entertained in 1457 in a ruined house between Mark and Oye (the boundary between Calais and Burgundian territory) in a sumptuous feast.[32] This was before he entered his paternal and maternal inheritances. On his embassy to Rouen in June 1467 he took a magnificent company of esquires, ushers, pages, archers, heralds and trumpeters, which greatly impressed his hosts.[33] If in the mid-fifteenth century economies were made in most aristocratic household expenditure, Warwick was a notable exception, and seen to be an exception. It is possible that, at his zenith, his household appeared to rival that of the king in size and splendour, and may have contained as many as 200 persons, with 150 people in attendance at any one time. One should not be surprised if Warwick's expenditure on his household alone did not approach £4,000 per annum in the 1460s.[34]

We can only identify a few of these household men, the closest of his servants who were often entrusted with the most confidential business. Some prospered. Otwell Worsley, possibly the son of William, of Warwick, was, it appears, a later steward. In May 1461 he was sent to St Omer to brief the duke of Burgundy on recent events, and appears to have delivered the earl's personal version of the battle of Towton. He was shortly to become Warwick's deputy warden of the Cinque Ports and then took over the command of a contingent of the Calais garrison.[35] John Otter, who was given a place as an usher in the Exchequer under Thomas Colt, was often engaged in Warwick's financial matters, becoming a customer of London in 1458, after tunnage and poundage were granted to the earl to help pay for the keeping of the seas and subsequently at Southampton. He was frequently an agent managing matters to do with his ships. In 1465 he had a general authorization to act on Warwick's behalf. It could be, though there is no proof of this, that he was the household treasurer/cofferer. At the end of his master's life he was at Calais, apparently serving in the garrison. The list of aliases given by him for the pardon he received on 9 August 1471 reveal the breadth of his interests. He was of Calais, soldier, and late of Warwick, 'yeoman', late of Ulskelf, Yorkshire, his place of origin, 'gentleman', late of London, late of Ham and Walthamstow in Essex, where presumably he had acquired property, late of Westminster, in association no doubt with his post as usher of the Exchequer, and late of Sandwich.[36] Robert Neville, Warwick's secretary after 1461, became one of his principal diplomatic intermediaries, as were Warwick herald and Calais pursuant. But for the most part we know little about the most intimate of Warwick's servants, those who staffed his private office as it were.

In addition to maintaining his household, he built and maintained his own navy, the capital cost of which has been estimated at almost £3,000. In 1469 he undertook a major refit, or built a replacement of his severely damaged flagship, The Trinity.[37] He probably also maintained an arsenal; at least, this is suggested by his purchase of gunpowder charged to the Middleham receiver's account in 1465–6.[38] And then there was the cost of fees of retainers, annuities and other concessions of rent above and beyond the foresters, parkers, reeves and bailiffs deducted at source. At Middleham in 1465–6 this came to over £200 – more than 20% of revenue.[39] It probably ran at something like this proportion at Penrith and elsewhere. A further drain was the cost of royal service, especially military and diplomatic, the salaries, allowances and expenses of which were frequently delayed or never paid at all, and thus had to be met from private income. Warwick had a heavy burden here. One needs to bear in mind too that conspicuous expenditure was an integral part of aristocratic lifestyle; little or no thought was given to saving. Income, and beyond, was for spending. All aristocrats depended on credit, raised on anticipated estate revenue or on anticipated royal payments, and built up debts which were not finally settled, if at all, until after death.[40]

While no balance sheet can be drawn up, it is apparent that in 1461–71 Warwick received and spent on a huge scale. The management of the earl's finances, the administration of his estates and the maintenance of all his many interests was a major undertaking. When we consider the complexity of his manifold diplomatic, political and personal commitments, we should not think simply of Warwick the man. We should envisage an organization. He authorized major decisions, and we know in some detailed instances, from the small body of correspondence that has survived in his name, that he intervened personally. But he could not possibly have handled all matters, and indeed would not have wished to deal with the many routine matters concerning household management, estate administration, acquisition of property and legal disputes: he employed others to do this. Much of the exercise of his lordship, such as acting as feoffee (trustee) for a client, carrying out arbitrations in disputes which were referred to him, or dealing with the stream of appeals for his patronage, for which for a few years after 1461 he was doubtless bombarded, must surely have been filtered by and delegated to others. His council and officers dealt with this business most of the time on his behalf. When we refer to 'Warwick', beyond his political, diplomatic and military actions, we should envisage a corporate body acting in his name. It is perhaps appropriate to think of his position as being, in this respect, not unlike that of the king, who was both a person and an institution: the 'crown'. It was not only Warwick the man but also Warwick the 'earl': his household and council that appeared in the early 1460s to be an alternative focus of power to contemporaries.[41]

Warwick's council was composed of his principal household officers, senior lawyers, experienced administrators and his leading retainers, clergy as well as laymen. It had neither a fixed membership, nor a fixed meeting place. It probably met frequently in London, especially after 1461 when Warwick's affairs took him to and from the north, the West Midlands and Calais. It was first recorded sitting there as early as 1450–1, no doubt on an occasion when the earl was in the capital; in December 1467 it was in session there when the earl himself was in the north.[42] Like the royal council, of which he himself was a member, it was a fluid body at which attendance varied according to business and availability. And there were probably what we would call committees, meeting especially at Warwick, Middleham, Cardiff, Carlisle and Calais to coordinate local affairs. His Richmondshire council, for instance, met at Richmond Castle on 22 April 1465 to settle leases of vaccaries in Arkengarthdale. Four years later the bailiff of Crakehall had to produce a warrant authenticated by signet and sign manual dated 5 March 3 Edw IV (1463) to allow him not to be charged for the farm of the Rand which had been granted to Sir John Conyers rent free. Conciliar memory was long, and record keeping assiduous. Thomas Witham and others had issued a mandate on behalf of the earl of Salisbury concerning free rents for which the feodary was answerable at the audit of account in 29 H VI (1451); this was produced at the audit in 1469 to justify collecting rent unpaid since the earl's death.[43] Finally there would also have always been a small body of councillors in personal attendance. The key link was his secretary, the names of two of whom are known: Richard Fisher and Robert Neville, a distant cousin.

We have a glimpse of who Warwick's most trusted councillors were in 1463, after he had inherited his mother's estates at the end of 1462, and thus finally united all the property that descended to him. At this moment he made a new will (a copy of which has not survived) in which he nominated eleven men as his feoffees and to whom he granted, as the royal licence subsequently issued on 14 June 1463 states, 'castles, manors, lordships, lands, rents and services' to the yearly value of £1,000 'to pay his debts and to fulfil his will after his death'. The feoffees were his brother George, then bishop of Exeter and chancellor of England; his one-time brother-in-law, John Tiptoft, earl of Worcester, constable of England and lately treasurer; the two chief justices, Sir Robert Danby (Common Pleas) and Sir John Markham (King's Bench); three prominent retainers, Sir Walter Blount, Sir James Strangways and Sir Walter Wrottesley; and four senior administrators in his service, Thomas Witham, Thomas Colt, Henry Sotehill and William Kelsy.[44]

Two characteristics of this body of men stand out. The first is the extent to which many of them were also the king's men, demonstrating how fully, at the beginning of Edward IV's reign, king and earl were as one. Not only was Tiptoft the constable of England, but he was also steward of the king's household. George Neville, of course was the chancellor of England. Colt and Blount, were also much engaged in royal service.[45] Equally remarkable is the fact that the two chief justices were close to Warwick too. Additionally, if not a royal servant, Sir James Strangways had been the speaker of the House of Commons in 1461–2. To these men we could add Richard Illingworth, chief baron of the Exchequer, styled as the earl's councillor in 1466.[46] All of them were no doubt also engaged on other baronial councils.

The second characteristic is the dominance now of men from the north, and in particular the Neville patrimony in north Yorkshire. If George Neville, who was to become archbishop of York two years later, is included as a member of the family, there were now six men, the majority, drawn from the old Neville affinity. Colt, Strangways, Danby, Sotehill and Witham had served the earl's father. Sir James Strangways of West Harlsey, North Riding, had been a retainer of the earl of Salisbury since 1447, and before that had served his mother, Warwick's grandmother, in the important role of a feoffee of Middleham and her other jointly endowed estates until her death in 1440. He too was one of Salisbury's executors. He fought at and survived Wakefield. He was retained by Warwick with a fee of £20 paid from Middleham. He was sheriff of Yorkshire several times, the last being in 1468/9. He died, aged 65, in 1480.[47] Sir Robert Danby of Thorp Perrow, a justice of common pleas from 1452, was an executor of the earl of Salisbury, as well as councillor, feoffee and executor for other members of the family. He was dismissed as chief justice by Edward IV in 1471, and died as a result of a hunting accident in 1474.[48] Thomas Witham of Cornburgh, close by

Sheriff Hutton, another executor of the earl of Salisbury, had been his steward of Sheriff Hutton as well as steward of the Yorkshire estates of Lord Latimer under the earl's guardianship. A clerk in the office of Thomas Colt as Warwick Chamberlain in 1450, he was appointed chancellor of the Exchequer by Salisbury as treasurer in 1454, and was restored to the office for life in 1460, confirmed in 1461. Pardoned after the rout of Ludford, he continued in Warwick's service, especially in the lordship of Sheriff Hutton. He served on the bench for the East Riding during the Readeption. In his will of 1475 he remembered the earl and countess of Westmorland as well as the earl and countess of Salisbury with a substantial bequest for prayers for their souls, but not, perhaps out of political expediency, the earl and countess of Warwick.[49] The fourth Yorkshireman was Henry Sotehill. He had been in Warwick's service before 1449, moving with him to the midlands then. He was a lawyer, who appears to have had West Riding origins. Retained by the duchy of Lancaster, he was appointed Warwick and his father's deputy as steward of Pontefract in 1458 and as steward of all the north parts of the duchy in 1460. His clients included the duchy of York, Sir John Fastolf and later Sir William Plumpton. He became king's attorney in 1461 and was of the quorum of the West Riding bench continuously until 1475, when he was also dismissed as king's attorney.[50]

Perhaps the most important of these northern councillors was Thomas Colt. A lawyer, probably born in Carlisle, he was an established Neville servant by 1447, escheator of Cumberland and Westmorland in 1448, and a JP in Cumberland from 1448. He was in the service of the earl by 5 April 1449, when Warwick received his first independent royal grants in the north, of a third of the lordship of Egremont in Cumberland and the manor of Deighton in Yorkshire, on the surrender of his father. The sureties for these transfers were Thomas Colt, then resident at Middleham, and Henry Sotehill. Colt may already have enjoyed a post in the Exchequer. His election as one of the MPs for Carlisle in November 1449 was probably secured to further the younger Richard Neville's claims in the earldom of Warwick, in which he was by then involved. He was appointed Warwick chamberlain of the Exchequer, the hereditary gift of which office lay with the earls of Warwick, on 7 December 1450, but shortly after removed, not to be restored until the spring of 1454. He was frequently active as a mainpernor for the earl (with Witham in 1450) in the early 1450s. He was a witness to the new borough charter granted to Cardiff in March 1451.[51] Colt's career flourished as a result of his connection with the earl, and perhaps specifically his Exchequer office, which he held for the rest of his life. He was subsequently retained both by the duchy of Lancaster and by the duke of York, whose councillor he became, and for whom he was acting as a mainpernor by bill of the treasurer (Salisbury) at Westminster on 19 July 1454 (as of Middleham) with Witham (in his capacity as chancellor of the Exchequer), as of London.[52]

It is possible that Colt became more closely attached to York than to Warwick thereafter. He was in the field at Ludford, fled to Ireland with the duke and was attainted at Coventry. His importance in Yorkist circles was acknowledged by his being identified in the indenture of Sir Baldwin Fulford to keep the seas in February 1460 as one of the rebels for whose capture Fulford was to be especially rewarded. He fought at Wakefield where, he later alleged, he was sought out with murderous intent and wounded by Roger Thorpe, son of Sir Thomas Thorpe, for the part he had played in the imprisonment of the father in 1454. He was thereafter granted Colby Hall and £2,000 in compensation. An executor and administrator of York's estate, he was subsequently made chancellor of the earldom of March by Edward IV and served on the royal council. In the early 1460s, however, he remained close to Warwick. He was appealed to with Henry Sotehill as one of the earl's learned counsel in the summer of 1462. He was one of his feoffees and executors in 1463, a guardian of the county palatine of Durham, 1462–4, more one suspects in Warwick's interest than the king's, and was in receipt of a fee of £10 per annum from Middleham in 1465–6. In the last two years of his life (he died in 1467), he was much engaged in diplomacy on both the earl's and the king's behalf. He acquired the manor of Netherhall in Roydon, Essex, which he rebuilt as a modern moated brick house as his principal residence, as well as Norton in Enfield; on his death he held lands in eight counties.[53]

It may be that the close involvement of these northern councillors as executors of Warwick's father (and probably of his mother), who had only recently died, explains in part their prominence, but this does not detract from the fact that, after 1461, the earl's Neville roots had superseded his countess's Beauchamp connections. The longest serving, most trusted and loyal in his service of all these feoffees, however, was Sir Walter Wrottesley of Wrottesley, Staffordshire. He was made Warwick's deputy as hereditary steward of Worcestershire in 1451, was on hand at Ludford, and fled with the earl to Calais after the rout. He fought through the campaigns of 1460–61, being knighted it appears at the coronation of Edward IV. He was liberally rewarded, primarily with properties in the midlands confiscated from the attainted earl of Wiltshire. His standing with the earl was such that he served as pantler at the enthronement feast of Archbishop Neville in 1465. He can be glimpsed occasionally as an active councillor in the 1460s, as in November 1464 when he and colleagues attended to business at Cardiff, or in 1467 when he received payment for the earl's diplomatic expenses.

Wrottesley succeeded Thomas Colt as Warwick chamberlain of the Exchequer in that year. He was with Warwick in March 1470, his brother Henry being one of the emissaries to the king, and fled with him to Calais. He and Henry were among those proscribed. He may have returned to England briefly in 1470 and had a hand in the death of John Tiptoft, earl of Worcester, in revenge for the execution of Henry at Southampton earlier in the year. If so, he was back in Calais early in 1471 as Warwick's lieutenant there with Sir Geoffrey Gate. He thus did not fight alongside his lord at Barnet, as no doubt he would have wished. After protracted negotiations he surrendered Calais to Lords Hastings and Howard in August 1471, having secured a pardon for himself and his men, but on returning to England he was arrested on a trumped-up charge and committed to the Fleet. There he died on 10 April 1473, and was buried in the Greyfriars at London, the customary burial ground of prisoners. It was with good reason, and some understatement, that seventy years later John Leland commented of him that he was 'great with the earl of Warwick'.[54]

Not all of these feoffees survived, like Wrottesley, to carry out their duties, should they in the event have been allowed to do so. It is uncertain which of the feoffees of 1463 would have counted as the earl's principal councillors at the end of his life. Not Tiptoft: he was wholly a king's man later in the decade. As constable he had presided over the trial and execution of Warwick's captured servants at Southampton in May 1470, including Henry Wrottesley and Richard Clapham, and was executed himself in November on the earl's orders. Earlier in Warwick's career, however, Tiptoft who had been his brother-in-law, appears to have been active on Richard Neville's behalf. As a councillor or perhaps feoffee of Barnard Castle in February 1456 he sued by attorney in the Durham palatine court eighteen tenants of Barnard Castle and its constituent manors (Denton, Headlam, Langton, Longnewton and Piercebridge) for detinue of rent. He was, however, out of England between 1458 and 1461, on pilgrimage to Jerusalem and studying at Padua. He was recalled by Edward IV, and by 1463 was already more of a king's man than the earl's, although he served alongside him in Northumberland both in 1462 and 1464.[55] Blount was even more distinctively a servant of the house of York. He had first served the earl as marshal of Calais in 1458, and was treasurer there after 1461. In 1464, however, he was recalled by Edward IV to become treasurer of England and promoted to the title of Lord Mountjoy in 1465. His brother Thomas suceeded to his post in Calais. Mountjoy sought sanctuary during the Readeption; his son William died of wounds fighting for the king at Tewkesbury.[56] Even Colt might have faced a difficult choice of masters had he lived longer. But the number of those still on the earl's council probably included Danby, Witham and Markham (dismissed by Edward IV in 1469), as well as George Neville and the faithful Wrottesley. By this time, Lord Wenlock and Sir Geoffrey Gate, both key figures at Calais, were also prominent in Warwick's council, as also was Henry, Lord FitzHugh. For a short while, Sir William Parr was another high in the earl's confidence after 1463, until he deserted the earl in 1470,[57] The northern and Neville domination was not significantly diminished in the last years of his life.

Answerable to the council, and often councillors themselves, were the local administrators, the names of whom are occasionally thrown up, most frequently as stewards of the earl's lordships. One can include Sir Walter Scull of Holt (Worcestershire) who was steward of his Worcestershire estates in 1464. They were almost always significant local gentry in receipt of fees of £10 and over. Because of the paucity of surviving estate records, we know little of the earl's financial administration, far less than for his father-in-law. It may well be that William Kelsey, of such seniority as to be a feoffee and executor in 1463–4, was then his receiver-general of England: he is to be found renewing rentals in Canford and Hanley. His receiver of Glamorgan in 1464 and again 1469 was Thomas Throckmorton;[58] his receiver at Middleham, Richard Conyers, was brother of the steward and constable, Sir John Conyers. These men were responsible for the bailiffs, reeves, rent collectors, foresters and parkers who actually ran the estates. At Middleham, for instance, there were some thirty men, including the chief gardener and janitor, on the pay roll; they in their turn no doubt employed assistants and workers, paid from their fees.[59] A considerable number of men were directly dependent on the earl.

Beyond the household and estate administration, Warwick commanded a substantial following, or affinity. This radiated out from formally feed men retained by contract for service in both war and peace, through less formally bound annuitants, to the numerous swarm of men moving in and out of his orbit who were described as 'well willers' or 'well wishers', and who might perform occasional service in exchange for ad hoc reward. Warwick's men were known by the wearing of his livery or his badge, the ragged staff. Writing at the end of his life, John Rous, who was in a position to know, commented that in 1483 Henry Stafford, duke of Buckingham boasted that he had as many men wearing his badge of Stafford knots as had the earl of Warwick men wearing the ragged staves. But, Rous added, in reality they were greatly inferior in number.[60] Retainers and well willers were to be found wherever Neville held estates and royal office. We have incomplete evidence about those he formally retained, or to whom he paid annuities. A handful of indentures themselves are still in existence; only for the lordship of Middleham does a list of fees paid to retainers survive. We are even denied a long list of followers punished in 1471, since Edward IV halted proceedings. Some indication is to be found in pardons of 1470 and 1471, but these do not add many names.[61] Professor Carpenter identified 41 Warwickshire-based men who served the earl in one capacity or another. A slightly greater number, of approximately 45, can be identified in the north west and Yorkshire.[62]

Occasional news reports sent to members of the Paston family give some indications of the numbers on which the earl could call. In 1454 John Stodeley reported that the earl was expected to arrive in London with 140 (seven score) knights and squires 'beside other meyne [following]'. It had also been reported to Paston that Warwick had attended the Leicester parliament in May 1450 with

400 men. John Bottoner informed John Paston that Warwick's father, the earl of Salisbury, came up to London in 1458 with eighty knights and esquires in a company totalling 400 men. These may have been eighty of his indentured retainers and annuitants accompanied by their own servants. If these numbers are at all reliable (and they are likely to be exaggerated), they indicate that father and son could bring out 200 retainers before 1461, and by implication that the earl alone could muster that number thereafter.[63] The number may well have increased at the end of the decade. John Warkworth commented that after George Neville was removed from the office of chancellor (in 1467) 'the earl of Warwick took to him in fee as many knights, squires, and gentlemen as he might, to be strong'. One was Robert Cuney of Western Coyney, Staffs, whose indenture was sealed at Warwick on 25 September 1467.[64] It is possible, therefore, that, not including the Calais garrison, Warwick might by then have had a similar number to the 200 indentured retainers and annuitants feed by Gaunt in his last decade.[65]

Richard Neville, at the height of his career, got, spent and retained on a massive scale. His occupation of the earldom of Warwick between 1449 and 1471 coincided with the great slump of the fifteenth century. The revenues he received from his estates were probably at their lowest level in the century. On the other hand, from the end of 1462 he had inherited the best part of what had once sustained four separate earldoms. This more than compensated for any decline of income in each. He stood out spectacularly from all his peers and was able to spend and attract followers on a scale which none of his contemporaries could match. While, in absolute terms, his level of income and expenditure may have been lower than magnates of his standing in earlier times, in comparative terms it was as great, if not greater. There had probably not been a subject so magnificent to his contemporaries in the lavish display of his wealth, or the number of men at his command, since John of Gaunt. At a time when aristocratic families and those dependent on landed income were feeling the pinch, he was a man of seemingly unlimited resources. After 1461 only the king could outshine him, and it appeared to many contemporaries that his glow was as great as his sovereign's.

6

Lordship and Loyalty: East Anglia and the West Midlands

The scale of Warwick's presence in England in terms of men and resources is apparent if not precisely known. Warwick's affinity was formidable, far outstripping that of any other subject at the beginning of the 1460s, almost rivalling the king's own. It was one thing, however, to have men in his service and resources at his disposal; it was another to exercise lordship effectively. The provinces in fifteenth-century England were ruled by a partnership between the king and great subjects. The king, whose authority was supreme, did not have the resources to govern directly. He did so through the power and authority of his greater subjects: the magnates, noblemen of comital rank or above who held significant lordships and estates and commanded significant numbers of men as tenants, retainers and well-willers. As Bishop John Russell intended to remind members of parliament in 1483, 'The politic rule of every region well-ordained standeth in the nobles'.[1] Effective government depended on the ability of the king to work with these magnates, but he needed also to command their obedience and respect. The effective, or politic, rule depended on the king's ability to assert his authority. For his part, a magnate seeking to be a significant and powerful figure in the realm (and not all did or could) needed both to maintain favour at court and to sustain his influence in the provinces. His capacity to reward and promote his men, to keep them loyal to him, depended in part on whether he could channel royal favour in their direction. Favour at court greatly increased a magnate's capacity to do favours for his men; a large following in the country enhanced the significance of his presence at court.[2]

Good lordship was expected of a lord: the phrase was ever on the lips (and pens) of contemporaries. The political world moved on the basis of the reciprocal relationship of lordship and service. Honour and respect were evaluated against the proper performance of either lordship or service. A lord was the centre of a fluctuating circle of dependants, employees, retainers, tenants, neighbours and general 'well willers' who expected to benefit from his largesse and influence and who were in return willing to undertake tasks for him. In an exchange of reciprocal obligations, favours were done for services rendered. A lord's 'worship', the standing and respect in which he was held, depended in part on the effectiveness with which he exercised his lordship. It was not simply a matter of mutual advantage: good lordship was a public virtue; an integral part of the value system. No magnate could afford to neglect it. On it stood not just his political power but also his reputation and honour.

Good lordship and the effective rule of the country in which a magnate had interests was achieved not just by advancing one's own men, but additionally by ensuring that they, their fellow gentry and their dependants lived harmoniously. It was not always easy so to do because disputes, especially over property where title was uncertain and contested were never far from the surface. Such disputes often erupted into violence, commonly alongside the pursuit of a case at law. The best lordship tried to avoid taking sides and sought to avoid maintaining the cause of a retainer against one who was not. Lords sometimes did intervene, to browbeat courts on behalf of their men, but the practice, if never eradicated, was widely condemned. It was usually in a lord's greater interest to secure peaceful settlement of disputes, often through arbitration backed up by legal agreement, and thus be seen to be a reconciler rather than fomenter of conflict.

In considering the effectiveness of Warwick's lordship we will concentrate on three of the principal areas where his estates lay and in which he could be said to have exercised politic rule: the West Midlands, the north west and northern Yorkshire. There were other areas where Warwick was a significant landholder and might have aspired to be a significant presence but about which our knowledge is scant. One is the area of south-west Hampshire, south-east Dorset, southern Wiltshire and southern Somerset, which one might call Wessex, which were the heartlands of the Montagu earldom of Salisbury, and were focused on the lordships of Christchurch and Canford. Warwick inherited these estates after his mother's death in 1462. Unfortunately, very little material remains on which to base a discussion, and what little there is has not as yet been subjected to detailed scrutiny. It may be, however, that he did not exert himself in this area beyond the necessary management of the estates. And after 1467, the evidence suggests, it was a part of England in which George, duke of Clarence played a far more prominent role. In so far as it was mobilized in Warwick's cause in 1469–71 it was by Clarence, not him.[3]

One area, however, where we know that Warwick would have liked to have played a bigger role was in South Wales. As lord of Glamorgan, Abergavenny and other marcher lordships in Powys he was a significant presence. Between 1449 and 1453 he asserted his control, especially of Glamorgan, by violence when necessary, and almost certainly called on its resources to support him in men and materials. After the Yorkist victory in 1460 he secured the grant of the keeping of the marcher lordships of Newport, Hay, Brecon, Huntingdon (Herefordshire) and Goodrich during the minorities of the duke of Buckingham and earl of Shrewsbury, whose fathers had been killed at Northampton. However, after Edward IV became king, Sir William Herbert of Raglan, created Lord Herbert, supplanted him. Herbert had in fact been Warwick's steward and sheriff of

Glamorgan in 1449–53. He had served York and Warwick well in the marches in 1456 and in the wars of 1459–61. On 8 May 1461 he was made chief justice and chamberlain of South Wales and the offices and custody of the estates, previously granted to Warwick, were transferred to him subsequently. Herbert was responsible for securing Wales for the new dynasty and was rewarded accordingly, and at the expense of Warwick.[4] It appears that Neville, who had to accept this curb on his ambition and limitation of what he could personally undertake, deeply resented Herbert's promotion. As soon as he overthrew him at Edgecote in 1469 and recovered control of the government, Warwick rewarded himself with Herbert's offices in South Wales, though he was only able to enjoy them for a matter of weeks and probably never entered them. Throughout the 1460s Warwick was frustrated in his attempts to extend his power in South Wales. It seems he did not visit Glamorgan at all in the decade, and although he continued to raise revenue and to rule his marcher lordships, they seem to have become peripheral to the exercise of power.

We will thus focus, in our discussion of Warwick's lordship and his position in the provinces of England, on the West Midlands, the north west and northern Yorkshire. The effectiveness of Warwick's lordship in these three regions is open to question. Professor Carpenter concluded in her study of the relationship of the earl with the gentry of Warwickshire that, as a consequence of the failure of his lordship, only in the Readeption could they be persuaded to show a solid allegiance to him and that after his death they quickly realigned themselves. In his study of Cumbria in the later fifteenth century, Dr Booth argued that Warwick failed to attract the same level of committed support as his father enjoyed and, as a consequence, was deserted in his final hour. And Professor Hicks once bluntly stated that the northerners never rose at all in his support, implying that even they were disenchanted.[5] The possibility that Warwick's fall was caused, at least in part, by the desertion of his men, and that this might have been the consequence of the failure of his lordship, thus needs to be considered.

Before looking at the contentious issue of the West Midlands, we will visit a county which was not at the heart of his interests, where his landed presence was minimal, yet where local gentry were nevertheless anxious to secure his good lordship: Norfolk. We are able to do this because of the exceptional survival of the Paston Letters. They reveal, in a way that is not possible in those regions where he was dominant, the manner in which his lordship was negotiated. They are, perhaps, additionally indicative of Warwick's standing and influence elsewhere in England where similarly he had only a relatively minor presence, for, at the height of his power, Warwick's lordship had an impact in most parts of the realm and not just those where he had a prominent presence.[6] The earldom of Warwick possessed the small lordship of Saham Toney in the east of Norfolk. Under the terms of Richard Beauchamp's will, this was placed in the hands of trustees to build his chapel at St Mary's Warwick and other works. Technically Richard Neville did not hold it. However, it is clear that the trustees acted on his behalf in the administration of this and the other enfeoffed properties.[7] In addition, the earl acquired two properties: 'manors' called Bowles and Walcotes, in Little Snoring, near Walsingham in 1454. He also held the advowson of Little Snoring.

Shortly after he entered the earldom, Neville wrote to his 'right trusty and well beloved friend' Sir Thomas Tuddenham asking him if he could help him with a loan. Tuddenham was at the time one of the regime's key men in the county, and the new earl himself part of that same inner circle. Perhaps in hopes of securing the loan, Warwick lauded praise on Sir Thomas 'for there is none in your country that we might write to for trust so well unto you; for as we be informed, you be our well willer, and so we pray you of good continuance'.[8] One suspects that this is a case where the earl's council rather than Richard in person was the initiator in this fishing trip. Tuddenham's well willing did not continue for long. After Warwick had sided with Richard of York, he became an ill willer. On 19 April 1458 (?) the earl wrote to the feoffees (in London?), Thomas Hugford, William Berkeswell and Nicholas Rody, informing them that he had restored Sir William Oldhall to the office of steward of Saham. Oldhall, who was described in terms appropriate to a retainer, had been appointed to that office before he was accused of treason and arrested in 1452. Although he escaped to sanctuary, he did not recover his freedom until after St Albans in 1455. He subsequently 'stood in trouble thorough the labour and pursuit of his not wellwillers (sic.), Sir Thomas'. And indeed Tudddenham had 'not been friendly but demeaned him strangely unto us'. The feoffees were requested to make sure that Oldhall enjoyed the office and received the fee.[9]

By this time Warwick had already approached John Paston, another not particularly enamoured of Tuddenham. On 23 August 1454 he wrote from Middleham concerning his purchases of the property in Little Snoring and asked him to show good will and favour to him and his feoffees in the property, so 'that I may by your friendship the more peaceably enjoy my foresaid purchase'. Moreover, he added, that in this matter he would do him a singular pleasure and 'cause me to be your right good lord, which sometime shall be to you available by the Grace of God'. Warwick (or his council), it is worth noting, approached Paston.[10] The offer was taken up, and for the next fifteen years Paston, his sons and his associates did what they could to draw on this proffered good lordship. In their correspondence they kept up a steady stream of reports of the earl's whereabouts and affairs, most dramatically of the fight at sea in 1458 in which John Jerningham participated, and of the berating of Rivers at Calais in 1460. Friar Brackley claimed in 1456 to be close to Richard Fisher, the earl's secretary, but one wonders whether he really was.[11] Four years later, in a letter from

Norwich to John Paston when he was attending the parliament which made
Richard of York heir to the throne, Brackley wrote in his idiosyncratic, excessive
and barely understandable way:

> God safe our good lord Warwick, all his brethren, Salisbury etc from all false covetousness
> and favour of extortion, as they will flee utter shame and confusion. God save them and
> preserve from treason and poison; let them be aware of the pity of God; for if ought come
> to my lord Warwick but good, fare well ye, fare well I, and our friends! For by the way of
> my soul, this land were utterly undone, as God forbear etc.[12]

He followed up a few days later with some advice for Paston to pass on to the earl.
Referring to Jeremiah 8: 8–10, he wrote: 'I would mine Lord Chancellor [George
Neville] and my special Lord Earl, *utinam* Duke, of Warwick, with all their trew
affinity, schould remember this text which is Holy Scripture'. A full and almost
incomprehensible exegesis follows.[13] What Paston made of all this, and the earl
himself, in the unlikely event of the message being passed on, we can only surmise.
Warwick probably appreciated more the military service he received. Paston's
somewhat dubious relative, Thomas Dennis, fought for him in the battles of
1460–1; Paston's younger son John III served under him, in the company of the
duke of Norfolk, in the north of England in the winter of 1462–3.[14]

Paston probably looked for the earl to assist in the matter of Caister. Before
Easter 1460 Brackley semed to believe that after Warwick returned to England in
triumph (about which he seems to have been sublimely confident), he would sort
things out for him. But Warwick refused to be drawn. In fact, like so many of his
contemporaries who doubted Paston's honesty in his claim to be the beneficiary
of Sir John Fastolf's will, he does not seem to have done much for Paston as he
struggled to get his hands on Fastolf's inheritance. In October 1460 Margaret
Paston was anxious about her husband's failure to persuade Warwick to write a
letter on their behalf in respect of a hearing at Bungay. John was advised in May
1461 to approach 'my lord of Warwick, the which is your good lord' to move the
king in his favour. If he did, the king was not moved. Thomas Dennis asked in
vain for Paston to put in a good word to the earl for him in the same month.[15]

Paston seems additionally to have had to accept that Warwick pursued
interests that clashed with his. That same year, John Taverham, a Paston tenant
who claimed to be wrongfully disseised of his property in Taverham, also
complained that his mother-in-law's possession of a property in Attylbrigge was
threatened by the earl who had commanded certain gentlemen to enter it.[16] It was
even less likely that he would have been able to persuade the earl to help Elizabeth
Mountford to recover part of her jointure at East Lexham from Edmund Rowse
who had already enfeoffed the earl, Sir Walter Gorges (Oldhall's son-in-law) and
others in the property. Elizabeth was a kinswoman of Margaret Paston. Warwick
had been responsible for the summary execution of her husband at Calais in

1460. Elizabeth besought her nephew, as she styled him, 'to take great labour upon you to inform my lord's good lordship of the trouble' and find out

> 'whether that my lord will abide the feoffment made to him or not; and that it shall please my Lord that I may have right as law requires, for I trust to God by such time as my Lord shall be informed of the truth by you, that his Lordship will not support the foresaid Rows against my right'.[17]

It was a forlorn hope: the deed was done. Paston, even if he did approach the earl on her behalf, had little chance of countering the support enjoyed by Rowse. My lord's good lordship, in this instance, lay elsewhere.

And finally In January 1466, not long before his death, Paston was approached by Sir John Felbrigg. Felbrigg complained that his appeal to Warwick and the advice of members of the earl's council in his attempt to recover Felbrigg Hall from John Wymondham had cost him dear. He wished not to offend his lord's lordship so turned to Paston for assistance, especially in labouring Warwick. This too was apparently of little avail since ultimately Felbrigg sold out to Wymondham. Sir John Paston, who succeeded his father in 1466, for all his greater charm, fared no better with the earl. He was advised by an anonymous correspondent in October 1468, when the earl's standing at court was no longer so great, to speak with the archbishop of York, George Neville, in respect of a subpoena, and reported that it was widely known what the archbishop and Warwick had said openly in the king's chamber to the duke of Norfolk, in the duke's favour, over Caister.[18] But Sir John was to find a more effective lord in the earl of Oxford, especially after the Readeption of Henry VI.[19]

John Paston I, who had first, it seems, been approached by Warwick, found in the event that his lordship did not do him much good. Warwick had other interests in the county and other followers such as Rowse to whom he showed more favour. It was perhaps because of John's stubborn pursuit of his contested claim to the Fastolf inheritance that Warwick, as well as others, kept him at arm's length. What the letters show, however, is that even in this county, one of his more remote areas of interest, Warwick had a presence, advancing the causes of his favoured servants, whose good lordship was frequently sought. The correspondence also indicates how much has been lost to historians in respect of his lordship in other parts of the kingdom where his interests were concentrated, especially the West Midlands.

Warwick was directly associated with the West Midlands as a lord for longer than anywhere else: for twenty-two years. This is where he first emerged as a significant figure, even before he was 21, and where the core of his comital estates lay. Besides Warwick itself, his wife inherited the castles of Elmley and Hanley in Worcestershire. With them went some three dozen separate manors and other properties concentrated in southern Warwickshire and Worcestershire. He also held other lands in east Staffordshire, including Walsall, and Gloucestershire, most significantly Tewkesbury. His father-in-law had held sway in this region. The Warwick 'interest' had been maintained more or less intact throughout the intervening ten years before Neville acquired the earldom, through two minorities and the brief majority of his brother-in-law Henry, duke of Warwick, who died in 1446. Richard Neville rapidly retained key men from families who had a tradition of service to the Beauchamp earls: Lord Ferrers of Chartley, who died, however in 1450; Thomas Burdet of Arrow; Sir Humphrey Stafford of Grafton, who also died in 1450; Sir Baldwin Mountford of Coleshill; Thomas Throckmorton of Coughton; Sir Edward Grey of Astley; William Berkeley of Weoley; and John Rous of Ragley. He also retained the notorious Sir Thomas Malory.[20]

As well as the above, the earl brought some men from the north of England with him – men, one assumes, who were already in his personal service. These were Richard Clapham (a relation perhaps of Thomas of Beamsley in the West Riding retained by Warwick in 1464–5), John and Robert Otter, and John Middleham, all of whom acquired property in Warwickshire, and Thomas Colt. Colt's appointment to Warwick chamberlain of the Exchequer in 1450, which so dramatically launched his career, led to immediate local conflict. If nothing else, the fee of £52. 3s. 4d was worth contesting. John Brome of Baddesley Clinton had been granted the office by Henry, duke of Warwick, shortly before he died and had been confirmed in office by Henry VI. Brome, a man who had already made many enemies, was embroiled in a violent dispute in his native town of Warwick before he crossed swords with the new earl's nominee to the chamberlainship. Reinstated almost immediately to the post early in 1451 through the influence of the rival claimants to the earldom, he was the victim of several attacks on his lands by Warwick's men in 1451–2. Brome, not surprisingly, was driven into the camp of those who came to oppose the earl and his followers in the West Midlands.[21] However, it is noticeable that during the crises of 1450–52, during which Earl Richard was steadfastly loyal to the court, he was able to call out significant retinues from the West Midlands (and probably South Wales) in support of the crown. He did so twice in the early summer of 1450, to attend the parliament at Leicester in May and a month later to confront Cade and his rebels; and in February 1452 he responded to the king's call for support with a substantial body of men to face York at Dartford. Even more impressive is the report of John Stodeley of 19 January 1454 that the earl, now in alliance with the duke of York, would have one thousand men waiting for him at London, as well as the fellowship that he would be bringing with him. Many of the same men were, no doubt, in the force recruited at Warwick a year or so later that fought under his command at St Albans on 22 May 1455. In these years, Earl Richard repeatedly called up significant numbers of men from the resources of the earldom concentrated in the West Midlands and South Wales.[22]

Yet the relationships that Warwick developed with the prominent gentry of the area were far from straightforward. It has been argued that he showed singular lapses in judgement in dealing with the conflicts and feuds besetting the gentry of Warwickshire, that he came close to losing control of his affinity because of his personal incompetence as a lord, and that, by favouring his own retainers, he alienated those he should have won over. He took the wrong sides in the blood feud between Stafford of Grafton and Harcourt and in the quarrel splitting the Mountford family; and he fell foul of the duke of Buckingham. The mistakes he made and his inability to assert his authority between 1449 and 1454, it has been concluded, were to dog him till the end of the decade. Matters went from bad to worse after 1461.[23] These are challenging judgements, with more general implications for the quality of Warwick's lordship elsewhere, which demand careful consideration.

Gentry disputes over property, involving material interest and honour, were frequent in fifteenth-century England. They were waged at law and by direct violent action. The line between going to law and taking the law into one's own hands was fine. Violence was justified if one believed one was acting with justice on one's side. And, not surprisingly, in such disputes both parties tended to believe that justice was indeed on their side. Warwickshire was by no means the only county to be troubled by conflicts, often pursued by force, in the mid-fifteenth century. The weakness of royal authority was as much to blame as failures of lordship if they ran out of control. We should keep in mind the warning that an affinity was neither monolithic nor a machine for the enforcement of a lord's will, but a series of individual relationships conditioned by the circumstances of both lord and retainer. Control over the gentry was more the exception than the rule. Some parts of the country were easier to rule than others.[24] Lords, especially great magnates like Warwick, were frequently absent, and if they were new to a county, and unfamiliar with its local politics, as was Warwick in 1449, they were even more handicapped. Their authority was mediated through their local councillors who were familiar with the circumstances, and their councillors had their own interests and relationships to consider. It was not, therefore, a straightforward question of the new earl exercising his personal authority over the gentry in the West Midlands, it was an authority negotiated case by case in the light of contending interests.

The Stafford/Harcourt blood feud had begun in 1448, before Richard Neville inherited the earldom, with an assault on the Staffords at Coventry by Sir Robert Harcourt and his men, in which Stafford's son, Richard was killed. In May 1450 Sir Humphrey had led a band, including Thomas Burdet, in an attack on Robert Harcourt's seat at Stanton Harcourt in Oxfordshire. Warwick served on the commission of oyer and terminer appointed soon afterwards. Harcourt was bailed by a group of courtiers and received a pardon on 25 May 1451. Stafford had been killed by Cade's men in 1450 less than a month after he attacked Stanton Harcourt; by Michaelmas 1451. Harcourt was himself retained by Warwick, becoming the steward of his Oxfordshire estates from that Michaelmas, and emerging by the 1460s as an important councillor of the earl. It has been suggested that paying annuities to Stafford and Burdet would have been a waste of money, if, subsequently, Warwick also backed Harcourt. But perhaps there is another explanation. It is quite possible that the retaining of Harcourt was part of an attempted pacification of the feud after Sir Humphrey's death, the details of which have not survived. Certainly no more disturbances occurred between the two families until Stafford's sons, both legitimate and illegitimate, took their revenge in London, shortly after the Readeption of Henry VI, by killing Harcourt on 14 November 1470.[25]

The Mountford family quarrel arose out of William Mountford's decision, shortly before his death on 6 December 1452, to disinherit Baldwin, his son by his first marriage, in favour of Edmund, his son by his second marriage. Edmund and his mother sought the lordship of the duke of Buckingham and the earl of Wiltshire in whom they enfeoffed Coleshill and Ilmington (Worcestershire), which they promptly occupied. Sir Baldwin, who had been retained by Warwick at the end of 1451, contested the settlement. Violence ultimately ensued, and with Warwick's backing, Baldwin was in possession of both estates by July 1454, having conveyed his right in Ilmington, to the earl. An attempt at arbitration in 1454, in which the earl of Salisbury participated, sought a partition, but failed. Sir Baldwin's son, Simon, who was retained by Warwick by 1456–7, took up the cause from his unassertive father who took holy orders in 1460–1. During the later 1450s Simon was imprisoned by Edmund's backers and was induced to surrender his claim. In 1461, however, with the reversal in political fortunes, he was able to recover the family property.[26]

It is possible that retaining Baldwin in 1451, whom Warwick knew would be disinherited, was 'an extraordinarily misconceived step', because it drove William and Edmund into the arms of Buckingham and that, as a consequence of this decision to back the weaker side, by the time William Mountford died at the end of 1452, Warwick was powerless to prevent the appointment of a commission of inquisition post mortem led by Buckingham, which found in Edmund's favour.[27] Whether or not the Mountford issue led immediately to estrangement from the duke of Buckingham is hard to determine. It is not clear when the breach between the two occurred, but the role played by the duke at St Albans suggests that relationships between the two were not improved by it.[28] One might wonder, however, whether it really was misconceived to support the eldest son and rightful heir to Mountford. Warwick himself faced the challenge from Richard Beauchamp's elder daughters: there was something to be said for making a public demonstration of his support for the strict rights of inheritance within the old

Beauchamp affinity. And he was surely party to the attempts to find a peaceable settlement when the opportunity arose in 1454. Moreover, one might also bear in mind his youth, lack of local knowledge and comparative inexperience. He surely took the advice of experienced and knowledgeable councillors in these matters, councillors who had been long in the service of the earldom and knew local society far better than he did.

While he was accepted as earl, Neville nevertheless had yet to establish his personal position in local society. Moreover, other lords, such as Lord Sudeley and Lord Beauchamp of Powicke, had well-established connections and were figures to whom the gentry had recently turned for lordship. Both of them had been custodians of the Beauchamp inheritance during the minority of 1446–9.[29] Politically, they had been the key local figures in the absence of an adult earl and the prospect of a long minority. It had not been expected that the young Anne Beauchamp would die. It is not surprising, therefore, that Neville found it difficult to establish his personal authority when he first arrived. Furthermore, between 1449 and 1453, Warwick's principal concern was to secure his possession of the earldom. The tensions, rivalries and conflicts in local society in the early 1450s were, in part, a reflection of the uncertainty of the ultimate fate of the Warwick inheritance. It now seems cut and dried, but it was not so at the time. We might note, too, that it was only at the end of 1453, after the removal from the scene of the duke of Somerset, who had been the principal pursuant of the elder daughters' claims, that Warwick's hold on the earldom began to look secure. It was only then that the earl was able to begin to restore greater harmony in Warwickshire.[30]

Between 1454 and 1456, once the earl was fully established in the West Midlands, strenuous efforts were made, often through the earl's good offices, to pacify local disputes. After 1456, however, two, possibly linked, developments undermined his position in the region. One was his appointment to the captaincy of Calais, secured in the summer of 1456 and to which his attention shifted. It has been calculated that he was resident in Calais for almost 10 months between midsummer 1457 and midsummer 1458.[31] The second development was the decision of Margaret of Anjou, who emerged as the de facto leader of a resurgent court party in 1456, to build up her own power in the region. She did so on the basis of her own dower lands, especially Kenilworth, and her possession of the prince of Wales' estates, exploiting the traditional link of princes of Wales as earls of Chester with Coventry. She acted through the agency of the prince of Wales' council.[32] Both Coventry and Kenilworth were within ten miles of Warwick. The king came down to Kenilworth in August 1456. The assertion of the queen's new role was marked by an elaborate royal entry to Coventry on 14 September,[33] and given substance by a council meeting held there in October on the eve of which new officers of state were installed. The earl was resident at Warwick after the council. He and his countess received the king at St Mary's church. Nevertheless, tensions were high: it was reported that an attempt was made by Somerset to 'distress' York and that the following month Somerset and other peers tried to seize the earl.[34]

The move of the king's court to the West Midlands almost continuously from August 1456 to September 1457, and again from mid-1459 for several months, and the queen's adoption of Coventry as a second 'capital' are usually explained in terms of the reconstruction of Lancastrian power away from London; but it also had the secondary effect of neutralising Warwick in his own territory. Simon Mountford was arrested and imprisoned during the October 1456 council meeting and the compromise reached two years earlier discarded. Probably as worrying for Earl Richard was the recruitment of Thomas Throckmorton into the queen's service as attorney-general to the prince on 28 February 1457.[35] Other retainers were also tempted to desert the earl, including Thomas Burdet who was granted the deputyship of his hereditary shrievalty of Worcester at the Coventry parliament of 1459, and Walter Scull, who with Throckmorton was ordered to hold Worcester on behalf of the crown in March 1460.[36] Warwick is not known to have visited the West Midlands between November 1456 and July 1460, after the battle of Northampton. No doubt his councillors and estate officials managed his affairs as best they could, but his absence could only have further damaged his authority in the region.[37]

The earl set about recovering his position in July and September 1460. The Waurin Relation reported that Warwick was welcomed back enthusiastically by the local gentry, who complained to him of the depredations of the duke of Somerset a year earlier. He presided at a quarter session at which some of the offenders were indicted.[38] He was back under arms at Coventry in March 1461, before advancing north to fight at Towton. He had probably raised troops there. After the Yorkist victory Warwick enjoyed complete domination of the midlands. Not only had Queen Margaret been defeated, but also the duke of Buckingham, the earl of Wiltshire and Lord Sudeley had been removed.

Yet following this triumph, it has been claimed, Warwick came even closer to losing control of the old Beauchamp affinity. A series of disputes between prominent officers and retainers seemed quite beyond his control. In one, involving his own man Richard Clapham, the earl failed either to secure his victory or a satisfactory arbitration. The most serious conflict developed between Sir Simon Mountford and Clapham, which came to a head in 1465 with an attack on Clapham's lands at Alspath by Mountford, in which one of Clapham's servants was killed. Unable to settle the dispute informally, the earl was appointed to head an oyer and terminer which sat at the end of August. This did not resolve matters and a further attempt at conciliation proved futile. This dispute seems to have divided his affinity down the middle. It was not apparently until Warwick put his backing behind Mountford that some degree of harmony was restored, although this did not prevent the murder of John Brome of Baddesley Clinton by John Herthill, one of Warwick's men, in November 1468. During the upheaval caused by the Readeption two old scores were settled: the sons of Stafford murdered Robert Harcourt and Nicholas Brome murdered John Herthill. It is indeed hard to see that Warwick offered effective lordship in the West Midlands after 1461.[39]

The earl himself may well have been unable to choose between two important men, Clapham and Mountford. If it were true, as it would appear, that his own council was also divided, it would have been even more difficult to handle the worsening situation. This would have been particularly so because of his heavy personal commitments elsewhere early in the reign of Edward IV: in the north, at court, in royal council and in diplomacy. Fleeting visits to Warwick, made frequently between 1464 and 1467, were insufficient to enable him to attend to the problems consistently. It was not until he became estranged from court in 1467 that he might have been able to give more time. It is perhaps significant that thereafter he finally reasserted some degree of authority over his squabbling retinue by finally putting his weight behind Sir Simon Mountford.[40]

Furthermore, when it came to renewed civil war in 1469, Warwick seems to have been able to rely upon his following in the West Midlands, even though the exercise of his lordship had been fraught. The earl was confident enough in his authority to make Warwick and Coventry his centre of operations in 1469 and 1470. Edward IV was first held at Warwick after his capture in July 1469; the earl spent the Christmas season there in 1469–70. He was there again in March 1470, raising a force to challenge Edward IV a second time, and he set out from there to link with his northern men when he heard of the defeat of his ally Sir Robert Welles at Losecoat Field. It was to Warwick and Coventry that he and Clarence first marched when they returned in triumph, and it was to Warwick and Coventry that he withdrew in March 1471 to rally his men once more and confront the returned Edward IV.[41] Neville seems to have had little difficulty in calling out his men in March 1470 and March 1471. Some of the more prominent among them, including Sir Edward Grey, Richard Clapham and John Herthill, were proscribed by Edward IV as they fled the kingdom after the debacle of Losecoat Field. There were desertions, however. One who switched sides once more was Thomas Throckmorton. Throckmorton had made his peace with the earl in 1461, and had been made his receiver of the lordship of Glamorgan in 1464, but on 25 April 1470 it was he who was commissioned to seize the property of Grey, Clapham and Herthill in Worcestershire. Another who did not stand by the earl at this moment was John Beaufitz, who was the commissioner for Warwickshire.[42]

A year later the earl called once again upon his midland support. On 25 March

1471, as soon as he heard of Edward IV's landing in Yorkshire, Richard Neville, who was then at Warwick, called upon the service of his retainer Henry Vernon of Haddon in Derbyshire. Assuring Vernon of his trust in him and indicating how well he would be rewarded, the earl requested him to bring all the men he could raise to Coventry. His anxiety was revealed, however, in a postscript in his own hand: 'Henry I pray you fail not now as ever I may do for you'.[43] But fail him he did: Vernon, who was also in communication with the duke of Clarence and earl of Shrewsbury, stayed at home. But what of others? According to the *Arrivall*, Edward IV

> Determined to keep the next and right way towards his said great rebel, the earl of Warwick, the which he knew well was departed out of London, and had come into Warwickshire, where he bestirred him, and in the countries near adjoining, to assemble all that he might, to the intent to have made a mighty field against the King and to have distressed him.[44]

In the event he might not have raised as many as he might have hoped, for although he 'had assembled greater number than the king had at that time', he withdrew into Coventry. The *Arrivall* also drew attention to the fact that Warwick was constituted lieutenant of England for Henry VI. One might not take too seriously the claim that he could not raise troops through good will but had to resort to the threat of death.[45] On the contrary, his strength, especially in the last six months, owed as much to his rediscovered Lancastrian credentials as it did to the breadth and depth of his personal following. He raised men from his estates,[46] and almost certainly by commissions of array, but how many and which of his retainers fought in his final battle is not known. On the field of Barnet itself, Warwick was to a considerable extent dependent on the Lancastrian wing commanded by the earl of Oxford, which included contingents raised by other Lancastrians such as the duke of Exeter and Viscount Beaumont. It was as Lancastrians and retainers of John, earl of Oxford, not as followers of the earl, that the brothers John Paston fought for Warwick at Barnet.[47]

7

Lordship and Loyalty: the North

One reason, perhaps, why Warwick failed to assert his authority over his quarrelling West Midland affinity after 1461 was that his interests had reverted to the north. His father died on the last day of 1460. He entered his estates and offices in the west march and Yorkshire, which were the roots of Neville power, in April 1461. The basis of Warwick's power in the north west, to begin in Cumbria, lay in the office of warden of the west march and the captaincy of Carlisle, and in the lordship of Penrith in the far south of Cumberland. He had held the west march in survivorship with his father since 1446. Possession of the office was confirmed by Edward IV in 1461. It has been assumed that, after the overthrow of the houses of Percy and Clifford in 1461, Warwick held complete sway in the counties of Cumberland and Westmorland. After he was granted the honour of Cockermouth and the hereditary shrievalty of Cumberland in 1465, and the Clifford lordships of Brougham, Pendragon and Brough, his hold on the west march appeared even more overwhelming.[1]

But the depth of Warwick's support in the north west is problematic. The Neville landed interest in the region was relatively modest. It focused on Penrith, first granted to the earl of Westmorland in 1397. Salisbury did not have outright possession of Penrith, with its outliers in the vicinity of Carlisle, until after his mother's death in 1440. Until then he was a tenant, for which he paid rent to his mother. And for three years from 1441 he had sub-let it to Bishop Lumley, who was then warden. From 1451 he additionally enjoyed the custody of Bolton in Allerdale and related manors of his incapacitated brother George, Lord Latimer. This was neither a substantial nor a long-standing territorial presence in the north west.[2]

The authority of the Neville family derived primarily from the office of warden of the west march and captaincy of Carlisle. Salisbury held these offices from 1420 to 1435 and then again from 1443. It is not entirely clear why he surrendered the office in 1435, but it was probably linked to difficulty in receiving payment and the challenge to his mother's possession of Penrith mounted by his half-brother the earl of Westmorland. Only after he had come to terms with the earl in 1443 did he take up the office again for ten years. His possession was confirmed by the re-grant of 1446 in survivorship with his heir, the then 18-year-old Sir Richard Neville, to run for twenty years from 1453. He was also able to secure preference at the Exchequer in the payment of his salary. The terms of agreement between the Nevilles, father and son, and Sir Thomas Neville as their lieutenant in November 1457 reveal that they set aside various local revenues from Penrith, the forest of Inglewood (which Salisbury held by royal grant) and elsewhere to help make up his peacetime salary of £333 6s. 8d. The implication of this arrangement is that the salary itself was set aside for the general expenditure of the two earls.[3] Warwick himself seems never to have been actively engaged in the affairs of the march from 1449 until after his father died. He was virtually a stranger there in 1461.

To establish his authority in Cumberland, the earl of Salisbury had challenged both the Cliffords and the Percys for supremacy. He had first taken on the Cliffords, who held Brougham close by Penrith. The Cliffords were handicapped in the first half of the fifteenth century by two minorities and it had not proved too difficult for Salisbury to supplant them.[4] But the Percys, who dominated the west of the county, were too powerful to be displaced. As a result, until the outbreak of violence between the younger sons of the two families after 1450, the two earls had maintained an uneasy partnership, reflected most clearly in the nominations of sheriffs and the elections of MPs. After the first battle of St Albans of 1455, in which both the second earl of Northumberland and Lord Clifford were killed, the hold on the west march and the Neville domination of Cumberland was temporarily made more secure. Nevertheless, Neville presence in Cumberland was comparatively recent and remained precarious when the heirs of those killed at St Albans, the third earl of Northumberland and John, Lord Clifford, threw their support behind Queen Margaret against Neville, father and son.[5]

Salisbury had done his best to build up a following in the march. After his restoration to the wardenship in 1443 he retained Ralph, Lord Greystoke (1446) and Walter Strickland of Sizergh (1448); Sir Thomas Parr was associated with the earl and his circle from 1430 and was retained as steward of the Westmorland estates of his brother Lord Latimer. However, retainers from his first period as warden, Sir Henry Threlkeld (1431) and Sir Thomas Dacre (1435), had died before 1458. Salisbury also brought into his orbit Roland Vaux of Triermain, who was pardoned 5 April 1460 as of Penrith, and his former ward and son-in-law, Richard Salkeld of Corby, sheriff 1457–8 and a commissioner to restore order in Cumbria with other Neville men in November 1460.[6] An indenture with Sir Richard Musgrave of Hartley in 1456 implies that his grandfathers, Sir Richard Musgrave and, on his mother's side, Sir William Stapleton of Edenhall, were already retained from the lordship of Penrith, for after the first of their deaths his fee was to be raised from ten marks to £10, and after the second to 20 marks. However, an additional clause was entered in this contract which protected Musgrave's existing commitments to John, Lord Clifford (his father-in-law) and Thomas, Lord Dacre in their 'own proper matters', but bound him 'not to assist the said lords nor either of them in his person, his men, with counsel nor otherwise against the said Earl'. If he did 'labour as an entreator for the weal of any such matter', it was added, the earl would not take displeasure.[7] This is not an indenture negotiated by the earl from a position of strength. His vulnerability was revealed in 1459–60 when Clifford was granted the wardenship with Dacre's son as his deputy.

Warwick's possession of the wardenship of the west march, under the terms of the 1446 grant, was confirmed by Edward IV at Middleham in May 1461. His younger brother Sir Thomas, who had been their deputy, had been killed at Wakefield in 1460. He seems to have recognized that he now needed to extend his influence and strengthen his authority in Cumbria. The necessity would have been brought home to him by the loss of power in 1459–60, the siege of Carlisle in June 1461 and the initial refusal of Lord Dacre to submit. He thus undertook a round of new retaining in the early 1460s. Sir Richard Salkeld had, it was stated six years later, 'rescued' Carlisle, probably in command of the garrison during the siege. Appointed sheriff of Cumberland later that year, he was probably constable of Carlisle castle. Neville also retained the services of members of two prominent Carlisle families, John Denton and John Aglionby. Henry, Lord FitzHugh was probably Warwick's lieutenant by 1464, Lord Montagu having been so since 1461. Among those newly retained were John Vaux of Caterlen on 20 April 1461; Sir John Trafford of Trafford and Stretford, Lancashire in May 1461; John Fauconer, gunner on 24 June 1461; Robert Warcop of Langholme, Cumberland, son-in-law of Sir Richard Musgrave the elder (a relation of whom was to become receiver of Penrith); Christopher Lancaster; Thomas Sandford of Askham; and Thomas Blenkinsop of Helbeck, Westmorland, all on 27 April 1462. Their number almost certainly still included Sir Richard Musgrave the younger, who was in 1462 appointed constable of Brougham, Pendragon and Brough, the Clifford lordships forfeited to Warwick, and Christopher Moresby who was his steward of Penrith in the late 1460s. Musgrave, Sandford and Lancaster were brothers-in-law; Warcop a cousin.[8]

The immediate context of this retaining was the continued need to defend the far north from both Lancastrian rebels and Scottish incursions. The four indentures of April 1462 were made on the eve of a raid into the west march of Scotland that summer and the opening of negotiations with Mary of Guelders, the Scottish regent. The provision made for the warden of the west march, even after it was enhanced for Warwick by Edward IV, could never have paid for a permanent Carlisle garrison of much above 20 men at arms and 40 archers at full strength.[9] It was probably, in reality, much less. That Warwick was concerned to strengthen it after the siege is demonstrated in the clause in the contract with the gunner, Fauconer, who was to have his table for him and his man in the castle paid by the earl.[10] But defence of the border with Scotland did not depend on a garrison at Carlisle. Some contracts with retainers make it clear that service against the Scots was expected. Care was taken in Musgrave's contract, for instance, to ensure that he did not receive wages of war during times of peace.[11] The defence of the border thus depended not on a permanent garrison in Carlisle, but on the ability of the warden's retainers to raise their tenants and dependants quickly in times of emergency. By this means an army of reservists was made available; an army, which, of course, could also be turned against rebels or even the crown itself.

It may be that the most trusted of Warwick's servants in the north west were those commissioned on 28 February 1462 to arrest and imprison remaining Lancastrian sympathizers who were going about inciting insurrection and making seditious speeches in Northumberland, Cumberland and Westmorland. They were Sir Richard Musgrave, Roland Vaux, Richard Salkeld, Sir William Parr, his brother John and Sir John Huddleston.[12] Sir William Parr of Kendal and Sir John Huddleston of Millom were perhaps the closest to the earl. Sir William's father, Sir Thomas, had ridden with Salisbury to Ludford in 1459, had fled to Calais with him and been subsequently attainted. He survived Wakefield but died the following year. William, knighted in 1462, was the eldest of Sir Thomas's surviving sons. His younger brother, John, found more favour at court as a knight of the body and it was he, not William, who was granted the hereditary office of sheriff of Westmorland forfeited from Lord Clifford. Although there is no direct evidence of his having been retained by Warwick, Sir William served under him on border commissions and with other retainers to agree terms with the Lancastrian garrisons holding out in Northumberland in 1464. By 1466, when he and two of Warwick's councillors, William Berkeley of Weoley and Sir Walter Wrottesley, entered bonds to repay a debt of £40 to John, Lord Dudley, he appears to have entered the earl's inner circle – a development further suggested by his somewhat hasty marriage to Thomas Colt's widow, Joanna (or Joan) after Colt's death in 1467. Thereafter he resided chiefly at her dower house of Netherhall in Essex. On 20 July 1468 he nominated the earl as the chief feoffee of Kendal in a joint enfeoffment to him and Joan and the heirs of their body, in which Henry Sotehill also acted as a feoffee.[13] A year later, on 1 July 1469, ten days before the marriage of Clarence and Isabel Neville and less than a month before Edgecote, he revised the enfeoffment to include Clarence, and to incorporate men more closely associated with Warwick, including Richard Redman of the Levens and Harewood, and other associates of the earl from Richmondshire.[14]

Huddleston was probably as close to the earl as Parr. The lord of Millom, on the west coast of Cumberland, he was sheriff four times, twice in 1463–4 and 1468–9, as well as Parr's fellow MP in 1467–8. He escaped prosecution after Ludford, being able to purchase a pardon on 10 December 1459. Knighted in 1461, he was in the same year granted the offices of lieutenant of the honour and constable of the castle of Cockermouth by Edward IV, then in the king's hands from forfeiture from the earl of Northumberland, almost certainly at the suit of the earl. He reconfirmed Henry Thwaites in office as receiver-general on 3 August, the first of a series of grants confirming offices held by Percy servants. He probably remained in post after Cockermouth was granted to Warwick in 1465, and was additionally steward of the neighbouring Neville of Latimer manor of Bolton in Allerdale from 1461. He initially shared the administration of the Percy estates in Cumberland with Richard Salkeld, who held the stewardship of the manors lying between Cockermouth and Carlisle. His son Richard was married to Warwick's illegitimate daughter Margaret in 1465, on whom the earl settled lands to the value of over £6 per annum in Coverdale. He himself acquired property in Teesdale through his second wife, Jane Stapleton. He was liberally rewarded in 1461, being made porter of Newcastle upon Tyne, and granted the Clifford properties in Skelton and Lamunby, Cumberland and forfeited property of Richard Kirkeby as well as offices in Cockermouth.[15]

Yet Warwick was himself largely an absentee warden and lord of Penrith. There is no record of his having visited Carlisle or having been in Cumberland after 1462. He was a more frequent visitor to Middleham throughout the decade and may well have dealt with matters that needed his personal attention from there. He relied at first on his brother John, Lord Montagu until his promotion to the earldom of Northumberland in 1464, and on Henry, Lord FitzHugh thereafter. But doubt has also been raised about the frequency with which FitzHugh resided at Carlisle. No sooner formally retained as lieutenant in 1466, he received permission to leave the country on pilgrimage.[16] In the event, and increasingly one suspects, Warwick depended on Sir Richard Salkeld, Sir William Parr and Sir John Huddleston to rule on his behalf. But the earl's remoteness after 1462, following his absence before 1461, may well have hindered the development of any deep personal commitment to him beyond a relatively narrow circle.

Neville might have sought to strengthen his position in Cumberland and Westmorland by encouraging his trusted retainers to undertake their own retaining, even though this was strictly speaking illegal. This seems the best interpretation to put on two indentures made by Thomas Sandford in January 1468 and April 1469. In the first, Sandford retained William Bradley, yeoman, for life, so that he, his friends and all that 'he may cause and distrain (streyn)' take part with him in return for his good mastership and one mark a year. In the second, John Clibburn of Bampton, gentleman, was retained for life to serve him, except against the king, his own father, brethren and Sir Thomas Curwen, with all his men and tenants for a fee of £2 p.a. The date of 24 April is suggestive because it was just two months before Robin of Redesdale's rebellion.[17]

In the early reign of Henry VI, Cumbria had been as disorderly and disturbed by gentry disputes as was Warwickshire in the 1450s and 60s. The family of

Lancaster was ranged against Thornburgh; Threlkeld against Crackenthorpe. This feuding culminated in the murder of Robert Crackenthorpe in 1438. Peace was made in the following decade, only for a feud between the Parr and Bellingham families to erupt, which culminated with them taking opposite sides in 1459.[18] Another long-running dispute existed between the Salkelds and Sandfords.[19] It seems, however, that these disputes were in abeyance or brought under control after 1461. Many of the participants, or descendants of the participants, were absorbed into the Neville affinity, or like the Bellinghams removed from the scene and their estates granted to others, including Parr. The gentry of Cumberland and Westmorland were a particularly cohesive group with close ties of kinship. As well as leading to bitter disputes over property, as happens between kin, these networks could also work to restore harmony.[20] But it is to be doubted that Warwick himself was directly the agent for keeping the peace. In 1465 Sir John Huddleston and others arbitrated between Pennington and Lamplugh; in the same year arbiters including Richard Salkeld, Thomas Curwen and Hugh Louther acted in a dispute on John Salkeld and others' part against Thomas Sandford, who nominated Parr, Huddleston and Lamplugh to act on his behalf.[21] The shared service to the earl provided the context for peace to be maintained between Salkeld and Sandford, but Warwick's lordship was at arm's length. His principal servants and councillors were responsible for maintaining the peace on his behalf.

There was a further dispute in the region which Warwick's servants could not handle and which ultimately had significant repercussions for the earl. Sir James Harrington of Hornby in Lonsdale was a retainer of the earl, paid from Middleham, and had earlier been retained by Salisbury, as had his father, who had been killed at Wakefield, before him. They were both handsomely feed.[22] After the deaths of his father and elder brother, Sir James was embroiled in a feud with Lord Stanley over possession of his principal seat. His brother had died leaving two daughters. Sir James claimed to be the heir male under an entail; the two daughters, supported by Lord Stanley, one of whom was to be married to his son Edward, claimed as heirs-general. Harrington occupied the castle. An award was made against him in 1466 and confirmed in 1468, but he refused to surrender the castle. Warwick was caught in a dilemma, for, while Harrington was his retainer, Stanley was his brother-in-law and a man he could ill afford to alienate at the end of the decade. He seems, as he did in Warwickshire, to have tried to find a compromise, presiding over an arbitration in 1468 which satisfied neither party.[23]

Warwick had strengthened the Neville affinity in Cumberland and Westmorland after 1461, but he was never closely associated with the north west. His position there was not as deep rooted as in northern Yorkshire, focused on the lordships of Middleham and Sheriff Hutton. It is to be noted that not only were several of the retainers of indenture with Cumbrians in1461–2 sealed at Middleham, but also that some of the fees paid to them were to be charged to the revenues of that lordship.[24] The importance of north Yorkshire to the earl from 1461 is confirmed by fact that three of the men who were nominated his feoffees and executors in 1463 were long-standing Neville retainers, two of whom had served not only his father but also his grandmother, the countess of Westmorland. Alongside these should be placed Sir John Conyers, steward and constable of Middleham and Richmond for the earl, another who, with his father Christopher and numerous relations, served three generations of Nevilles. Conyers was perhaps most influential as the earl's factor in Richmondshire, coordinating the administration of his lordships there and being something of a recruiting sergeant for his affinity. Christopher, the father, was another of those who executed the earl of Salisbury's will. Other sons of his, William and Richard, were retained by the earl, Richard as the receiver. Sir John's eldest son, another John, was killed at Edgecote. Only marginally less numerous and less important locally were the Metcalfe family of Nappa who, like the Conyers, served Neville grandfather, father and son. Miles, a rising lawyer was Warwick's attorney-general by 1464–5 when he was feed from Middleham. Richard Pigot, serjeant-at-law, of nearby Clotherholme by Ripon was retained of counsel by the earl in the same year and was the earl's understeward of Knaresborough. His rewards included the farm of the manor of Deighton (a royal estate first granted to Warwick in 1449) and the chief messuage of South Cowton for £26. 13s. 4d in 1462 for twenty years. He also counted the bishop of Durham, the priory of Durham and the city of York among his clients.[25]

These men, all Warwick's local councillors, stood at the heart of a tight-knit community of lesser peers (Henry, Lord FitzHugh of Ravensworth, John, Lord Scrope of Bolton, and John, Lord Scrope of Masham) and gentry, several others also retained by the earl, many closely related by blood, and further linked by the traditional bonds of the lordship of Richmond, two-thirds of which were in the earl's hands. The seigneurial rights in the liberty of Richmond had been held by the Nevilles since 1399 with but a short break between 1425 and 1435. They were consolidated by the earl's father in 1445 and 1449 with grants, first with remainder to the heirs of his body and then extended to tail male, with the reversion of the dower of one-third held by the duchess of Bedford since 1435. These included the profits of justice within the liberty, whatever the court in which they were levied, local or not.[26] The feudal structure of this lesser liberty was still meaningful. The sixty-three knights fees, now in the hands of twenty-seven feeholders, grouped under three sub-tenants of the lordship, known as the Middleham, Marmion and Constable's fees, held respectively by Neville, FitzHugh and the Scropes, still had meaning for the payment of commuted castleguard, fines and wards. The five wapentake courts were administered by the steward of Middleham who, as bailiff, acted in place of the sheriff of Yorkshire in the liberty. Warwick stood to inherit in full 'the liberty, honour and lordship of Richmondshire', as it was styled, on the duchess' death. It is clear that he exercised seigneurial authority as if he were the earl of Richmond. The continued vitality of the liberty ensured that Richmondshire in the mid-fifteenth century was a remarkably cohesive aristocratic society, in which the vertical ties of lordship, the horizontal network of kith and kin and the vestiges of feudal structure all reinforced each other. After 1460, Richmondshire was the heartland of the Kingmaker's appanage.[27]

This does not mean that there were no disputes within the liberty, but it does appear that the mechanisms for resolving disputes worked smoothly and successfully. Richmondshire stands out in stark contrast to Warwickshire for its lack of conflict, riot and violent disorder. One case might illustrate this. Richard Clervaux of Croft was in dispute with Thomas Fitton of Carwaden in Cheshire over a rent from his lands. In 1463 they agreed to accept the arbitration of Sir James Strangways and John Nedeham, a justice of common pleas. It was agreed that Clervaux would buy out Fitton's claim. At Croft, on 15 June, Fitton quit his claim in the presence of Strangways, Sir John Conyers, Thomas Mountford (another Warwick retainer) and two other local gentry. Then the party travelled over to Harlsey where the agreement was finally sealed and a contract for the payment completed. The agreement settled the issue. The involvement of Conyers and others in the formalities marked a communal seal of approval. Warwick was not personally involved, but a group of his councillors, acting on his behalf, maintained social harmony.[28] On another occasion Neville seems to have exercised his good lordship in person on Clervaux's behalf. Clervaux had been a promising esquire of the body in the service of Henry VI, and, although he withdrew from court in 1450, he continued to be a loyal subject. He was one locally who was prepared to participate in the administration of the lordship of Middleham when it was forfeited to the crown in 1459. He became under-steward to John, Lord Clifford, and was granted as a reward Warwick's forfeited royal manor of Deighton. He made his peace after 1461 without apparently needing to seek a royal pardon. But at the end of 1462 he was summoned to join the royal army preparing to subjugate the Northumbrian castles. However, he was excused service on appeal because, as the king wrote

> We, having been informed by our right trusty entirely beloved cousin of Warwick that you be vexed with such infirmity and disease that you do not have any power to labour without great jeopardy, we [sic] of our grace especial in consideration of your said impotence and at the instance of our said cousin have pardoned you.

By such magnanimity Warwick was able to heal the wounds of 1459–61 in northern Yorkshire.[29]

Warwick's presence in the north east was not restricted to Richmondshire. It extended to the lordship of Sheriff Hutton, where a similar but smaller

1. There are five surviving contemporary and near contemporary visual representations of Richard Neville; on Richard Beauchamp's tomb, in the Salisbury Roll, the Rous Roll, the Beauchamp Pageant and in the Besançon Ms of the Short Arrivall of Edward IV. An image in the founders' and benefactors' book of Tewkesbury Abbey (Bodleian Library, Oxford, MS top. Glouc. 2, f 36v) is almost certainly, by the costume and beard, mid-sixteenth century. The mourner (above) portrayed on the eastern end of the south side of the Beauchamp tomb is identifiable from the coat of arms beneath it as Richard Neville. The tomb was in construction during the 1450s and Neville himself was closely involved with the trustees responsible for the building and furnishing of the Beauchamp Chapel. The face, albeit suggesting an older man, could well be a likeness modelled on life. (*Marilyn Roberts, St Mary's Church, Warwick*)

2. The Salisbury Roll, containing painted figures of successive earls of Salisbury and their countesses by means of heraldric display, was almost certainly completed to mark the occasion of the burial of Warwick's mother, Alice and the reburial of his father and brother at Bisham Abbey in February 1463. Richard Neville is represented wearing a surcoat blazoned with his arms. No attempt is made at a physical likeness. One peculiarity is that the tinctures of the Neville arms (gules, a saltire argent) are reversed. This, it has been suggested, was deliberate: an additional form of differencing to the label which is also displayed on his arms to indicate that he was of the junior line of Ralph Neville, earl of Westmorland. (Ann Payne, 'The Salisbury Roll of Arms, c.1463', in D. Williams, ed., *England in the Fifteenth Century* (Woodbridge, 1987), pp. 188–9, 195–6). (*By kind permission of His Grace The Duke of Buccleuch & Queensberry, KT*)

3. The roll compiled in 1483–5, during the reign of Richard III by John Rous, chaplain of Guy's Cliffe, Warwick, contains 64 figures, drawn in pen and ink, each with coats of arms painted on banners and shields, some with helms, crests and supporters. While the banner above him depicts his full arms as earl of Warwick, Richard Neville himself is represented as earl of Salisbury, a title he did not hold until 1461. He carries a shield emblazoned with the arms of Montagu, earl of Salisbury. Above his right shoulder is the Montagu helm, bearing a griffin; above his left is the helm of Neville, bearing a bull. At his feet lie a Neville bull and a Montagu eagle. The eagle, quartered on the shield is an eagle displayed vert. That painted at his feet is a representation of the same device. The representation of Warwick as earl of Salisbury, rather than as earl of Warwick, is reinforced by the opening lines of the biographical note immediately below which stress that Sir Richard Neville was by his father's and mother's inheritance earl of Salisbury, and by his lady and wife earl of Warwick. Even though he was earl of Warwick before he became earl of Salisbury, and the title of Warwick was superior to Salisbury, Rous it seems considered him to be subordinate to his patron, the countess, heir of Beauchamp. In the portrait of the countess Anne Beauchamp, which precedes Neville in the roll, she is depicted with a bear at her feet. In the text the opening two words 'Dam Anne' are written in bold letters. She is described as of royal blood and her status as whole sister and heir of Henry Beauchamp, duke of Warwick, is emphasized. No attempt is made at a likeness. (*British Library, Add MS 48976*)

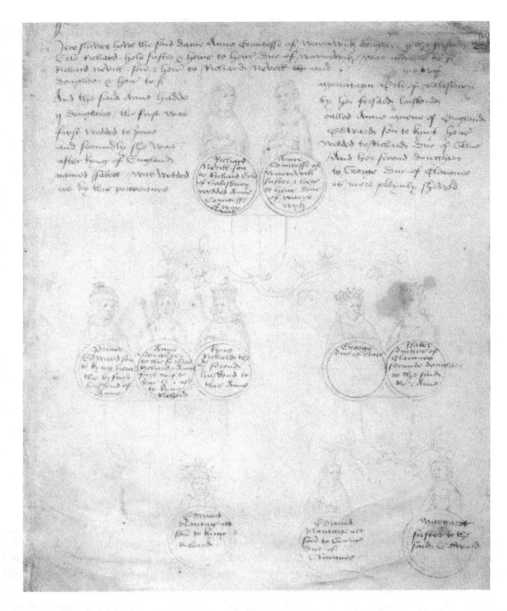

4. The last page in the pictorial biography of Richard Beauchamp, called Warwick (known as *The Beauchamp Pageant*) was almost certainly commissioned by his daughter, Anne, the widow of Richard Neville in 1483–5. Warwick is represented above a roundel beside his countess, to whom he is pointing, 'the whole sister and heir to Henry, duke of Warwick', stressing that he owed his title to her. The detail of the shield has not been completed. It it is to be noted that their daughter, Anne, described as queen of England, is deliberately and falsely identified as the elder of their two daughters. Their grandson is also portrayed in the pageant as 'Edward Plantagenet son to King Richard'. The faces in the pageant are different, which suggests that an attempt at likenesses might have been made. (*British Library, Cotton MS Julius IV, article 6, f. 28*)

5. See also cover illustration. The depiction of the Battle of Barnet in the Besançon version of the *Short Arrivall* was painted about ten years after the battle. Edward IV's men are shown wearing white roses, Warwick's the ragged staff. Edward IV himself is identified by the crown on his helm and the royal coat of arms on his shield and horse. In the background the royal banner rides high, in the foreground Warwick's overthrown banner lies on the ground. The banner, in which some pigment has oxidized, is that of Beauchamp quartered with Newburgh (ascribed to the legendary Guy of Warwick). This is the same banner as used throughout the Beauchamp pageant to identify his father-in-law, Richard Beauchamp. It is not known whether Neville did indeed use the same arms, or whether the artist assumed he did. Warwick in flight on a white horse is shown to the right, being chased down by a knight with a raised sword. On his back he bears a shield with the same arms as the banner. Unlike the scene as depicted in the other illuminated version of the *Arrivall*, the Ghent version, which is a more stylized representation of cavalry clashing head on, this emphasizes the story in circulation when it was executed that Warwick fled from the battle. This information is not to be found in the text itself. (*Besançon Municipal Library, MS 1168, f.2 detail*)

6. This illustration of a battle at sea from *The Beauchamp Pageant* has a cryptic rubric: 'Howe Erle Richard in his commyng into England wanne ij greet carykkes in the see'. It is placed chronologically between his embassy to the Council of Constance in 1414–15 and his campaigning in France in 1417. His 'coming into England' could have been in May 1415, or later in October when he evacuated the sick and wounded from Harfleur. He did not participate in the battle of the Seine in 1416. The rubric could equally be applied to one or more of Earl Richard Neville's escapades in 1458–9. Given that the *Pageant* was executed for Countess Anne Beauchamp some years after Richard Neville's death it might be that this pageant, on an otherwise obscure incident in her father's career, was included because it recalled, as does the rubric, her husband's most famous exploits. The mainsail is blazoned with the same arms of Beauchamp and Newburgh, and shields display the ragged staff, as were also depicted in the Besançon illustration of the battle of Barnet executed but a few years earlier. (*British Library, Cotton MS Julius E IV, 6 f.18v*)

7. Warwick would almost certainly have been familiar with the legend of Guy of Warwick from the traditions of the Beauchamp family, the tapestries celebrating it at Warwick Castle and his association with Guy's Cliffe where a statue of the hero stood. It is highly likely that he and his countess owned a copy of the romance. A key incident in the tale is the story of how Guy rescued England under King Athelstan from the depradations of the giant Colbran, a Viking champion, which he killed in single combat. It may be that Warwick saw himself in a similar role as England's saviour. In this early fourteenth century depiction Guy is represented as a pilgrim. (*British Library, EIV 6. f. 18v*)

8. The late-fourteenth-century style statue of Guy of Warwick as a warrior, carved out of the rock face of the original cave, dominates the chapel at Guy's Cliffe created by the earls of Warwick in the fifteenth century. No doubt the shield originally bore the arms attributed to the legendary founder borne by Richard Beauchamp and possibly also by Richard Neville. The building, which fronted the cave, was completed in the first year of Richard Neville's tenure of the earldom in 1449–50. According to John Rous, Neville planned to transform it into a collegiate establishment. The fan vaulting, visible in the photograph, may have been Neville's work for he was said by Rous to have buttressed and vaulted the cave which was in danger of collapsing. (*English Heritage*)

cluster of gentry, including the families of Gower and Constable of Bosall, as well as that of Witham, were long-standing servants of his house, and into the lordship of Barnard Castle, north of the Tees, which he had held as earl of Warwick since 1449. It reached into the West Riding through duchy of Lancaster office, including the stewardships of Pontefract, Knaresborough and Tickhill. His personal position was buttressed by his Neville kinsmen. Custody of the Neville of Latimer lands of Snape, Well and Danby passed to him in 1461. His unfortunate uncle, George lived until 1469. George's son, Henry was retained by Warwick and paid a generous fee from Middleham. He was killed at Edgecote in 1469. Warwick's uncle William, married to the heiress of Fauconberg with lands concentrated in north-eastern Yorkshire around Skelton, Stokesley and Yarm, served alongside him in 1459–63. He died in 1463, but his estates descended through his two daughters to the sons of Strangways and Conyers.[30]

Not only were the offices Warwick had held jointly with his father immediately confirmed by Edward IV, at Middleham, early in May 1461, but also for two years, until succeeded by his brother John, Warwick was warden of the east march as well as of the west. He benefited personally from the destruction of the Percys and Clifford by the grants of the lordship of Topcliffe (fee simple in 1462, tail male in 1465), and of both families' property in Craven (including Skipton). The Percy property added over £200 to his net income in 1467–8. The Percy estates in Northumberland were granted to John Neville when he was created earl in 1464, effectively bringing that county firmly into Neville hands. The other Percy lands in Yorkshire, apart from Wressle, which was also granted to John Neville, were settled on the king's younger brother George, duke of Clarence, but it would appear that until the later 1460s Warwick exercised a decisive influence over them.[31]

At the same time Warwick recovered influence within the county palatine of Durham, which the Nevilles had monopolized during the pontificate of Warwick's uncle Robert between 1437 and 1457. He had faced down a challenge to the possession of Barnard Castle from Bishop Booth to whom it had been ceded in 1459. In 1462 he had his revenge when Booth's temporalities, in other words the county palatine and the episcopal estates, were sequestered. Thomas Colt was one of the three guardians appointed by the king. The new administration, which lasted for fifteen months, was heavily Neville in character. John was made lay steward, an office he occasionally exercised in person, and both he and the earl were placed on the Durham bench. Although Booth was restored in April 1464, he was a chastened man. John Neville remained steward until 1467, and until the very end of the decade Warwick's influence in palatine affairs continued. But of all the enhancements of Neville ascendancy in the north perhaps the translation of George Neville to the archbishopric of York in March 1465 was the most significant. In addition to spiritual authority, he exercised direct temporal power in his liberties of Ripon, Beverley and Hexham.[32] From 1465 Warwick, his two brothers and his principal retainers dominated the counties of Yorkshire, Durham and Northumberland. John Warkworth wrote later in respect of the disgrace of Archbishop Neville in 1473, 'he and his brothers had the rule of the land, and gathered great riches many years'; and so they certainly had in the north east of England.[33]

Warwick's retainers naturally benefited from the flood of Lancastrian confiscations after 1461. Sir Robert Ogle, created Lord Ogle, whose fees charged to Middleham were increased on Warwick's succession, was appointed steward of the Percy lordships in Northumberland and granted the forfeited Tailboys properties of Redesdale and Harbottle. Sir Robert Constable of Bossall became steward of Spofforth and Sir John Conyers steward of Topcliffe. William Burgh of Brough was made constable of the Percy castle of Prudhoe in 1462; his son John another Middleham retainer, was later sub-steward of Topcliffe. These offices were in Warwick's gift; Sir Thomas Gower received the riding forestership of Galtres, probably on the earl's petition. Others received the custody of the estates of the children of Percy followers killed at Towton: Sir William Parr of the Hotham lands and John, Lord Scrope the Bigod lands and the marriage of the heir, Ralph. His lordship was truly beneficial to his north Yorkshire retainers in the early days of Edward IV's reign.[34]

Some indication of the further attraction of Warwick's lordship beyond his own retinue after 1461 is revealed in the surviving Plumpton correspondence. Sir William, whose estates in Yorkshire, Nottinghamshire, Derbyshire and Staffordshire were valued in 1479 at over £290, was steward, constable and chief forester of Knaresborough, in which his seat of Plumpton lay, for life from 1439, and the steward of the nearby Percy lordship of Spofforth and other Percy lordships in Yorkshire from 1442. It seems that after he was granted the reversion of the stewardship of Knaresborough, and especially after the death of the second earl of Northumberland in 1455, the earl of Salisbury had sought to build up his own rival following in the lordship, retaining among others Richard Roos of Ingmanthorpe, near Spofforth, and Ralph Pullan of Scotton, and had also harassed the sitting steward, Plumpton. In 1459 a group of his followers disrupted a meeting at which Plumpton read a royal proclamation, and later in the year Pullan, Robert Percy of Scotton and others, who had been involved in that disturbance, mustered with the earl at Boroughbridge en route for Ludford. Plumpton was in the royal army. In 1465 Percy was to bring an action against Plumpton in chancery, accusing him of having ransacked his house and having sought to murder him after the rout of Ludford. Plumpton also fought on the Lancastrian side at Wakefield. He was commanded to raise the men of Knaresborough for Henry VI on 12 March 1461. He was said to have been captured by the earl of Warwick at Towton; his second and only surviving son died on the field. He himself escaped attainder only by compounding with Edward IV by a recognisance of £2,000 on good behaviour on 13 May. He was held responsible with others, mainly retainers and tenants of the earl of Northumberland, for the murder of Salisbury at Pontefract. The widowed countess, seeking redress, entered a formal appeal in May 1461. For this he was bound in another £1,000 to await the award of her and her three surviving sons. He was, it seems, at Warwick's mercy.[35]

Not surprisingly, Plumpton was unable to raise the sums demanded of him and so surrendered himself to the Tower two months later. He secured letters of pardon in February 1462, and was released, but on condition that he did not leave London. Eighteen months later he faced fresh charges that he had been in treasonable correspondence with the king's enemies, that he had harboured them coming out of Scotland, and that he had rejoiced at the king's discomfiture. These charges, which have the ring of truth, can only refer to the renewed risings in Northumberland in April 1463. Tried before a court of chivalry, convened by the constable, the earl of Worcester, shortly before Christmas, he was acquitted, pardoned, declared a true and faithful subject, and allowed to return north in January 1464. Given Tiptoft's position then as one of Warwick's councillors, and his subsequent reputation, this might seem to be a remarkably generous judgement.[36]

By this time, however, Warwick had shown clemency. Indeed, by the mid-1460s Plumpton was serving as Warwick's constable at Knaresborough and, as 'his right trusty and well beloved knight', was desired by the earl to go to arbitration in a dispute with another of the earl's well willers, Robert Scarborough, over possession of a property in Spofforth called Spencer Close.[37] Plumpton's correspondence between 1461 and 1464 reveals something of the way in which he ingratiated himself with the earl and the role of several intermediaries. While he was in the Tower, Justice Bingham wrote to him proposing arbitration in a long-standing dispute with Sir Henry Pierpoint over property in Nottinghamshire that had led to two tit-for-tat murders in 1457. The fellow arbitrator was the soon-to-be Chief Justice Markham. Agreement was reached in February 1462. He also received a series of letters from his neighbour, Brian Roucliffe, third baron of the Exchequer, mainly concerned with the disputed terms of the contract of marriage between Plumpton's daughter, Elizabeth, and Thomas Beckwith's son William. On 14 October Roucliffe reported that he had 'communed' on his behalf with John Tiptoft, earl of Worcester. Thomas Colt, he added, wanted to be paid for his services. A year later, on 26 November 1463, an agreement was sealed between Plumpton and Roucliffe for the marriage of the elder of Plumpton's granddaughters and heiresses, Margaret, to Roucliffe's son John. When Roucliffe wrote again from Cowthorpe a month later to Plumpton in London, it was from his 'serviceable brother'. Thanking Plumpton for his innumerable comfortable

letters, he expressed his delight that 'you now take your disport at your liberty'.
'And as touching my lord', he continued, 'I shall ride to M to him within these 4
days and do my part'. What suit it was that Roucliffe was to pursue with Warwick
at Middleham is not known, but it might well have been to do with the earl
receiving him into his favour now that he was free, a path made easier since the
death of the countess of Salisbury. Godfrey Green reported on 14 February that
Roucliffe had laboured effectually on Plumpton's behalf in other suits: perhaps
he had in this as well.[38]

Roucliffe was not the only line to Warwick. Over the winter of 1462–3
Plumpton was negotiating with Henry Sotehill for the marriage of his younger
granddaughter Elizabeth to Sotehill's son John, a contract sealed on 11 February
1464. In addition to Roucliffe, Tiptoft, Colt and Sotehill, three of Warwick's
nominated feoffees in 1463, were in a position to ease Plumpton into Warwick's
service as well as to dismiss charges of treason. It is not surprising, therefore, that
when Plumpton enfeoffed his estates himself in June 1464, Roucliffe, Sotehill,
Pigot and Sir Walter Blount were among his feoffees.[39] Sir William found friends
in high places close to Warwick, both to enable him to escape prosecution for
murder, attainder and forfeiture after 1461, and to enable him to find favour
with the earl. He was, one suspects, made to grovel. His plight gave Warwick
the opportunity to display magnanimity towards his erstwhile enemies, and
was perhaps designed to encourage others who had fought against his family in
the recent feud with the earl of Northumberland to make their peace. Another
who did so was Sir Richard Tempest of Bracewell, retained by Warwick for a fee
of £10 charged to Topcliffe on 8 January 1467.[40] Warwick also provided a route
for reconciliation for the Tunstall brothers, sons of Sir Thomas of Thurland,
Lancashire and Bentham in the West Riding. While Sir Richard, the head of the
family, remained a diehard Lancastrian until the surrender of Harlech in 1468,
when he sued for a pardon, his younger brothers William and Thomas both came
to terms with the regime and joined Warwick's service earlier. Their paths were
eased by their mother, Eleanor FitzHugh, and their half–sisters, Lady Margery
Conyers and Lady Elizabeth Strangways. William was retained by Warwick in
1465; Thomas was a feoffee for Sir John Conyers in 1469.[41]

Plumpton lived to regret the marriage alliances which helped him off the
hook. At the end of the decade he revealed his own secret marriage to Joan
Wintringham in 1463 and the existence of a legitimate male heir, Robert, hitherto
believed to have been illegitimate by Roucliffe and Sotehill. His own political
sympathies perhaps remained Lancastrian: one of the few letters kept by him
giving news of political events in the 1460s was from Godfrey Green in London
on 9 December 1468 in which he reported in detail on the arrests of the earl of
Oxford and other Lancastrian sympathizers, in tones which suggest that he knew
the reader would have sympathy for them. By August 1470 Plumpton was in the

service of the restored Henry Percy, earl of Northumberland, and it is clear that during the months to follow he was one of those who, with the earl, kept his head down. Warwick had not won him over.[42]

When relations with Edward IV first became strained in the winter of 1467–8, it was to Yorkshire that Warwick withdrew. When he began to plot rebellion, by 1469 at the latest, it was to his men in the north, and in particular his affinity in northern Yorkshire, that he turned. Warwick's repeated rebellions in the last two years of his life tested the loyalty of his northern men in whom he most trusted. Was he able to depend on them? Did they answer his calls to arms? In the summer of 1469, it appears, they were united behind him. Robin of Redesdale's rising in June 1469 was essentially a north-eastern affair. Described by Warkworth as 'a great insurrection in Yorkshire of divers knights, squires and commoners', it was coordinated by Warwick's men. It has not been agreed who precisely masqueraded as 'Robin'. It was said to be a member of the Conyers family, William of Marske or Sir John himself. From the pseudonym, it might just as conceivably have been neither of these but Robert, Lord Ogle, lord of Redesdale, who died, it seems, of wounds sustained at Edgecote a month later. Other casualties included Sir Henry Neville and John Conyers, son and heir of Sir John, and of lower status, probably alongside his master's heir, Richard Nicholson of Hornby. It was not just men from Richmondshire and elsewhere in the north east who fought at Edgecote. They were joined by men from the north west led by Sir William Parr. According to Waurin, Parr and Sir Geoffrey Gate played a particularly prominent role in the attack on the earl of Pembroke.[43]

The story of the involvement of men both from the north west and Yorkshire in the Lincolnshire rebellion nine months later is considerably more complex. It would appear that Parr and a contingent raised by him in the west march joined Clarence and Warwick in the midlands before Sir Robert Welles was routed at Losecoat Field, for it was Parr who acted as Warwick's intermediary and conducted negotiations for a safe conduct and pardons on the earl's behalf with Edward IV at Doncaster on 19 March. Sir Walter Wrottesley had been the earl's emissary to Newark three days earlier. But, unlike Wrottesley, Parr did not flee with the earl to France. Instead he made his peace with the king and on 7 May was appointed the king's lieutenant of the west march and the city and castle of Carlisle, superseding Warwick. In the summer he and the newly restored Henry Percy, earl of Northumberland, were engaged in negotiations with Scottish commissioners.[44] There were several possible reasons for Sir William's turn of coat. His brother John, an esquire of the body, had been at court throughout the decade; his youngest brother Thomas was already serving the duke of Gloucester. Both John and Thomas had fought at Edgecote, but on the king's side, and were in the king's entourage after Losecoat. They had had the opportunity at Doncaster to persuade their brother to change sides. The well-informed, if hostile, Chronicle of the Lincolnshire Rebellion, composed after Sir William had deserted Warwick, hints as much in the king's reported suggestion that he should not return to Warwick's camp but, as his duty and allegiance demanded, should stay and serve his king.[45] It is quite possible that it was John, who had already sought to raise troops for the king in Westmorland, of which he was sheriff, who persuaded his brother to abandon Warwick. By the time that Sir William submitted to the king he would also have known that Warwick's Richmondshire men, led by Lord Scrope and Sir John Conyers, had thrown themselves on the king's mercy at York and been pardoned.

Warwick and Clarence still hoped that the earl's Richmondshire following would be able to confront the king. On 19 March, having received the king's rejection of safe conducts and pardons, they left Chesterfield for Lancashire, trusting to receive support there that would enable them 'out of Yorkshire [across the Pennines] to have assembled so great a puissance that they might have been able to have fought with the king's highness in open field'. They hoped in vain, for Edward IV knew of 'the commotion in moving people in Richmondshire by the stirring of lord Scrope and others, sent by the said duke and earl for that cause with many letters'. Thus, he himself raised troops to the north of them, in Westmorland and Northumberland, to follow them, and ordered Montagu, who had not joined his brother, to confront them. Having heard of the king's victory, the Chronicle recounts, and 'thinking by the manner of the said earl of Warwick writing sent thither in his own name only, to array the people, that their stirring should be against the king', as well as fearing the king's advance against them, they 'left their gathering and sat still'. Over the weekend of 22 to 26 March their leaders prostrated themselves before the king at York. Lord Scrope, Sir John Conyers and others who 'had laboured, specially provoked and stirred the people … freely submitted them to the king's grace and mercy, and humbly besought him of his pardon and grace: and also of their free wills, unconstrained and undesired', they confessed that they had risen on Warwick's command and would have led their men to encounter the king at Rotherham. This, the author added, they affirmed to be true by solemn oath on the sacrament.[46]

One may wonder whether the confessions made were so completely of their unconstrained free will, for they were surely very much desired so as to demonstrate Warwick's treason and duplicity. Moreover, in claiming that they were so freely made, the author could once more point up the king's own authority over his great subjects as well as his magnanimity in pardoning them. The hard reality is revealed in the conclusion. A plan for Welles to have joined Warwick and Clarence at Leicester, allowing the king to advance north, so that they 'might have been between the king and the south parts, and enclose him betwixt them and the power of the north', had failed.[47] The author offers a complex explanation. While one can see why, in a document to reassure others of the king's continued and undiminished authority, he would wish to stress the overriding loyalty of even Warwick's men to the king and their readiness to abandon the earl, in reality one suspects that this was not a major consideration. They sat still and left their gathering not because they refused to follow Warwick on his authority alone, but because they were outmanoeuvred.

It is not surprising, therefore, that few Richmondshire men were proscribed in the following month when commissions were appointed to seize the possessions of Warwick and Clarence and their supporters. Those listed, who had in the interim not taken advantage (as had Parr, Gate, Scrope and Conyers) of the offer of a pardon, were the most prominent people who had marched with the earl and his son-in-law from Coventry. They included Sir Walter Wrottesley and his brother Henry and the brothers William and Thomas Huddleston. Also named were two who had been killed fighting for the earl on Edgecote field nine months earlier: John Conyers, son of Sir John, and Robert Strangways, son of Sir James. Sir Henry Neville was not included, since by this time the custody of his son and his father had been removed from Warwick.[48]

Although the plan to trap Edward IV between the earl's men marching from the midlands and his Yorkshire men advancing south had failed in March 1470, it was repeated with success later in the year. The list of those from Yorkshire who were pardoned on 10 September as having been in Henry, Lord FitzHugh's company included at least twenty men from some of the most substantial families of Richmondshire and Cleveland, several being retainers of Warwick, or relations of retainers, and many being connected with Sir John Conyers. The steward of Middleham and Richmond and constable of both castles was a key figure in all these risings. His son died at Edgecote; he submitted in person at York and his kinsmen and neighbours played a significant part under FitzHugh's leadership in July/August.

As revealing is the list of those who rose in Cumberland in August 1470, for it shows that Sir William Parr's desertion had divided Warwick's following in the north west. Sir Richard Salkeld, 'late constable of Carlisle', twenty-one 'gentlemen' from in and around Carlisle, principal among them being several members of his own and the Aglionby, Denton, Skelton, Vaux and Lancaster families, as well as a large number of yeomen from the county, were pardoned in one list. Separately, Sir Richard Musgrave's brothers, William, and Nicholas, as well as his sister-in-law, Joan, and several yeomen of Edenhall also sued for pardons.[49] Not surprisingly, Salkeld was restored to Carlisle and appointed sheriff of the county during the Readeption, but there was little more that Warwick attempted then, other than to restructure the commission of the peace. Sir William Parr was able to lie low: his younger brothers had fled into exile with Edward IV.

Where Sir John Huddleston and his connections stood in all this is more difficult to discern. Like Parr he seems to have supported Warwick in March

1470. His two sons, William and Thomas, were proscribed on 25 April as they fled the kingdom with Warwick, but John himself took advantage of the king's offer of a pardon, issued at Southampton on 5 May, two days before Parr was made lieutenant of the west march.[50] He was more circumspect later in the year, turning out neither for king nor for earl. The release of Henry Percy on 27 October 1469 and the subsequent restoration of his estates perhaps provide a clue to Huddleston's stance. As lord of Millom he had long-standing connections with fellow gentry of West Cumberland who moved in Percy circles before 1461. As lieutenant and constable of Cockermouth after 1461 he had worked with members of the Percy affinity, such as Thwaites and Thomas Lamplugh, who had been kept in office by the crown and then Warwick. These men had bent with the political wind. Christopher Curwen of Workingon, the son of another Percy retainer, with Lamplugh and Huddleston, had joined Edward IV's host which had been raised to recover the Northumberland castles at the end of 1462, and subsequently served under Warwick's command. They were quick to rejoin Henry Percy after his restoration. At Cockermouth on 16 December, Percy, assuming to himself the title of earl of Northumberland to which Edward IV had not as yet restored him, retained Curwen for life with a fee of over £7 to be paid in part from the rents of Allerdale. Huddleston seems to have remained in post as constable of Cockermouth under Percy until 1471, when he was replaced by Sir John Pennington. In compensation, he was granted custody of the lordship of Egremont from 1 May 1471, that is between the battles of Barnet and Tewkesbury.[51] The evidence suggests that, like Parr, he abandoned Warwick in 1470.

On landing on the Yorkshire coast with Edward IV in March 1471, John Parr must surely have made swift contact with his brother Sir William, as a result of which Sir William, with Sir James Harrington, raised a band of 600 men, according to the *Arrivall*, 'well arrayed and habled [trained] for war'.[52] They joined the king within a few days at Nottingham. Harrington's decision to join Parr almost certainly followed from the realignment of royal offices in northern Lancashire in the autumn of 1469. The young Richard, duke of Gloucester was granted duchy of Lancaster lordships and offices, removed from Lord Stanley, in October 1469. Tension developed between Stanley and Gloucester, there being 'variance' between them, it was said, in March 1470. That month Gloucester was in residence at Hornby, Harrington's seat, having evidently by then taken his side. In the summer Gloucester was installed as warden of the west march, with Parr as his lieutenant already in post. Stanley took advantage of the Readeption to lay siege to Hornby, but failed to take it. Not surprisingly, therefore, Harrington opted to join Richard of Gloucester in the king's party in March 1471 rather than his erstwhile lord, the earl of Warwick, whom he perhaps believed had failed him. Parr and Harrington may have also been joined by Christopher Moresby, who was subsequently knighted on the field of Tewkesbury, as well as by Thomas Huddleston. Huddleston's sons, who had been with Warwick a year earlier, were to fight for Edward IV in the company of Richard of Gloucester, possibly at both Barnet and Tewkesbury. Thomas was killed at one of the battles, as was Thomas Parr, and both were remembered by the duke in prayers for their souls six years later.[53] These were significant desertions from Warwick's cause.

However, they were not the only men of Cumbria arrayed and 'habled' for war in the spring of 1471. John Neville, Marquess Montagu, was following up the king, with a growing body of men. Among them may well have been a contingent from Cumberland and Westmorland which included several of the men who had come out with Salkeld the previous August. On 20 July 1471 Sir William and the newly dubbed Sir John Parr, Sir Thomas Strickland and Sir Christopher Moresby were commissioned to arrest and bring before the king and his council Sir Richard Musgrave's younger brothers, Sir Lancelot Threlkeld, Thomas Sandford, Thomas Skelton, William Lancaster and four members of the Bellingham family who had a long-running feud with the Parrs. A day or two earlier Sir Richard Musgrave himself and Sir Richard Salkeld, who had been sheriff of Cumberland during the Readeption, had received pardons.[54] No prosecutions followed, possibly because it had already been decided not to attaint Warwick and because several of these men had found a new lord in the duke of Gloucester, now warden of the west march. Unlike Yorkshire, loyalties in the north west were seriously divided in 1470–71.

We are left finally with the question as to why the men of Richmondshire did not fight at their lord's side at Barnet. It is hard to believe that they deserted him at the eleventh hour. The *Arrivall* provides the answer. According to the author, a northern contingent did fight in the battle, for he recounted how the earl of Oxford fled, 'in his flying, fell in company with certain northern men, that also fled from the same field'. One can assume that these had fought with Montagu, and might have included Salkeld, Musgrave and others from Cumberland. More crucially, no force of Richmondshire men intercepted Edward IV's small party when it was at its most vulnerable in Yorkshire. The author is aware of this and devotes a long passage to its explanation. Warwick was reliant on Montagu, who was at Pontefract, to raise his men. 'Truth it is, that he [Montagu], neither had not, nor could not have gathered, nor made a fellowship of number sufficient to have openly resisted him'. Edward IV advanced through Percy territory. Percy sat still, his men likewise. They would fight neither for Edward IV nor against him. They would certainly not fight for Montagu, 'neither for his love, which they bare him none, nor for any commandment of higher authority'. They had not loved John Neville since 1453. They would have followed Northumberland, but he, although he had secretly declared himself for Edward IV, knew that his men would not follow him in this cause for they remembered still what they had suffered at Towton. The earl of Northumberland's inaction and Montagu's powerlessness had a knock-on effect further north. As the author commented, 'his sitting still caused the city of York to do as they did, and no worse, and every man in all those north parts to sit still also, and suffer the King to pass as he did, not with standing many were right evil disposed of them self against the King'. Among those in all the north parts who were so evil disposed were, one supposes, the men of Richmondshire.[55] Besides which, given the circumstances in southern Yorkshire, it was not possible for them to array and advance quickly to intercept Edward IV on his landing.

They did eventually rise, but too late to affect the outcome. After the battle of Tewkesbury, some six weeks later, the king being at Worcester heard that 'certain his rebels of the north parts began to make commotions and assemblies of people against him'. He determined immediately to confront them, but as he was recruiting a new army at Coventry he learnt that 'they of the north' had heard of the decisiveness of his great victories and that he was preparing to march against them, and 'not having any of the Warwick's, or Neville's, blood, unto whom they might have resorted, as they had done afore', knowing that Northumberland would resist them on the king's behalf, their leaders who had begun to raise the people, gave up and submitted to the earl. York, other towns and countries did likewise. By 13 May the king knew that in York and other divers parts of the north the rebellion was over. The author makes it seem a significant movement. He is unfortunately vague about its leaders and focus.[56] Its timing, however, makes it seem as though it began after Barnet. It is a puzzle that they did not attempt to rise earlier so that they could join Montagu on his march to the battle. It was too late, but it reveals that in the spring of 1471 the far north, and most likely Richmondshire, was not completely inactive in Warwick's cause.

There is nothing in Warkworth's account to suggest that, in retrospect, the earl's recent recruiting of additional retainers proved futile in 1469–71, or that Neville was subsequently abandoned by the new retainers he reported. Indeed, he makes it explicit that it was his belief that it was the desertion of the duke of Clarence that was his destruction, rather than the failure of the earl's own men to fight for him.[57] One or two notable exceptions aside, Warwick's men remained loyal to their lord until the end. Somewhat paradoxically, in the region where his relationships with the local gentry had been most difficult (the West Midlands) he was consistently able to call upon substantial support in 1469–71, while in the region where his following was strongest and his standing greatest he could not, because of circumstances, always bring it out. Geography played a significant part here. The West Midlands were closer to the centre of gravity in the kingdom. Moreover, Warwick's personal presence there at critical moments probably ensured a better response to his appeals locally for support than if he had been more distant. Every individual to whom Warwick appealed in his hour of need made an individual choice, according to personal circumstances and judgement. There were always several factors in play. In particular, all men knew that their primary allegiance lay to the crown and that it was treason to follow their lord in rebellion. This affected decisions in 1469–70. In the spring of 1470 Edward IV set out to portray Warwick as a man acting without royal authority and to argue that his affinity would not follow him as a consequence. In the north west of England Edward IV made significant gains in detaching Warwick's most senior followers from him. We should not underestimate the impact of Sir William Parr's decision to put the king before the earl. This, and the restoration of the earl of Northumberland, effectively undermined the earl's hold on Cumberland and Westmorland. Parr was not the only one Edward IV sought to turn. He made a tempting offer to Sir Simon Mountford in Warwickshire, which was declined. He believed he had won over Lord Wenlock at Calais; he had certainly turned Gaillard de Duras, the second in command, who subsequently prospered in royal service.[58] Edward IV used his superior authority as king astutely and effectively in 1470 to undermine Warwick's position. After Warwick's rapprochement with the house of Lancaster, royal authority became more complex, with men having a choice of dynastic allegiance. As we have seen this was particularly beneficial to Warwick in the West Midlands.

Politics thus came into it. So too did the sheer uncertainty of military planning and campaigning. In medieval campaigns matters rarely went to plan, particularly if they included crossing the Channel. The effects of adverse or favourable winds on both parties significantly affected the outcome of the war in the spring of 1471. Ultimately, however, the inability of the Yorkshire men to act in time, then, to support Warwick may have cost him his life. It will probably remain a puzzle as to why they did not mobilize until after Barnet had been fought and lost. One would have expected them to have moved earlier or not at all. We can understand why they were constrained on Edward IV's first landing. They were hindered by particular local circumstances. Yet there is perhaps no more eloquent a testimony to the loyalty of these men to their lord than that they rebelled after his downfall, when political expediency would surely have suggested lying low. The same considerations apply to the Calais garrison, which also mobilized in Warwick's defence after his death. It is the particular circumstances of Calais, the earl's position as captain there and his relationship with the garrison, burgesses and merchants of the Staple to which we now turn.

8

Calais and the Keeping of the Seas

Warwick did not depend alone on men and resources drawn from his estates in England and Wales. For most of his political career, from 1456 to his death, he was captain of Calais. Its possession was as important politically and militarily to him as any of the parts of England and Wales in which he had a significant landed interest. It was the base of the only substantial permanent armed force in the territories held by the crown. Although Warwick's position depended on royal grant, he was continuously in post for fifteen years. The length of his tenure at Calais gave him an opportunity to develop a rapport with the garrison, the burgesses and the merchants of the Staple who dominated the town's economy and to make it, in effect, his own. Warwick's interests were not restricted to Calais and its pale. It was important, commercially and militarily, for the crown, the staplers, and not least the captain and garrison at Calais, to command the straits of Dover. Warwick was keeper of the seas from 1457 to 1465, and from 1460 warden of the Cinque Ports. With these additional offices, the earl was in an ideal position to control the narrow seas. When considering his captaincy of Calais, therefore, we should encompass the Straits of Dover and seaboard of eastern Kent and Sussex. Command of the seas and a high profile in south-eastern England were vital military and political assets in 1459–61 and continued to be crucial thereafter. Neville fully appreciated the political and military advantages the captaincy of Calais and the keeping of the seas conferred. Was he able to make the most of them?

Calais was more than the town itself. The marches extended 18 miles along the coast from Wissant, near Cap Gris Nez, in Picardy to Gravelines to the east in Flanders, and some eight to ten miles inland. The town, at the centre, was protected by its castle, walls and Rysbank Tower at the entrance to the port. The eastern marches were low, water-logged country; the west hilly and woody. It was surrounded entirely by territory held by the duke of Burgundy, Flanders to the east, Picardy to the west. The boundaries of the English-held territory were originally protected by a string of forts, west to east, of Sangatte, Guînes, Hammes and Oye. Sangatte had been destroyed in the war of 1436 and Oye lost permanently.[1] The only other settlement of any size was Mark just to the east of Calais on the road to Oye. The captain of Calais was also the king's lieutenant as governor of this small enclave of English-held France. He was not only the military commander, charged with the defence of Calais and its marches, he was also its civilian governor with power to hear criminal and civil cases.[2]

Calais was the last toehold of the English conquest in France and had been in English hands since 1347. York's propaganda since 1450 had focused on the allegation that since his rival, Edmund, duke of Somerset, had been responsible for the loss of Normandy he could no longer be trusted with the defence of Calais. In 1455 it followed that Warwick as York's ally and his nominee could be relied upon. The threat to Calais was real. In 1452, having reconquered Gascony, Charles VII of France began preparations for an assault on the last enclave. After he had dealt with the English resurgence in Gascony in 1453 he was free to mount a further attempt. In November 1455, and again in June 1456, James II of Scotland proposed to Charles that the time was ripe for a coordinated attack on England. But Charles VII was diverted by growing internal tensions and was equally fearful of an English descent on Normandy or Guyenne. When the French did attack, in August 1457, it was in the form of a dawn raid on Sandwich, Warwick's principal supply base for Calais, not on Calais itself.[3] Relationships with the duke of Burgundy were also tense when Warwick took up his command. There was frequent cross-border raiding and other infringements of the truce.[4] Warwick's was a genuine military command. As a demonstration of his commitment he resided there for nine months of the year from midsummer 1457 to midsummer 1458.[5]

The captain indented with the crown to provide soldiers for its defence. The long-established size of his retinue was 260 men, including the captain himself, his lieutenant and marshal. The crown indented with others to provide garrisons for the castle, 50 men including its commander; Rysbank Tower, 18 men; Hammes, 41; and Guînes 100. When Warwick first took up his command in 1456, between 1462 and 1466, and perhaps at other times during his captaincy, his ordinary retinue was reinforced by a 'crew', or temporary company, of a further 300 men recruited directly by him. Thus, in all, there were 600 men under his direct command and a further 209 men in retinues commanded by other captains answerable to him as governor of Calais.[6] These soldiers served at different rates of pay as men-at-arms on horseback (one shilling a day, the equivalent of £18. 2s. 6d. a year), men at arms on foot and mounted archers (8d. a day or £12. 1s. 8d. a year) and archers on foot (6d. a day. or £9. 1s. 3d. a year). They were all paid, through the captains by whom they were recruited, by the crown. Bearing in mind that £10 a year was considered by some contemporaries to be a sufficient clear income from land to support the lifestyle of a gentleman, these were exceptionally well-paid men. A place, or 'room' in the Calais garrison was well worth having and the men themselves not mere soldiers. In addition those serving in the garrison, especially at the higher rates of pay of men at arms, were able, and perhaps expected, to recruit additional men at their own cost.[7] In

1474 Sir John Paston, joining the garrison under Lord Hastings, sought to hire four archers under his own wages and wearing his livery for 4 marks (£2. 13s. 4d.) a year. This was almost the same rate as customarily paid to foresters, who frequently served as archers in English armies, and was not far short of what would support a man of yeoman status.[8] If other, higher paid, men at arms were accompanied by just two of their own archers, half the number thought appropriate by Paston in 1474, the number of serving men could have been at least 1,500 men. This was a significant military force, apparently at the disposal of the captain.

Initially Warwick's command over the garrison and its officers was not strong and his personal standing with them understandably weak. He inherited both deputies and soldiers. When he first indented as captain in 1455 he also indented for the garrisons in the castle and Rysbank Tower: Lords Welles and Rivers, the serving captains of those garrisons were dismissed, but not until after 16 March 1456, when they were included in the commission to receive the command on the earl's behalf. Guînes and Hammes, however, remained in the hands of Sir Thomas Findern and Sir John Marney who, like Welles and Rivers, had taken up their commands in 1451 when the duke of Somerset had become captain. The earl appointed his uncle, William Neville, Lord Fauconberg, an experienced general who had served in France since 1436, as his deputy, probably in de facto command of the castle and tower. Another of his principal officers was Sir Edmund Mulsho, also an experienced captain who had served in France under York in 1441–6 and was one of the duke's principal councillors. Both Fauconberg and Mulsho had been sent by York to take control of the garrison after the battle of St Albans and were largely responsible for conducting the subsequent long-drawn-out negotiations with the garrison, including Richard Woodville, Earl Rivers. This protracted bargaining was necessary to achieve a smooth transition.[9] Sir Edmund Mulsho was possibly given his office of marshal at York's request. He died in 1458. His brief service in Calais seems to have brought him closer to Warwick, for he appointed the earl an overseer of his will and left to him a suit of armour given him by the Dauphin.[10] He was succeeded as marshal by Sir Walter Blount, also a man 'borrowed' from York. In October 1458 Warwick wrote to the duke asking permission to appoint Blount, permission that was given, but in the first instance for one year only.[11]

One understandable concern of the existing, well-paid, men of the garrison was that Warwick would replace them. On 13 December they were assured by the council that Warwick would not dismiss them, but bring in reinforcements, offer an amnesty for all previous offences and guarantee not to take reprisals for past allegiance to Somerset.[12] Thus the earl agreed to retain most of the existing soldiers in Calais, the castle and the tower in his service, including the veteran Andrew Trollope. Trollope had fought in the French wars since 1425, had been Lord Rivers' lieutenant in 1441, and then served no less a man than John Talbot, earl of Shrewsbury, in command of Falaise in 1448–9. Like many such veterans he was recruited to Somerset's service at Calais in 1451, becoming the porter, in command of the defence of the town gates.[13] Calais was garrisoned by experienced, well-paid soldiers, but, they were not men personally committed to the new captain. The major challenge facing Warwick when he took possession in 1456 was to win them over. The earl was no doubt confident that he could do so, both those directly under his command and those in the independent garrisons of Guînes and Hammes. He presented himself as a loyal servant of the crown, above partisan politics, coming to defend the last English outpost in France facing imminent attack. Yorkist rhetoric in part determined such a non-partisan approach.

When he finally took up the post, Warwick's trump card was that he and York had resolved, temporarily at least, Calais's horrendous financial problems that had left the garrisons unpaid, and often mutinous, in recent years. In the early fifteenth century the cost of maintaining Calais had been calculated as £12,000 in peacetime, £19,000 in war. This was an enormous sum, and the garrison's wages were almost invariably in arrears, and often never paid. Income was raised on a mint in Calais until 1403 and by the customs paid on the shipment of wool through the Staple based there, and through which all but the most northern of English wool merchants were required to trade. Earlier in the fifteenth century a system had been devised whereby the staplers paid their customs directly to the captains. This however collapsed in mid-century as exports of wool declined and a bullion famine seriously reduced the quantity of cash in circulation. The government resorted to borrowing from the staplers to pay for the garrison, in return for allowing them to ship wool customs free. But this did not offer a long-term solution. By 1456 the crown owed the merchants of the Staple just under £40,000. In addition, past captains were owed substantial sums for unpaid wages: the duke of Buckingham nearly £20,000 up to 1451, repayment of which had been assigned to the customs at Sandwich; six years later Somerset's executors settled for nearly £23,000. As a result of hard negotiation over many months in 1455–6 a new deal was struck with the company. All the debts were paid by the Company of the Staple, either in cash or in wool, and repayment was scheduled to specific appropriations of customs. The garrisons were pardoned for all offences, primarily mutiny and seizing wool for themselves. All their arrears of pay were settled. Moreover, Warwick was paid his first quarter's pay in advance. He and the garrisons started with a clean sheet.[14]

From the outset Warwick also assiduously built up a network of support extending from Calais across the channel through the Cinque Ports to Canterbury and south-east Kent. He had been aware of the value of this from the moment he took up his command. Throughout the period of his captaincy the town depended on supplies from England. Sandwich was the most important supply point. Sandwich also became, after 1459, a place of shipment for wool to Calais, upon which the whole prosperity of the Staple and thus the financing of the garrison depended. Even though he did not secure the office of warden of the Cinque Ports until November 1460, he had quickly established good relationships with the townsmen. As early as May 1457, it was reported, he had formally thanked the men of Canterbury and Sandwich for their support in victualling Calais and prayed them to continue.[15]

As keeper of the seas between 1457 and 1465, Warwick had responsibility for the defence of the coasts of England, and in particular the southern and south-eastern shores, which were the most vulnerable to French attack. He was first appointed in October 1457, in response to the recent French raid on Sandwich, and perhaps reluctantly, by a government that, after the failure of the duke of Exeter as admiral to take effective action, recognized no alternative. The keepership was renewed on 13 February 1462 for three years at the same time as the earl was renegotiating his command at Calais and when there were renewed rumours of French raids.[16] It was an emergency military command, albeit for an emergency which lasted for eight years, and not a permanent royal office. Warwick appears not to have been so anxious to hold the office of Admiral of England, which was more an administrative than an operational post, responsible for assembling ships, recruiting and disciplining sailors. The admiral was not usually a fleet commander expected to lead his ships in battle.[17] Earl Richard did become Admiral of England when Edward IV took the throne; his lieutenant and commissary general, John Aleyn, was involved in a case concerning the ownership of a skiff later in the year. But on 30 July 1461 his brother William was granted the office during pleasure and on 14 October 1462 the king's youngest brother, Richard, duke of Gloucester, who was already styled 'admiral of the seas' in August, was granted the office for life. Neither grant represented a threat, and Richard of Gloucester was subsequently to be in his guardianship.[18]

The terms of the commission in 1457 reveal its military significance. He was to safeguard the sea continuously from 1 February to 31 October every year with a maximum of 5,000 and a minimum of 3,500 men in arms, in as many ships as he thought necessary, which he was authorized to commandeer, with wide powers to impress men and purvey stores. He was to resist the king's enemies, and to do them all the hurt he could. He could offer his own safe-conducts, follow the laws of war and take the usual spoils and shares of his men's spoils. He himself built up his own fleet of 12 ships by May 1458; he had at least 10 in commission in 1462–4. His flagship was the *Trinity*, but he also took command of the principal royal ship, the *Grace Dieu*, which was refitted in 1462. He suffered losses, most seriously of the *Trinity*, which was damaged in battle off the Breton coast in 1462, and captured by pirates from St Malo in 1465. She was probably returned to him through the later intervention of Louis XI, and was refitted in 1469. Warwick's personal fleet was a formidable force through which he commanded the Channel.[19] He did not hesitate to use it, against neutral as well as enemy shipping.

Warwick's naval actions in 1458–60 have been conventionally described as piracy. While this is how his victims undoubtedly saw it, it is perhaps a misleading word to use. There had been irregular warfare on the seas between England and France since the fourteenth century. It had been particularly intensive in the early part of Henry IV's reign. It had been brought under control after Henry V's conquest of Normandy in 1417–20, but had revived in 1435–9 when England had been at war against both France and Burgundy. Merchants and shipowners were regularly licensed to protect themselves, to keep the seas and retain prizes: in short, to be privateers. Captains then and later had not been too scrupulous in distinguishing between neutral and enemy shipping. Even without licence, seamen from all the English, French, Breton, Flemish and Scottish ports along the Channel (and along the North Sea coast of England) attacked other shipping and each other. So lawless were the seas that merchants preferred to travel in convoys, whether to or from the Baltic, Spain or the Mediterranean. This was no protection for the Hanseatic Bay Fleet, seized by English privateers in 1449. The Straits of Dover were particularly dangerous. It seems as though Calais men, especially garrison members, were not exceptional in waging private warfare on the sea for personal gain, or to compensate for unpaid wages. Andrew Trollope had taken to piracy in 1454 to pay for his wages, and again had seized Hanseatic ships early in 1457. The definition of enemy shipping was loose. At a pinch any foreigner would count, and in the atmosphere of the late 1450s, when feeling against Hanseatic, Genoese and other merchants trading in London and Southampton ran high, their ships on the high seas were seen as fair game and were attacked without discrimination. But Italian ships carrying wool under special licence of the crown, which was thus avoiding the Staple, were particularly vulnerable. Such was the attack on Italian ships in the Thames estuary early in 1457, which was made specifically to recover the wool for merchants of the Staple and was considered legitimate by them. Warwick, as captain, was charged with investigating these and later attacks on shipping, including attacks by ships acting under the command of his lieutenant, Lord Fauconberg.[20]

Yet Warwick's instructions were specific. Neither he nor any of his retinue were 'in no manner [or] wise [to] despoil, wrongfully hurt, or give any unlawful occasion to any of the king's friends, allies or any having his safeguard'. And 'he was to put him in his full devoir and diligence to let all other whatsoever they be … that would wrongfully hurt' the king's subjects, allies, or friends.[21] From the beginning of his captaincy it appears he turned a Nelsonian eye to the actions of his subordinates. But by May 1458 it was apparent that the earl himself was authorizing and participating in these actions. In 1458–9 at least four convoys of 'neutral' shipping were attacked. In 1460 it was reported that 'daily as my lord has any knowledge of an enemy, anon my lord makes his ships to sea'. Warwick's actions won him renown, but were prompted by the need to pay his soldiers so as to retain their loyalty; to recover some of the lost revenue for the staplers, especially by seizing ships carrying wool; and to demonstrate that he was an effective and vigorous military commander.[22]

The financial situation in Calais rapidly deteriorated. The crown was quite unable to find the resources to pay Warwick and the other captains. Within four years of his appointment the arrears had risen again to over £37,000. The government of Henry VI also continued to offer licences to Italians to ship wool without passing through the Staple, which deprived the staplers of trade and diverted customs revenue away from the settlement of debts. By 1458 they were feeling the commercial pinch. At the end of the year the crown, once more firmly under the control of Warwick's enemies, reached agreement with them that it would issue no more licences, would punish smugglers and authorize the company to negotiate with Duke Philip to establish exclusive trading rights with Flanders. In exchange £4,000 per annum was diverted from Calais to the household.[23] This agreement only served to exacerbate the mounting financial problems facing the garrison. But by the end of 1458 the breach with the court was permanent and Warwick had already taken the law into his own hands.

In the event Warwick was only partially successful in winning the loyalty of the garrison. He had not done enough by September 1459 when he led a contingent to join his father and York in confronting his enemies at court. Andrew Trollope's desertion with part of the retinue, when it became apparent that they were to fight the king himself, proved to be a crucial moment in the campaign. As the author of Gregory's Chronicle, who was particularly interested in military matters, recalled, it was 'olde sudyers' who went with Trollope over to the king's side.[24] Those who deserted were not those who were in Warwick's personal retinue, but men who had been kept on in 1456. However, there were other veterans among those who remained in Calais in 1459 who did adhere to the earl. In June 1460, the Lancastrian government, which had failed to recover Calais by force, empowered the duke of Somerset to receive all rebels there into his grace, with exceptions that included not only two men who had helped Warwick and the earl of March escape from Devon – John Courtenay (one of the many sons of Sir Philip of Powderham) and John Dinham – but also two eminent Calais burgesses and staplers, John Prowde and Richard Whetehill, both of whom had been on the commission to receive Calais on Warwick's behalf on 16 March 1456.[25]

The battle for Calais over the winter of 1459–60 reveals how bitterly divided those who had served there in the previous decade had become. The duke of Somerset, appointed captain on 9 October even before Ludford, attempted to take it at the end of the month. According to the Waurin Relation he arrived too late, only hours after Warwick himself had returned. He was beaten off. Denied access, he and some of his men landed on the coast to the west and made their way to Guînes, still commanded by Sir Thomas Findern. Hammes, too, under Sir John Marney, declared for Somerset. It is noticeable also that those who sought to reinforce the duke from the Cinque Ports were predominantly men who had served his father: Rivers, the treasurer of Calais, Sir Gervaise Clifton, and Osbert Mountford, who had been in command of Rysbank Tower between 1451 and 1454 and who had also been one of those commissioned in 1456 to receive the captaincy on Warwick's behalf. Mountford's summary execution on the sands in front of the Tower in June 1460, after he had been captured at Sandwich, suggests that he might have been one who, like Trollope, had deserted Warwick at Ludford. That fate had already befallen such men who had fallen into his hands earlier, and others from the garrison continued to slip over to Somerset in Guînes during the winter.[26] As deeply divided as those who had had 'rooms' in the garrison were, it is noticeable that neither side went to the extreme of bombarding the fortifications. There was skirmishing, including an action at Newnham Bridge between Calais and Guînes, but no assaults. Indeed, immediately the Yorkist earls had seized control of the government in the summer of 1460, Warwick himself sailed back to Calais to negotiate with Somerset the surrender of Guînes and the duke's own safe-conduct to prevent him handing it over to Charles, count of Charolais, the heir to the duke of Burgundy.[27] Hammes, however, remained in the hands of Sir John Marney and was not reduced to obedience until the summer of 1461.[28] In contrast to Calais, so confident was he of his command of the sea, that Warwick sailed with a significant part of his fleet to and from the town to Ireland to confer with the duke of York in the spring of 1460, and so great was his reputation as a naval commander that the duke of Exeter, sent to intercept him, refused to engage.[29]

At the same time the staplers had little choice but to back the earl. They depended for their trade on secure communication between London, Sandwich and Calais. They thus benefited from Warwick's command of the sea and had every reason to support him, especially after he recovered his fleet from Sandwich in January 1460, even though it was increasingly difficult to secure repayments of their loans. The decision taken at the Coventry parliament in November 1459 to suspend all trade with Calais while it was in Warwick's control, and to extend the embargo in December to prohibit all supply of foodstuffs to the port, effectively drove them into his arms. Significant numbers of them made loans to Warwick, in effect financing his invasion of England in July 1460.[30]

The earl also benefited from the cordial diplomatic relationships he had established with the duke of Burgundy. On his arrival as captain, Warwick immediately initiated a round of negotiations with the duke's representatives, meeting them between Oye and Mark in July 1457. A grand banquet was held for the Bastard of Burgundy. The result was that the duke agreed to make concessions to reduce tension. A dialogue was subsequently maintained. All this stood the earl in good stead. No sooner had he fled back to Calais in the autumn of 1459 than, on his own initiative, he opened negotiations, first at Gravelines and then at Calais, for extending the official truce between England and Burgundy. He came to agreement early in December, forestalling a Lancastrian embassy. According to the Waurin Relation, the duke agreed to supply Warwick from Flanders. These contacts were maintained after the return to England in July 1460; they were never broken.[31]

The full account given in the Waurin Relation of events in Calais in 1459 and 1460 seeks to give the impression that the earl was much loved there. When Warwick and his company returned to Calais at the end of October 1459, we are told, they were welcomed joyfully by Fauconberg, the soldiers, staplers and mayor of the town, and a special service of thanksgiving was held in Notre Dame de Saint Pierre. When a herald arrived the same night from Somerset, demanding admission for his master, he was told that they wished to have no captain but Warwick. The burgesses and merchants determined to stand by Warwick; when Rivers and others were brought as prisoners it was decided not to bring them into the town, for they distrusted the commons, who loved them not; and so were kept prisoner in the castle for their own protection. Before Warwick set off for Ireland to consult with York, the burgesses, merchants and soldiers all of one accord ('d'un commoun acord') pledged fidelity to the remaining lords and begged the earl to return as soon as he could. The informant appears to have travelled to Ireland with Warwick for he gave details of what happened, especially on the return journey, but made only passing reference to the anxieties of those left at Calais. When the earl finally returned, everyone was much relieved, including 'all those of the town, men as well as women, who welcomed him with much joy'. They requested him 'all of them, because of the great love they bore unto him' to deal with the garrison at Guînes that had been harassing them. He asked for their patience, since in the face of French and Burgundian hostility it was unwise, he explained, to lay siege to Guînes. All agreed, therefore, that it was best for him to invade England.[32]

The favourable view is transparent. The Relation had earlier assured the reader that Warwick governed the town and its *pays* better than any of his predecessors. It is at pains not only to show how popular Warwick was as a consequence, but also to suggest that he consulted with the 'people' of Calais, 'ensamble' seeking 'commun acord'. There is, however, a sub-text of anxiety. It is admitted that desertions to Guînes continued; Warwick felt it necessary to make the representatives of the town pledge their loyalty to his fellow lords when he went to Ireland; murmurings during his long absence were noted; the earl had to defend his actions, and especially his decision not to assault Guînes, in formal debate with 'all the community of the town' (tout le commune de la ville). The sub-text therefore suggests a position of weakness, in which the earl and his advisers were uncertain of the reliability of either soldiers or the staplers. His position was not as strong as the report wished to imply. However, one can perhaps also discern behind this the skill with which the earl handled a difficult situation so as to sustain himself in a divided town.

After the Yorkist victory in 1461 Warwick made sure that he had full control of Calais, the seas and the Cinque Ports, and men on whom he could rely in command of every garrison. He had learnt by bitter experience of the dangers of divided loyalties. Already, in November 1460, he had secured the office of warden of the Cinque Ports with the constableship of Dover Castle. This was confirmed immediately after Edward IV became king. In December 1460 the keepership of the seas had been renewed for an interim period of six months. In February 1462 the earl reindented, on the same terms as before, for a further three years from the preceding St Martin in winter (11 November). And Edward IV acceded to his request to become captain of all the separate garrisons at Calais, including Guînes and Hammes in April 1462.[33] Warwick probably anticipated that he would largely be a absentee captain in the foreseeable future. Apart from a possible brief visit at the beginning of March 1462, his only sustained residences recorded thereafter until 1469 were in March–April and again May–July 1465, when he was negotiating with duke Philip of Burgundy.[34] Before departing after this second stay, he issued ordinances for 'the pleasure of God, and our said sovereign lord and for the assured governance and prosperity of the said town and march', with the aim of assuring the 'good and politic governance and defence of the town' in his absence. One clause laid down that all captains, councillors and officers should attend and obey his lieutenant in his absence, which was, one assumes, anticipated to be most of the time after 1465. The rest dealt with crime, retaining and discipline, and with an attempt to clamp down on the licentiousness of members of the garrison.[35]

Warwick now appointed men in whom he had absolute trust to be his deputies. Fauconberg, created earl of Kent in 1461, notwithstanding his many other obligations, may well have continued to serve as Warwick's deputy. He had been back in Calais on 31 January 1461 from whence he wrote to the duke of Milan, signing himself lieutenant.[36] John, Lord Wenlock was possibly Warwick's lieutenant as captain and governor by April 1463, a few months after Fauconberg's death, and certainly by 1466. Wenlock seems to have first come under Warwick's spell when passing through Calais in 1458 on an embassy to both Charles VII and Duke Philip, and had committed himself openly to the Yorkists in 1459. After 1460 he was much employed in government business, especially diplomacy, and was often absent from Calais.[37] Warwick's treasurer from 1460, immediately after the battle of Northampton, was Sir Walter Blount, promoted from his post of marshal to replace Sir Gervase Clifton. On Blount's promotion to the treasury of England in 1464, his brother Thomas took his place. Warwick's marshal was now Gaillard de Duras, a Gascon exile in English service, who had been attached to the garrison before 1460. Richard Whetehill, a Calais merchant, who had stood by him stalwartly in 1459–61, was first the controller of the garrison and then lieutenant of Guînes by 1466. Otwell Worsley, who had been a senior household officer before 1461, having been the earl's deputy warden of the Cinque Ports in the early 1460s, was lieutenant of the town walls and gates and Rysbank Tower by 1466. In the same year, John Courtenay was the porter. There were subsequent changes. Duras was replaced, after his desertion in 1470, by Sir Geoffrey Gate, and early in 1471 Sir Walter Wrottesley succeeded Wenlock.[38]

Finance remained a major problem in the early 1460s. At the beginning of Edward IV's reign the inherited arrears of wages were calculated as over £37,000. An allocation of parliamentary subsidies was set aside to pay for some of this. There was never enough money to pay the wages of the garrison and mutiny was again threatened in 1462. The garrison could hardly revert again to piracy. In 1464 Edward IV diverted much of the subsidy earlier voted for an attack on Scotland to the costs of Calais. The staplers continued to lend substantially to the crown, but little of what they lent came back to pay the garrison. The realization that it was going to prove extremely difficult to repay these loans, as well as the awareness that, on their own, loans did not secure regular payment of the garrison, led to the Act of Retainer in 1467 which made the Company of the Staple solely responsible for the payment and maintenance of the garrison out of customs and subsidies levied by them in Calais.[39]

In the immediate aftermath of the seizure of the throne the threat from France increased. In 1461 Pierre de Brézé had successfully occupied Jersey; the Channel Islands were in French possession for the next seven years. In June 1462 in the Treaty of Tours the new French king, Louis XI, agreed to give financial and military assistance to Margaret of Anjou. To win French support she was willing to concede the Channel Islands and Calais. There was a general alert in southern England in the summer of 1462. Rumours of an imminent siege of Calais reached the Pastons in July. In the event, Louis XI's designs on the town were frustrated by the refusal of the duke of Burgundy to allow passage for his troops, but for two or three years the danger seemed real enough. Early in 1462 Warwick was preparing to undertake more conventional warfare on the sea against the French when he was called back to the north to deal with further Lancastrian disturbances. In his place, William Neville, now earl of Kent, commanded his fleet, which raided Le Coquet and the Île de Ré and, according to a report which reached John Paston, fought a great battle against a fleet of Spanish, Breton and French ships, of which they took fifty prizes.[40]

After 1464 Calais was no longer at risk from attack. Warwick's commission as keeper of the seas expired early in 1465. He nevertheless continued to maintain his personal fleet. When war was again being planned against France, the appointment of Earl Rivers as keeper on 7 October 1468 was no doubt particularly galling. Warwick seems simply to have ignored it. He was himself fitting out a ship at Newport in 1469, and undertook a major refit and relaunch of the *Trinity* at Sandwich in the same year. Undeclared war in the Channel revived in 1468–9. The corporation of Sandwich paid for soldiers serving him against a great fleet of France in the Downs, in which action, or another, they captured a ship called 'Columbes'.[41] As his relationship with Edward IV deteriorated, continued command of the Channel was vital to Neville. In July 1469 it enabled him to cross to and from Calais freely for the wedding of Isabel Neville and the duke of Clarence. In 1470 he cruised in the Channel attacking shipping for a month or two before being finally driven by a Burgundian fleet to seek refuge at Honfleur in July. His fleet carried him to England in September 1470, and then continued to operate at sea under the command of the Bastard of Fauconberg, even after his death.[42]

In the mid-1460s, as the military threat slackened, Calais grew in importance as a base for English diplomacy. It was always important to maintain good relations with the duke of Burgundy, whose territories encircled the English enclave. Members of the garrison were not averse to raiding into Burgundian lands to compensate for the loss of wages. Thus march days, the arrangements of safe-conducts, meetings to settle compensation, and negotiations to confirm truces ensured continuous contact between representatives of the two sides. It was particularly important for the English to keep the lines of communication open, for Calais was the principal gateway to continental Europe. In the early years of Edward's reign Calais became the base for Warwick's own independent diplomatic activity. He issued his own credences to his servants there, notably Richard Whetehill, Louis Galet and John Water, the Calais pursuivant, in negotiations with Burgundy and France. One of them, or another agent, dined with the papal legate, Francesco Coppini at St Omer in late April 1461, and passed on the legate's frequently proffered advice to the earl and Edward IV. Coppini described him as an ambassador, but as Dr Meek has pointed out, these men were not officially accredited. At one level Warwick's agents based in Calais were continuing the necessary day-to-day contact with Burgundy and France to maintain good relations with them. They enjoyed considerable local autonomy. In 1464, for instance, Whetehill was in negotiation with French envoys at Abbeville over the treatment of French prisoners at Guînes, assuring them that there was no need to refer matters to his king. In effect, as Dr Meek has suggested, Warwick maintained a consulate at Calais engaged in a continuous exchange of views with the French and Burgundians as Edward IV's representative.[43] At another level, however, given Warwick's prominence, it is not surprising that they became involved on their master's own behalf, and with the knowledge and agreement of the king, in larger-scale diplomacy. They ran messages to and from Warwick to Charles VII, Louis XI and Philip the Good, and were themselves appointed to formal embassies. Thus, in 1463 and 1464 Whetehill and Galet joined Bishop George Neville and Lord Wenlock in an important embassy to Hesdin and St Omer. It was Wenlock, Whetehill and Warwick herald who were negotiating with Louis XI over the projected match for Edward IV with Bona of Savoy when the king announced he had married Elizabeth Woodville.[44] There can be little doubt that these contacts laid the ground for Warwick's later independent, and subsequently treasonable negotiations with Louis XI, which culminated in the rapprochement with Margaret of Anjou in the summer of 1470.

By July 1469, when Waurin himself visited the town, Warwick was apparently in total command of Calais. The chronicler was at the time collecting material for his history of England. Warwick had promised that if he came to Calais he would treat him kindly and find him a man who would give him all the information he wanted. The earl seems to have been alert to an opportunity to have his version of recent events recorded. It would seem, however, by Waurin's own account, that he only had a brief meeting with the earl and, in the event, received little information either from him or his man. It was suggested that he should return again in two months. Waurin's visit coincided with the marriage of Isabel Neville with the duke of Clarence, when Warwick was deeply engaged in plotting to overthrow Edward IV. Unfortunately, Waurin did not note anything he observed while he was there, only that the earl was busy with some great matters. He does not even seem to have discovered what those great matters were. All he tells us is that the earl paid his expenses and gave him a beautiful hackney. Warwick was generous in his largesse, but not of his time.[45]

Commynes was more forthcoming in his later account of *his* visits to the town in the following year. He was then 23, and newly in the service of Charles the Rash, duke of Burgundy. He went to Calais several times in the summer of 1470, Commynes recalls, as the emissary of the duke, who was then at St Omer and later Boulogne. He was also sent back there later in the year after the Readeption. Commynes may not be the most reliable witness. Apart from any lapses of memory, he was also obsessed with observing the trickery and deceits involved in political intrigue. His account is coloured by this; indeed it is presented as an exemplar. One perhaps also has to take into account his admission that this was the first time that he had been engaged in such diplomacy and that at the time he knew little of the ups and downs of the world.[46] He had several interviews with Lord Wenlock. It seems that he was convinced by Wenlock's later statement that he had denied Warwick entry to Calais for the earl's own safety. Wenlock claimed then, three months later, after Warwick had concluded his treaty with Margaret of Anjou and Louis XI, that at that time Calais was full of treason, and that in particular the marshal, Duras, had turned against the earl. Wenlock claimed, so Commynes wrote, that he had advised Warwick to go to France and that he would have Calais for him when the time was ripe, or so he said to Commynes some time after the event, even though for three months Commynes had believed that he too had abandoned Warwick. Earlier Wenlock had sworn on oath to Commynes that he was true to Edward IV, who had made him his lieutenant, as was the garrison and town. Commynes discovered Wenlock's dissembling when he advised him to rid the town of the remaining household servants of the earl, some twenty or thirty of them, whom he had warned could lead a rising in the town. At this point Wenlock admitted to his collusion with Warwick and instructed Commynes to pass a message to the duke of Burgundy asking him to lift his blockade of the earl at Honfleur.[47]

When Commynes returned in November 1470 he found a garrison preparing for war. They were already raiding the duke's territories in Picardy; it was necessary now to have a safe-conduct and he needed Wenlock's personal intervention to secure one. He was met courteously by the captain of Guînes (Whetehill). When he arrived at Calais he now found everyone wearing the badge of the ragged staff and Warwick's livery, and signs on the houses proclaiming the new Anglo-French alliance. He was told that within a quarter of an hour of the news of the Readeption reaching the town, everyone had put on the earl's livery. Warwick's household men whom he had advised Wenlock to banish, he now observed, had the greatest influence in the town. He undertook his mission of confirming the truce between Calais and Burgundy and of agreeing reparations for the pillaging by the garrison before returning again to the duke.[48]

It is almost impossible to know from Commynes' account whether Wenlock had indeed been playing a double game in the summer of 1470. Maybe Commynes himself was never sure. He told an anecdote of a double-dealing English lady passing between Edward IV and Clarence who, the event revealed, successfully pulled the wool over Wenlock's eyes.[49] In a world in which everyone was double-crossing each other you could not know whom to believe. Edward IV no doubt himself believed that Wenlock had turned his coat; just as Sir William Parr had done. Duras certainly did and he prospered in royal service after 1471. The impression Commynes gives of the majority of the burgesses, merchants and soldiers of the garrison, however, is that their outlook was very much the same as a decade earlier: they bent with the political wind. But a core, and perhaps a dominant core, was fiercely loyal to Warwick. It was these men who seem to have been in a position to determine which way Calais would go. It was the deep-seated loyalty and commitment to the earl of these twenty or thirty household servants and their dependants that was crucial.

In 1471 Calais stood out for Warwick, even after his cause was lost. It may be significant that from the beginning of that year his principal men in post were Gate and Wrottesley; Wenlock had left to join Margaret of Anjou's army waiting to sail to England. What game was he really playing? It was Gate and Wrottesley who sent a contingent to England under the command of Sir George Broke, but not according to John Warkworth until early May, after they would have heard of the defeat at Barnet. This company of 300 men was carried to England by the Bastard of Fauconberg, who had been cruising in the Channel in command of the late earl's fleet. However, after they failed to take the city of London, as they had hoped, they withdrew to Sandwich and took ship back to Calais.[50] For the following two months they held out against Lord Hastings, who came over to Calais in June to recover the town for King Edward. It is not at all clear why they did not invade England and raise Kent earlier that year, in particular to assist Warwick at Barnet. It may be that they were outmanoeuvred by Edward IV who had already reached London before they could sail. It may be that the wind was against them at the critical moment (the same wind that kept Margaret of Anjou in port further down the coast). Or it may be that they were under orders to defend Calais from possible attack by the duke of Burgundy – all too possible. For whatever reason, they left it too late.

Many of the thirty-three men who were included in the pardon negotiated by Wrottesley and Gate before they surrendered early in August were surely among the twenty or thirty household men of the earl who had remained in Calais throughout the crisis, some of whom would have made the attempt on London in May. Included in their number were Lord Clinton, Roland (recte Otwell?) Worsley, 'late lieutenant of Rysbank Tower', John and Robert Otter, John Courtenay, porter (portitor), Robert Warmyngton, treasurer's clerk, Richard Whetehill, lieutenant of Guînes, and his son Adrian who succeeded him as controller. The aliases given by them allow one to place them in their Calais context. Twenty-three identified themselves as 'soldiers' of the town, or of Calais, or of Guînes, and four as late soldiers of the town or of Guînes, indicating whether they were currently serving, or had at one time served, in the garrison. A further man was identified simply as of Guînes. As many as fourteen were, or had also been, burgesses, two of them mayors and one other alderman. In addition, one man was the collector of rents and farms, another the clerk of the great hall (town clerk?). Ten of these men were, or had been, both soldiers and burgesses. A further nine identified themselves as merchants of the Staple, several of whom, unsurprisingly, had also been burgesses. Three, Richard Whetehill, John Courtenay and Thomas Walden, had been, at one time or another, all three. They formed the core of the garrison, burgesses and merchants of the Staple who were committed personally to Warwick. Their property interests in England suggest that they were drawn from throughout the realm, with a slight, and unsurprising tendency to focus in the south east. But there were also two with connections in Carlisle and two with

Northumberland. One was, it seems, French (Robert Osclyffe) who had no other place of association other than Guînes; and one, Sir George Bisipate, 'Greke', was late of the city of Constantinople.[51]

Two of those pardoned had received protections from legal actions when joining Warwick's retinue in the late 1460s: Thomas Walton, or Walden in 1467, and John Colt, described as merchant and gentleman of Newcastle upon Tyne and London in 1468. In his pardon in 1471, Colt still used the aliases of merchant of Newcastle and London, but also acknowledged being known as 'yeoman' of Northumberland and a 'gentleman of London and Essex'. He was probably Thomas Colt's brother. His links with the earl can be traced back to 1463. On 24 January 1464 he received a grant from the king in consideration of his having bought victuals in Northumberland for his household when he was expected at York, to the sum of over £50 from his own money. He was granted revenues from the confiscated lands of Sir Ralph Grey said to be in the same county. The lands in Sedgefield, Newlands, Consett and Whickham, were in fact in the county palatine of Durham. They were at the time in the king's hands, having been sequestered from Bishop Booth. One of the king's three guardians was Thomas Colt.[52]

By far the most intriguing was Anthony de la Toure, 'of the town of Calais, "soldeour", alias burgess, alias clerk, alias gentleman'. He is surely the same Antonio della Torre who came first to England in Francesco Coppini's embassy from the pope in 1460. According to Coppini a 'good Milanese', he was described as his gossip and friend. He established himself in the service of the Yorkist lords, and especially Warwick, soon after their recovery of power in England in July 1460. He was in London with them, and by 15 August was an esquire of the body and servant of Henry VI, although in reality servant of Warwick, and nominated the king's envoy to the pope. As ambassador, he travelled to Milan and Rome in the autumn of 1460, and back again to England by the beginning of the next year. In January 1461 he carried more letters from Warwick, Coppini and Lord Fauconberg to Milan, leaving Calais after 31 January. Although expected to return soon by Coppini, he did not set out on his journey until 14 June. Certainly back in London by 23 September, he was once more in communication with Coppini in Paris. He disappears from the Milanese correspondence in 1462. The last letter of his to Sforza was written from Bruges on 25 March of that year, and in it he styled himself as envoy of King Edward and the earl of Warwick. And then there is silence.[53] We may conjecture that he remained in diplomatic service as ambassador to Milan and Rome, but at some time after 1467 committed himself to Warwick. During this period, one assumes, he took up residence in Calais and at some point joined the garrison, without abandoning his diplomatic role in Warwick's service.

Should these have been the men to whom Commynes referred, as is likely, several of whom held important posts in Calais and Guînes, it is not surprising that he suspected that they could betray the town to Warwick if the chance arose in the summer of 1470, and that he noticed that they exercised considerable authority the following November. By 1471, after fifteen years, the earl had established a committed personal following in Calais. The principal officers of the garrison and a number of burgesses and merchants of the Staple were his men and were prepared to defy King Edward IV even after their lord was dead. These were the men that mattered. We will never know what game Wenlock was playing in the summer of 1470, but his ambivalence and Duras's desertion apart, Calais, in the hands of Warwick's committed servants, ultimately stood four square with him.

PART THREE

Fame

9

The Idol of the Multitude

From the moment he took up office as captain of Calais Warwick drew on the Cinque Ports, Canterbury, and the towns and villages of eastern Kent for supplies and military assistance. His actions in the Channel as keeper of the seas won him considerable popularity with the commons, especially the inhabitants of Sussex, Kent and London. London merchants and the commons of the south-eastern counties were both concerned about commercial prosperity, the protection of the trade route between London and the continent, and national pride – national pride in particular. The sympathetic author of Bale's Chronicle, writing in respect of 1458, stressed that 'no lord of the land took the jeopardy nor laboured for the honour and profit of the king and the land but only he'.[1] The Short English Chronicle's account of the same episode, adds that the earl seized at least seventeen ships laden with salt 'because they would not strike (their flags) in the king's name of England'.[2] At the end of Henry VI's reign he became, in short, a national hero.

It is not surprising, therefore, that Richard Neville mobilized the commons in his cause. In 1459, 1460, 1469, 1470 and 1471 they rose in his support. In the aftermath of Edward IV's victory in 1471 a short poem now entitled 'The Battle of Barnet' was addressed to the commons of England who were implored to change their ways. Turn away (convertimini) from Warwick, they were exhorted; turn to your true and sovereign lord, Edward IV, to whom victory had been granted by God. 'Convertimini, ye commons, & drede your kyng'. 'He ys gon', they were reminded, 'that louyd diuision, mortuus est'. Turn back to your sovereign lord, who is another Arthur. Yet the author characterized Easter Day, the day of his death, as a tragic day, a day in which a great man had lost his life.

> 'Allas!' may he syng that causyd all thys,
> Sorow and care causyd many a day.
> Orate pro anima, that he may com to blys
> Ye that be hys frendys, yow prestys, to pray.[3]

It is a remarkably frank and conciliatory line to take, more in sorrow than in anger, more imploring than commanding. The victorious king and his advisers recognized that although they had won the battle, they had still to recover 'the hearts and minds' of his subjects.

The admission that Warwick enjoyed greater popularity than Edward IV is also to be found in the *Arrivall*, which is not only careful to avoid explicit denigration of Warwick's chivalric reputation, but also to acknowledge the high regard in which he was held by the commons. It describes how the earl's and his brother's body were put on display at St Paul's for the people to see, so that false claims could not be made that he was alive. Since 'many of them were wont to be towards the Earl of Warwick', the display was intended to stop new 'murmurs, insurrections, and rebellions' being made in his name, such

> 'as many days had led to great inconveniences' spread 'by his subtle and malicious moving' which were 'seditiously sown and blown about all the land' ... 'whereof, as is commonly said, right many were towards him, and, for that intent, returned and waged with him'.[4]

Here, however, in a text intended for overseas circulation, it could not be admitted that Warwick was indeed popular, only that he had craftily misled the commons. The Crowland chronicler, who had lived through these events, remarked fifteen years later on how Edward IV, after he had dealt also with his brother the duke of Clarence in 1478, was so secure on his throne that he could rule autocratically once 'all those idols had been destroyed to whom the eyes of the common folk, ever eager for change, used to turn in times gone by'. 'They regarded', he added, 'the earl of Warwick, the duke of Clarence and any other great man who withdrew from royal circles as idols of this kind'.[5]

Historians have tended to accept that Warwick cynically exploited the restless commons for his own seditious ends. This interpretation is expressed most cogently by Professor Hicks. Through a close examination of the various manifestos and poems in circulation, no fewer than eight identified for 1459–60, he dissects the 'ideology of reform' current in the mid-fifteenth century to which the Yorkist lords and Warwick in particular appealed. He argues that the Yorkist lords sought popular support in 1460 because they were denied access to their own power bases and had very little committed backing among the rest of the peerage. They were thus driven by circumstances to launch a popular rebellion; the campaign of 1460 was 'a popular uprising focused and directed by the great nobility'. In the process, 'Warwick was required to metamorphose from great magnate into popular demagogue'. He espoused the ideology of reform in 1459–60 merely as a means to secure power. When in power he did nothing to advance it; instead, he and his allies just helped themselves to rewards and entrenched themselves in office.[6] The same hypocrisy recurred a decade later. Popular grievances were again exploited by a ruthless noble leadership for its own ends. The earl's very public opposition to the king's favourites and policies distanced him and cleared him of complicity.

He stood in 1469 for the same as a decade earlier and appeared in the popular eyes as the consistent advocate of the common weal. So well had Warwick gauged the popular mood that he can be said to have represented it. That does not determine whether he sincerely stood for their interest, or cunningly manipulated them.

But the answer to the rhetorical question is not in doubt. 'Others', he concludes, 'were (in the future) to appeal directly to public opinion and to peddle public grievances as the cloak for their own private gain'.[7]

Thus the prevailing view is that Warwick became a demagogue out of desperation to advance his own cause. He was a cynical rabble-rouser. There was even something demeaning and distasteful in the manner in which a great nobleman such as Warwick exploited popular grievances. But was it so straightforward? A fuller examination of the nature of popular politics in fifteenth-century England, and of popular political ideology and its language leads to a more nuanced understanding of Warwick's 'demagogy'. First, however, we need to establish the nature and extent of the earl's popular standing. Writing in the early sixteenth century of the mayoral year that ran from 1468 to 1469, Robert Fabyan, the author of the *Great Chronicle* of London remembered how the 'earl was ever had in great favour of the commons of this land'.[8] He placed the comment in that year as a preliminary to the renewal of popular rebellion associated with the earl in 1469. He was probably not aware of the strictly contemporary report of the French agent, William Moneypenny, who informed Louis XI in 1468 that Warwick had never been so popular. When he passed through town and countryside it seemed to people that God had descended from the skies. They greeted him with cries of 'A Warwick! A Warwick!' His standing in the public eye was not one iota diminished since 1460–1 when he was 'much loved by the commons of Kent and of London', because he promised to reform the 'hurts and mischiefs and grievances that reigned in this land'.[9]

A surge of popular support in London and the Home Counties had borne him through the revolution of 1460–1. The *English Chronicle* recounts how in the summer of 1460 the commons of Kent had beseeched the Yorkist lords in Calais to come to their aid. The lords were, according to this highly favourable account, surprised when the people of south-eastern Kent flocked to Lord Faunconberg after he occupied Sandwich as a beachhead. We are to believe that the Yorkist lords only decided to launch their bid for power when they knew the true hearts of the people.[10] It may indeed be that they were surprised by the scale of the turn-out. It swept them through London to the field of Northampton. They left London, noted the Short English Chronicle, with 'much other people of Kent, Sussex and Essex'; 'there was much favour to the earl in the field', added the author of Gregory's Chronicle, who had ordered that the commons were to be spared.[11]

After the victory Warwick was greeted ecstatically wherever he went. According to the Waurin Relation, on his return from a brief visit to recover Guînes from the duke of Somerset in August, the crowds came out again to welcome him at Sandwich. From there he progressed to Greenwich to be received by Henry VI and then, after several days at court, he went on to London. There he was welcomed by great numbers of lords and people who came out of the city to meet him. With them were children carrying great banners and extolling him as if he were God. And so he made his way into the city, escorted to his lodgings. To him there came the mayor, burgess and merchants to thank him for all he had done for their benefit and to offer great gifts, amongst great celebration.[12] This could be seen as merely an exaggerated account, were it not for the fact that it bears strong resemblance to a joyous entry such as was usually reserved for monarchs. The king, it is clear, was not with him. The banners, the extolling of his virtues, the escort through the city, perhaps along the traditional route, all suggest that this is what was laid on for him as if he were in fact a king returning in triumph.[13]

And so it continued. It was reported to Milan on 14 February 1461 that Warwick had left London four days earlier with a great concourse of people from Kent and the surrounding districts to face the rampaging Lancastrian host.[14] His volunteers and levies were no match, however, for battle-hardened veterans on the field of the second St Albans. Nevertheless, despite the defeat, the earl was still able to capitalize upon his popularity in London and the Home Counties to return to London and make Edward IV king. The crucial factor, Gregory commented, was 'the love and favour that the commons had unto him'.[15] In particular, as these accounts all stress, it was the commons of Kent, with their tradition of dissent and unrest, who loved and favoured him most.

How much beyond London, Kent and neighbouring counties this popularity spread is hard to determine. According to Gregory's Chronicle again, the earl sent letters 'unto many places of England how they were advised [purposed] to reform the hurts'.[16] It extended to Norfolk. In October 1460, when the future of the Lancastrian dynasty was being considered in parliament, Margaret Paston wrote to her husband John, then one of Norfolk's MPs, that there was great talk in 'this country' of the desire of my lord of York. What was said she did not report, except that 'the people report full worshipfully of my lord of Warwick', adding that 'they have no fear here but that he and others should show too great favour to them that have been rulers of this country before time'. Clearly she hoped that the days of Tuddenham and Daniel were over, but it was to Warwick rather than York that she understood people looked. Friar Brackley said much the same in his ramblings from London. The popularity did not diminish. Writing to her husband in some despair five years later about the 'too horrible a cost and trouble that we have now daily', Margaret suggested that he should try anything for relief, even an appeal to the duke of Norfolk, for 'the people love and dread him more than any other *except* the king and my lord Warwick'.[17] On the other hand, disturbances aimed at the new regime in 1462 suggest that the earl's popularity did not extend to Gloucestershire and North Somerset.[18]

In the north of England Warwick's popular standing was paradoxically more ambivalent. It has to be remembered that he rarely visited the north between 1449 and 1461. His father, who dominated Yorkshire in these years, was murdered at Pontefract on the last day of 1460 because, it was said, the commons loved him not.[19] The account given of Edward IV's campaign in 1471 by The *Arrivall* asserts that the Nevilles were still unpopular in southern Yorkshire a decade after the battle of Towton. Robin of Redesdale's rising in 1469 was not a genuinely popular movement, and earlier risings in Yorkshire seem to have had a distinctly anti-Neville colour.[20] It may well be that the more they experienced his seigneurial lordship, the less enamoured were the commons. The West Country and West Midlands rose in force in the autumn of 1470 to welcome Warwick and Clarence's return in the cause of the house of Lancaster. 'Immediately the earl landed', the Milanese ambassador to the court of Louis XI reported home, 'countless multitudes thronged to him'.[21] It is not clear how much of this was a reflection of the Kingmaker's personal standing, or of his new Lancastrian credentials. It was still, at the end of his life, in the south east that Warwick was most highly regarded. There was a show of support for him at the beginning of the Readeption and then, too late, under the Bastard of Fauconberg, a last futile rising in his cause in Kent and Sussex in May 1471.

Warwick became popular in London and the south-east after he became captain of Calais. There was no doubt a considerable degree of self-promotion involved. One might suspect, for instance, that as kings did, so he arranged the welcome he received in London in August 1460. The poems in his praise were not entirely spontaneous. Contemporaries offered different reasons for the phenomenon. Robert Fabyan suggested it was 'treating'. He recalled that he kept open house everywhere he went, but drew particular attention to how in London meat cooked in his house was supplied to every tavern for distribution.[22] Olivier de la Marche was more cynical. De la Marche was a frequent ambassador to Edward IV from Burgundy in 1469–70, during which he no doubt picked up the view circulating at the English court, and which he recorded in his memoirs later. There were three main reasons why Warwick had a hold on the city of London and the realm. The first was that by flattery and false humility he won the hearts of the people of London. The second was that he pandered to English chauvinism. As warden of the Cinque Ports (not captain of Calais) he allowed great robberies of strangers, because he was beloved of pirates whom he protected. Thirdly he owed 3 or 4,000 écus to divers citizens of London who were anxious that he should continue to prosper so that his debts might one day be repaid.[23]

De la Marche's observation about the debts owed by him to Londoners is germane. Most of the merchants of the Staple were Londoners, half a dozen of them handling most of the export of wool through the city. The backing of the staplers in Calais was also the backing of a significant element in the city. Bale remembered that the city had contributed to the cost of reinforcements sent to the town in October 1457, 'to the rescue of Calais and comfort of the earl of Warwick, being then there for the safeguard thereof'.[24] The earl's actions in 1458–9 had been to their benefit. In the mid-1450s there was considerable resentment of the privileges enjoyed by alien merchants, especially Italians and Germans (the Hanse), and serious rioting in 1456–7, instigated, it has been argued, by the staplers. One particular issue that incensed them was the granting of licences to Italians to ship wool other than to the Staple. Although the crown had acknowledged the Staple's monopoly, it nevertheless continued to grant these lucrative loopholes. The crown was particularly concerned not to lose the heavy customs dues that Italian merchants paid, especially as the revenue from customs was shrinking dramatically at the time. And, considering the manner in which the garrison was paid, diversion of customs revenue, was loss of pay. One of the more notorious acts of piracy by the Calais garrison, an attack on shipping in the estuary of the Thames in February 1457, was in fact a seizure of wool being exported under such licence by Italian merchants. Matters did not improve subsequently: the crown continued to grant licences at the expense of the Staple. The final straw was the ban of exports of wool to the Staple enacted by the Coventry parliament. By 1460 most of the leading citizens were Yorkist, or to be more precise, Warwick sympathisers. The earl, by his direct actions in the Channel, seemed to be the only one prepared to stand up for the interests of the city. No wonder he was treated to a joyous entry.[25]

By 1469, however, despite de la Marche's cynical view, it would seem that the love affair between the London mercantile elite and Warwick was over. It is noticeable that he himself kept away from the city in 1469–70; he did not return there until after the Readeption of Henry VI; his defence of the restored Lancastrian regime was conducted from the midlands. Edward IV, on the other hand, made straight for London on his return in 1471, was welcomed by the citizens and rewarded with their stalwart defence of the city against Fauconberg's rising. The reason may well have been Warwick's preference for a French alliance, made a reality in 1470. The commercial interests of the city were bound up with Flanders. Richard Neville was no longer the protector of the trade route between London and the Low Countries. London's interests were best served by the close ties that Edward IV established with Charles, duke of Burgundy after 1467.[26] Thus in the final years of his life Warwick came to rely more heavily on the commons of the countryside and small towns of the south-east, especially Kent and Sussex. The tensions between the two constituencies, London's elite and the commons of Kent, which had erupted in 1450, resurfaced. His popular base narrowed.

It is easy to assume that, excepting the mercantile elite of London in 1459–61, the commons with whom Warwick was popular in the countryside, small towns and the city were the poor and dispossessed, 'ever eager for change', always ready to rise in rebellion and itching to indulge in looting and mindless destruction. Such, it is supposed, was the multitude of which Warwick was the idol. It was the view of the 'establishment'. In 1459, the *Somnium Vigilantis* responded to the claim in the defence of the Yorkist lords that they enjoyed the favour of the people dismissively: they are for the most part full of 'opinionable conceits, and not of truth'. Popular favour does not make them right. Everyone knows of the 'great variableness of the people and of the incertitude of their opinions'.[27] The 'people' are fickle and worthless. It was the line taken by Walsingham in 1381, and again, vividly, by the London merchant who was the author of Gregory's Chronicle in his account of Cade's revolt. The commons of Kent, he reported,

> made a field, ditched, and staked well-about, as it had been in land of war, save only [the way in which?] they kept order among them, for as good was Jack Robyn as John at the Noke, for all were as high as pig's feet ... Then they put all their power unto the man that named him captain of all their host.[28]

They were the scum of the earth. Later, when they returned and attacked London, looted and murdered citizens, in his self-righteous outrage, the author 'wot [knew] not what [to] name it for the multitude of riff raff', which acted as men 'that had been half beside their wits' and who 'in that furnish they went, as they said, for the common weal of the realm of England'.[29] A swinish multitude could not possibly represent the common good. It is a view that has been expressed down the centuries and has commonly coloured the reporting of direct action by public protest. We need, however, to look beyond the hostile and stereotypical representation of the many-headed monster and examine more carefully the character of popular politics in the mid-fifteenth century.

There are two aspects to consider: the social structure of fifteenth-century England and the nature of popular political participation. English rural society below the level of gentility was not composed of one homogeneous mass of common people. During the preceding century, following the Black Death and catastrophic population decline, there had been a general rise in the living standards of those who were skilled labourers in regular employment, tenant farmers, artisans and craftsmen. Paradoxically, the per capita wealth of English people increased while national income declined. As the fifteenth century progressed, right through the ultimate defeat in France in mid-century, the disposable income of ordinary men and women grew. This is shown in improved housing, a growth in horse ownership, an increase in the consumption of meat, dairy products and ale, the acquisition of decencies such as brass and pewter vessels, and more time spent simply in leisure. There was widespread amelioration as the benefits of a redistribution of income spread down the social order. New definitions were adopted for that social order, and given legal form by the Statute of Additions of 1413. Men below the level of gentleman were to identify themselves in any legal transaction as yeoman, or husbandman, or labourer or by their craft. The stratification was not in itself new, but it is clear from the end of the fourteenth century that a recognizably modern occupational structure existed in the countryside. The greatest beneficiaries were what came to be called the middling sort: yeomen, substantial husbandmen, self-employed craftsmen, small-scale traders, shipmen, brokers and factors (many employed in the cloth industry which flourished in the countryside where costs were lower).[30]

People such as these, as well as the gentry and the great city merchants, came to have a voice in the affairs of the realm. They were the leaders of their communities in normal times, many of whom enjoyed the parliamentary franchise and several of whom served as churchwardens, bailiffs, constables, local jurors and tax collectors. Some as representatives of small boroughs, even sat in the House of Commons. The forty-shilling franchise in the counties, in place since 1430, established a widely based electorate. They were the persons on whom crown, lords and church relied to transmit their views, rally support, enforce common and customary law locally, and collect taxes. They were increasingly literate, in English, if not in the Latin used by the clerical and intellectual elite. Governments wooed them by bills, by manifestos, through pulpits and by display. They admired Henry V, especially his aggressive foreign policy and more effective enforcement of law and order. They were prepared to pay heavy taxes to provide for the vigorous defence of the realm. By the same token, they were critical of governments that wasted taxation in futile wars, abused power and failed to maintain order. They were accustomed to using the procedure of parliamentary petition to seek amends and to air social and economic grievances. Moreover, they mediated and articulated a public opinion and political awareness that extended through oral and ritual culture to labourers, servants and the unskilled in urban and rural societies. It is a mistake to assume that there was no popular, in the sense of non-elite, participation in fifteenth-century politics. On the contrary, ordinary men, and to some extent women, were continuously engaged in political action.[31]

Thus there was a well-informed and engaged political constituency beyond the narrow confines of the nobility and the ruling elite. By the middle of the fifteenth century there was not only wider political participation beyond the ruling elites, but also a wider dimension to political thought, a perception that there were matters which were accepted as being of concern to all. This was expressed usually in English as the 'common weal', or in Latin as the 'res publica'. The expression and circulation of these ideas in the vernacular was a new phenomenon in the mid-fifteenth century. They were now extended beyond privileged gentle and intellectual circles to encompass ordinary men and women. The language of politics was democratized, and the gap between aristocratic and popular ideologies was narrowed. In 1381 the language of protest was archane and cryptic, deliberately mystifying.[32] By 1450 there was a shared language and a shared ideology expressed in a common vernacular. The language of parliamentary politics and the rhetoric of parliament as a representative institution was familiar; petitioning was widely practised. There was what has been called a 'representational hierarchy' through which the needs of the common weal could be met by informal and formal channels of normal politics. One or two commentators, such as Thomas Gascoigne, were exceptionally prepared to acknowledge the manner in which protestors represented themselves as the king's true liegemen petitioning in arms for reform and the correction of abuses as a legitimate part of the political process.[33]

And if normal, indirect, representative procedures failed, local elites were prepared to take direct action in protests, demonstrations and full-scale uprisings. One shared characteristic of these many manifestations of popular action is that a prominent part was played in them by the local elites – the more substantial villagers, manorial and parish office holders, jurors and constables who were responsible in emergencies for raising and leading the local militias, trained and practised in the use of arms. They were the very people who had gained most from economic and social amelioration, yet, even though they had the most to lose, as the record of prosecutions, enquiries and pardons reveals, they also led their communities in protest against government action when they were driven to it. Just as in happier times they stood by the crown, so in less happy they articulated grievances and led protest in defence of a proper order of society that they believed to be threatened by bad government. In times of stress and government failure, as had happened in the late fourteenth century and happened again in the mid-fifteenth century, when 'representative hierarchy' failed, direct action in defence of the common weal was believed to be justified. In their own eyes they represented the 'true commons'.

Furthermore, in the mid-fifteenth century there were very real economic and commercial anxieties. Between 1450 and 1470 the English economy suffered a severe recession, especially a commercial slump in the south and east, for which the government was blamed. Loss of the control of the Channel after 1450 and growth of attacks on English shipping particularly affected shipmen, merchants and producers, both of wool for direct export and cloth. There was a virtual stop of trade in the late 1450s.[34] This caused real poverty. A protectionist pamphlet, in the form of a poem, in circulation at the time, called for the best wool to be kept back for cloth production so as to help impoverished spinners, carders and weavers to give 'the pore pepyll livying in dystress' decent wages.[35] There were multiple and deep-seated grievances against the government in mid-century into which Warwick tapped.

The familiarity with parliamentary process of those who were 'as high as pig's feet' is shown in the first of the manifestos they drew up in 1450. Clause 8 complained about collectors of the fifteenth, clause 13 complained that the people of Kent did not enjoy free election in choosing knights of shire, 'but letters have been sent from divers estates to the great rulers of all the country, the which embrace [influence] their tenants and other people by force to choose other persons than the common will is'. Self-evidently this is a complaint of the enfranchised, the forty-shilling freeholders. They also objected to the manner in which the chosen knights of the shire had, in effect, 'now late' sold the office of collector of subsidy to their own profit.[36] The list of complaints drawn up at Blackheath, now in Magdalen College, reveals a clear awareness of constitutional theory, asserting that the king was not above his laws, as his coronation oath confirmed, and that he could not tax his subjects at will without the consent of parliament.[37] These are people with a sophisticated grasp of politics, fully cognizant with political processes, and actively participating in politics as suitors at law, taxpayers and parliamentary electors.

This point was acknowledged by the author of the English Chronicle, who commented that Cade was a 'subtle' man, for he

> said that he and his company were gathered and assembled for to redress and reform the wrongs that were done in the realm, and to withstand the malice of them that were destroyers of the common profit, and for to correct and amend the defaults of them that were the king's chief councillors; and showed unto them the articles of their petitions concerning and touching the myschiefs and misgovernance of the realm, in the which articles was nothing contained but that was rightful and reasonable, whereof a copy was sent to the parliament held that time at Westminster. Whereof the said captain desired that such grievance should be amended and reformed by the parliament, and to have answer again of the same articles.[38]

Thus, Cade and his demonstrators presented themselves as petitioners in much the same way as public protestors from the Levellers to the Chartists subsequently did. They believed in a right to public protest. The fact that such interest was shown in the articles of petition they produced, and that several copies have survived, one being sent to Sir John Fastolf, suggests that there was not only some sympathy for their ends, but some understanding of their means.

Those who led direct action in Kent, Sussex and neighbouring counties in 1459–61, in 1469–71 and again in 1497 came from the same backgrounds and shared the same outlook. Moreover, it is highly likely also, that those who followed Warwick in arms in these years were the same local militias of 'fencible' men, raised by their elected constables of hundred and parish, who had turned out in 1450. There was a well-established and familiar system whereby these communally elected men of modest means were responsible for ensuring that local persons of military age were regularly mustered and reviewed and, in response to commissions of array, for calling them out. Those fit for military service were expected to provide their own equipment as archers or even men-at-arms, according to means, at their own expense. They were for the most part, therefore, drawn from the ranks of the substantial husbandmen, yeomanry and mere 'gentlemen'. In Bridport in 1457, 180 men were mustered, of whom 120 had their own 'harness', including salet and jack (helmet and protective jacket) and one a full suit of plate armour. There was thus, county by county, a force of semi-trained and armed men ready to be mobilized by their local constables. Furthermore, the bearing of arms in fifteenth-century England, at gentry and sub-gentry level, was itself perceived as conferring a political voice, and if all else failed, the use of force to assert that voice was sanctioned. It is what York and his colleagues consistently claimed throughout the 1450s. Indeed it was fundamental to the notion of a just war. Just as kings and nobles could claim the right to use violence to make good their rights and secure justice, so also, claimed the commons, could they. There was, therefore, an inextricable link between political engagement, the bearing of arms and direct action in defence of the common weal.[39]

There is a clear indication that this was the case in 1460–61 and again in 1471 in the repeated use of the word 'host' to describe the insurgents who followed Warwick and subsequently the Bastard of Fauconberg. Bale's Chronicle, once more particularly revealing, describes how on 2 July 1460 Warwick, his father and the earl of March came to London with 500 horsemen and led 'an ost' of footmen of the commons of Kent, Sussex and Surrey, numbering 60,000 (a huge exaggeration) who first camped outside the city beside St George Barre, but after negotiations the following day, were permitted to pass through the city to St John's Field, near Smithfield, and then on to Northampton. This was a host, or an army, by implication raised by the constables of hundreds and parishes.[40] According to one account, an advance guard from the Calais garrison, reinforced by Kentish levies, also decided the battle of Edgecote in 1469.[41] In May 1471 it seems the men of Kent, raised by Fauconberg in the last rising in Warwick's name, were mobilized through the same mechanism. Warkworth tells how Sir George Broke and Fauconberg, with the help of other gentlemen, raised up all Kent. His 'host' of 'good men [goodmen, men of worth] well harnessed [equipped]' was more than 20,000 strong.[42] The *Arrivall* likewise describes it as a 'host', but in its view many of its number were unwilling conscripts. They clearly were arrayed men, for 'such, especially, as were able in persons, if they had array, and might not wage to such as would go, they were compelled by like force, to lend them their array, and harness; and such as were unharnessed, aged, and disable, and of honour, they were compelled to send waged men'. The fact that subsequent pardons of 79 men, of whom 3 ranked themselves as esquires, 28 as gentlemen,

20 as yeomen and 9 as husbandmen as well as 2 artisans and 17 men from the Cinque Ports, were identified by the hundred in which they lived, powerfully reinforces the impression that Fauconberg, as self-styled captain of Kent, used the system of array to mobilize the militia. As in Cade's Revolt, two decades earlier, some of the yeomen and husbandmen may have been the constables themselves.[43]

When we consider Warwick, therefore, we should see him in relationship with this world of popular political participation, and in terms of an established discourse of public politics, of the perceived legitimacy of direct action in defence of the common weal, and linked to the well-established system of mobilizing county levies led by and substantially composed of the same ranks of men. In 1470 Warwick addressed this constituency as the 'worshipful, discreet and true commons of England'. The phrase 'true commons' has a long pedigree, stretching back to 1381.[44] It had been recently used in the petition of the 'only commons' (of the commons alone) drawn up by the Yorkshire rebels of 1469. The petitioners described themselves as the 'true and faithful subjects and commons of this land', assuring the lords spiritual and temporal that they intended only the 'weal of the king and the common weal of the land'.[45] The use of the word 'worshipful' in this document is also striking, as the polite term of address for respectable persons. It implies recognition of the real standing of the local elites, acknowledges their own perceptions of themselves, and demonstrates that Warwick was fully aware that he was targeting this particular section of the community. He had experienced Cade's Revolt at first hand and, one assumes, remembered well the rebel demands and the rhetoric they deployed. Like all his peers, he could not have avoided being aware in the early 1450s of the public discourse of the common weal.

The rebels in 1450 had appealed to York. In what was possibly their final manifesto, the 'true commons of Kent' called upon the king 'to take about him a noble person, the true blood of the Realm, that is to say the high and mighty prince, the Duke of York, late exiled from our sovereign lord's presence'.[46] York, however, was careful to distance himself from the direct action of the true commons. Although he was later to espouse the cause of reform, he always did so as an aristocratic reformer, not as one who condoned direct popular action. His stance might be parodied as being tough on insurrection, and tough on the causes of insurrection. When, in 1453, Warwick threw in his lot with York he implicitly endorsed the duke's rhetoric. By 1459, however, he seems to have moved significantly further than Duke Richard in appealing directly and explicitly to this public arena. The true novelty lay in the manner in which he now espoused and endorsed direct action. He was far more willing than the duke to place himself at the head of the true commons in defence of the common weal.[47]

The articles of September 1459 were published in Kent quite independently of York, when the earl was on his way from Calais to a rendezvous with the duke and his father in the midlands. They drew attention to the manner in which the common weal and good politic laws had been subverted, how the king's household had lived extortionately on the backs of the people, and to the threat that now existed to the kingdom from its enemies. They explained how, 'for the tender love that we bear unto the common weal and prosperity of this realm and secondly to the king's estate', they intended 'to go unto the presence of our said sovereign lord, and as true subjects and liegemen, lovers of the said common weal', to petition him ['to show ... as lowly as we can'] to reform his government and restore the prosperity and peace of the realm. This was the language of popular protest. An attack on the abuses of the household repeated the fifth complaint of the commons at Blackheath nine years earlier against 'the king's menial men, servants of household'. Another set of complaints from 1450, those preserved at Magdalen College, were recycled virtually verbatim (the only difference of substance is that clause 14 is divided into two). They were entered by John Vale in his memoranda book as 'the articles of the commons of Kent at the coming of the earls of March, Warwick and Salisbury from Calais to the battle of Northampton'. Whereas, York had been careful to distance himself from popular complaint in 1450, Warwick and his fellow lords were happy to give them their imprimatur.[48] In their own letter written to the archbishop of Canterbury, Thomas Bourgchier, according to the near contemporary *English Chronicle*, addressed at large to the 'Commons of England', the lords focused on their own grievances and how they had been excluded and proscribed wrongly by their mortal and extreme enemies. They also stressed how the commons had been impoverished by heavy taxation, which had nevertheless not prevented the loss of Normandy, Anjou, Maine and Gascony.[49]

It is surely not accidental that in 1459 Warwick and his fellow lords declared that they acted first for the common weal and secondly for the king's estate, in that order.[50] Their justification for direct action first and foremost in the name of the common weal, and thus in the tradition of popular politics, raised fundamental questions. In the autumn of 1459 a counter-argument, known as the *Somnium Vigilantis* ('A Dream of Vigilance'), possibly composed by Sir John Fortescue, was drawn up to justify the condemnation of the Yorkist lords for treason at the Coventry parliament. It addressed six claims attributed to them, including in particular that it was reasonable and worshipful to take up arms ['to expose oneself to great jeopardy of goods and life'] to 'intend [attend to] the common wealth of the realm'. Against this, it was argued at length that the principal guarantee of the common weal was, and could only be, due obedience to the sovereign and his laws. Only the sovereign could ensure that the realm was governed according to the common good and not for private interest. Moreover, the recent rebellion, and rebellion it was, had set out not to procure the common good, but to subvert it. The lords had but pretended reformation

of wrongs and extortions. And even if the public good of the realm had in any
way been neglected, what authority had they to reform it without the king's
commission?[51]

As Dr Watts has pointed out, this is a powerful statement of the prevailing view
of the overriding and unlimited authority of the crown. Nothing but obedience
to the king could be justified, and especially not in the name of the general good
of the body politic. There could be but one authority, the crown.[52] Whether or
not Warwick and his allies in the summer of 1460 did pretend a reformation of
wrongs for their own private ends is as irrelevant as the question as to whether
those who exercised royal authority in the king's name were thereby inevitably
acting in the common good. Both sides were pursuing private interests, and
especially personal power. But the conflict was couched in terms of the common
good, and thereby raised significant and fundamental constitutional issues. The
Somnium Vigilantis may have insisted that there was only one answer, but it is
clear that there was an alternative, popular perception of the roots of authority
in the realm, which Warwick at this time espoused, and which was evidently,
as the length and care of the rebuttal testifies, taken extremely seriously by the
defenders of unlimited monarchical authority.

In 1470 Warwick repeated the message, but with subtle variation. Respect for
the crown and an appeal to nationalism loom larger. God and our deeds will
judge, he and Clarence declared 'to the worshipful, discreet and true commons of
England', how they had been badly treated, notwithstanding that they had always
had true hearts and tender zeal for the 'weal of the crown' and 'the advancing of
the common weal of England' and for the 'reproving of falsehood and oppression
of the poor people'. They had been exiled, they claimed, by covetous and seditious
persons about the throne, more concerned with self-advancement than with
looking to the 'majesty royal or to the thing public of the true commonalty
of the said realm', as they knew by experience.[53] Concern for the king's estate
('weal of the crown', 'majesty royal') now came *before* the common weal ('the
thing public'). More stress is also given in these complaints to the threat to the
kingdom from its enemies abroad. In 1460, in the middle of civil war, Warwick
and his fellow lords reminded the people of Kent that Henry VI's governments
had been responsible for the loss of France, a point made ten years earlier, but
they also drew upon memories of more recent events and threats to England from
France, stressing how their enemies at court had conspired with the French to
dislodge them from Calais, and even alleging that 'the same lords would put the
same rule of England, if they might have their purpose and intent, into the hands
and governance of the said enemies'.[54] The same claim was repeated in 1470. The
realm, Warwick and Clarence asserted, was in danger of being 'alienated and
governed by strangers and outward nations'. Indeed, the 1470 letter ended with
the rounding peroration that they would in short time return to restore justice,

overthrow tyranny and redeem for ever the realm from 'thraldom of all outward nations and make it as free within itself as ever it was heretofore', with the aid of Almighty God, the Virgin Mary and St George.[55]

The emphasis in the proclamation by Warwick and Clarence when they landed in England in August 1470 is again somewhat different. The surviving version of this document is a composite. The first three clauses, which survive in a separate version, is a call to arms to depose the 'great rebel', Edward IV, and restore the 'most noble and Christian prince our most dread sovereign lord King Henry VI, very true and undoubted king of England and of France'. Edward IV is now the destroyer of the 'good, true commons'. Earl and duke promise 'reformation', 'for the common weal', but under the authority given to them by Queen Margaret and Edward, Prince of Wales. They offer a pardon to all who rally to the cause, and command all able-bodied men between the ages of sixteen and sixty to join them. There then follow four clauses dealing with military discipline, clearly designed to reassure the population at large.[56] The emphasis is now on Henry VI's absolute right first, the common weal second. While this reflects the stance taken ten years earlier in the *Somnium Vigilantis*, that only through absolute obedience to the crowned king can the common good be served, it is clear that the appeal to the common weal had not been abandoned altogether.

It should cause no surprise that Warwick was prepared to go along with this shift of emphasis: needs must. One should hesitate, however, before dismissing Warwick as being totally opportunist. The articles drawn up by Sir John Fortescue in the name of the prince of Wales for the interim government of England in 1470–1, when Warwick acted as the king's lieutenant, reveal a thoroughly reformist stance for the 'good public of the realm'. No rewards are to be paid until a council is established to consider all petitions in the light of the king's needs. The constitution of this continual council established for the good of the realm and not the private profit of its members, is set down; its authority is established in matters touching the rule of the realm, especially in matters of grants, above that of the king. So that,

> 'the king not be counselled by men of his chamber, of his household, nor other which can not counsel him, but the good public shall by wise men be conducted to the prosperity and honour of the land, to the surety and welfare of the king, and to the surety of all them that shall be about his person, whom the people have often times slain for the miscounselling of their sovereign lord.[57]

It is charged not only to manage the king's own livelihood and household, but also to regulate the economy, and administer the law. One may note, too, that the public good once more seems to take precedence over the surety and welfare of the king.

Clearly there were very special circumstances in which the government of the kingdom and the management of the king's household were placed in the hands of a continual council. During the Readeption, as both the court in exile and Warwick knew, the king was in no condition to govern his kingdom. He was now, if he had not been before, totally incapacitated. Whereas before 1461 the fiction was maintained that the king could govern, now it was not. Moreover, it was clearly in the interests of the court in exile, the queen, the prince and their advisers, to do their utmost to circumscribe Warwick's freedom of action before they themselves returned to England. Furthermore, it is made explicit that these arrangements were strictly temporary, for the last clause declares that 'it is thought good that it will please his highness to forbear all this first year the keeping of his worshipful and great household'.[58] We cannot know what further arrangements might have been made had the restored regime survived, but we can doubt that an attempt was being made to curtail the absolute authority of the crown permanently.

Nevertheless, there are elements in this temporary settlement for the government of the kingdom which are consistent with Warwick's own past position and the pre-1461 critique of the crown. This particularly lies in the recognition that the king had been profligate in his distribution of patronage, and that he had been misled by evil councillors. To some extent, the provisions can be read as an acknowledgement of the essential correctness of the Yorkist critique, as set out in various manifestos before Duke Richard laid claim to the throne. York, Dr Watts has proposed, attempted to construct a new authority based on parliamentary approval in 1455–6 and the far-reaching Bill of Resumption, which was the occasion of the end of his second protectorate, resembled Fortescue's later blueprint for a government which envisaged conciliar rule in place of the personal sway of the monarch.[59] If this were so, it would have been quite possible for Warwick, who had been at York's shoulder at the time, to claim that his essential quarrel with the house of Lancaster before 1460 had now been settled. He could have argued that his concerns for the good of the common weal were now to be met; and indeed promised to be met, in a more sustained and direct way than they had ever been under Edward IV. It was thus open to contemporaries to interpret Warwick's actions as consistent; indeed, should they have so chosen, they could have presented this as the culmination of Warwick's campaign for the reform of government for the common weal.

Warwick may have been convinced by Sir John Fortescue's argument, by historical example, that the kingdom of England would prosper if such a ruling council could be established and the king be guided by it. The earlier manifesto put out by Warwick and Clarence before they returned to England might also owe something to Fortescue's writings, especially in its stress on the 'majesty royal' and 'thing public'. The views developed by Fortescue in exile and encapsulated in his later works, bear strong resemblance to some of the complaints advanced by the Yorkist lords in 1459–60, which themselves set out, in essence, the notion of England as a mixed monarchy – that the king is neither above his law nor free to put his subjects at jeopardy nor take their goods without the assent of parliament. There might thus have occurred a coming together of ideas in a new approach to the government of the realm which went some way toward recognizing the complaints of the commons in the 1450s. Since the Readeption lasted but six months there is no way of knowing whether a new direction might have been taken.

As we have seen, the extent of Warwick's popularity, fully recognized by Edward IV after his death, became a matter of grave concern. The same argument was mounted by Edward IV against Warwick in 1470–71 as had been advanced in the *Somnium Vigilantis* in 1459. His rebellions, far from being in defence of the common weal, were a threat to it.[60] The only certain way to ensure the common weal was obedience to the king. The tone may initially have been more pleading than commanding, but the message was the same. After 1471, when Sir John Fortescue's ideas for a refoundation of the monarchy were put into practice as royal policy, the focus was on the recovery of the crown's finances and the need to prevent another Warwick emerging to challenge its authority. A firm line was drawn under public politics. The people, Bishop Russell asserted in one of his draft parliamentary sermons for 1483, 'stood afar'.[61] Their representation was, and should remain, indirect and virtual. Direct action, it was insisted once again, could never in any circumstances be justified. Warwick's espousal of public politics was ultimately perceived as a threat to the established order. The lid was now firmly closed on the Pandora's box which he had opened. Thus, he was represented as a traitor and idol of the multitude, who, in refusing to accept anything but his domination of the kingdom, did not hesitate to stir up popular rebellion.

It was not that easy, however, either to suppress public politics or to expunge the memory of the earl as a champion of the true commons. Public petitioning, often admittedly by vested interests in the name of the common good, was widespread in early sixteenth-century England. A distinction was drawn, however, between the act of petitioning and gathering in any number, which was deemed an unlawful assembly. Nevertheless, in both the Pilgrimage of Grace and Kett's Revolt, the commons, who were well able to articulate a political view and organize themselves to advance it, seem to have taken the line that forming 'camps', or assemblies, which were peaceable and did not threaten violence, were lawful. On these occasions, however, and this marked a significant change, they now spoke only as loyal subjects and never in the name of the true commons.[62]

It was in this context that Warwick's image as a champion of the commons was still alive in the mid-sixteenth century, some eighty years after his death. It is to be found dramatized in a monologue put into the earl's mouth in the 1559 edition of the *Mirrour for Magistrates*. The reader is enjoined to imagine the earl's body lying in St Paul's, in his coat armour, as depicted in the (now lost) portrait over the entrance door to the Jesus chapel at the south end of quire, and to hear him recite an apology for his life. He reminds the audience of his greatness, honour and prowess. But this was not all: he was more than a great man of chivalry

> The truth of all I will at large recite,
> The short is this: I was no hypocrite.
>
> I never did nor sayd, save what I mente
> The common weale was still my chiefest care.

And there follows a five-stanza paean of praise of his selfless commitment to the common good. Particular emphasis is given, somewhat bathetically, to the promptness that he paid his creditors and his concern to make sure his soldiers and workmen were paid on time. Because 'the people' saw that he dealt justly and minded the common weal, they were ready to 'spend their substance, life, and blood' on his behalf. And so, when he saw the realm decayed under Henry VI, he sought to mend the state. His moral, from which the reader should learn, is that those who seek popular approval must ensure their actions match their words,

> For upright dealing, dets payd and poore sustyned,
> Is meane wherby all hartes are throwly gained.

This is, the author concludes, the greatest of all the virtues of a man of authority. It is quite a remarkable mirror to hold up, and very much of a piece with current mid-sixteenth-century debate. At the end, an authorial comment is added: 'I think the Earl of Warwick although he were a glorious man, hath said no more of himself than what is true.'[63] These stanzas in the *Mirrour for Magistrates* may well be influenced by the writings and concerns of the 'common wealth men' of a decade or so earlier, of Robert Crowley, John Lever and Sir Thomas Smith. Yet Warwick, it seems, could still be evoked as a model for the aristocratic reformer such as Thomas Seymour, duke of Somerset, who had also espoused that cause in Edward VI's reign.

The modern historian may not be so easily swayed that the earl said no more of himself than that that was true. For a start, the appeal to the public good was not the only rhetoric he employed in his final years. John Vale, who copied them, had no doubt that the articles of the 'only commons' associated with Robin of Redesdale's rising in 1469 were 'devised, made and desired' by Warwick and his allies. These are notable for their threat of deposition by likening the circumstances to those that led to the destruction of Edward II, Richard II and Henry VI. Although the articles express concern for the common weal, the impoverishment of the commons and the collapse of law and order, the burden of the three clauses is the manner in which the named courtiers led by Earl Rivers had seditiously led the king astray. It is more in the tradition of aristocratic complaint against the evil ministers of the crown than the complaint of the true commons for reform of the realm.[64] Moreover, during the long and difficult negotiations with Margaret of Anjou at Angers in July 1470, the burden of Warwick's excuse and answer to the queen was, in the summary we have, that he was prepared to abandon Edward IV and depose him, not because he had neglected the common weal, but because of 'the evil terms that the king has kept him'. His earlier reply to Margaret that his actions a decade earlier were justified on the grounds that she had tried to destroy him and that he had acted in self-defence is a completely different justification, drawing upon the chivalric discourse rather than the discourse of the common weal.[65] Warwick's rhetoric was deployed according to need and circumstance: defence of the common weal, complaint against evil ministers or an affront to his honour.

There is little doubt that Warwick's actions reveal that he pursued his own aggrandizement, that he was aware of the political advantage to be gained by mobilizing popular support, and that he was inconsistent. It is, however, a simplification to insist that Richard Neville whipped up popular dissent merely to further his own ambition or for political advantage. Warwick understood that politics were a public matter, which extended beyond the confines of the court, the houses of parliament and the circles of the landed, clerical and urban elites. He acknowledged the reality of the participation of those who were not gentle. He responded to the pressure of the public more directly and more dramatically than any of his contemporaries. He was no doubt able to make up for the lack of aristocratic support at critical moments by having a 'people's army' at his back. No metamorphosis was required. He was a man capable of taking the unusual path, as his preference for a Francophile foreign policy testifies. It is conceivable that Warwick was sincere in his concern for the common weal, and was not able to act on his beliefs until 1470. It is conceivable, but unlikely. What matters more than his motivation, however, is that he gave voice and credence to an alternative view of politics and of the constitution, in which the commons did not stand afar. He did not just respond to the pressure of the public: he endorsed and validated the idea that political engagement extended beyond the narrow confines of the political elite. He was almost alone of the magnates of his time in recognizing and engaging with this wider political world. Precisely because he was such a powerful and charismatic figure, his espousal of a populist stance presented a profound threat to the political and social order. No wonder there was a reaction after 1471. However, so great was his impact that the memory of Warwick as a man committed to the cause of the true commons persisted in the popular imagination, to emerge again in public discourse in the mid-sixteenth century.

10

The Flower of Manhood

Polydore Vergil, who had probably spoken to men who had known Richard Neville, wrote as follows in respect of the earl on the occasion of the first battle of St Albans:

> He was a young man, not only marvellously adorned with virtues in deed, but also had a special gift, as it were by art, even from his infancy, in the show and setting forth of the same; for his wit was so ready, and his behaviour so courteous, that he was wonderfully beloved of the people. He was also liberal to all men, which helped him much to the attaining thereof. Moreover the haughtiness of his mind [his high-mind], with equal force of body, increased the same popular good will. By reason of which matters, the people were fully persuaded that there was no matter of so great importance which the said Richard was not able to undertake, wherefore he became within a while of such estimation that whither as he was inclined, thither also swayed the more part of the people.[1]

A significant element of Warwick's hold on popular opinion was his contemporary image as the pattern of nobility and an exemplar of chivalry. It was clearly revealed in his own lifetime. Writing early in Edward IV's reign, as we have seen, the author of Bale's Chronicle remarked more than once on Warwick's heroic standing: 'he was named and taken in all places for the most courageous and manliest knight living'; 'all the commonalty of this land ... so repute and take for as famous a knight as was living'.[2]

This viewpoint is reflected in, and was probably influenced by, the representation of Warwick in the Yorkist propaganda of the early 1460s. It is to be found in the verses circulated before the Calais lords landed at Sandwich in June 1460 and posted on the door of Canterbury Cathedral. The lords, readers were assured, were soon to rescue the kingdom, among them

> that noble knyght and floure of manhode, Richard,
> Erle of Warrewyk, sheelde of oure defence.[3]

It was stressed by the Waurin Relation. The anecdote is told that, on boarding ship for the flight to Calais after the rout at Ludford in 1459, Warwick and his party discovered that the captain and crew had not sailed there before. When he saw that his father and others were frightened [*effraer*], he was unabashed. He assured them that if they set sail it would please God and St George to get them safely to port. He took the tiller himself.[4] This image was only enhanced by the victories that followed. And so it was too in the early years of the new reign. Take for instance the poem that begins 'To have in mynde calling to remembraunce', composed perhaps in 1462–3 (Edward was crowned but there was further rebellion). The verses celebrate the Yorkist recovery of their right, but conclude with a prayer to St George and the Virgin to intercede in the present crisis, presumably in the far north.

> He it ys that schal wynne castelle, toune and toure;
> Alle rebellious undyr he schal hem brynge
> Richard the erl of Warwyk, of knyghthode Lodesterre,
> Borne of a stok that evyr schal be trewe,
> Having the name of prowes and manhoode,
> Hathe ay ben redy to helpe and resskewe
> Kyng Edward, in hys right hym to endewe.[5]

He was the guiding star of chivalry, the one on whom all hopes were fixed.

It was an opinion shared initially in Burgundian circles. Chastellain, writing in the mid-1460s, was unstinting in his praise: 'And for certain, among the great men of the world, this man is to be counted one of those, it seems to me, of whom one may write grandly and nobly, as much by reason of their prudence [*sens*] and valour as for their success'. He was a 'gentle knight, full of prudence and with all the virtues' and again a man 'about whom henceforth there will be told marvellous and noble tales, worthy of being forever remembered amongst men'.[6] We have a glimpse of how this perception of the earl was transmitted from England in the letter sent by Lord Hastings to Lannoy on 7 August 1463 describing the recent punitive raid into Scotland by the 'noble et valiant lord' after he had relieved Norham.[7]

A few years later the Burgundians were singing a different tune. In the winter of 1470/1 there was a real fear at the Burgundian court of invasion by the combined forces of Lancastrian England and France. This was first expressed in an outpouring of vitriolic verse and ballads disparaging Warwick, which circulated in the Netherlands in early 1471. 'Where else but to death are you rushing?' wrote Jean Mielot. 'Wherever you come, traitor, to break up the league between brothers [Edward IV and Charles, duke of Burgundy], through strife, deceit, by vice and fraud and snares, your fierceness leads you to folly and the savage Fates are spinning your last thread'.[8] After his defeat and predicted death, a series of satirical chivalric epitaphs mocked the earl, relishing in his overthrow as the just desert for his treachery.[9] But the really vitriolic condemnation came in the pages of Burgundian chronicles composed in the following decade. The continuator of Monstrelet's chronicle refers to his 'cunning treason and diabolic deception [trayson subtile and engen dyabolyque]'.[10] Chastellain now wondered how a king of France could take for a comrade in arms a low-born criminal Englishman so as to undo the house of Burgundy: no more writing grandly and nobly, no more marvellous and noble tales.[11] Jean Molinet focused on his thirst for blood and sowing of discord. Thomas Basin, referring to him dismissively as 'that perfidious man' [ille perfidus]', saw him as an expert in deceit, the ideal instrument for Louis XI. Even Waurin, who had earlier been a great admirer of Warwick, modified his opinion. He now wrote that he was a man without courage, a crude and cunning traitor and claimed to be shocked that such a high prince as he could behave as he did.[12] If there is one thing linking all these texts it is the idea of dishonour. Warwick was now, in short, a disgrace to the ideals of chivalry.

As it transpired, the image of Warwick as a disgrace to the order of chivalry proved impossible to sustain in England. John Rous, in his portraits of the earls and countesses of Warwick, first drawn up, in English, during the reign of Richard III, reverted to the theme of twenty-five years earlier. The earl, whom he had served and whose widowed countess he still served, was 'a famous knight and excellent greatly spoken of throughout the most part of Christendom'. We know where the exception lay. Moreover, despite his end, 'his knightly acts had been so excellent that his noble and famous name could never be put out of laudable memory'.[13] They would *never* be forgotten, Rous might have been thinking, despite the recent efforts of Edward IV. It is perhaps telling that this praise was written after Edward's death and during the reign of his brother Richard, who had spent three years as an impressionable adolescent in the earl's household. One might also suspect that Rous echoed the views of his patron, the countess, who at more or less the same time commissioned the 'Beauchamp Pageant', a homage to her father, the last Beauchamp earl.[14] Had she seen her late husband, as the earl had perhaps seen himself, as the heir to her father's chivalric excellence?

It may not, therefore, only be because Warwick died a loyal Lancastrian and mortal enemy of the house of York, that Tudor accounts honoured him as a chivalric hero. Polydore Vergil, who began to collect information for his history in the first decade of the sixteenth century, spoke to men who had been in exile with Henry VII, as well as the king himself. He tells the story that in 1467 Warwick decided to depose Edward IV and restore Henry VI. In an entirely invented scene and speech he has the earl persuade his brothers, George, archbishop of York, and John, Lord Montagu, to join with him in the cause of the 'holy man', King Henry, whose own son was of great promise in contrast to Edward IV 'given wholly to follow sensuality and already shunning all honest exercise [ie, martial acts]'. Warwick draws attention to the way Edward has disparaged the honour of their house, has forgotten that they exalted him and had recently slighted him 'to the intent that the honourable renown which we have gotten amongst all the nobility of this land, partly by prowess of our parent, partly by our own travail, might be utterly diminished, depased [impaired] and in no reputation'. By linking the honour and renown of Neville lineage to the morally superior cause of Henry VI, Vergil recruited them to the cause of Henry VII, his true successor.[15] Appropriately, in Vergil's pages, Warwick dies a noble death, with no hint of the cowardice to be found in Yorkist or Burgundian-influenced accounts. He delivers a stirring address to his troops before the battle at Barnet, 'to fight for the liberty of their country against a tyrant who had wickedly invaded the royal seat'. In the battle, 'The earl, remembering his renowned virtue and prowess, resisted valiantly', and he is killed fighting manfully. 'This end had Richard earl of Warwick, which after so many sundry chances, happened unto him through haughtiness [highness] of courage long before his time by course of years'. It is, in essence, the version repeated by Hall, in places almost word for word, which became enmeshed in the standard sixteenth-century picture of the earl.[16] Neither traitor nor coward, he was once more the pattern of nobility.

This view reached a wider and popular audience through works such as the *Mirrour for Magistrates*. Drawing on Hall, the author has the earl recount how he loyally served the duke of York 'in feldes right manly fought', and then his son Edward, who achieved his father's ambition of the throne, only to find himself deceived by him. Shocked by a king 'so bent to lust' and so lacking in good faith, he determined to make amends and restore Henry VI. But fortune deserted him and at Barnet he and his brother were slain.[17] They died manfully:

> For we to harten our overmatched men
> Forsoke our stedess, and in the thickest throng,
> Ran preacing furth on foote, and fought so then,
> That down we drave them wer they never so strong.
> But ere this lucke had lasted very long:
> With number and force we were so fowlye cloyed.
> And rescue fayled, that quite we were destroyed.[18]

The enduring English memory of Warwick for decades after his death was as a famous knight.

The question facing the historian is not really whether the earl did, or did not, live up to the highest ideals of chivalry. Warwick was perceived by contemporaries and succeeding generations in terms of chivalry. He was praised or criticized in relation to this set of values. Comments about him in his own lifetime and afterwards were framed by reference to them. One might say that all perceptions of him, friendly and hostile, were part of the chivalric discourse. Polydore Vergil had heard that he had a special gift, as it were by art, in the showing and setting forth of chivalric virtues. If he deliberately modelled and presented himself on the pattern of chivalry, as well he might, he would have drawn upon the treatises that provided instruction and the courtly romances which celebrated chivalry, and with which he would probably have been familiar since his infancy. A romance which he surely knew well, if not since childhood then since he moved into the Beauchamp circle, was 'Guy of Warwick' with its tale of distant travel and stirring feats of arms performed by the legendary founder of the family, which climaxed with him being the saviour of the realm in the reign of King Athelstan. The Guy of Warwick legend remained a potent point of reference for his father-in-law and probably for him himself.[19] The one book with which Warwick is certainly identified was a handsome copy of 'Lenseignement de Vraie Noblesse'. This was one of the standard treatises compiled in the first half of the fifteenth century, drawing heavily on the work of Ramon Lull, which stressed the connection between chivalry, the noble lifestyle and lineage.[20] Warwick's contemporaries are also likely to have used treatises and romances such as these as points of reference. The five different qualities celebrated in romances in the fifteenth century provide a useful peg on which to hang a discussion. They are: 'franchise', the free and independent bearing that is visible testimony to the combination of good birth and virtue; 'courtoise', behaving towards others in the correct, courtly manner; 'largesse', open-handedness, generosity and magnanimity of spirit; 'loyauté', both to those above him and below him; and, above all, 'prowesse', courage, valour, and the performance of feats of arms on the field of battle.[21] Warwick's honour was evaluated in the light of these qualities. What evidence is there of the earl living up to them?

One can be fairly confident that Warwick displayed 'franchise'. His whole career and the admiration in which he was held were to a large extent determined by this. He was independent, even of kings. He first made his mark acting as a free agent without regard to royal authority in command of Calais and keeping the sea in 1457–60. To some extent his exploits then, which instantly won him celebrity and renown, were reminiscent of knight errantry. More dramatic was the very making and unmaking of kings. This was, from a chivalric perspective, the supreme mark of his 'franchise'. The phrase is conventionally credited to the Scottish churchman and historian of Britain, John Major in 1521: 'Of him it was said that he made kings [*regum creator*] and at his pleasure cast them down'.[22] But contemporaries were convinced that he had made Edward IV king. Commynes later said as much in his memoirs: 'The earl of Warwick governed king Edward in his youth and directed his affairs. Indeed, to speak the truth, he made him king and was responsible for deposing King Henry'. So too did Chastellain, who commented that Edward was king by virtue of the earl, and that his fortune and glory at the beginning of his reign owed all to the earl, without whom nothing in the realm was done.[23] There was, too, in Commynes' reminiscences a touch of admiration for the man who had defied kings, as there remained in the heart of his fellow Burgundian, Waurin. This image grew stronger after his death. The Flemish monk, de But, writing in the years 1478–88, considered that the earl behaved like a third king and added, 'I call Richard the 'third king' because in England his reputation was so great that having deposed Henry VI, he made king in his place Edward of York, Earl of March, and then again by his doing Edward was chased away and Henry VI restored'.[24] The same sense of awe at his greatness soon appeared in English accounts. John Rous, who had served him as a chaplain, wrote, in 1483–5, in an encomium, that 'he had all England at his leading and was dreaded [revered] and doughted [considered doughty] through many lands'.[25] There is no ambiguity here. This was praise. The *Mirrour for Magistrates* took it up:

> ...
> hast thou heard or read,
> Of any man that did as I have done?
> That in his time so many armies led,
> And victory at every voyage wunne?
> Hast thou ever heard of subiect under sonne,
> That plaaste and baste his soveraynes so oft,
> By enterchaunge, now low, and than aloft?[26]

From the chivalric point of view, the capacity to act independently of kings, the achievement of having controlled the kingdom, and the power to have been able at his pleasure to cast kings down was treated with awe. They are marks of his greatness in the minds of these contemporaries and near-contemporaries. Kingmaking was admired not condemned: it was the supreme demonstration of Warwick's 'franchise'.

'Courtesy', his personal behaviour in conformity with the aristocratic etiquette of his day can largely be assumed: Waurin, himself deeply imbued in the same values, noted that the earl received him well, meaning in the right form.[27] Two instances concerning the honouring of the dead may be cited. One was the earl's attendance at the funeral of Lord Scales in July 1460. Scales had been murdered by Thames boatmen as he sought to find sanctuary at Westminster Abbey after escaping from the Tower. It was, the author of Gregory's chronicle, ever alert to matters of honour, commented, 'great pity that so noble and so worshipful a knight, and so well approved in the wars of Normandy and France should die so mischiefuously'. Warwick and his father, his enemies that summer, were, according to the Waurin Relation, displeased, and ensured that he was buried with full military honours.[28] More fully documented as a ritual conducted with full chivalric panoply was the re-internment of the bodies of Salisbury himself and his younger son, Thomas, along with the burial of the countess at Bisham on 14 February 1463. The elaborate rituals for the disposing of the dead earl's coats of arms, sword, crest and helm, as well as the customary appearance of a man fully armed on horseback, followed by the offering of the arms and horse to the church, were recorded by the heralds present who had orchestrated proceedings. The account was subsequently adopted as the model for the correct burying of an earl. The event was a display of family power and honour, and was marked by an elaborate roll of arms created at the same time in celebration of the Neville lineage.[29]

'Largesse' is well documented by English and continental contemporaries, who noted the magnificent household kept by the earl and the scale of his generosity. Warwick made a deep impression by the lavishness of his table, both while entertaining Burgundian ambassadors in 1457, keeping open house wherever he travelled, and also most excessively at the enthronement feast of George Neville as archbishop of York at the end of September 1465. On the last occasion, two to three thousand persons participated in a celebration which lasted at least a week and during which approximately 25,000 lbs of beef, just over 24,000 lbs of mutton and about 15,000 lbs of pork were consumed. The guest list included all the great and the good of the north, as well as the mayor of the Calais Staple. This was display on a gargantuan scale, designed to demonstrate the power and wealth of the Neville family, but it was mounted according to the strict protocol of such events.[30] In the summer of 1467, Waurin reported, when the French ambassadors, whom the earl had escorted to England, were snubbed by Edward IV, 'he determinedly maintained his honour, for he entertained them in the grand manner'.[31] Four years later, on Trinity Sunday, 12 June 1469, the commissioning at Sandwich of Warwick's flagship, the *Trinity*, 'de nuovo fieri fecit' [rebuilt or newly built] was conducted in a style which impressed the monks of Canterbury Cathedral Priory, including a service of blessing, sung mass and a lengthy banquet on board. The wedding of Isabel Neville and George, duke of Clarence celebrated at Calais a month later, of which no account has survived, was probably even more extravagant.[32] Warwick did not stint.

Magnanimity of spirit, however, presents a conundrum. Warwick, it has been remarked, was a serial killer. He has been blamed for introducing a new level of brutality into war and politics in the mid-fifteenth century.[33] Beginning with the killing of Somerset, Northumberland and Clifford at St Albans in 1455, it is argued that he did not hesitate to murder his opponents. The execution of Osbert Mountford and two servants by shipmen on the sands of Rysbank in June 1460 has been cited as the first instance of this merciless butchery. When he returned to London after Northampton the following month, he took command of the city, and sat in trial 'for treason' of Sir Thomas Browne and five servants of the duke of Exeter who had reinforced the garrison of the Tower. They were condemned and summarily executed in what was nothing short of a revenge killing.[34] Coppini had already reported to Milan that now the government was in

Warwick's hands it was thought that he would not stay his hand but put to death those that had acted against him.[35] His reputation had run before him. He and his brother John, Lord Montagu were similarly ruthless with a harvest of heads after the final destruction of Lancastrian resistance in Northumberland in 1464. Even Oman, one of his greatest modern admirers, conceded that he was 'reckless in blood'.[36] This was so, although he was not alone.

Chivalry was a code based on violence and recklessness in blood. Both sides were guilty of atrocities. The duke of Exeter had executed ten men at Sandwich in 1460 who were arraigned for sending supplies to Warwick. Sir Thomas Kyriel and Lord Bonville, who had been escorting Henry VI, were summarily executed by the Lancastrians after their victory at the second St Albans, even though, it was said, the king had granted their protection. Accounts favourable to Warwick completed soon after were shocked by the manner in which the king's protection was so callously ignored by the Lancastrian captains.[37] In 1470 the treatment of Warwick's men by the constable, John Tiptoft, was even more shocking to contemporaries. In an attempt to recover his ship the *Trinity* from Southampton in March 1470, several of his leading men, including Richard Clapham, were taken prisoner. Tried and found guilty of treason before the constable's court, they were hanged, drawn, quartered and beheaded. In addition, however, their mutilated bodies were skewered on stakes for display. According to Warkworth, this added indignity caused great offence, for which Tiptoft was 'greatly hated among the people'.[38] This was an increasingly bitter civil war in which tit-for-tat murders and brutality were increasingly common.[39]

Yet Warwick was capable of mercy as well as revengeful killing and summary justice. Sir Thomas Throckmorton, who joined Margaret of Anjou's service in 1457, was taken back into Warwick's service after 1461. Sir William Plumpton was accused of involvement in the murder of the earl's father at Pontefract, yet he was subsequently received into the earl's service.[40] The author of Gregory's Chronicle repeats an anecdote that clearly amused him, but also throws light on Warwick's chivalric credentials. When Pierre de Brézé withdrew with his Franco-Scottish army from Northumberland early in 1463 one man stayed behind, who was a taborer [a drummer], to 'meet with' Warwick. He stood on a hill playing his drum and piping as merrily as he could. Until Warwick came up to him he would not yield his ground. One pictures a man taunting the earl and courageously defying him with his music. There and then, the story continues, he became my lord's man; 'and yet [still] he is with him full good and to his lord'. The earl clearly appreciated such pluck. The story, of course, has the hallmark of a fiction, echoing as it does the chivalry of romance and the flamboyant gesture, but its telling reflects well on Warwick, and in the hands of a man who had a particular interest in martial matters, suggests that it was founded on report.[41]

It may be that Warwick's worst excesses were linked to a sense that the victims deserved their fate because they had been disloyal. Deserters from the Calais garrison had been put to death in the autumn of 1459; Osbert Mountford and his fellow victims might have also have been deserters. He was almost certainly Andrew Trollope's brother-in-law, and was a member of the Calais garrison in 1457 when Warwick took up the post of captain. He seems to have been in England in December 1458 when an order was issued for his arrest, perhaps in connection with the fracas that occurred at Westminster the preceding month. The possibility exists that he was one of those who, with Trollope, deserted Warwick in September 1459.[42] The seriousness with which disloyalty by a trusted servant was treated is revealed in the court martial and degrading execution in 1464 of Sir Ralph Grey, who as a one-time retainer of the house of York had turned his coat.[43] The bitterness with which the earl subsequently pursued Henry, duke of Somerset, might have been linked with the reported promise made by the duke when he surrendered Guînes to Warwick in August 1460 that he would never take up arms against him again.[44] All these touch on the code of chivalry, which might have been seen to justify such brutal responses.

If Warwick were particularly unforgiving and high-handed in relationship to those he believed had betrayed him, the problematic question then arises concerning his own 'loyauté' to his kings. This was a complex political world, in which men on both sides frequently broke their word and betrayed each other. But Warwick stands accused of disloyalty on a grand scale. Treachery and perfidy were the complaints of the Burgundians after 1471. It is hard to deny this. It transpired that he was not born of a stock that would be ever true to Edward IV. Warwick's own defence, which he articulated in the long and difficult negotiations with Margaret of Anjou at Angers in July 1470, was couched in terms of his honour. The burden of his excuse and answer to the queen was, in the summary we have, that he was prepared to abandon Edward IV, and depose him, because of 'the evil terms that the king has kept him'. Edward had dishonoured him. His earlier reply to Margaret that his actions a decade before were justified on the grounds that she had tried to destroy him and that 'there in he had not done but that a noble man outraged and disparaged ('dispeired') ought to have done', is redolent with chivalric righteousness and suggests that he believed that his honour was at stake.[45] This is, in essence, the justification given later by Vergil in the invented speech in which the earl persuades his brothers to join him in rebelling against Edward IV.[46] Moreover, the argument could be mounted, and was indeed implied later, that Warwick, far from betraying Edward IV in 1470, admitted the error of his ways and returned to his first and true lord, for which he made atonement on the field of Barnet.

Finally, and most contested, there is the question of 'prowess'. Warwick, one Yorkist poem proclaimed, had 'the name of prowess and manhood'. And prowess, valour on the field of battle, was at the heart of the chivalric ideal. After his death, however, the story began to circulate that Warwick was a coward. He was accustomed to lead in battle on horseback so as to avoid becoming involved in the fighting. Fifteenth-century English commanders, most notably Henry V, John, duke of Bedford and now Edward IV, as his apologists endlessly stressed, fought on foot alongside their men in the thick of the press. Prowess was demonstrated by trading blows with your enemies, toe to toe. Commynes later drew attention to Warwick's supposed lack of stomach for the battle:

> The earl of Warwick was not used to dismounting to fight for, after bringing his men in to the battle, he used to mount his horse. If the battle was going well for him he would throw himself into the fray, but if it were going badly he would make an early escape.

At Barnet, however, he was counselled by his brother, Montagu, 'who was a very courageous knight', to dismount and send away his horses. 'So it happened the earl was killed this day.'[47] English chroniclers were more circumspect. John Warkworth told a complex tale which has no mention of his supposed preference for hanging back. Montagu attempted to double-cross Warwick, and a man of the earl 'fell upon hiym and killed him. And when the Earl of Warwick saw his brother dead, and the Earl of Oxford fled, he leapt on horse-back, and fled to a wood by the field ... where was no way forth; and one of King Edward's men had spied him, and one came upon him and killed him, and despoiled him naked.'[48] The *Arrivall* was even more restrained; it opted to stress Edward IV's personal courage, merely stating at the end that the earl was killed 'somewhat fleeing'.[49] A popular version in verse on the last campaign, 'On the recovery of the throne by Edward IV', was, however, more explicit. Despite his difficulties Edward drew up his army in battle before Coventry and challenged his enemy to battle. But Warwick was afraid, and his people also.[50]

Warwick fought in five battles on land, four of them in the field and one in the streets of St Albans. He defended Calais over the winter of 1459–60 and he campaigned vigorously in the north of England in the winter of 1462–3 to reduce the Northumbrian castles. It is important to acknowledge that, with the exception of attacks on Genoese, Castilian and Hanseatic fleets in the Channel, he fought only against other Englishmen in civil war. How much he personally engaged in hand to hand fighting, the 'shouting and crying, hewing of harness, hewing of helmets, roaring and rumbling' that was a battle (as written of Barnet) is unknown.[51] It was he who led the assault on the royal party at the first St Albans by breaking through the gardens to the High Street. He was, according to Gregory, 'hurt in his leg with an arrow' in the action forcing the river crossing at Ferrybridge on the day before Towton. We do not, it is true, read of him, as we do of his foe Andrew Trollope on the field of the second St Albans, standing his ground, taking on all comers, and killing fifteen men on the spot.[52] Trollope, one assumes, died endeavouring to repeat the feat on the field of Towton.

It was at sea that Warwick's reputation was made. As a naval commander he was, the Waurin Relation asserts, 'fort, sage et ymaginatif'.[53] On 29 May 1458 he attacked a flotilla of Castilian vessels; later in the summer he took on the Hanseatic bay fleet; in July 1459 he was reported to have attacked five Genoese and Spanish ships; and in June 1460 to have had a running battle with French ships from Dunkirk to Boulogne. These actions won him great fame. No wonder he was hailed that year as the 'Shield of our Defence'. Paston's servant, John Jerningham, participated in the attack on the Spanish fleet on 29 May 1458 and excitedly reported the experience to Margaret Paston three days later. They took on 28 ships with 12 of their own. In the running hand-to-hand battle that followed for six hours about 80 Englishmen were killed and, according to Jerningham, a further two hundred were wounded, but nevertheless the English killed and wounded considerably more Spaniards. No doubt in his excitement Jerningham exaggerated the casualties. For a while he was taken prisoner, but was rescued. Although they eventually came away with six prizes, Jerningham concluded that 'we were well and truly beat'. The author of 'Gough 10' gave slightly different details. Six vessels were sunk off Boulogne, sixteen fled, but were soon overhauled. Many of their people were slain and about 100 English.[54]

It is not certain, however, that Warwick was himself personally involved in all these naval actions. Jerningham reported in 1458 that Warwick had news of the approaching Spanish fleet and then went and manned his twelve ships. On the following day 'we' (the two fleets) met together at four o'clock in the morning (at dawn?). Jerningham did not specifically state that Warwick took personal command on board. The letter from Calais in June 1460 makes it clear that, on some occasions, he did not take to the sea himself, but sent others into action for he 'sent into the see divers carvels and balingers of war', and the writer added, 'thus daily as my lord has any knowledge of an enemy, anon my lord makes his ships to the sea'.[55] His personal engagement, however, is implied in other accounts. 'Gough 10' stated that the earl 'met in the sea' with the Spanish ships in 1458; the author of Bale's Chronicle also reported that in the summer of 1459 'he met in the sea' two great Genoese carracks and three great Spanish ships. The English Chronicle implied also that he fought with them in person. In this engagement, too, Edward Grey wrote to Sir Thomas Findern, six or seven gentlemen of his household with divers other yeomen (also of his household) lost their lives.[56]

Bale was right, too, to identify Warwick and his men as performing great feats of arms at this action in July 1459. For, with the exception of the Grace Dieu and the Trinity the earl had only small ships, balingers and carvels, at his disposal. Only the two great ships were big enough and equipped to chase, bombard, grapple with and then board the carracks and great ships of Spain. Despite the odds, and at some cost in lives, he took one carrack and the three great ships, as well as breaking the mast of the other carrack that escaped. The same courage and daring was shown in the battle reported by Jerningham the previous year, of which 'as men say there was not so great a battle upon the sea this 40 winters' (that is since the battle of the Seine in 1416). According to Jerningham, in this action Warwick's men took on sixteen great ships of the forecastle in the Spanish fleet with but five ships of the forecastle of their own. Against such odds no wonder there was such loss of life and, as Jerningham concluded, the English came off the worse. It is in these two actions that Warwick won his chivalric reputation. One can be reasonably certain, because of the fame that Warwick won on account of them that he was personally engaged.[57] Ten years later, in the summer of 1470, according to the Chronicle of Flanders, he was once more at the head of a large and evil company of pirates from England, who fought the Rochelle fleet of Flemings, Dutchmen and Zeelanders in a fierce battle on 20 April 1470, in which he captured forty ships. Another fight with Hollanders occurred off Cap Gris Nez on 29 May. Eventually, the chronicler recorded, he was routed and driven ashore in Normandy by the Burgundian fleet, captained by Hendrick van Borsele, lord of Veere. His courage was particularly noted even by this hostile chronicler, who was moved to acknowledge that in September 1470 he bravely risked going to sea in a terrible storm.[58]

There was no choice of holding back from the fighting at sea. Was the accusation that he kept a safe distance on horseback when fighting on land a libel? It could hardly have been the case that he was on horseback at the first St Albans when he led his troops through the gardens. The account of the battle of Northampton given in the Waurin Relation clearly implies that he fought on foot at the head of his battalion, 'hand to hand' for three hours. No doubt there is poetic licence over the duration of the mêlée, but we are to be left in no doubt that Warwick was in the thick of it. Even though it was written to cast a favourable light on the earl, the author is unlikely to have invented his personal engagement. The Burgundian, de But, conceded that Warwick dismounted to fight on foot at Towton.[59] Either the wound in the leg received the previous day, as reported by Gregory, was too slight to matter, or he displayed commendable endurance. However, Warwick escaped, presumably on horseback, from his first major defeat at the second St Albans.

Gregory's Chronicle gives an expert assessment of what went wrong that day. While the victors were in substance experienced soldiers, those under the earl's command were mainly new men of war, levies and footmen from the counties who had rallied to Warwick a few months earlier. They 'lacked good guiding [leadership]'; everything on the Yorkist side was 'sick and out of order'. They took up, and then abandoned, a good position, the scouting was incompetently conducted, the guns, of which there were many, were poorly positioned, and other engines of war placed to protect the archers did not work effectively and did more to impede than to help them.[60] Others remarked on the chaos in Warwick's army at the second St Albans. The *English Chronicle* drew attention to the 'indisposition of the people of the King's side [i.e. Warwick's], that would not be guided nor governed by their captains'.[61] And news sent to Milan immediately after the defeat stressed that Warwick's men lacked fortitude, and that the leadership of the earl of Arundel and duke of Norfolk was inadequate.[62] On 9 March, Prospero Camulio from France gave a further gloss. Some of Warwick's men deserted and the earl was worn down. He decided to quit the field and thus fought his way back towards the town with 4,000 men (his own, no doubt in reality much smaller, retinue) but then found himself facing even more of the enemy. Trapped, and fearing more treason, he got away as best he could. The account is garbled, but confirms Gregory's statement that it was only 'through great labour' (that is by fighting) that he escaped from the debacle.[63] These accounts do not suggest lack of personal courage, whether on foot or on horseback.

If Warwick did remain on horseback it is possible to put a different gloss on it. Edward Hall writing in the mid-sixteenth century commented, though with what foundation one cannot tell, in respect of Barnet that, 'the earl of Warwick, which was wont ever to ride on horseback, from place to place, from rank to rank, comforting his men, was persuaded to relinquish his horse and try the extremity by hand strokes'.[64] One might note that, fourteen years after Barnet, both Richard III and Henry VII commanded their troops at Bosworth on horseback, standing slightly apart from the main battles. The loser in that battle, whatever else was said of him, was not accused of cowardice. Commanding on horseback in the manner described by Hall later became the accepted practice of generals. It is conceivable, if Hall had heard correctly, that the story of the earl's cowardice, which was surely unfounded, derived from him being one of the first to adopt this practice, in sharp contrast to the more traditional practice of Edward IV.

If we may doubt the charge of cowardice, in the light of defeats at both the second St Albans and Barnet, we might, however, question Warwick's effectiveness as a commander in the field. There is evidence that he was capable of conducting a successful campaign. John Paston III's letter home on 11 December 1462 gives a vivid report of the reduction of the Northumberland castles. The sieges had begun the day before. Alnwick was invested by the earl of Kent and Lord Scales; Dunstanburgh by Worcester and Sir Ralph Grey; Bamburgh by Montagu and Lord Ogle. Warwick was based at Warkworth from which he coordinated the action. 'He rides daily to all these castles to oversee the sieges; and if they want victuals, or any other thing, he is ready to purvey it for them to his power'. The king was at Durham. He had placed the duke of Norfolk, in whose company Paston was serving, in charge of supplying the army from Newcastle. Only the previous day they had taken victuals and ordinance up to Warkworth.[65] Paston seems to have been impressed. Warwick's attention to detail is revealed in the letter he wrote to Edward IV from Newcastle, probably later in 1463, advising the king of the importance of logistics, having a powerful train of artillery and ammunition, and purveying sufficient victuals in advance if he were to undertake an invasion of Scotland.[66] It is not clear that Edward IV needed a lecture from the earl on these matters, but the letter shows that Neville was fully aware of what was needed to mount a campaign.

Warwick, the campaign to recover the castles in December/January 1462–3 also reveals, was fully conversant with the code of warfare. Warkworth, who may have drawn on local memory, remarked that when the Scots did finally appear before Alnwick to relieve the castle, Warwick's army 'removed from the siege and were afraid; and the Scottish host supposed that it had been done for some gain, and they were afraid'. However, he continued, had the Scots attacked, they might have routed the English who had been so long in the field (a month) and 'were grieved with cold and rain, that they had no courage to fight'.[67] And so the garrison came out of the castle and left with the relieving army. It may well be that a month-long campaign in northern Northumberland in the middle of winter had taken its toll, but Warwick's action was in fact consistent with the convention of a day having been fixed for the relief of a siege. If the enemy appeared, the besiegers drew up in battle plan to await their attack. This was how it was done. It was not in his interest to attack the relieving army: he drew up in defensive array, challenging *them* to attack *him*. That terms were agreed for the surrender of the castle and the safe and honourable withdrawal of the garrison was standard practice. There was no need to impugn cowardice on the English side. Warwick achieved his objective without further loss of life.

The earl showed considerable interest in artillery, perhaps acquired during his first extended stay at Calais in 1456–8: Calais was well provided with guns. Some of this ordinance was brought over to England in 1460. The author of Bale's Chronicle observed the duke of York and earl of Salisbury set out from London to restore order in the north in December, followed by 'one called Lovelace, a gentleman of Kent, with great ordinance of guns'. These were the guns deployed somewhat ineptly at the second battle of St Albans. Warwick employed a gunner at Carlisle in 1462; he kept an arsenal at Middleham. He recovered his artillery at Bristol, abandoned there six months earlier, in September 1470. These guns were deployed at Barnet, but again to little effect. The earl's interest in artillery and his attempt, if largely unsuccessful, to use them in the field is clear.[68] It is apparent, however, that as a general he stood in stark contrast to Edward IV. Warwick was the more cautious, more deliberate, and more innovative, but ultimately less successful; Edward was the more daring, more decisive, and always led from the front in personal combat, carrying all before him in his battles. At sea, on the other hand, Warwick seems to have shown more of these qualities and to have been more at home. He should perhaps be remembered as a competent, if cautious, general, but as a daring sea captain.

It is difficult to reach the bottom of any chivalric reputation in the fifteenth century; much of it lay, as Vergil observed, in the art of self-fashioning. Even contemporary, or near contemporary, reports of feats of arms, displays of prowess, or demonstrations of honour, were fictionalized in the telling. Having the *name* for prowess, being *reputed* a famous knight, being *taken for* the manliest knight living was tantamount in itself to being so. Chivalry was mainly about performance, reputation and image, rather less about the substance that lay behind it.[69] There is inevitably a degree of circuitousness. But there can be little doubt that in Warwick's lifetime and for generations to come, embittered Burgundian commentators aside, he was indeed taken to be the model of chivalry. We need also to remember that in all ages there is usually a contradiction between the ideals by which prominent men are expected to guide their lives, the way they are represented (and represent themselves) as having done so, and the realities of the actions they take. Chivalry as a code was no exception. Warwick was unsurprisingly a flawed hero. Contemporaries were fully aware of the difficulty of living up to its ideals and the contrast between them and reality. The greatest of English works on chivalry, Thomas Malory's *Morte D'Arthur*, composed during Warwick's lifetime, and with the predicaments facing the earl and his contemporaries in mind, is just such an exploration of its inherent limitations and contradictions. It may also contain cryptic reference to Richard Neville.

The work, completed in the ninth year of Edward IV's reign (4 March 1469– 3 March 1470), when Sir Thomas Malory was a prisoner in Newgate, is a compilation with some authorial interpolations undertaken from four French and two English sources recounting the tales of various knights.[70] It is given some degree of unity and a common narrative structure by Malory, especially in its final book, by a focus on the final years of Arthur himself. It purports to be a history, in the sense that the author adopts the pose of retelling of what had really happened. It is however, through its fictions, a discourse on knighthood, as an ideal and in practice. On one level, it is an account of a legendary lost world; on another it is a lament for the debased and fallen times in which the author lived; and on yet another, especially in its last pages, it is a recognition that knighthood never lives up to its ideal and that the best end for all knights is to hang up their harness and retreat from the world into a hermitage or monastery. Although this was a well-established trope concerning the relationship between knighthood and religion, it nevertheless recognizes the ultimate hollowness of the military code of chivalry as well as the contradictions inherent in its highest ideals.

The date of completion, attested by the author himself, his own connections with the earl of Warwick and his tantalizing contemporary references have given rise to speculation that it contains allusions to the politics of the recent past and that it is, in some respects, an allegory of his times. But if this is so, in what respect?

It seems to be accepted that the author was Sir Thomas Malory of Newbold Revel, Warwickshire. He served under the earl of Warwick in the Northumberland campaign of the winter of 1462–3, but in whose company it is not known. Sir Thomas was a man with a violent and disruptive record, who spent two long periods in prison because of his crimes, during the second of which he wrote the work.[71] He was a member of the higher ranks of gentry society, though how typical he was of the mid-fifteenth century is hard to know. He fits one stereotype of the violent lawlessness of the era, but the weight of modern scholarship has led historians to suppose that in reality, in this respect, he was untypical. He was also, self-evidently, literate and well-read in chivalric romance. In the twenty-first century we find it difficult to accommodate a cultured thug. But we need to grasp that in the fifteenth century there was no such contradiction in terms: chivalry was a cult of violence, it celebrated it. If the author was Sir Thomas of Newbold, we know that he had been a retainer of the earl, although he seems to have left his service in the mid-1460s. The generation from which those who served and fought with Warwick were drawn was accustomed to taking the law into its own hands. It could be argued that they brought their chivalric values, earlier in the century exercised by their fathers on the fields of France, into domestic affairs. The Paston Letters, and the tribulations of that family in Norfolk between 1440 and 1475, reveal that violence was one of the accepted means of pursuing a claim to property. Indeed, one particularly violent associate, Thomas Dennis, who was murdered in 1461, had like Malory fought for Warwick. Not everyone behaved as Malory or Dennis did, but few were shocked by them.[72]

Perhaps the work itself, and especially its final pages, completed in the second of his long periods of imprisonment, represent the author's own coming to terms with the mismatch of his own violent actions and the ideals of the order to which he professed to belong by his knighthood. It may be of importance that it was written between 1468 and 1470, years of renewed uncertainty and political conflict in which, of course, Warwick was a major player. It is by no means certain why Malory was incarcerated again in the late 1460s and was specifically excluded from the two general pardons of 14 July 1468 and 22 February 1470. One interpretation is that he was caught up in the Lancastrian plotting which surfaced in 1467. Peter Field, who like others before him supposed that he was a prisoner in the Tower, argued that he was imprisoned in 1468, without charge, in connection with the Cornelius conspiracy, and was the only conspirator who did not secure a pardon.[73] Anne Sutton has more recently argued that since he was imprisoned in the Newgate his offence was less than treason, probably for further offences such as assault and forcible entry, or serious trespasses of such nature, for which Newgate was the customary prison.[74] But imprisonment in Newgate rather than the Tower on a lesser charge, or no charge (for no evidence of a charge exists) does not necessarily preclude suspicion of treason. In 1471 Sir

Walter Wrottesley, one of Warwick's principal lieutenants, who had negotiated a pardon with Edward IV, was arrested on a trumped up-charge of debt, committed to the Fleet and died there in 1473. He, like Malory, was buried at the Greyfriars. In truth we do not know why it was so important to keep Malory in prison, even perhaps after the Readeption. His offences, whatever they were, seem to have been equally embarrassing to Edward IV and to Warwick. We do know, however, that the work was completed by 3 March 1470,[75] *before* Warwick became a Lancastrian again, and *before* the author knew of the Lincolnshire Rising and its consequences. In other words, it was finished before the breakdown between Edward IV and Warwick was complete, but during the period when their relationship deteriorated to the point of breakdown.

Malory adapted the Arthurian stories for an English setting as well as for English readers. He made specific references to English locations and to the England familiar to his readers.[76] The key passage in which Malory reveals that he is aware of a correlation between the legendary world he is recreating and his own times comes towards the end of the last book. He tells how, when King Arthur was in France fighting a great war against Sir Lancelot, Sir Mordred, whom he had left as his regent (he identifies him as chief ruler of England), usurped the throne and, claiming that Arthur was dead, sought to marry Guinevere, who refused. Arthur made peace in France and returned to recover his throne. It is worth recounting the passage in full:

> Then came there word unto Sir Mordred that King Arthur had raised the siege from Sir Lancelot and was coming homeward with a great host to be avenged upon Sir Mordred. Sir Mordred made writs unto all the barons of this land, and much people drew unto him. For then was the common voice among them that with King Arthur there was never other but war and strife, and with Sir Mordred was great joy and bliss. Thus was King Arthur depraved and evil said of. And many there were that King Arthur had brought up of nought, and given them lands, that might not then say him a good word. Lo ye Englishmen, see ye not what a mischief there was here? For he that was the most king and noblest knight of the world, and most loved the noblest fellowship of noble knights, and by him they were all upheld, and yet might not these Englishmen hold them content with him. Lo thus was the old usages of this land: and men say that we of this land have not yet lost that custom and usages of this land. Alas, this is a great default of us Englishmen, for there may nothing please us no term.[77]

The people were better pleased with Sir Mordred than King Arthur at this time. 'The most part of all England', he continued, 'held with Sir Mordred, the people were so new fangle'.[78] Battles followed which King Arthur won. Fortune swung: people returned to Arthur and said that Sir Mordred's war on him was wrong. A third battle was to be fought. Sir Mordred raised many people in the south-eastern counties, and those that loved Sir Lancelot threw in their lot with Sir Mordred. The night before the battle Sir Gawain came to Arthur in a dream and warned him that should he fight he would be slain; rather, he should come to an accord with Mordred, for within a month Sir Lancelot would come to him with all knights, rescue him and slay Sir Mordred. So, the following day, an accord was reached in which Sir Mordred was to have Cornwall while Arthur lived, but after his death all England. But the accord collapsed and they fought: Mordred was slain, but Arthur received what ultimately proved to be his mortal wound. 'Ah Sir Lancelot', said King Arthur, 'this day have I sore missed thee. And alas that ever I was against thee, for now I have my death'. From this moment Arthur prepared for his end. He returned his sword to the lake and withdrew to the vale of Avalon where he died, while his one remaining knight, Sir Bevidere, became a hermit and Queen Guinevere withdrew to the nunnery at Amesbury. When Lancelot returned, he found Guinevere and Bevidere in their retreats, and he too, proclaiming, 'Alas, who may trust this world', joined the hermitage.[79]

Malory invites his readers to draw a contemporary comparison between the events in his tale, especially the relationships between King Arthur, Sir Mordred, Sir Lancelot and recent happenings in England. The problem lies in determining what comparison he had in mind. It is not difficult to find broad parallels. It has been proposed, for instance, that the work contains a parable about what happens to a kingdom divided against itself, especially when there is dissension among the peers. Gawain, Lancelot and Mordred, each in his turn is presented as an over-mighty subject. Arthur is faced with the dilemma of having to choose between two over-mighty subjects, and makes the wrong choice.[80] It has been argued more specifically that Malory figured Arthur as Edward IV.[81] Certainly in respect to Edward's penchant for the Arthurian cult, his own military skills and his promotion of jousting, one can see that Edward himself might well have done so. But the text hardly supports such an interpretation.

It could be argued that there was some correspondence between Mordred and Warwick, especially his popularity in the south-east and his complaint that under Arthur there had been nothing but strife, reflecting almost verbatim the earl's propaganda of 1469. But it is equally true of Richard of York and the 1450s. More tellingly, however, no contemporary reader with any knowledge of recent history could fail to note that York, like Mordred, had been 'regent' in the king's 'absence', that he had attempted to usurp the throne, that an accord had been agreed in which he became the heir to the throne and granted the patrimony of the prince of Wales (which included Cornwall), that the accord had failed, that York had been killed and that the king had been incapacitated. It can be objected that Henry VI was no Arthurian figure. He was hardly 'the most king and noblest knight of the world, and most loved the noblest fellowship of noble knights'.[82] Yet John Vale, the servant of Sir Thomas Cook who was caught up in

Lancastrian conspiracy and accused of treason in the summer of 1468, and was one of the witnesses alongside Malory to the deathbed testimony of Thomas Mynton in the gaol on 29 April 1469, expressed a high opinion of the king in his short chronicle of the reign from his coronation to his death. He was, he wrote, 'right glorious and royal many of those years he reigned in great nobility, worship, wealth and prosperity' until he was ruled by those who were not of blood royal but 'brought up of nought' which caused not only his 'fall most dolorous', but also execrably 'many and divers great mischiefs, losses, insurrections and civil battles'.[83] Moreover, it could well be argued that Malory had not just Henry VI in mind, but the Lancastrian dynasty as a whole, including the heady days of Henry V and Henry VI's early minority, when indeed, in retrospect, the kingdom had seemed to enjoy once more the legendary days of Arthur.[84]

If this is so, the allusions to recent events could be said to have ended with the death of Mordred (York) and the incapacity of Arthur (the Lancastrian dynasty), in 1461. But it is hardly surprising that a man so untrustworthy as to be excluded from two general pardons, whatever his offence, would refrain from making any allusion to events after Edward IV came to the throne that might be construed as a criticism of the reigning king. Moreover, when the work was completed in 1469–70, it surely looked as though there was little possibility of a revival of Lancastrian fortunes. Readers still loyal to Lancaster could always hope that Arthur had not died, but was in another place whence he would come again. And certainly it could have been said with Henry VI in mind: 'Yet I will not say that it shall be so: but rather I would say, here in this world he changed his life'.[85] Mentally by this time, he was indeed in another place. The notion that Henry VI, whilst here in this world, had changed his life when he suffered his first bout of mental illness became an established facet of the burgeoning belief in the king's sanctity.

Where in all this could Warwick have stood? It has been proposed that Malory perceived him as another Lancelot, whose prowess makes him the paragon of knighthood.[86] Lancelot, let us not forget, is also deeply flawed. He betrays Arthur in his affair with Guinevere. He makes war against him. When Mordred first deposes Arthur, the most part of his knights support Mordred, but Lancelot declares he will never fight personally against Arthur; only other knights, especially Sir Gawain over whom he triumphs. His principal quarrel is with Gawain. Even in his treason he never disparages Arthur's honour. He is not responsible for the downfall of the round table. Lancelot ultimately repents his betrayal and makes atonement, although he is too late to save Arthur. His life ends in penance. This uncannily reflects Warwick's own version of his actions in 1459–61, before his defeat at the second battle of St Albans, and his fateful decision to support the deposition of Henry VI. His personal quarrel with Somerset, not the king, was highlighted by contemporary commentators.[87] Furthermore, it might not be entirely fanciful to see Guinevere as standing for the kingdom to which Arthur is married, the realm over which he exercises sovereignty.[88] If so, her adultery with Lancelot could take on a coded meaning as a reference to Warwick's popularity and representation of himself as the champion of the true commons of England. Lancelot excused himself to the king in these words:

> How be it, it hath liked her [Guinevere] good grace to have me in favour and cherish me more than any other knight; and unto my power again I have deserved her love, for oftentimes, my lord, ye have consented that she should have been burnt and destroyed in your heat, and then it fortuned me to do battle for her' ... 'And at such times, my lord Arthur ... ye loved me and thanked me when I saved your queen from the fire, and then ye promised me for ever to be my good lord. And now methinketh ye reward me evil for my service'.[89]

No allusion is straightforward. The fire to which the fictional Guinevere would have been committed would have been her punishment for her adultery. The fire to which England might have been subjected could be construed as the feared punishment on the rebellious commons of Kent in 1450, or French attacks on England, against which Warwick had valiantly protected the kingdom. The relationship between Warwick, his allegiance to the king and the commons was complex, just as the relationship between Lancelot, Arthur and Guinevere was complex. It is not utterly impossible that Malory had such memories of the 1450s in mind as he looked back to the fall of the house of Lancaster. If thus Malory was inviting readers to see near contemporary parallels in the tale he weaves in the last two books, it might be that he wished us to see Henry VI as a sadly incapacitated Arthur, York as Mordred and Warwick, a Lancastrian at heart, as Lancelot, the very pattern of chivalry. However, Malory would have been indulging in wishful thinking about the earl's ultimate repentance and atonement for his betrayal.

The *Morte D'Arthur* is a work of literature, which one reads as a historical parable at one's peril. It is allegorical and allusive. One might suppose, though, that its threnody for the collapse of chivalric fellowship and despair concerning the inability of the author's contemporaries to live together in peace reflects not only recent happenings, but also the longer turn of events since the reign of Henry V. The tragedy of Lancastrian England was the manner in which the fellowship created by Henry V disintegrated. Malory was looking back over his lifetime, not just the last decade. More significant, perhaps, is the portrayal of the anguish of the world. Rights are seen to lie on different sides. The players are all too limited human beings caught up in the dissolution of a world that they cannot fully comprehend or handle. Actions stem from a mixture of high and low motives. Perhaps this is where the real insight lies. If we think of the author in his relatively comfortable imprisonment, aware of political events as he worked on his version of the Arthurian tales, one can perhaps see that he was composing a non-judgemental contemplation of a tragedy unfolding, the outcome of which he would not live to see.

Warwick fits into the tangled and world-weary view of chivalry encapsulated in the *Morte D'Arthur*. He was at the centre of the chivalric discourse in the mid-fifteenth century. It may be that the contradictions implicit in his career and behaviour helped bring home to some contemporaries the shortcomings of the chivalric ideal as an ideology for political society. Excessively praised earlier in his career by English and Burgundian commentators alike, he was viciously condemned by some of his erstwhile admirers at its end. Malory, the author of the *Morte D'Arthur*, did not see things so starkly in black and white. Even if it does not contain coded allusions to Warwick and recent history, the book's tone provides a key to a more nuanced perception of Richard Neville as the flower of manhood.

11

Conclusion

Warwick died at the age of 42. His last will and testament has not survived. His surviving executors, of whom presumably Archbishop George Neville was the most senior, seem not to have been able to secure probate. John Rous, possibly another executor, noted that in his testament he bequeathed his body to be buried in St Mary's Warwick, alongside his father-in-law, but that 'for all that', he was buried at Bisham.[1] It seems that Rous was right about his intention, for in 1463 Warwick had secured a licence to add to the endowment of the chapel, and in 1469 conveyed property there to establish another chantry for the soul of Richard Beauchamp. Under the same licence he also added to the Despenser endowment at Tewkesbury and the college at the original Beauchamp seat of Elmley. He identified strongly with the lineage and associations of his earldom and the person of his celebrated predecessor.[2] It is possible, too, that provision for his own soul included lavish post-mortem endowment. If so, a significant proportion is likely to also have been directed at the Beauchamp foundations, especially the new chapel at St Mary's and the chantry at Guy's Cliffe.

The fabric of the magnificent Lady Chapel had largely been completed by Richard Beauchamp's executors before Richard Neville entered the inheritance. However, it took another fifteen years to provide the fittings and furnishings. Besides the choir stalls, lecterns and reredos, the principal fitting was a bronze-gilt tomb for his father-in-law, with its distinctive hearse at the very centre of the chapel. The tomb chest was commissioned in 1447; the contract for the lattern hearse made in 1454. Work was still being done on it in 1457 when payments were made to the marbler, founder and coppersmith. The tomb was probably not finished until 1459; the final payments for all fittings not made until 1464. The chapel then lay empty. It was not until 1475 that it was consecrated and the remains of Richard Beauchamp translated. As we have seen, Neville worked closely with the trustees who were responsible for the building of the chapel.[3] They seem to have seen themselves as answerable to him. Neville's influence can perhaps be detected in the tomb itself. He is portrayed along with other mourners on its side. Over half of the shields identifying the mourners include the arms of Neville, but the pace of work slowed down significantly under his stewardship. One reason may have been the early uncertainty over Neville's position as earl; another might have been a desire not to wind-up the trust precipitately because some of the property would revert to Anne Neville's elder sisters. And it is puzzling that, while he ensured that his own father was lavishly reburied at Bisham, he did not show the same zeal in undertaking the reburial of his countess's father.[4]

Richard Neville may have been more interested in Guy's Cliffe. John Rous, who as one of the chantry priests there had reason to know, noted that he 'purposed to have endowed' Guy's Cliffe for more priests and distressed gentlemen (that is transform it into a collegial almshouse on the model of St Cross at Winchester), to have vaulted and buttressed the cave there which was in danger of falling in, and to have had an image of Sir Guy painted in it. The painting would have been in addition to the statue, which still exists, which was already there. His intention was to build on Richard Beauchamp's foundations. He had converted the hermitage into a chantry with two priests, and had provided in his will for the building of a chapel; the tower was completed in 1449–50.[5] While these ambitions to add significantly to his father-in-law's plan did not materialize, they suggest a more personal involvement than with the Lady Chapel. Rous was not moved to record any planned post-mortem northern bequests of a similar character, but St William's College, York, founded in association with George Neville, was perhaps his most significant endowment during his life. In 1461 the college received licence to acquire lands to the value of £100 p.a. for its endowment.[6]

In 1465 Warwick additionally received licence to endow a chantry at the church of Olney in Buckinghamshire for a priest to say prayers for the souls of himself, his countess and the king.[7] His widow lived until 1492. Having landed at Weymouth in the train of Margaret of Anjou on the day of his death, she hastened into sanctuary at Beaulieu Abbey. There she was kept for two years under guard, pleading to whoever would listen for their support in securing her release and the restoration of her rights. At length, in 1473, she was taken into the care of Richard of Gloucester, who had married her daughter Anne, and was removed to Middleham Castle, where she was probably able to live a more normal life, but still denied her rights. She was disinherited by Edward IV so that his brothers could share the spoils of the Warwick inheritance. Only after the succession of Henry VII did she receive any kind of justice, and that on the condition that she 'voluntarily' made over her inheritance to the crown. Little is otherwise known of her. She seems to have been close to her husband, although this did not prevent him fathering at least one illegitimate child. She shared his exiles with him in 1459–60 and 1470, though it appears she did not enjoy living in Calais. In the summer of 1460 it was reported that 'my lady of Warwick comes but little abroad but keeps her always in the castle'.[8] She was a great promoter of her father's name and reputation, commissioning the Beauchamp Pageant later in her life, and may well have encouraged her husband to identify with the Beauchamp traditions in the early years of his earldom, although after 1460 he balanced this with his inherited Neville interests. She was much admired by John Rous, who was of the same age. He stressed in his note on her that she was by true inheritance countess of Warwick and that she had suffered great tribulation for her lord's sake (as she had). He picked out that she was 'free of her speech to every person familar [i.e. of her household, and presumably especially him] according to her and their degree'. He recorded too that she was glad to be with women that 'travailed of child' and was 'full comfortable and plenteous there of all things that should be helping to them'.[9]

She and Richard Neville had but two daughters: Isabel, born in 1451, who married Clarence, and Anne, born in 1456, who was married to Edward, Prince of Wales. It is perhaps because after 1465 Warwick despaired of producing a male heir that he became obsessed with making first one and then the other of his daughters queen of England, an ambition he was to achieve posthumously when the younger became queen as the consort of the third Yorkist king, Richard III. His grandson and granddaughter, the children of Duchess Isabel, both met violent ends. Edward, earl of Warwick was incarcerated by Henry VII and met his death on the block in 1501, accused of having dabbled in treason with the captive Perkin Warbeck. It was said that he was simple, but he was probably just unworldly, having spent most of his life in close confinement. His sister, the countess of Salisbury, was executed by a vengeful and insecure Henry VIII when she was in her eighties. Warwick's male heir, his nephew George, duke of Bedford, the son of John Neville, Marquess Montagu, was disinherited and died aged 18 while in the care of Richard, duke of Gloucester. The residual heir to the Neville estates, Richard, Lord Latimer, accepted that he would not be allowed to make a claim. Thus after 1483, when Richard III became king, most of the great Neville inheritance reverted to the crown.

What lived on was Warwick's reputation, initially sustained by his widow and her chaplain John Rous. The admiration of many contemporaries for Warwick as an exemplar of chivalry, and the awe in which his achievements were held by them, lasted long after his death. Men continued to write grandly and nobly of this great man of the world for a further three centuries. Shakespeare was one of those who henceforth, in Chastellain's words, told marvellous and noble tales of him.[10] He created a portrait of Warwick firmly grounded in this heroic tradition in *Henry VI, Parts 2 and 3*, in which the earl is presented as the pattern of true nobility. In his very first appearance, Salisbury's 'valiant son' bewails the surrender of Maine in 1446:

> Those provinces these arms of mine did conquer;
> And are the cities that I got with wounds,
> Deliver'd up again with peaceful words?[11]

The dramatist neatly conflates him with his father-in-law, merging the reputations of both earls of Warwick into one fictitious person. It is this composite 'great Warwick' that inspires and holds the Yorkists together following the duke of York's death. After defeating the Lancastrians at Towton, Warwick declares that he will lead Edward IV to London to be crowned king and then immediately be off to France to arrange for his marriage.[12]

Shakespeare's reduction of the subsequent action into little more than six months is also significant. In three quick scenes he moves the action from the coronation, through the capture of Henry VI, the marriage to Elizabeth Woodville, to France, where Warwick is negotiating with Louis XI for the hand of Bona of Savoy as Edward's queen. Messengers arrive bearing news of Edward's wedding to Elizabeth Woodville. Warwick is infuriated and immediately switches sides. He has been dishonoured, he proclaims,

> And to repair my honour lost for him,
> I here renounce him and return to Henry.

Thus he declares

> I was the chief that raised him to the crown,
> And I'll be chief to bring him down.

Yet then, at the end his true motive is revealed;

> Not that I pity Henry's misery
> But seek revenge on Edward's mockery.[13]

He had been ill-used.

The sudden change of heart is a Damascene moment. By eliding nine years from 1461 to 1470 into but a few months, Shakespeare enhances the sense that Warwick, a man of honour and pride who suddenly saw the error of his ways in temporarily deserting the house of Lancaster, was not truly a Yorkist. His Yorkist association becomes a momentary aberration. This sense is enhanced by the conflation of him with his father-in-law who had been Henry VI's own guardian and tutor. And so Edward is forthwith deposed by Warwick; in stage time he has hardly been on the throne a year. Warwick returns to England and greets Edward as duke of York and tells him he is not fit to be a king.[14]

Thereafter, as the action unfolds, the earl moves to his honourable and courageous death, the punishment for his short-lived desertion of Lancaster, musing in the manner of the time on the emptiness of earthly fame and wealth. He remembers the power he once wielded:

> For who lived king, but I could dig his grave?
> And who durst smile when Warwick bent his brow?
> Lo, now my glory smeared in dust and blood!

My parks, my walks, my manors that I had,
Even now forsake me, and of all my lands
Is nothing left me but my body's length.
Why, what is pomp, rule, reign, but earth and dust?
And, live how we can, yet die we must.[15]

The composite Warwick is truly the hero of *Parts 2 and 3* of *Henry VI*, another tragic chivalric hero, brought low by the debased times in which he lived. In a realm of inadequate kings, it is the great aristocrat who takes the helm. Although he found fault with Edward IV for failing 'to study for the people's welfare',[16] he was not, however, in Shakespeare's script, the champion of the commons. This aspect of the legend, prominent in the mid-sixteenth century had been expunged. Only fleetingly is it subsequently recalled.

In the seventeenth and eighteenth centuries, especially after 1660 with the emergence of England as an aristocratic oligarchy, his status as an exemplar of the aristocratic ideal became embedded. His earliest biographer, Thomas Gainford, in his *Unmatchable Life* published between 1618 and 1624 described him as 'Great by reason of his hospitality, riches, possessions, popular love, comeliness of gesture, gracefulness of person, industrious of valour, indefatigable, paynstaking'. Some of these attributes Gainford seems to have invented, but he paints him as the perfect aristocrat.[17] Thomas Carte took up and repeated the theme of Warwick's popularity. The wealthiest and most powerful man in the realm, 'he deserved all the popularity he enjoyed'.[18] It was, however, the early eighteenth-century French historian of England, Paul de Rapin de Thoyras, whose history was translated and widely circulated, who best captured this sense of aristocratic admiration for the great earl. He stressed his personal courage. He elaborates a story that at Towton he killed his horse and kissed the hilt of his sword and swore that, though the whole army should take to flight, he alone would defend the king's (Edward IV's) cause.[19] He was the proudest lord that had ever been in England. That is, he stood out the most. Pride in this sense was justified and ennobling. The contempt shown to him by Edward IV was an affront to his dignity (literally an affront to his dignity as a great lord), which 'much increased his disgust'. Edward IV's attempt on the chastity of one of his daughters, found first in Vergil and taken up by Hall, Rapin's principal source, if true, gave him a stronger reason to have hated Edward. Thus it was that the earl 'had the honour of restoring Henry to the throne, after having deposed him, and of pulling down Edward, who had been raised entirely by his means. Wherefore, he was commonly called The King-Maker'.[20] It was a matter of honour to have made amends. And finally he fought courageously on foot in the thickest of his enemies and fell covered with wounds. 'Such was ... the end of the famous Earl of Warwick, who since the beginning of the quarrel between the Houses of Lancaster and York, had made in England the greatest figure any subject had ever done before him.'

In a word, he had made and unmade kings as he pleased. Nothing more glorious could be said of a private man, if true glory consists in an excess of power', which we should surely understand as 'the exercise of power'.[21]

The author was an exiled Huguenot, who landed with William of Orange at Torbay in 1688 and subsequently served in Ireland for four years, fought at the Boyne and was wounded at the siege of Limerick. He became the governor of the son of Hans Willelm Bentinck, first duke of Portland. His history was widely read. It was controversial: one incensed critic described it as anti-monarchical, anti-church and 'singing of anarchy and levelling'. Perhaps this explains why he admired Warwick so much. He too had participated in an act of kingmaking. But above all, as a one-time soldier and a nobleman, he most admired Warwick as the epitome of fifteenth-century nobility. His work became the established history of England, especially after its rapid translation by Nicholas Tindal, until it was superseded by Hume's history thirty years later.[22] The admiration for Warwick should occasion no surprise. Maurice Keen has drawn attention to the 'independence of spirit that was the pride of the nobilities of the *ancien regime*, and which preserved them from ever fully acknowledging their subservience to state authority'.[23]

The enlightenment transformed the assessment of the Kingmaker. There ceased to be innate virtue by birth into the aristocracy. True glory no longer existed solely in the exercise of power. David Hume described Rapin's work as despicable in style and content.[24] He disagreed fundamentally with his assessment of Warwick. He wrote in the first volume of his *History of England*, completed in 1761, a prequel to his *History of Britain* from 1603, that Warwick was 'the greatest as well as the last of those mighty barons that formerly overawed the crown and rendered the people incapable of any regular system of civil government'.[25] 'In many respects', John Robertson has concluded, 'the *History* adhered to the norms of what in the eighteenth century was thought of as a "civil history", concentrating on one nation's constitutional developments'.[26] Hume had no time for the old aristocracy. He perceived the growth of commerce and the arrival of Protestantism to have fostered a love of liberty. Warwick was a hindrance to these developments. Modern interpretations of Warwick begin with this magisterial judgement. Hume's perception formed the basis of that of the great historians of the later nineteenth century. It followed for Stubbs that Warwick hardly came 'within the ken of constitutional history' and for James Gairdner that 'his removal was a blessing for his country'.[27] Thenceforward he was presented in a line of historical works as dangerous, restless, over-ambitious, selfish and treacherous.[28]

There have always been exceptions: Lord Lytton in his romantic novel of 1843, *The Last of the Barons*, though he called on Hume for his title, drew on Rapin for his history. Warwick was a hero, 'a man who stood colossal amidst the iron images of the Age – the greatest and the last of the old Norman chivalry – kinglier in pride, in state, in possessions, and in renown, than the king himself'.[29] Charles Oman accepted the modern approach, but reversed the judgement. He argued that Warwick would have made a perfect minister for Henry VI had he espoused peaceful means. He was hard working. It was as a statesman and administrator that he left his mark. And no statesman had ever been so consistently popular with the mass of the nation. His whole career was possible because the majority of the nation not only trusted and respected him, but also honestly liked him. It was because he was the greatest landowner in the country that he could fulfil this role. He was far-sighted in foreign policy. He was not only a great nobleman but also a man in touch with the people. He had but two flaws: he was 'reckless in blood' and worse, morally, he was treacherous. But against this we must set his fifteen long years of honest and consistent service:

> He will still not compare unfavourably with any other of his time. Even in that demoralised age his sturdy figure stands out … Cast into the Godless time of the Wars of the Roses, [he was] doomed to spend in the cause of a faction the abilities that were meant to benefit a whole nation.[30]

One assumes that Oman wrote as a good Protestant, rather than colloquially, about the godless times of the Wars of the Roses. Here then is the lost leader of the late-nineteenth-century conservative party (not, of course, a faction). If only Warwick had lived in Oman's time; if only Oman's great aristocratic contemporaries had had half the earl's ability.

A more overtly nationalist and quirky line in respect to Warwick's 'far-sighted' foreign policy is to be found in I. D. Colvin's *The Germans in England, 1066–1598*. Written in 1915 and published by the National Review, Warwick is one of the few heroes of our earlier history who had seen that Germany had always been interfering in English affairs for political and commercial gain. A 'terrible enemy' of the Hanseatic League, he heroically took on the Germans and pioneered an Anglo-French accord to resist them. Edward IV, on the other hand, sold himself to the national enemy. Warwick was not just an unscrupulous noble; if one applies 'the German key' we discover that he was the champion of the 'Patriot Party'. Warwick died in vain attempting to fortify England against the German danger.[31]

No one else has followed that line. Paul Murray Kendall also saw Warwick as super hero, but of a different kind. He fashioned himself as the flower of manhood, identified himself with the figure he persuaded the world to believe him to be, and acted out his own legend in his own lifetime. He made himself the hero of his own saga, a man who reached higher than he was able to grasp, who poisoned his character in the course of reaching, and 'who ignored the shackles of his time and reached for what he dared to call his own'. He was an adventurer

– a surcharged moment of human experience. It was men's imaginations that
he stamped. But in the passing of time, he paid the price of becoming a legend
by almost ceasing to be a man (whatever that means). In effect, this is an
interpretation developing Polydore Vergil's judgement that the earl fashioned
himself from an early age as a figure of chivalry; as such it anticipates Greenblatt's
theory of Renaissance self-fashioning.[32]

Yet even the most enthusiastic among modern historians, except perhaps
Colvin, seem to have found Warwick wanting in one important respect: the lack
of contribution he made to the growth of the English state. Oman concluded that
'For England's sake it was perhaps as well that he fell at Barnet'. Kendall conceded
that 'Warwick left no enduring print upon the English state'. And the refrain
has been taken up later in the twentieth century. 'He put his own needs of the
moment above the needs of the kingdom as a whole.' 'His *unconstructive* career',
Colin Richmond has observed, 'has not found favour in our sight'. Michael Hicks
remarks in passing on the admiring place *surprisingly* reserved for Warwick in
so many histories.[33] This common refrain shared by critics and admirers takes
us close to the reason why since the eighteenth century Warwick has not found
favour in our sight. So deeply are the Whig perceptions ingrained that we find
it surprising that he was admired by contemporaries and earlier historians, and
conclude that his career was unconstructive because it left no imprint on the
emergence and development of the English state; indeed it actually hindered it.
He did not ultimately serve the greater good of England.

In the modern tradition, inaugurated by Hume and enlarged by late-
twentieth-century scholars, especially those who carry a particular torch for
Edward IV, Warwick has been recast as a threat to England's manifest destiny. In
truth, England's history has been interpreted and debated since the eighteenth
century in terms of the extent to which it enhanced and advanced, or alternatively
retarded and hindered, this remorseless growth of the state. It went without
saying that the monopoly of arms and the use of force should lie with the state;
it passed without question that all steps to unify the kingdom were for the good;
and it followed naturally that the crown must be mightier than any subject, and
the rule of law, *its* law, supreme. It is this perspective that has dominated the
historical writing on the greatest of fifteenth-century subjects, the Kingmaker,
for the last two and half centuries. He had a disastrously destabilizing effect on
English politics between 1455 and 1471, at the epicentre of the Wars of the Roses.
These wars and the period in which they occurred have long been interpreted
as the prime example of what can go dangerously wrong in England when the
authority of the crown and central government collapses. Anarchy is a condition
worse even than the tyranny of the crown itself. And Warwick was a prime mover
in the creation of anarchy.

The very sobriquet 'Kingmaker' itself is taken today to encapsulate the idea that he was a man who exceeded his rightful place and role, a man who took it upon himself to be the arbiter of the crown, not its subject. Whereas for Commynes and others it was a mark of greatness, for Hicks it appears as 'a title that overturned his renown amongst contemporaries'.[34] Thus, in a crown-fixated history of England, he stands as an exemplar of all that a subject ought not to be: one so powerful and so arrogant that he had the temerity to think that he was above kings. Rather than submit to any king, he would find another who would be more amenable.

The idea that Warwick had, in effect, undermined the crown came to underpin the prescriptions of Sir John Fortescue and the circle who were to undertake the task of rebuilding royal authority in England after 1471. Warwick was the most recent, and perhaps the mightiest, of a line of over-mighty subjects. It was the manner in which over-mighty subjects such as Warwick had aspired above their status as subjects and subverted the realm, which was at the heart of the problem. No over-mighty subject should be allowed to threaten the crown again.[35] This became embedded in early Tudor policy towards its greater subjects and the provinces, for the manner in which great lords had built up regional *hegemonies* in the mid-fifteenth century was perceived to have been particularly subversive. There were to be no more Warwicks.

Warwick was, thus, not just a troublesome individual: he has also come to be perceived to be symptomatic of a structural weakness in the realm that threatened the power and authority of the crown in the fifteenth century. Historians, as a whole, have endorsed both Fortescue's analysis of the problem (though not always agreeing on what his analysis was) and have praised the crown for the steps it took to restore its authority (though again not always agreeing as to which were the more significant or who is to take the credit), in what is generally still called the foundation of a new monarchy after 1471; that is after Warwick. We should be careful not to oversimplify this picture. As we have seen, there are indications that Warwick himself was espousing this same cause in the short life of the Readeption. It is possible that he returned to England armed with Fortescue's remedies, which had first been drafted as advice for Edward, Prince of Wales, and was prepared to introduce them. If this were so, one may suppose that the new monarchy would have happened anyway; it is an irony that in the event it was he, and not the usurping Edward of York, who came to be condemned for threatening the future development of the state. As it turned out, however, how could Warwick possibly fit constructively into this modern approach to our national history? He *had* to be the last of the barons.[36]

There is no arguing with the fact that Warwick the Kingmaker was exceptional in his defiance of the crown. Holding what had in earlier times been the most part of the substance of four separate earldoms, he enjoyed wealth and exercised influence on a scale arguably never matched before or since by a nobleman who was not directly of the royal blood, and that at a time when the crown itself was weak. It was this fortuitous conjunction of circumstances that made him, in effect, the arbiter of English politics for fifteen years. It could be said that he lacked that quality for which his father was noted: prudence. He was a consummate intriguer, dissembler, and manipulator. His birth, wealth, and status placed him unavoidably at the centre of affairs; his erratic course was determined as much by self-preservation as by self-aggrandizement. His vast inheritance stood on shaky foundations, each element open to counter-claim. It was thus essential for him to retain influence at court so as to ensure untroubled possession. Furthermore, his grievances against an immature and inexperienced Edward IV were real. In the later 1460s he and his brother George were pushed aside by a faction led by the queen's father, Earl Rivers. Yet Warwick and Edward became estranged because, in the last resort, the king could not rule indefinitely under the shadow of his mighty subject, while the earl, on his part, could not accept any diminution of his special status and power. It is not simply that Warwick was arrogant, haughty, acquisitive, and ambitious (all of which as a great aristocrat he was by nurture, if not by nature). He had good cause to be aggrieved by 1467. He may genuinely have believed that England's future lay in close diplomatic and commercial ties with France. This was an eccentric and unrealistic policy, but it might not have been adopted solely as a mask to cover insatiable ambition or an assertion of his independence. His appeal to popular support, however, even if it derived from a genuine concern for the common good, could not but be perceived to threaten the very fabric of the social order. There is little doubt that if his career is looked at from the point of view of the ship of state, Warwick was a loose cannon on its gun deck.

There is, however, an alternative way of seeing his career, which views it from a different perspective than the emergence of the English state. And that is to see him, as contemporaries largely saw him, as a great European prince. During his meteoric career he dazzled the courts of northern Europe with his power and flamboyance. His contemporary Burgundian historians, men who met him, thought of him as a great European figure. Commynes called him a 'prince' and saw him on the same level as the great rulers of his day whom he knew – Charles the Rash, Louis XI and Edward IV. He recalled meetings he had attended between the Emperor, the king of France, the king of Castile, the king of England, the duke of Burgundy and duke of Austria. Among such meetings was one between Warwick and Duke Charles, which, according to his rule of international relations, led to immediate dislike. 'I think', he concluded, 'that great princes should never see each other if they want to remain friends'[37] Warwick was one of those great princes. And to another Burgundian he was quite simply the third king.[38] This is the measure of the impression that the earl made on his Burgundian, and we suppose other European, contemporaries.

Warwick's possessions certainly gave him, after 1460, the resources and manpower of a petty prince, and his lifestyle gave substance to that image. His magnificent household was almost a separate court; he was granted, or arranged for himself to be given, something akin to a joyous entry into London in the summer of 1460. At the height of his power he held all the military commands of the kingdom: he was warden of both marches in the north, captain of Calais and keeper of the seas. His fleet was the largest naval force in England; with it he waged independent war. Between 1457 and 1464 he could, in theory, call upon something approaching 8,000 men to fight for him on land and sea. His claim after 1457 as keeper of the seas on tunnage and poundage, backed up by the nomination of his own revenue collectors delivering the revenue direct to him without account at the Exchequer, entitled him to a share of crown revenue. At the height of his power his council, which may have sat permanently in London, was barely distinguishable from the king's. The chancellor, both chief justices, the treasurer and chancellor of the Exchequer were all his men too. The extraordinary enthronement of Archbishop George Neville in 1465 could have been mistaken for a Neville attempt to upstage the coronation of Queen Elizabeth Woodville. Representatives of the houses of Burgundy and France treated with him as both the representative of the king of England and as the independently-minded captain of Calais. It was but a short step from this, and the perception of his special status which both Charles the Rash and Louis XI held, and which he did nothing to counter, to treating with him as a separate power, which is what eventually happened in 1470. It is not surprising that, at the beginning of Edward IV's reign, several contemporaries thought that he was the real ruler of England.

There is certainly no doubt about the supremely self-confident manner in which Earl Richard acted on the national and international stages. By 1460 he was indispensable to Richard, duke of York. It is noticeable that all the contemporary sources give pre-eminence to him as the dynamic element in the Yorkist camp. By the time Edward IV was first on the throne, barely of age and with limited experience, and most of that gained at Warwick's side, it is not surprising that Warwick was in charge. He was England's Caesar. And he was not slow to inculcate that image. He made himself a celebrity, in particular a chivalric celebrity. He made sure that the world knew about his exploits in the Channel. They won him renown in 1458 when the English public, after the recent debacles in France, was in need of heroes. If seen today, as the government then saw them, as acts of piracy, they were also seen at the time, by his friends, as old-style chivalric feats of arms in the spirit of English knighthood. Here we see in sharp focus the difference between the modern and the medieval perception of his actions. In modern eyes, to have preyed on the ships of neutrals in a time of peace without the authority of his own king is both illegal and insubordinate – an indication of his threat to the unity and stability of the state. In contemporary eyes, it was possible to justify his actions in terms of prowess and honour. If Malory saw him as the modern Lancelot, this was in part due to the earl's skill in representing himself as such a figure.

Warwick did indeed act as though he was at the head of a state within the state. From the time that he established himself at Calais he was acting quasi-autonomously. A comparison with the Valois dukes of Burgundy comes to mind. Of course the dukes of Burgundy, subjects of the kings of France, did succeed in setting up what was, in effect, an independent state. Warwick could not approach this, but perhaps he aspired to a status and role that was inspired by it, and which separated him from the rest of the English nobility. He acted as though he believed that he had separate authority. He made himself an independent political figure in England with a substantial popular following, essentially beholden to neither Lancaster nor York. Warwick never saw himself as merely a subject of Edward IV: he was never a Yorkist in the sense that he depended on the dynasty. Rather, one may imagine, he took it for granted that the dynasty depended on him. Thus from 1467 at the latest, he could easily envisage political life without Edward IV, first toying with the idea of promoting the duke of Clarence, but always, one suspects, aware that a Lancastrian restoration was an option. The *bouleversement* at the end of his career was a logical culmination of it. By the same token, his defeat by Edward IV in 1471 allowed the crown to re-assert and strengthen its grip on exclusive political authority in England, and opened the way for the further extension of the centralized state. This is why he soon became a hero for those in the following centuries who, for different reasons, resisted the centralizing and autocratic tendencies of the crown and why, in more modern times, he has been castigated as a danger to the growth of that state. We do not know much about his personality, but his hold on the contemporary imagination suggests that he had what today are called charisma and leadership qualities. He also cultivated celebrity. What this great gleaming star represented in his life and after-life is as important to understanding the course of English history as what he was. He had the temerity to put himself on a par with kings and to outshine them. For so doing he was at first greatly admired and later roundly condemned by posterity.

Appendix 1

Attempts on the Earl's life, 1456–59

It is extremely difficult to establish how many attempts to 'distress' the earl were made between 1456 and 1459. The evidence is as follows:

1. The author of Bale's Chronicle, who we have seen was particularly interested in him, later recalled that on Friday 5 November 1456 he came to London and that on the same day, before he arrived, the dukes of Exeter and Somerset (Henry, the heir of Edmund), the treasurer, the earl of Shrewsbury, and Lord Roos, with others, 'rode against him to have distressed him'. But he was forewarned and forearmed (he 'purveyed a remedy against their malice') and passed safely into the city. (Flenley, 'Bale', p. 144) The author is specific about the date: the fifth of November did indeed fall on a Friday in 1456. Yet the evidence for Warwick's itinerary suggests that he remained in the West Midlands in the first two weeks of November. He was at Warwick on 30 October and again on 16 November, when he entertained the king (Hicks, *Warwick*, p. 130). In terms of Warwick's movements, however, the following year, 1457, when he would have been coming up to London from Calais for a great council meeting would seem to fit better. Moreover, this is one of the points in the narrative at which the author remarks on Neville's fame and popularity. Although this is being recorded in retrospect, Warwick's fame and popularity were barely established in 1456. Maurer (*Margaret of Anjou*, p. 149) accepts 1456, but Griffiths (*Henry VI*, p. 809) and Hicks (*Warwick*, p. 132) settle for 1457. There is no doubt, however, that the Nevilles were the target of attack by their enemies in the autumn of 1456. There was a confrontation between Sir John Neville and the duke of Somerset in London in December 1456 ('Gough 10', p. 159; GC, p. 189).

2. The Gough fragment ('Gough 10', p. 160) recounts how, after mid-Lent 1458 on Thursday (9 March), Somerset and Northumberland with their 'meyny [following] harnessed and arrayed in form of war went to Westminster to the intent to have met with the Earl of Warwick there but certain lords seeing it went against the Earl met him in his barge in Thames and so returned him again and so nothing was done, blessed be God; and it was said that Warwick said he would to Westminster on the morrow manger of [despite] them all'. This, if it happened, accords with the knowledge that Warwick did

not arrive from Calais for the conference until mid-February. Some of the details, however, are similar to accounts of other attacks, as in Bale's story of an attempt to ambush him a year earlier, and also to the accounts given of the fracas at Westminster eight months later. It is also seems unlikely that such an attack would have been attempted while negotiations which led to the Loveday Award were in progress, without having had an effect on their outcome.

3. Almost all accounts include the fracas at Westminster in November 1458 at which, it was later claimed, an attempt was made on his life, although details differ. Something happened, but exactly what is not clear. If more than a brawl that began between the followers of the lords, it may have been an attempt to arrest him, not to assassinate him. (See above pp. 37–8).

4. The *Great Chronicle* (p. 190) states that Warwick was involved in a brawl after Candlemas 1459 (2 February). The details suggest that this was almost certainly the November incident but misdated. It adds, for instance, that he was to be arrested for this labour – that is the disturbance in the precinct of the household – and that lords who were his friends protected him and saw him safely to his barge at Westminster wharf. The author would seem to be following Bale and Rawlinson B. 355.

We will never know how many attempts, if any, were made on the earl's life. We might suspect that the earl went out of his way to claim on more than one occasion that he had narrowly avoided an assassination attempt. It is noticeable that all the alleged attacks took place in the vicinity of London and entered the tradition of London historical writing. It is possible that repeated claims that his life was in danger were part of his successful campaign to win support and sympathy in the city.

Appendix 2

Some problems of dating, 1457–59

Historians face considerable difficulty in pinning down some of the basic narrative of the last years of Lancastrian England. Professor Hicks has proposed a significant redating of four events: an oath by York and Warwick not to resort to force; an attack on a Genoese and Spanish fleet; the dating of a letter by the earl of Salisbury; and a conference at Middleham in which Salisbury determined to take York's 'full part'.

1. **The oath not to use force** (*PROME*, xi, pp. 455–8: *RP*, v, p. 347)
   Johnson, pp. 178–9, Wolffe, pp. 309–10, Maurer, pp. 144–5 prefer March 1457. But Griffiths, pp. 800–01; Storey, pp. 180–1, and Watts, pp. 335–6, place this at the October 1456 council. Hicks, pp. 157–9, argues on the basis of the chronology presented in the 1459 act of attainder, the sole source, that it was in June/July 1459. The chronology, however, is confused. The statement in the parliamentary indictment is that at a Coventry council meeting sometime after St Albans, York received a final warning after Buckingham had intervened and requested the king not to show any more leniency to him, and that at the same council first he, and then Warwick, swore on the holy Gospels and signed an 'act' that they would not act again against the royal estate or disturb the realm. It was also 'remembered' how after the grace shown to York, Warwick and Salisbury, they brought about the appalling act concerning the execrable and most detestable deed done at St. Albans: a reference surely to the exculpatory act of the summer of 1455. Was this 'remembered' in 1459 or earlier at the undated Coventry council meeting? Nevertheless, the narrative continues, 'yet that your subjects should think ye called no thing to mind of time passed' the king made Warwick captain of Calais (1455/6, undoubtedly *before* the Coventry council) and keeper of the seas (late 1457). Despite these and other benefits and graces the duke and earl continued to demonstrate their envy. Moreover, it repeated, the oath and assurance given by Warwick, signed by his own hand and sealed with his seal, which was appended to the act, was not to be forgotten. Was this the first oath, or another made later? All these things having been done, it concludes, the king, trusting the tranquillity and obedience of the Yorkist lords, sent for them 'divers times to come to [his] council', which they either disobeyed or feigned trivial excuses to avoid; and,

while continuing in malice, they remained a distance from each other until the appointed time to rebel. After this preamble, the indictment moves into a detail account of what happened in September–October 1459.

York, Warwick and Salisbury remained a distance from one another (York in the marches, Warwick at Calais and Salisbury in the north) from the middle of 1457. If the oath-taking were dated to the summer of 1459 it is hard to see how the lords had time to refuse to come to council meetings 'divers times' before September of the same year. Furthermore, It is hard to see how Warwick could have been at Coventry in June/July 1459. Most of the summer he was in Calais. According to Bale he was in Kent in June, gathering a great fellowship and navy with which to attack the 'fleet of Spain' and at the beginning of July met with the Spanish ships (147). Benet (Chronicle, p. 223) recounts that he was summoned to the council meeting but refused to go. At it, according to him, not only were all three lords indicted, but also the archbishop of Canterbury and the bishops of Ely and Exeter; the earl of Arundel and Viscount Bourgchier were also condemned on the queen's advice. Those indicted, Griffiths suggests, were non-attenders (p. 847, n. 274). Upon hearing of the indictment, according to Benet, the lords determined to go to the king's presence, but the king withdrew to Nottingham. Vaughan and Oldhall, York's councillors, who were later indicted for an act of treason on 1 July at Garlickhythe, may have been communicating with Warwick in Calais (*PROME*, xii, p. 461). Maurer points out (163) that if they were indicted, there seems to have been no overt follow up.

Thus the meetings in the autumn of 1456 and the spring of 1457 remain the more likely occasions for the oath-taking. On balance, I prefer March 1457 because of the difficulty reconciling the evidence of Buckingham's intervention on York's behalf in October 1456 (*PL*, iii, p. 108) with the statement that he led the delegation requesting the king to issue a final warning to the duke. This may well have taken place six months later. The earl's presence in March 1457 is likely as he was still in England and plausibly at Coventry.

2. The attack on a Spanish and Genoese fleet

Hicks (p. 147) also proposes that the attack on a convoy of Spanish and Genoese ships in the Channel in July 1459, recalled by Bale (p. 147) and seemingly for later in the year by The *English Chronicle* (p. 81) was in fact in 1458. But Bale unambiguously states that the earl met with them on the sea at the beginning of July 1459. The *English Chronicle* has no precise date, but places it at the time of the Coventry parliament, which might be too late in the year for a convoy to be sailing for the Baltic. This account reads: 'In the meantime, the earl of Warwick, having a strong and mighty navy, kept the strait sea [straits of Dover], and faught with the Spaniards and killed many of them and took there (their/ three?) great vessels and a carrack of Jene [Genoa], and got in them great riches'. The details, however, confirm that this is the same action as reported in Bale ('the said earl of Warwick met in the sea 2 carracks of Jean and 3 great Spanish ships and he scomfited [discomforted] and took one carrack and the 2 great ships and slew much people and broke the mast of the other carrack, which escaped'. Moreover, they are remarkably similar to those contained in a letter of 9 July 1459 from Edward Grey to Sir Thomas Findern reporting action against two Genoese carracks and three or four Spanish ships, (Richmond, 'Domination of the Channel', p. 7).

3. **Salisbury's letter to the prior of Arbury** (J. H. Flemming, *England under the Lancastrians*, 1921, pp. 128–9)

An undated letter of the earl of Salisbury to the prior of Arbury near Coventry, written from London on 7 March, thanks him for his intercession with the queen on his behalf and asks him to continue to assure her of his 'right fervent desire to know and feel' her good ladyship towards him, 'her humble true servant'. He asks him to reassure her that he will keep his promise and refers to her recent letter to a council meeting in the cause of 'rest and unite', of which he had heard. He further asks him to deny on his behalf recent charges of disloyalty against him, by those of 'right high estate', which disloyalty he never imagined, thought, or said ever in all his life. Hicks (pp. 155–6) assigns this letter to 1459, after the earl had decided irrevocably to support York in rebellion. The letter is dated by Maurer to 1454 (pp. 216–21), but it could equally fit 1457, if the great council at which York and Warwick, but not Salisbury, were required to take oaths were held that year. Its tone leaves no doubt that the earl still valued the queen's good ladyship, and was affronted by the accusation of disloyalty. On the other hand, it implies that she was already a figure with considerable political influence, which suggests a date after 1455.

The promise that Salisbury had made could well refer to negotiations which were almost certainly taking place in the spring of 1457 for the marriage between his son Sir John and Isabel Ingoldisthorpe, which was celebrated on 25 April, and for which the Nevilles found £1,000 as well as a jointure of several manors from the Montagu inheritance. Salisbury and the queen were later in dispute over the release of Isabel's estates. In 1460 Sir John Neville and Isabel Ingoldisthorpe secured an act in parliament cancelling and securing recompense for moneys he had forfeited to the queen as recognizances. The queen had claimed that Isabel, who was 14 at the time of the marriage to Sir John, was under age and that she had the right to keep her inheritance, which she had for two years; Neville claimed that at 14, as a married woman, she was of age to enter her inheritance. Neville had agreed under duress on 27 June 1458 to make payments of £100 every half year until Whitsun 1463 pending the resolution of the case (*PROME*, xii, pp. 542–5).

4. Salisbury's conference at Middleham

In respect of the commitment given by the earl of Salisbury to York, to be found in Whitaker's *Richmondshire*, ii, p. 167, published in 1823 from a deed then at Hornby Castle, Lancashire, but which no longer exists, I see no reason why the date he transcribed (1458) should be doubted. And as Maurer points out (p. 162), even though the document itself was composed some thirty years later, the incident recalled is of integral importance to it and is unlikely that the date would have been remembered inaccurately.

The net effect of his redating of these events is that Professor Hicks offers a significantly different narrative of the period from November 1458 to August 1459, giving considerably greater emphasis to the supposed indictment of the Yorkists at the Coventry council of June/July 1459 and, as a result, proposing that York, Warwick and Salisbury did not finally decide to take co-ordinated direct action until as late the end of July. Since none of the evidence is conclusive this is possible, but my judgement is that, on balance, the evidence leads to the reconstruction I present here, which is that the oath was made in March 1457, the decision to confront the court once more was taken in November 1458, perhaps even before the fracas at Westminster, and that during 1459 both sides were preparing for what they intended to be the final confrontation.

Notes

Notes to Preface

1 D. Grummitt, 'Calais 1485–1547: a study in early Tudor Politics and Government', University of London PhD thesis, 1997 and *idem, The Calais Garrison: War and Military Service in England, 1436–1558* (Woodbridge, 2007); E. L. Meek, 'The Conduct and Practice of English Diplomacy during the Reign of Edward IV (1461–83)', University of Cambridge PhD thesis, 2001; Visser-Fuchs, 'Warwick and Waurin: two case studies on the literary background and propaganda of Anglo-Burgundian Relations in the Yorkist Period' (University of London PhD thesis, 2002); P. W. Booth, 'Landed Society in Cumberland and Westmorland, c.1440–1485: the politics of the Wars of the Roses', University of Leicester PhD thesis, 1997; M. C. Carpenter, *Locality and Polity: a study of Warwickshire Landed Society, 1401–1499* (Cambridge, 1992). I am particularly grateful to David Grummitt for allowing me to consult the typescript of *The Calais Garrison* in advance of publication.

2 Hicks, *Warwick, passim* but especially pp. 31–63, 144–5 and 250–1. See also other essays and articles listed in the bibliography.

3 Ibid, in which pp. 31–219 take the story from 1449 to 1461; pp. 220–311 from 1461 to 1471.

4 See R. A. Griffiths, *The Reign of Henry VI: the Exercise of Royal Authority, 1422–1461* (1981); G. L. Harriss, *Shaping the Nation: England, 1360–1461* (Oxford, 2005), pp. 617–49, C. D. Ross, *Edward IV* (1974); C. L. Scofield, *The Life and Reign of Edward the Fourth*, vol. 1 (1924); R L. Storey, *The End of the House of Lancaster* (1966); J. L. Watts, *Henry VI and the Politics of Kingship* (Cambridge, 1966); B. P. Wolffe, *Henry VI* (1981).

5 A. J. Pollard, *Late Medieval England, 1399–1509* (2000), pp. 127–68, 267–96; *idem, The Wars of the Roses* (2nd edn, 2001).

Notes to Introduction

1 *PL*, iii, 322, pp. 74–5.

2 Ibid.

3 C. Ross, 'Warwick the King-maker', in *History of the English Speaking Peoples: the Wars of the Roses* (Purnell Partworks: BBC Publishing, 1969), pp. 891–4; The same sentiments are to be found in more muted form in *Edward IV* (1974).

4 J. R. Lander, *Government and Community: England, 1450–1509* (1980), pp. 221, 229, 245, 253, 308; M. C. Carpenter, *The Wars of the Roses: Politics and the Constitution in England, c. 1437–1509* (Cambridge, 1997), pp. 173, 181.

5   D. Hume, *The History of England* (1871 edn), iii, 160–1and see below pp. 194.

6   Charles Oman, *Warwick the Kingmaker* (London, 1891), pp. 236–43; P. M. Kendall, *Warwick the Kingmaker* (London, 1957), pp. 8, 272, 281, 324. For further discussion of these works see below pp. 195–6.

7   Kekewich *et al. John Vale's Book*, p. 49.

8   Hicks, *Warwick*, at pp. 6, 161, 183, 311, 313.

9   *Chronicle of the Rebellion in Lincolnshire, passim; Arrivall, passim; Historical Poems of the Fourteenth and Fifteenth Centuries*, ed. R. H. Robbins (New York, 1959), pp. 226–7.

10   L. Visser-Fuchs, 'Warwick and Waurin: two case studies on the literary background and propaganda of Anglo-Burgundian Relations in the Yorkist Period' (University of London, PhD thesis, 2002), pp. 20–21, 47–87, 94–141.

11   *The Crowland Chronicle Continuations, 1459–1486*, ed. N. Pronay and J. Cox (Gloucester, 1986), *passim*.

12   *The Mirrour for Magistrates*, ed. L. B. Campbell (Cambridge, 1938), pp. 254–5.

13   For the speech put into Warwick's own mouth see below, pp. 164, 170, 174.

14   See, for example, *Eng. Chron*, pp. 78–90; *Political Poems and Songs relating to English History*, ed. T. Wright, ii (Rolls Series, London, 1861), p. 270; Chastellain, *Oeuvres*, iii, pp. 318–20; v, pp. 22–3. See also below, pp. 167–8.

15   L. Visser-Fuchs, '"Warwick by Himself": Richard Neville, earl of Warwick, "the Kingmaker", in the *Recueil des Croniques D'Engleterre* of Jean de Waurin', *Publication du Centre Européen d'Etudes Bourguignonnes* (XIVe–XVIe s., 41 (2001), 145–56, hereafter 'The Waurin Relation'.

16   Waurin, *Recueil des Croniques*, v, 543–6.

17   L. Visser-Fuchs, 'Jean de Waurin and the English Newsletters: the *Chronicle of the Rebellion in Lincolnshire*', *Nottingham Medieval Studies*, vlvii (2003), 217–35; *idem*, 'Edward IV's Memoir on Paper to Charles, Duke of Burgundy: The So-called "Short Version of *The Arrivall*"', Ibid, xxxvi (1992), 167–205.

18   It is not known who the author of Bale's Chronicle was. For discussion of the text see C. L. Kingsford, *English Historical Literature in the Fifteenth Century* (Oxford, 1913), pp. 95–6; A. Gransden, Historical *Writing in England, II, c.1307 to the Early Sixteenth Century* (London, 1982), p. 233; M-R. McLaren, *The London Chronicles of the Fifteenth Century: a Revolution in English Writing* (Cambridge, 2002), pp. 33–4.

19   Bale's Chronicle, pp. 123–4 (Scottish campaign); p. 125 (Pont de l'Arche); p. 146 (riots), p. 150 (Scales).

20   Ibid, p. 144. Hicks, *Warwick*, p. 132, has this in 1457, but the author placed it in the November at the beginning of the mayoral year 1456–7. For the problem of identifying the alleged attempts on Warwick's life see below, Appendix 1.

21   Bale's Chronicle, p. 147.

22   Hicks, *Warwick*, p. 6.

Notes to Chapter 1: Premier Earl, 1428–55

1   *Oxford DNB*, 40, p. 528.

2 A. Emery, *The Greater Medieval Houses of England and Wales, 1, Northern England* (Cambridge, 1996), pp. 368–72.

3 *The Chronicle of John Hardyng*, ed. H. Ellis (1802), p. 1.

4 Hicks, *Warwick*, pp. 26–9.

5 Ibid, pp. 29–30; R. L. Storey, 'The Wardens of the West march towards Scotland', *EHR* lxxii (1957), pp. 605–6.

6 *Oxford DNB*, 40, pp. 516–19; M. Arvanigian, 'Henry IV, the Northern Nobility and the Consolidation of the Regime', in G. Dodd and D Biggs, eds, *Henry IV: the Establishment of the Regime, 1399–1406* (Woodbridge, 2003), pp. 117–38; M. J. Devine, 'Richmondshire, 1372–1425' (University of Teesside PhD thesis, 2006), pp. 215–50.

7 *Oxford DNB*, pp. 40, 520–1, 521–2, 525; R. B. Dobson, *Durham Priory 1400–1450* (Cambridge, 1973), pp. 185–90; A. J. Pollard, 'The Crown and the County Palatine of Durham, 1437–94', in Pollard, ed., *The North of England in the Age of Richard III* (Stroud, 1996), pp. 72–5.

8 Devine, 'Richmondshire', pp. 18–47; A. J. Pollard, 'Richard III, Henry VII and Richmond', in *Worlds of Richard III* (Stroud: Tempus, 2001), pp. 117–18; *CPR, 1441–6*, p. 429; *CPR, 1446–52*, p. 281; see also Hicks, *Warwick*, pp. 19–20.

9 *Oxford DNB*, 39, p. 579; 40, p. 520; A. J. Pollard, *North-Eastern England during the Wars of the Roses* (Oxford, 1990), pp. 245–84; M. A. Hicks, 'Cement or Solvent? Kinship and Politics in the Fifteenth Century: The Case of the Nevilles', *History*, lxxxiii (1998), 33–46; J. R. Lander, 'Marriage and Politics in the fifteenth century: the Nevilles and Woodvilles, in *idem, Crown and Nobility, 1450–1509* (1976), pp. 95–8; For the careers of Warwick's uncles see *Oxford DNB*, 40, pp. 488–9 (Edward); pp. 540–1 (Robert); pp. 546–8 (William).

10 *Oxford DNB*, 40, p. 528; For the careers of Warwick's brothers see *Oxford DNB*, pp. 40, 492–5 (George), pp. 508–10 (John). See also below, p. 73.

11 For this and the following paragraph see M. A. Hicks, 'Between Majorities: The "Beauchamp Interregnum", 1439–49', *HR* 72 (1999), 27–43; *idem, Warwick*, 33–35. For a different interpretation see M. C. Carpenter, *Locality and Polity: a Study of Warwickshire Landed Society, 1401–1499* (Cambridge, 1992), pp. 399–436.

12 Hicks, *Warwick*, p. 39; J. L. Watts, *Henry VI and the Politics of Kingship* (Cambridge, 1996), p. 258. For Talbot see, A. J. Pollard, *John Talbot and the War in France, 1427–1453* (Royal Historical Society, 1983 and Pen and Sword Military, Barnsley, 2005), pp. 63–6. Salisbury was single-minded in the protection of his daughter's and then his son's prospects, even against his own brothers. Not only did he prevent Bergavenny from entering Abergavenny and neutralize the Latimer claim to a share of the Warwick inheritance, he also frustrated Robert's attempt to recover Barnard Castle for the bishopric of Durham in 1439 (Pollard, *North-Eastern England*, p. 148).

13 Hicks, *Warwick*, p. 36–41; *idem*, 'The Beauchamp Trust, 1439–1487', *Richard III and his Rivals*, pp. 340–1; Carpenter, *Locality and Polity*, pp. 440–6; Pollard, *John Talbot*, pp. 131–3.

14 Hicks, *Warwick*, pp. 43, 51, 77–8, 97, 129, 170, 225.

15 Ibid., pp. 48, 77, 96–7; History of Parliament Trust, London, unpublished article on John Brome II for 1422–61 section by S. J. Payling. I am grateful to the History of Parliament Trust for allowing me to see this and other articles cited hereafter in draft. See also below, p. 99.

16 Hicks, *Warwick*, pp. 39, 41, 76, 82, 100, 132; T. Thornton, 'The English King's French Islands: Jersey and Guernsey in English Politics and Administration, 1485–1642', in *Authority and Consent in Tudor England*, eds G. W. Bernard and S. J. Gunn (Aldershot, 2002), pp. 197–200; History of Parliament Trust, London, unpublished article on John Nanfan for the 1422–61 section by Hannes Kleineke; *CPR, 1452–61*, p. 439.

17 Ibid., pp. 42–3, 45–9, 78.

18 Ibid., pp. 37–8, 43, 46.

19 Ibid., pp. 46–7, 49, 75–8, 82, 129, 226; for Cardiff and Glamorgan, pp. 59–60.

20 Carpenter, *Locality and Polity*, p. 687; Hicks, 'Beauchamp Trust', pp. 337–351; *idem*, *Warwick*, pp. 50–1. John Throckmorton was the son of John who had served Beauchamp and had died in 1445. I owe this clarification to Linda Clark.

21 Hicks, *Warwick*, pp. 53–62. The earl was in Glamorgan in the autumn of 1449, at Warwick for Christmas and there again on 21 March, 8 June and 1 August 1450, and at Cardiff on 1 October (ibid., pp. 43–5).

22 For characterizations of Henry VI, which range from the completely docile, through the occasionally active and well intentioned, to the vindictively spiteful, see Watts, *Henry VI*, *passim*, esp. at p. 104; R. A. Griffiths, *The Reign of Henry VI* (1981), esp. at p. 253 and Wolffe, *Henry VI* (1981), pp. 132–3. Hicks, *Warwick*, *passim* portrays him as an active monarch. For the problem of understanding Henry VI as a king see A. J. Pollard, *Late Medieval England 1399–1509* (Harlow, 2000), pp. 116–18.

23 *CPR, 1446–52*, pp. 235–6; Watts, *Henry VI*, pp. 211, 258–9.

24 Hicks, *Warwick*, pp. 44; *PL*, ii, p. 148; J. H. Bloom, 'A Letter from the "Kingmaker"', *Notes and Queries*, 12th series, v (1919), 120.

25 For these events see Griffiths, *Henry VI*, pp. 686–91; Hicks, *Warwick*, pp. 69–75; P. A. Johnson, *Duke Richard of York, 1411–1460* (Oxford, 1988), pp. 78–94; Watts, *Henry VI*, pp. 266–78, Wolffe, *Henry VI*, pp. 240–5. Watts, *Henry VI*, pp. 276–7, n. 61 suggests that the earl owed the grant to York, and that his subsequent service on commissions to try Norman veterans for treason and those accused of spoliation of Somerset's goods in Feb. 1451 shows his sympathy for the duke. The timing of the grant, however, indicates that he was closer to the court and suggests that it was in recognition of his service in its interest.

26 Hicks, *Warwick*, pp. 79–82; Johnson, *York*, pp. 107–19 (Dartford); Griffiths, *Henry VI*, pp. 693–7 (Dartford) pp. 698–9 (Edmund Tudor).

27 *PROME*, xii, p. 229; *Warwick*, pp. 83–4; R. L. Storey, *The End of the House of Lancaster* (1966), p. 135; Wolffe, *Henry VI*, pp. 262–6.

28 Hicks, *Warwick*, pp. 84–5.

29 R. A. Griffiths, 'Local Rivalries and National Politics: the Percies, the Nevilles and the Duke of Exeter, 1452–55', *Speculum*, 43 (1968), 610; Hicks, *Warwick*, pp. 86–9; Pollard, *North-Eastern England*, pp. 256–7. Hicks, *Warwick*, p. 88, points out that the conveyance was not in fact completed, for in the following year Cromwell put Wressle in trust for performance of his will. He suggests, therefore, that the marriage was not the cause of, but only the occasion for, the confrontation at Heworth. It is still possible that it had been the intention to settle Wressle on the couple. It is not clear what other reason there was for the quarrel to flare up so violently at precisely the same time in the summer of 1453.

30 Griffiths, *Henry VI*, pp. 719–25; Hicks, *Warwick*, pp. 90–2; Johnson, *York*, pp. 125–31; Watts,

Henry VI, pp. 302–8. For the quarrel between Cromwell and Exeter see S. J. Payling, 'The Ampthill Dispute', *EHR*, civ (1989), 881–907.

31 *PL*, ii, p. 298 (Stodely); Griffiths, *Henry VI*, pp. 72–6; Hicks, *Warwick*, pp. 94–9; Johnson, *York*, pp. 131–5; Watts, *Henry VI*, pp. 307–10; Wolffe, *Henry VI*, pp. 278–81.

32 R. A. Griffiths, 'The King's Council and the First Protectorate of the Duke of York', in *idem*, *King and Country: England and Wales in the Fifteenth Century* (1991), p. 317.

33 H. R. Castor, '"Walter Blount was gone to serve Traitors": The Sack of Elvaston and the politics of the North Midlands in 1454', *Midland History*, xix (1994), 21–39; Griffiths, 'Local Rivalries', pp. 612–24; Pollard, *North-Eastern England*, pp. 259–62

34 Griffiths, *Henry VI*, pp. 739–41; Johnson, *York*, pp. 152–3; Watts, pp. 312–14.

35 Hicks, *Warwick*, pp. 76, 100; Storey, 'Wardens', p. 605. And see above, p. 19.

Notes to Chapter 2: York's Lieutenant, 1455–60

1 R. A. Griffiths, *The Reign of Henry VI* (1981), pp. 741–2; Hicks, *Warwick*, pp. 113–14; B. P. Wolffe, *Henry VI* (1981), pp. 290–2.

2 C. A. J. Armstrong, 'Politics and the Battle of St Albans, 1455', *BIHR*, xxxiii (1960), 1–72 provides the fullest account. See also Griffiths, *Henry VI*, pp. 741–6; A. J. Pollard, 'The Battle of St Albans, 1455', *History Today*, 55.5 (2005), 23–29 and Hicks, *Warwick*, pp. 115–19.

3 Armstrong, 'St Albans', *passim*; Griffiths, *Henry VI*, pp. 746–51; Hicks, *Warwick*, pp. 119–23; Johnson, *Duke Richard of York, 1411–1460* (Oxford, 1988), pp. 158–68; J. R. Lander, 'Henry VI and the Duke of York's Second Protectorate, 1455–6', in *idem*, *Crown and Nobility, 1450–1509* (1976), pp. 80–1; Watts, *Henry VI*, pp. 317–23.

4 *PL*, iii, p. 44.

5 For this and the following paragraph see Griffiths, *Henry VI*, pp. 751–7; Johnson, *York*, pp. 168–73; Lander, 'York's Second Protectorate', pp. 82–90.

6 *PL*, iii, p. 75. In his musings on what would be the outcome of the third session, John Bocking enigmatically preceded his much quoted remark that 'the Queen is a great and strong laboured woman. For she spareth no pain to sue her things to an intent and conclusion to her power' with a cryptic comment that 'the resumption, men trust, shall forth, and my Lord of York's first power of protectorship stand, and else not, etc'.

7 *PL*, iii, p. 31.

8 G. L. Harriss, 'The Struggle for Calais: an Aspect of the Rivalry of Lancaster and York', *EHR*, lxxv (1960), 40–6.

9 For this and the next two paragraphs see Griffiths, *Henry VI*, pp. 772–5; Hicks, *Warwick*, pp. 126–30; Johnson, *York*, pp. 174–7; Helen Maurer, *Margaret of Anjou: Queenship and Power in late-medieval England* (Woodbridge, 2003), pp. 129–32, 144. Watts, *Henry VI*, pp. 327–8, 345 suggests that between 1456 and 1458 'The Nevilles opted for noble unity and the council of the lords in preference to the duke's adventures. In the ensuing years (1456–8), they and York went their separate ways.' This is to some extent based on the account in the Waurin Relation, which put a loyalist gloss on Warwick's actions (see above p. 4). Salisbury began to play a less prominent part in affairs, and was for much of the time in the north, but Warwick in these two years was preoccupied with Calais. I do not

see a parting of the ways in any other sense than that all three were differently engaged in different parts of the realm.

10 *PL*, iii, p. 108; 'Gough 10', p. 159. These are possibly reports of the same incident.

11 For discussion of the evidence of the alleged attempts on Warwick's life, see Appendix 1.

12 *PROME*, xii, pp. 456–7; Johnson, *York*, p. 179; Maurer, *Margaret of Anjou*, pp. 144–5. For my dating of the oath of loyalty see Appendix 2(1).

13 *PL*, iii, p. 118; Hicks, *Warwick*, pp. 130–1; Maurer, *Margaret of Anjou*, p. 147. See also Appendix 2(3).

14 Hicks, *Warwick*, p. 141.

15 Griffiths, *Henry VI*, pp. 775–85; Maurer, *Margaret of Anjou*, pp. 129–42, 148–51.

16 Hicks, *Warwick*, p. 142. See also below pp. 130–1.

17 Griffiths, pp. 815–16.

18 *CPR, 1452–61*, p. 390; Hicks, *Warwick*, pp. 131–2, 144.

19 For the Loveday see Griffiths, *Henry VI*, pp. 805–6; Hicks, *Warwick*, pp. 132–7; Johnson, *York*, pp. 180–5; Maurer, *Margaret of Anjou*, pp. 151–7 and 'Margaret of Anjou and the Love Day of 1458: a Reconsideration' in Douglas Biggs and others, eds, *Traditions and Transformations in Late medieval England* (Leiden-Boston-Köln, 2002), pp. 109–24; Watts, *Henry VI*, pp. 343–4; Wolffe, *Henry VI*, pp. 310–12. Historians cannot agree as to whose initiative it was: the king's (Griffiths, Johnson, Hicks), the queen's (Maurer), or the lords collectively (Watts). Hicks suggests that Warwick forced the pace in seeking to reach a settlement.

20 *PL*, iii, p. 125.

21 Ibid, Bottoner reported to Fastolf that Exeter took great displeasure that Warwick occupied his office and 'taketh the charge of the keeping of the sea'. So it seems that the earl had also been exercising the office of admiral. Six weeks later Bocking confirmed that Exeter resented Warwick's command of the sea and that he had been compensated after Warwick was confirmed in office (ibid, p. 127).

22 *Six Town Chronicles of England*, ed. R. Flenley (Oxford, 1911), 'Gough 10', p. 160; *CPR, 1452–61*. pp. 436–7.

23 Bale's Chronicle, p. 146; *The Chronicle of John Stone*, ed. W. G. Searle (Cambridge Antiquarian Society: octavo series, xxxiv, 1902), p. 73.

24 Hicks, *Warwick*, pp. 149–51; Wolffe, *Henry VI*, pp. 313–15; Stevenson, *Letters and Papers Illustrative of Wars of the English in France* (RS, 1864), i, pp. 367–9. Bishop Beauchamp claimed to have York's backing.

25 *PL*, iii, p. 130; *CPR, 1452–61*, p. 443. See also below, pp. 132–3 and 177–8.

26 *Letters of the Fifteenth and Sixteenth centuries from the Archive of Southampton*, ed. R. C. Anderson (Southampton Record Society, xxii, 1921), pp. 12–13.

27 It is dated 9 Nov. in *Eng. Chron.*, p. 77; 16 Nov. in Bale's Chronicle, p. 146.

28 Waurin, *Recueil des Croniques*, v, 272; J. Whethamstede, *Registrum*, ed. H. T. Riley. 2 vols (RS, 1872–3), i, p. 340; *The Brut or the Chronicle of England*, ed. F. W. D. Brie (EETS, original series, cxxxvi, 1908), ii, p. 526.

29 Stevenson, *Wars of the English*, i, pp. 368–9; *Eng. Chron.*, p. 78. There is further uncertainty as to whether the French report refers in fact to the November great council meeting. Hicks (154) suggests that the parliament, or great council, was one planned for January;

Wolffe (315) that it was either November or January; and Maurer (160), that it was the November meeting and that *Eng. Chron.* confused the date for the dismissal from Calais with October 1459. Confusion is added by the *Great Chronicle* which places the fracas itself after Candlemas (2 February 1459). See also below, Appendix 1.

30 Flenley, *Six Town Chronicles*, p. 113.

31 Bale's Chronicle, p. 146.

32 *PL*, iii, p. 228.

33 Gregory's Chronicle, pp. 203–4; H. T. Whitaker, *An History of Richmondshire* (1823), ii, p. 261; *CPR, 1452–61*, p. 470. John Bourgchier, Lord Berners was retained as sole constable. For discussion of the date of the 'Middleham Conference' see Appendix 2(4).

34 Watts, *Henry VI*, p. 349, n. 371; A. F. Sutton, *The Mercery of London: Trade, Goods and People, 1130–1578* (Aldershot, 2005), p. 257.

35 Hicks, *Warwick*, pp. 153–4.

36 *CPR, 1452–61*, pp. 487, 494–6; Griffiths, *Henry VI*, p. 813; Wolffe, *Henry VI*, p. 315. Maurer, *Margaret of Anjou*, pp. 163–4 doubts that preparations to destroy the Yorkists were being made.

37 *Eng. Chron*, p. 78; 'John Benet's Chronicle for the years 1400 to 1462', eds G. L. and M. A. Harriss in *Camden Miscellany*, xxix (Camden 4th series, ix, 1972), p. 223; *Rot Parl*, v, pp. 348–9 / PROME, xii, p. 461; Hicks, *Warwick*, pp. 156–8 has no doubt that the Yorkists were indicted with a view to later trial; Maurer, *Margaret of Anjou*, pp. 164–5 and Watts, *Henry VI*, pp. 350, n. 375 suggest that the account of the indictments was entered into the chronicle to justify the Yorkists' later actions.

38 For this and the following two paragraphs see Griffiths, *Henry VI*, pp. 817–23; Hicks, *Warwick*, pp. 162–9; A. J. Pollard, *North-Eastern England during the Wars of the Roses* (Oxford, 1990), pp. 271–2.

39 *Eng. Chron*, p. 79.

40 *John Vale's Book*, pp. 208–10.

41 Whetehamstede, *Registrum*, i, pp. 339–41.

42 Griffiths, *Henry VI*, p. 822; Johnson, *York*, p. 195; Ross, *Edward IV*, p. 21. For discussion of the route taken by Warwick see H. Kleineke, 'Lady Joan Dinham: A Fifteenth-century West Country Matriarch', in T. Thornton, ed., *Social Attitudes and Political Structures in the Fifteenth Century* (Stroud, 2000), pp. 75–7. The Waurin Relation tells the story that the lords requisitioned a boat in Wales to take them to Bristol, but once at sea demanded of the master of the vessel that he took them to 'the west'. The master, however, did not know those seas and was reluctant to sail in that direction, whereupon Warwick took the tiller himself and steered the vessel until they came to Guernsey (Waurin, *Recueil des Croniques*, v, 277). Given the evidence that Lady Dinham had supplied a vessel in south Devon (for which she was rewarded later by Edward IV), if the story has any truth, it may be that Warwick took command, not to sail all the way to Guernsey, but to cross the Bristol Channel to the north Devon coast.

43 PROME, xii, pp. 500–2; *CPR, 1452–61*, p. 568. Blount's pardon was issued on 20 December. By 31 January he had been declared a rebel (ibid, p. 568).

44 Griffiths, *Henry VI*, pp. 825–9; Hicks, *Warwick*, pp. 170–3; Pollard, *North-Eastern England*, pp. 272–8. Most grants touching Warwick's estates were of minor offices such as

parkerships granted to middle-ranking household men (*CPR, 1452–61*, pp. 541, 545–7, 569, 579, 581, 596). Sir Edmund Mountford was appointed receiver-general and steward of the lordships in Warwickshire and Staffordshire. He was also granted Sutton Coldfield for ten years (ibid, pp. 527, 534, 584). William Herbert, surprisingly, was entrusted with Glamorgan, Abergavenny and the marcher lordships (ibid, p. 549).

45   Griffiths, *Henry VI*, pp. 826–9; Hicks, *Warwick*, pp. 173–7. See also below pp. 133–6. The crown also met resistance in Glamorgan and the Welsh marches. On 5 February the prince of Wales, through his council, was granted 500 marks yearly from their issues so that he could retain knights and esquires there, on the grounds that the lordships were being detained from the king's possession by the adherents of the duke of York and earl of Warwick, of whom, surely, William Herbert was one. A month later Herbert had his powers to appoint all officers in Glamorgan and Abergavenny except constables and master foresters confirmed (*CPR, 1452–61*, pp. 574, 576).

46   Griffiths, *Henry VI*, pp. 859–63. For the battle see R. I. Jack, 'A quincentenary: the battle of Northampton, July 10, 1460', *Northants. Past and Present*, iii (1960–65), 21–25.

Notes to Chapter 3: England's Caesar, 1460–65

1   For accounts of events from the battle of Northampton to the November Accord see R. A. Griffiths, *The Reign of Henry VI*, pp. 866–9, P. A. Johnson, *Duke Richard of York, 1411–1460* (Oxford, 1988), pp. 207–18; Hicks, *Warwick*, pp. 180–90; C. D. Ross, *Edward IV* (1974), pp. 27–9.

2   Waurin, *Recueil de Cronicues*, pp. 308–18.

3   *Rot Parl*, v, pp. 375–83; PROME, xii, pp. 517–28.

4   The text, Bibliothèque Nationale, MS Fr.20136 fo 65, is cited in full by Johnson, *York*, pp. 213–14.

5   TNA, DL 37/32/79. The text is printed and discussed by M. K. Jones, 'Edward IV, the Earl of Warwick, and the Yorkist Claim to the Throne', *HR*, lxx (1997), 342–52.

6   *CSPM*, i, p. 27; *Eng. Chron.*, p. 78.

7   *CSPM*, i, pp. 21, 27. For Coppini see C. Head, 'Pope Pius II and the Wars of the Roses', *Archivum Historiae Pontificiae*, vii (1970), 149–73 and Margaret Harvey, *England, Rome and the Papacy, 1417–1464* (Manchester, 1993), pp. 193–211.

8   *CPR, 1452–61*, p. 647.

9   Johnson, *York*, pp. 218–23; A. J. Pollard, *North-Eastern England during the Wars of the Roses* (Oxford, 1990), pp. 279–82.

10 A. E. Goodman, *The Wars of the Roses: Military Activity and English Society, 1452–97* (1981), pp. 46–8; Griffiths, *Henry VI*, p. 872; Hicks, *Warwick*, pp. 15–16; H. E. Maurer, *Margaret of Anjou: Queenship and Power in Late Medieval England* (Woodbridge, 2003), pp. 192–7. See also below pp. 178–9.

11 Ross, *Edward IV*, pp. 32–4.

12 Ibid, pp. 34–36; Hicks, *Warwick*, pp. 218–19; *CSPM*, i, p. 61. Fauconberg had been in Calais on 31 January, where as lieutenant he wrote a letter of credence for Antonio della Torre on embassy from Westminster to Milan (*CSPM*, i, p. 47). I overlooked this evidence in my

article for the *Oxford DNB* in which I speculated that his absence from St Albans could have been because he was with Edward IV at Mortimer's Cross.

13   For the battle see Ross, *Edward IV*, pp. 36–8; P. A. Haigh, *From Wakefield to Towton* (Barnsley, 2002). For the casualties see PL, iii, p. 268; CSPM, i, pp. 62, 64.

14   *CSPM*, i, pp. 68–9 (my italics), 78; Commynes, *Memoirs*, p. 413.

15   Ibid, pp. 42, 46, 57, 74.

16   Gregory's Chronicle, p. 215.

17   *CSPM*, i, pp. 61–2.

18   Ibid, pp. 63–4.

19   Ibid, pp. 74, 97. Similar letters, it should be noted, were despatched to Archbishop Thomas Bourgchier, Henry, Viscount Bourgchier, their brother John, Lord Berners, George Neville and Fauconberg.

20   Hicks, *Warwick*, pp. 221–22, modifying Ross, *Edward IV*, p. 437; Pollard, *North-Eastern England*, pp. 286–8.

21   Pollard, *North-Eastern England*, pp. 285–6; Ross, *Edward IV*, pp. 45–8; Henry Summerson, *Medieval Carlisle: the City and the Borders from the Late Eleventh Century to the Mid Sixteenth Century* (Cumberland and Westmorland Antiquarian and Archaeological Society, Extra Series xxv, 1993), ii, pp. 46–7.

22   Hicks, *Warwick*, pp. 226, 239–40.

23   Pollard, *North-Eastern England*, p. 225; Ross, *Edward IV*, pp. 49–50; C. L. Scofield, *The Life and Reign of Edward the Fourth* (1923), i, pp. 246–9.

24   Warkworth, *Chronicle*, p. 2; *PL*, iv, p. 60; Hicks, *Warwick*, pp. 241–3; Pollard, *North-Eastern England*, p. 226; Ross, *Edward IV*, pp. 50–1; Scofield, *Edward the Fourth*, i, pp. 262–7. Warkworth included the castle of Warkworth in the strongholds that fell to the Lancastrians, but John Paston reported that it was Warwick's headquarters in the campaign that followed.

25   Pollard, *North-Eastern England*, pp. 292–3, 298–9.

26   Hicks, *Warwick*, p. 243; A. Payne, 'The Salisbury Roll of Arms, 1463', in D. Williams, ed., *England in the Fifteenth Century* (Woodbridge, 1987), pp. 187–93.

27   For this and the following paragraph see Pollard, *North-Eastern England*, pp. 226–7; Hicks, *Warwick*, pp. 244–5; Ross, *Edward IV*, pp. 53–7; Scofield, *Edward the Fourth*, i, pp. 290–2. The county palatine of Durham had been taken into royal hands in December 1462 and was in effect being governed by Warwick's nominees (Pollard, *North-Eastern England*, pp. 294–7).

28   For this and the next paragraph, Hicks, *Warwick*, pp. 245–7; Pollard, *North-Eastern England*, p. 228; Ross, *Edward IV*, pp. 58–61.

29   Jean de Waurin, *Anchiennes Cronicques d'Engleterre*, ed. E. Dupont (Société de l'Histoire de France, Paris, 1858–63), iii, p. 184; Commynes, *Memoirs*, p. 413.

30   Scofield, *Edward the Fourth*, i, pp. 320–9, 343–51.

31   Ross, *Edward IV*, pp. 85–91.

32   *CSPM*, i, pp. 113, 116; Waurin, *Anchiennes Cronicques*, ed. Dupont, ii, pp. 326–7; Edward Meek, 'The Conduct and Practice of English Diplomacy during the Reign of Edward IV (1461–83)' (unpublished Cambridge University PhD thesis, 2001), p. 129.

33   Hicks, *Warwick*, p. 253.

34 J. Leland, *Antiquarii de rebus Britannicus Collectanea*, ed. T. Hearne (1770), vi, pp. 2–4; Christopher Woolgar, 'Fast and Feast: Conspicuous Consumption and the Diet of the Nobility in the Fifteenth Century', in M. A. Hicks, ed., *Revolution and Consumption in Late-medieval England* (Woodbridge, 2001), pp. 23–5. The event was staged, as the detailed order of service stated, 'within the close of York' (*Collectanea*, vi, p. 7).

35 Jonathan Hughes, *Arthurian Myths and Alchemy: the Kingship of Edward IV* (Stroud: Sutton, 2002), pp. 176–84.

36 *Annales*, p. 783; Hicks, *Warwick*, pp. 234, 253, 258–9; Ross, *Edward IV*, pp. 92–6. For a modern, sympathetic reassessment of Elizabeth Woodville see A. F. Sutton and L. Visser-Fuchs, 'A Most Benevolent Queen?' *The Ricardian*, 129 (1965). The political impact of the marriages is discussed in J. R. Lander, 'Marriage and Politics in the Fifteenth Century: the Nevilles and the Wydevilles', *BIHR*, 36 (1963), 129–52 and M. A. Hicks, 'The Changing Role of the Wydevilles in Yorkist Politics to 1483', and in C. D. Ross, ed., *Patronage, Politics and Power in Later medieval England* (Gloucester, 1979), pp. 60–86.

37 *CSPM*, i, p. 131.

Notes to Chapter 4: The Third King, 1465–71

1 J. H. Munro, *Wool, Cloth and Gold: the Struggle for Bullion in Anglo-Burgundian Trade* (Toronto, 1972), pp. 159–61.

2 Commynes, *Memoirs*, p. 145; Crowland, p. 115. Commynes dates this to a meeting in 1469, but Crowland believed that 'the bitter hatred the earl bore for that man' was one reason why he was deeply opposed to the Burgundian alliance sealed in 1467. For diplomatic relations between 1465 and 1467 see C. D. Ross, *Edward IV* (1974), pp. 104–12; C. L. Scofield, *The Life and Reign of Edward the Fourth* (1923), i, pp. 402–32.

3 Hicks, *Warwick*, p. 254; Scofield, *Edward the Fourth*, i, pp. 413–15. For the involvement of Warwick's servants see E. L. Meek, 'The Conduct of English Diplomacy during the Reign of Edward IV' (Cambridge PhD thesis, 2001), pp. 125–32. See also below pp. 138–9.

4 Ross, *Edward IV*, pp. 110, 115.

5 Waurin, *Recueil des Croniques*, v, pp. 543–6, gives a detailed account of the manner in which Edward IV slighted the French ambassadors, keeping them in London for six weeks, and of the angry reaction of the earl. Meek, 'Diplomacy', 135; *CSPM*, i, p. 117.

6 Warkworth, *Chronicle*, pp. 3–4. One might be pardoned for drawing an early-twenty-first century parallel.

7 Hicks, *Warwick*, pp. 264–5; Ross, *Edward IV*, p. 118.

8 *CSPM*, i, pp. 121–2; Anthony Gross, *The Dissolution of Lancastrian Kingship: Sir John Fortescue and the Crisis of Monarchy in the Fifteenth Century* (Stamford, 1996), pp. 76–81. Waurin too picked up the rumour that Warwick was seeking to suborn Clarence as early as 1467 (*Recueil des Croniques*, v, p. 547).

9 Meek, 'Diplomacy', pp. 131, 136–7; Scofield, *Edward the Fourth*, i, pp. 440–4. Moneypenny's letters are published in Waurin, *Anchiennes Cronicques*, ed. Dupont, iii, 193 (16 Jan. 1468) and Morice, *Mémoires pour servir de preuves à l'histoire de Bretagne*, iii, pp. 159–61 (8 March 1468).

10 *CSPM*, i, p. 117.

11 Moneypenny's letters, n. 9 above; *Annales*, pp. 788–9; Ross, *Edward IV*, 118. It was at this time, the author of the *Great Chronicle* of London commented, that murderous tales were running in the city between Warwick and the queen's kinsmen (*Great Chronicle*, p. 207).

12 Moneypenny reported in January that Warwick had consulted with his brother John. It is of this period that Vergil later wrote of a meeting between the three brothers in which Warwick revealed to them his plan to break with Edward IV and restore Henry VI. The meeting may well have happened, and been remembered by one of Vergil's informants, but with a different outcome from that imagined by him (Polydore Vergil, *Three Books of English History*, p. 94). Hicks (*Warwick*, p. 269) concluded that 'there is no evidence that Warwick himself ever *seriously* considered turning Lancastrian' (my italics).

13 Hicks, *Warwick*, pp. 265–8; Ross, *Edward IV*, pp. 113,120–1; Tim Thornton, 'The English King's French Islands: Jersey and Guernsey in English politics and Administration, 1485–1642', in *Authority and Consent in Tudor England*, eds G. W. Bernard and S. J. Gunn (Aldershot, 2002), p. 202 and n. 68; *CPR, 1467–77*, p. 109.

14 *Annales*, pp. 789–90; Scofield, *Edward the Fourth* i, pp. 454–7, 459–62; M. A. Hicks, 'The Case of Sir Thomas Cook', in *Richard III and His Rivals: Magnates and their Motives in the Wars of the Roses* (1991), pp. 419–33; A. F. Sutton, 'Sir Thomas Cook and his "Troubles": an Investigation', *Guildhall Studies in London History*, iii (1968). One might also note that the commander of the garrison at Harlech was Sir Richard Tunstall, whose younger brothers were in Warwick's service and who himself was to receive a pardon a month after he surrendered the castle to the earl of Worcester in July. Not surprisingly, Sir Richard declared for the Readeption, being made Master of the Mint in place of Hastings. (Scofield, *Edward the Fourth*, i, 458).

15 Ross, *Edward IV*, pp. 122–3; Scofield, *Edward the Fourth*, i, pp. 480–2.

16 Leland, *Collectanea*, pp. 3–4. Oxford was seated next to John Tiptoft, earl of Worcester, who, as constable of England, had been responsible for the trial and condemnation of his father and brother. It would appear that the enthronement was also the occasion of a serious effort at reconciliation, perhaps at the archbishop's behest, which, as events in 1470 were to prove, was ultimately unsuccessful.

17 Ross, *Edward IV*, pp. 118–20, 125; Warkworth, *Chronicle*, p. 12; Morice, *Mémoires*, iii, pp. 159–6; *Great Chronicle*, p. 208.

18 *PL*, iv, p. 304; Ross, *Edward IV*, p. 128; Scofield, *Edward the Fourth*, i, pp. 488–90; Hicks, *Warwick*, p. 232.

19 A. J. Pollard, *North-Eastern England during the Wars of the Roses* (Oxford, 1990), pp. 303–5.

20 For this and the next paragraph see Ross, *Edward IV*, pp. 129–32.

21 *CSPM*, i, pp. 122, 132; M. K. Jones, *Bosworth 1485: Psychology of a Battle* (Stroud: Tempus, 2002), pp. 73–6, 206, n. 16 citing J. Calmette and G. Perinelle, *Louis XI et Angleterre* (Paris, 1930), pièce justicative, 30.

22 *PL*, v, p. 63; Ross, *Edward IV*, pp. 133–6; Pollard, *North-Eastern England*, pp. 305–6. Paston's reference to Oxford is the first evidence that he had been alongside his brother-in-law in the summer.

23 Ross, *Edward IV*, pp. 136–7; Scofield, *Edward the Fourth*, i, pp. 491–506; Pollard, *North-Eastern England*, pp. 306–7; *idem, Richard III and the Princes in the Tower* (Stroud, 1991), p. 47.

24   The principal source for this and the following paragraph is the *Chronicle of the Rebellion in Lincolnshire*, for the composition of which see Gransden, *Historical Writing in England, ii, c. 1307–the Sixteenth Century* (London, 1982), pp. 261–2 and L. Visser-Fuchs, 'Jean de Waurin and the English Newsletters: the *Chronicle of the Rebellion in Lincolnshire*', *Nottingham Medieval Studies*, xlvii (2003), 217–35. See also Ross, *Edward IV*, pp. 137–41; Hicks, *Warwick*, pp. 282–6; Pollard, *North-Eastern England*, pp. 307–9 and below pp. 119–21.

25   Ross, *Edward IV*, pp. 145–6 and below, p. 75.

26   Pollard, *North-Eastern England*, pp. 309–10; *CPR, 1467–77*, p. 209.

27   Visser-Fuchs, 'Warwick and Waurin: two case studies on the literary background and propaganda of Anglo-Burgundian Relations in the Yorkist Period' (Univerity College, London, PhD thesis, 2002), pp. 73–4; Hicks, *Warwick*, p. 287; *CSPM*, i, pp. 136–7.

28   *CSPM*, i, pp. 138–141; Louis XI himself wrote on 25 July that the marriage had been agreed (Scofield, *Edward the Fourth*, i, p. 530).

29   The *Manner and Guiding* is printed in *John Vale's Book*, pp. 215–17. While it dates the negotiations from 15 July, Bettini, who was on the spot, was nevertheless quite specific that both Warwick and Margaret arrived at Angers on 22 July. The question arises as for whom it was written. Hicks (*Warwick*, pp. 293–4, 299) describes it as 'Warwick's propaganda tract' designed to assuage his supporters. I find it hard to see this. The stress is on the toughness of Margaret's stand and how she made Warwick grovel, which is surely aimed at a Lancastrian audience, as Colin Richmond and Lucille Kekewich suppose (*John Vale's Book*, p. 48).

30   Scofield, *Edward the Fourth*, i, p. 530.

31   *John Vale's Book*, pp. 217–8.

32   Ibid, pp. 215, 18. Reference is made to the assurances Warwick is said *still to be giving* the king that he has considerable support pledged to him in England (my italics). *CSPM*, i, p. 142.

33   Ross, *Edward IV*, p. 147; Warkworth, *Chronicle*, p. 10.

34   Visser-Fuchs, 'Warwick and Waurin', p. 75; *PL*, v, p. 80; *John Vale's Book*, p. 218; A. J. Pollard, 'Lord FitzHugh's Rising in 1470', *BIHR*, 52 (1979), 170–5. The above account modifies some of the conclusions I reached in 1979.

35   Ross, *Edward IV*, pp. 147–52; Hicks, *Warwick*, p. 300. Montagu's change of coat followed his dismissal from the wardenship of the east march in the summer of 1470. Warkworth described how he declared that his late change of allegiance and reconciliation with his brother was because of the inadequacy of the compensation granted earlier to him when he had surrendered his forfeited Percy estates, which he reportedly described as a 'pie's nest' (pp. 10–11). In fact the compensation was generous. It is more likely that Warwick, and Archbishop George Neville, had persuaded him to return to the family fold.

36   *CSPM*, i, p. 143.

37   Ross, *Edward IV*, pp. 154–8; Hicks, *Warwick*, pp. 301–4.

38   *CSPM*, i, pp. 144–5; M. A. Hicks, *Anne Neville, Queen to Richard III* (Stroud: Tempus, 2006), p. 88.

39   Scofield, *Edward the Fourth*, i, p. 563; Hicks, *Warwick*, pp. 305–7.

40   Ross, *Edward IV*, pp. 159–60.

41   The principal source for Warwick's last campaign is the *Arrivall*, supplemented by Warkworth, *Chronicle*. Accounts are given in Ross, *Edward IV*, pp. 161–8; P. W. Hammond,

The Battles of Barnet and Tewkesbury (Gloucester, 1990), pp. 57–80, esp. pp. 72–80 for the battle of Barnet itself; Hicks, *Warwick*, pp. 307–10; Pollard, *North-Eastern England*, pp. 312–14. See also below pp. 104–5, 122–5 for discussion of his followers.

42   For the later resistance see *Arrivall*, pp. 31–40; Warkworth, *Chronicle*, pp. 19–22; Ross, *Edward IV*, pp. 173–5; C. F. Richmond. 'Fauconberg's Kentish Rising of May 1471', *EHR*, 85 (1970), 673–92; Pollard, *North-Eastern England*, p. 314; and below pp. 123–4, 140–3.

43   Warkworth, *Chronicle*, p. 21.

44   *CSPM*, i, pp. 131–2.

45   Visser-Fuchs, 'Warwick and Waurin', p. 85.

Notes to Chapter 5: Estates and Finances

1   *Rous Roll*, ed. W. H. Coulthorpe (1859, reissue Gloucester, 1980), p. 57.

2   TNA, SC/1085/20; Warwickshire RO, WCM 491.

3   R. H. Britnell, 'The Economic Context', in A. J. Pollard, ed., *The Wars of the Roses* (Basingstoke, 1995), pp. 41–64; J. A. Hatcher, 'The Great Slump of the Mid-Fifteenth Century', in Britnell and Hatcher, eds, *Progress and Problems in Medieval England* (Cambridge, 1996), pp. 237–72; A. J. Pollard, 'The North-Eastern Economy and the Agrarian Crisis of 1438–1440', *Northern History*, 25 (1989); T. B. Pugh, *The Marcher Lordships of South Wales, 1415–1536* (Cardiff, 1963), pp. 145–83.

4   M. A. Hicks, 'The Neville Earldom of Salisbury, 1429–71' in *idem, Richard III and His Rivals: Magnates and their Motives during the Wars of the Roses* (1991), pp. 353–63; A. J. Pollard, 'Richard III, Henry VII and Richmond', in *idem, The Worlds of Richard III* (Tempus:Stroud, 2001), pp. 117–19; M. A. Hicks, 'Cement or Solvent? Kinship and Politics in Late Medieval England: the Case of the Nevilles', *History*, lxxxiii (1998), 40. In addition, 8 manors from the Montagu inheritance had been settled on John Neville and Isabel Ingoldisthorpe on the occasion of their marriage in 1457 (Hicks, *Warwick*, p. 131).

5   C. D. Ross, *The Estates and Finances of Richard Beauchamp, Earl of Warwick* (Dugdale Society Occasional Papers, xii (1956), pp. 14–15, 18; A. F. J. Sinclair, 'The Beauchamp Earls of Warwick in the Later Middle Ages' (unpublished PhD thesis, London, 1986) p. 222, which puts the disposable incomes as slightly lower; *idem*, ed., *The Beauchamp Pageant* (Donington, 2003), p. 39.

6   M. A. Hicks.'The Beauchamp Trust, 1439–1487' in *idem, Richard III and His Rivals*, pp. 341–3; *idem, Warwick*, p. 225.

7   C. A. Rawcliffe, *The Staffords, earls of Stafford and dukes of Buckingham, 1394–1521* (Cambridge, 1978), pp. 113–14. T. B. Pugh, 'The Estates, Finances and Regal Aspirations of Richard Plantagenet (1411–1460), Duke of York', in M. A. Hicks, ed., *The Fifteenth Century II: Revolution and Consumption in late Medieval England* (Woodbridge 2001), pp. 74–7.

8   TNA, SC 6/1085/20.

9   In 1445–6 revenues of the fee simple estates were £861, which fell to £818 a decade later (TNA, SC 6/1122/3,4.); Harriss calculated that the tail male estates granted to the countess of Salisbury in 1461 were worth c. £275 in 1439 when they were purchased by Cardinal

Beaufort (*Cardinal Beaufort: A Study of Lancastrian Ascendancy and Decline* (Oxford,1988), p. 290, n. 48). For the recession in the cloth industry and the decline in rents in Wiltshire and neighbouring counties see Hatcher, 'Great Slump', pp. 240–5 and J. Hare, 'Regional Prosperity in Fifteenth-Century England: Some Evidence from Wessex', in M. A. Hicks, ed., *The Fifteenth Century II: Revolution and Consumption* (Woodbridge, 2001), pp. 114–15, 123–6.

10　Carlisle RO, D/lec 23/29; Alnwick, Syon Ms, X.I, Box 1, 2b, The income from Bolton in Allerdale and other estates in 1465–6 was c. £120, that for the Yorkshire estates in 1453–4, c. £180.

11　Durham University Library, Dean and Chapter, CC, 189808; J. M. W Bean, *The Estates of the Percy Family, 1416–1537* (Oxford, 1958), pp 46, 81, 111.

12　Cf Hicks, *Warwick*, p. 227.

13　TNA, SC 6/1122/4.

14　Rowena E. Archer, 'Rich Old Ladies: The Problem of Late Medieval Dowagers', in A. J. Pollard, ed., *Property and Politics: Essays in Later Medieval History* (Gloucester, 1984), pp. 15–35; *Oxford DNB*, 39, p. 584. The estates of John Mowbray, fourth duke of Norfolk, 1461–76 supported two dowager duchesses. They were valued at £4,000 p.a. in 1476; it has been calculated that he was left only £1,500. John, duke of Suffolk enjoyed less than £1,000 p.a. (*Oxford DNB*, 44, pp. 703–4) His mother, however, the redoubtable Alice Chaucer, enjoyed an income from her own inheritance, jointure and dower from three marriages of over £1,300 p.a. (ibid, 11, p. 247).

15　T. B. Pugh, 'Estates, Finances and Regal Aspirations', pp. 74–7; A. E Goodman, *John of Gaunt: The Exercise of Princely Power in Fourteenth-Century Europe* (1992), p. 344; S. J. Walker, *The Lancastrian Affinity, 1361–1399* (Oxford, 1990), p. 19; M. A. Hicks, *False, Fleeting, Perjur'd Clarence: George, Duke of Clarence, 1449–78* (Gloucester,1980), p. 180.

16　Commynes, *Memoirs*, p. 181 (80,000 crowns).

17　See below pp. 130–2 for Calais and the Keepership; Hicks, *Warwick*, pp. 145, 251; *Select Documents of English Constitutional History, 1307–1485*, eds S. B. Chrimes and A. L. Brown (1961), p. 273.

18　R. L. Storey, 'The Wardens of the Marches of England towards Scotland, 1377–1489', *EHR*, lxxii (1957), 606–7, 614; *CPR, 1461–7*, p. 45.

19　David Grummitt, 'Calais, 1485–1547: A Study in early Tudor Politics and Government' (London University PhD thesis, 1997), pp 40–1; G. L. Harriss, 'The Struggle for Calais: An Aspect of the Rivalry between Lancaster and York', *EHR*, lxxv (1960), 51–2.

20　*CFR, 1452–61*, pp. 199, 258; *1461–71*, pp. 72–3.

21　TNA, E 404/72/1, no.10.

22　*CPR, 1452–61*, pp. 177, 436, 439, 608 (Richardson); ibid, pp. 310, 430, 437, 439 (Gale) Both served as MPs, Gale at least four times for Dartmouth (J. C Wedgwood, *History of Parliament: Biographies of the members of the Commons House, 1439–1509* (1936), pp. 361, 715–16).

23　*CFR, 1452–61*, pp. 199, 258; *1461–71*, pp. 72–3; *CPR, 1461–7*, pp. 38, 88 (Sheldon) ibid, *145–61*, pp. 403, 494 (Auger). For Otter see below p. 84.

24　*CFR, 1452–61*, pp. 199, 258; *1461–71*, pp. 72–3. Pittlesden, from Plymouth, which he represented in the 1455–6 parliament, became a committed Yorkist. By successive grants in 1461 he was granted the keeping of 'Beuecombe' on the Isle of Wight for twelve years, became deputy butler to Lord Wenlock in Southampton and the receiver of the forfeited estates in the south-western counties of both the earls of Wiltshire and Devon(Wedgwood, *Biographies*, pp. 687–8; *CPR, 1461–67*, pp. 26, 94, 129; *CFR, 1461–71*, p. 14). Another who followed down that route was Richard Hanson, Warwick's collector at Hull from 1458, an alderman and MP six times for the town, including 1460–61, who was beheaded after Wakefield (Wedgwood, *Biographies*, pp. 12–13).

25   *CPR, 1461–7*, pp. 38, 188, 283; Hicks, *Warwick*, p. 145. Warwick's recent nominees in London and Southampton (Auger and Otter) were replaced by Tiptoft's and Stillington's nominees, including Pittlesden once more in Southampton (*CFR, 1461–71*, pp. 97–8). For trade and commercial relations with Burgundy see, Hatcher, 'Great Slump', pp. 240–5 and Britnell, 'Economic Context', pp. 44–6.

26   See David Grummitt, 'Public Service, Private Interest and Patronage in the Fifteenth-Century Exchequer', in L. S. Clark, ed., *The Fifteenth Century, III: Authority and Subversion* (Woodbridge, 2003), pp. 149–62.

27   CPR, 1461–7, p. 45.

28   Hicks, *Warwick*, pp. 239–40; and below, pp. 149–50.

29   Hicks, *Warwick*, p. 251.

30   C. M. Woolgar, *The Great Household in Late Medieval England* (New Haven, 1999) p. 93.

31   *Great Chronicle*, p. 207.

32   Chastellain, *Oeuves*, iii, p. 320.

33   Edward Meek, 'The Conduct and Practice of English Diplomacy during the Reign of Edward IV (1461–83)' (Cambridge University PhD thesis, 2001), p. 134.

34   Edward IV's household was 250–300 strong, but the impression may have been given by Warwick's entourage of an establishment every bit as splendid (Ross, *Edward IV*, p. 323). The Black Book of the Household set down 140 as the expected size of household of an earl, at a cost of £2,000 p.a. (A. R. Myers, *The Household Book of Edward IV* (Manchester, 1959), pp. 99–100). Neville almost certainly exceeded this. The norm for a duke was 240 men at £4,000 p.a., exceeded by the young duke of Clarence, the earl's protégé, in 1468. (ibid, pp. 96, 238, n. 69,70). John of Gaunt's financial records suggest that he maintained an establishment of 150 in his last decade and reveal that the expenditure on household and wardrobe fluctuated between £5,000 and £7,000 in the years for which evidence has survived in the 1390s, against a calculated net income of £10,000 (Goodman, *John of Gaunt*, p. 349; Walker, *Lancastrian Affinity*, pp. 11–14, 18). Exact comparison between Neville and Gaunt is impossible, but each made a similar impact on their contemporaries. For the retrenchment of noble household expenditure in the mid-fifteenth century see C. Dyer, *Standards of Living in the Later Middle Ages: Social Change in England, c.1200–1520* (Cambridge, 1989), pp 98–108 and Hatcher, 'Great Slump', p. 264. While a trend for an increase in household size has been detected at the end of the fifteenth century, Warwick was probably an exception among his contemporaries in its middle, which perhaps explains why the scale of his display was so noticeable. For further discussion of the noble household, and the methodological difficulties in calculating size and cost see Woolgar, *Great Household*, pp. 8–17, 197–202.

35   Hicks, *Warwick*, pp. 48–9; Meek, 'English Diplomacy', p. 119.

36 Hicks, *Warwick*, pp. 48, 62, 145, 172, 251–2; M. C. Carpenter, *Locality and Polity: A Study of Warwickshire Landed Society, 1401–1499* (Cambridge, 1992), p. 126, n. 113, 698; *CPR, 1467–77*, p. 291.

37 Hicks, *Warwick*, pp. 250–1.

38 TNA, SC6/085/20.

39 Warwick's level of expenditure on fees and annuities was probably more than his father's, for which see A. J. Pollard, 'The Northern Retainers of Richard Neville, earl of Salisbury', *Northern History*, 11 (1976 for 1975), 64–5.

40 Warwick does not seem to have spent significantly on building works. The raising of the roof of the great hall at Middleham to create a gallery may have been his work.

41 An appropriate comparison might be with Cardinal Wolsey at the height of his power in the 1520s.

42 Waurin *Recueil des Croniques*, v, p. 544 carries the story that in 1467, when he was rebuffed by Edward IV, Warwick expressed his displeasure to his council. He presumably summoned it, in London, to brief its members and to seek advice. See also Meek, 'English Diplomacy', p. 136, for the northern council later in the same year.

43 TNA, SC 6/1085/20; Lancs. R0, DDMa, p. 238, m. 6.

44 *CPR, 1461–70*, p. 270.

45 See below pp. 87–9.

46 *PL*, iv, p. 215.

47 A. J. Pollard, *North-Eastern England during the Wars of the Roses* (Oxford, 1990), pp. 132–3; J. S. Roskell, 'Sir James Strangeways of West Harlsey and Whorlton', *Yorkshire Archaeological Journal*, xxxiv (1958), 455–82.

48 Pollard, *North-Eastern England*, pp. 133–4, 203.

49 Hicks, *Warwick*, p. 58, n. 66; Pollard, *North-Eastern England*, pp. 137–8.

50 Joan Kirby, *The Plumpton Letters and Papers* (Camden 5th series, 8, 1996), pp. 338–9.

51 *CPR, 1446–52*, pp. 281–2; *CFR, 1445–52*, p. 131. *CPR, 1445–52*, pp. 157–8; Wedgwood, *Biographies*, p. 208, superseded by History of Parliament Trust, London, unpublished article on Thomas Colt for the 1422–1461 section by S. J. Payling; Grummit, 'Public Service', p. 159; Hicks, *Warwick*, p. 49, n. 69.

52 *CPR, 1452–61*, p. 158.

53 History of Parliament, 'Thomas Colt'; Wedgwood, *Biographies*, pp. 208–9, 849; *CPR, 1452–61*, pp. 572, 583; 591;Kirby, *Plumpton Letters*, pp. 307–8; TNA, SC 6/1085/20; C. F. Richmond, 'The Earl of Warwick's Dominance of Channel and the Naval Dimensions to the Wars of the Roses, 1456–1460', *Southern History*; 20/21(1987–9), 9–11; Susan James, 'Sir William Parr of Kendal: Part I, 1434–1471', *TCWAAS*, xciii (1993), p. 105, and n. 27.

54 George Wrottesley,'A History of the Family of Wrottesley: Sir Walter Wrottesley, 1464–1473' *Collections for a History of Staffordshire*, vi.ii (1903), pp. 216–43; Wedgwood, *Biographies*, pp. 274–5. The claim that he was a Knight of the Garter is almost certainly unfounded and there is no evidence that he ever sat in parliament. I am grateful to Linda Clark for this information.

55 TNA, Durh. 3/227/8d; *Oxford DNB*, 54, pp. 833–6.

56 *Oxford DNB*, 6, p. 315.

57 For Wenlock see below, pp. 136, 139–41; FitzHugh pp. 111, 121; and Parr pp. 100, 119–20.

58 Hicks, *Warwick*, p. 252; Wrottesley, 'Wrottesley', p. 220.

59 TNA, SC6/1085/20.

60 Alison Hanham, *Richard III and his early Historians* (Oxford, 1975), p. 122.

61 TNA, SC6/1085/20; 'Private Indentures for Life Service and War, 1278–1476', ed. Michael Jones and Simon Walker, *Camden Miscellany xxxii* (Camden 5th series, 3, 1994), pp. 165–72; 218, 290–2; *CPR, 1467–77*, pp. 214–16.

62 Carpenter, *Locality and Polity*, pp. 696–99; Pollard, *North-Eastern England*, pp. 126, 128–31, 288–91, 301–3; P. W. Booth, 'Landed Society in Cumberland and Westmorland, c. 1440–1485: the Politics of the Wars of the Roses (Leicester University PhD thesis, 1997), pp. 84–92.

63 *PL*, ii, pp. 148, 297, iii, p. 532. In 1454 Stodeley had heard that he would also have 1,000 men waiting on him besides the fellowship in his company. Stodeley's report, probably addressed to the duke of Norfolk, advising that he took similar precaution, makes it clear that those expected to be awaiting Warwick's arrival included tenants as well as servants.

64 Warkworth, *Chronicle*, pp. 3–4; Jones and Walker, 'Private Indentures', p. 172.

65 Walker, *Lancastrian Affinity*, pp. 14, 18; cf. the 190 identified to have been in Richard of York's service (Johnson, *Richard of York*, pp. 20, 228–31) and the 130 in the service of Humphrey, duke of Buckingham in mid-century (Rawcliffe, *Staffords*, 219–25).

Notes to Chapter 6: Lordship and Loyalty: East Anglia and the West Midlands

1 S. B. Chrimes, *English Constitutional Ideas in the Fifteenth Century* (Cambridge, 1936), p. 172.

2 For this and the following paragraphs see, G. L. Harriss, 'The Dimensions of Politics', in R. H. Britnell and A. J. Pollard, eds, *The McFarlane Legacy: Studies in Late-Medieval Politics and Society* (Stroud, 1995), pp. 2–10, 'The King and His Subjects', in R. E. Horrox, ed., *Fifteenth-Century Attitudes* (Cambridge, 1994), pp. 14–21 and *Shaping the Nation: England 1360–1461* (Oxford, 2005), pp. 198–200; M. A. Hicks, *Bastard Feudalism* (1995), *passim*, and *English Political Culture in the Fifteenth Century* (2002), pp. 141–80; R. E. Horrox, 'Service', in *eadem, Fifteenth-Century Attitudes,* and 'Personalities and Politics' in A. J. Pollard, ed., *The Wars of the Roses* (1995) and A. J. Pollard, *Late-Medieval England, 1399–1509* (2000), pp. 245–51.

3 M. A. Hicks, *False, Fleeting, Perjur'd Clarence: George, Duke of Clarence 1449–78* (Gloucester, 1980), pp. 170–90.

4 Ross, *Edward IV* (1974), pp. 76–7, esp. p. 76, n. 2 which details grants; T. B. Pugh, *Glamorgan County History, iii, The Middle Ages* (1971), pp. 197–8.

5 Carpenter, *Locality and Polity: A Study of Warwickshire Landed Society, 1401–1499* (Cambridge, 1992), pp. 499, 510, 515–16; P. W. Booth, 'Landed Society in Cumberland and Westmorland, c. 1440–1485: the Politics of the Wars of the Roses (Leicester University PhD thesis, 1997), pp. 108–13; Hicks, *Clarence*, p. 107.

6 Note, for example, that his brother George's 'wholesome counsell' secured the stewardship of Durham Priory's cell at Lytham in Lancashire for Sir William Stanley in April 1461

(M. K. Jones, 'Richard III and the Stanleys', in R. E. Horrox, ed., *Richard III and the North* (Hull, 1986), p. 35.

7   M. A. Hicks, 'The Beauchamp Trust, 1439–1487', in *idem, Richard III and His Rivals: Magnates and their Motives during the Wars of the Roses* (1991), pp. 345–6, 351.

8   *PL*, ii, p. 117.

9   P. B. Chatwin, 'Documents of 'Warwick the King-maker' in possession of St Mary's Church, Warwick', *Transactions of the Birmingham Archaeological Society*, lix (1938), p. 3. The year is not given. It could not have been before 1457 because Warwick was not in Calais in April 1456. It is unlikely to have been 1457. Neville was in Sandwich on 25 April that year: if he was about to come to England why send a letter from Calais? Rody died later in 1458.

10 *PL*, ii, p. 332.

11 Ibid, iii, pp. 32, 44, 86–7, 118, 125, 127, 204.

12 Ibid, p. 226.

13 Ibid, pp. 243–4. Rumour about Warwick's forthcoming promotion was ill-founded.

14 Ibid, iv, pp. 32, 59–60; C. F. Richmond, 'The Murder of Thomas Dennis', *Common Knowledge*, 2 (1993), p. 94; Helen Castor, *Blood and Roses: The Paston Family in the Fifteenth Century* (2004), pp. 185–6. The family had been reluctant to fight for the Yorkists before Edward IV became King (Castor, *Blood and Roses*, pp. 142–4)

15 Ibid, ii, 212, 246, 272, 274.

16 *PL*, iv, p. 8.

17 Ibid, iv pp. 22–3; C. F. Richmond, *The Paston Family in the Fifteenth Century: The First Phase* (Cambridge, 1990), pp. 154–56.

18 *PL*, iv, pp. 215, 304.

19 C. F. Richmond, *The Paston Family in the Fifteenth Century: Endings* (Manchester, 2000), pp. 136–41.

20 Carpenter, *Locality and Polity*, pp. 696–9.

21 Hicks, *Warwick*, pp. 48, 51, 62–3; Carpenter, *Locality and Polity*, p. 126, n. 13, 458; History of Parliament Trust, 'John Brome II'. See also above, p. 19.

22 *PL*, i, p. 298; Hicks, *Warwick*, pp. 44–5, 81. See also above pp. 22, 29–30.

23 Carpenter, *Locality and Polity*, pp. 451–66, esp. at p. 459.

24 Harriss, *Shaping the Nation*, pp. 195, 205–6.

25 Carpenter, *Locality and Polity*, pp. 456, 512; History of Parliament Trust, London, unpublished article on Sir Robert Harcourt for the 1422–61 section by S. J. Payling.

26 R. A. Griffiths, 'The Hazards of Civil war: the Mountford family and the wars of the Roses', *Midland History*, 5 (1981), 1–19, reprinted in *King and Country* (Hambledon, 1991), pp. 365–82, esp. pp. 366–73; Carpenter, *Locality and Polity*, pp. 456–82.

27 Carpenter, *Locality and Polity*, pp. 457, 464–5.

28 Professor Hicks was convinced that it did not occur until after 1456 (Hicks, *Warwick*, p. 52).

29 Hicks, 'Between Majorities: The "Beauchamp Interregnum", 1439–49', *HR*, lxxii (1999), pp. 33–5.

30 See above, pp. 24–6.

31 See above, pp. 31–2, below, pp. 130–1.

32   Helen Maurer, *Margaret of Anjou: Queenship and Power in Late Medieval England* (Woodbridge,2003), pp. 132–6.

33   Maurer, *Margaret of Anjou*, pp. 140–2; J. L. Laynesmith, 'Constructing Queenship at Coventry: Pageantry and Politics at Margaret of Anjou's 'Secret Harbour'', in L. Clark, ed., *The Fifteenth Century, III, Authority and Subversion* (Woodbridge, 2003), pp. 137–47.

34   Hicks, *Warwick*, p. 132; Maurer, *Margaret of Anjou*, p. 149. For the problem of dating this alleged attempt on Warwick's life see Appendix I.

35   R. A. Griffiths, *The Reign of Henry VI* (1981), pp. 777–90; Laynesmith, 'Constructing Queenship', *passim*; Maurer, *Margaret of Anjou*, pp. 127–36; Wolffe, *Henry VI* (1981), pp. 302–10.

36   *CPR, 1452–61*, pp. 587, 558, 566. Henry Everingham also had his annuity of 10 marks charged to Berkeswell ratified (ibid, 587); J. C. Wedgwood, *History of Parliament: Biographies of the members of the Commons House, 1439–1509* (1936), p. 853.

37   Carpenter, *Locality and Polity*, pp. 482–3. On the other hand Sir Robert Harcourt and Richard Clapham were among the 25 Yorkist supporters, assisted by persons of great might, who were picked out and condemned at the Coventry parliament for having distributed liveries against the law (*PROME*, xii, pp. 500–02

38   Waurin, *Recueil des Croniques*, v, p. 309; Hicks, *Warwick*, p. 185.

39   Carpenter, *Locality and Polity*, pp. 492–516 for the details. Professor Carpenter identifies three serious conflicts between Rous and Burdet, Verney and Dalby, and Clapham and Mountford which merged into one. It may be, as she implies, that the introduction of Clapham and other northerners into Warwickshire society exacerbated tensions.

40   Ibid, 499–508.

41   See above, pp. 65–72.

42   CPR, pp. 634, 635 also 6, 350. Throckmorton was adept at keeping on the winning side. He was back on the bench for Worcestershire under the Readeption, on 2 Jan. 1471, but had made his peace again with Edward IV soon enough for him to be appointed a commissioner of array in March 1472.

43   Historical Manuscripts Commission, *Report on the MS of the Duke of Rutland* (1888), i, pp. 3–4.

44   *Arrivall*, p. 8.

45   Ibid.

46   Hicks, *Clarence*, p. 107.

47   Richmond, *Paston Family: Endings*, pp. 136–44.

Notes to Chapter 7: Lordship and Loyalty: the North

1   Hicks, *Warwick*, p. 247.

2   A. J. Pollard, *North-Eastern England during the Wars of the Roses* (Oxford, 1990), pp. 250–1.

3   H. Summerson, *Medieval Carlisle: The City and the Borders from the Late Eleventh to the Mid-Sixteenth Century* (CWAAS, Extra Series, xxv, 1993), ii, pp. 405–8, 410–12, 443. One should note, however, that Salisbury had petitioned to be restored to the office on the expiry of Lumley's term, *Ibid*, 411–12.

4   R. L. Storey, *The End of the House of Lancaster* (1966), pp. 105–23.

5   Summerson, *Medieval Carlisle*, ii, pp. 437–44; P. W. Booth, 'Men Behaving Badly? The West March towards Scotland and the Percy-Neville Feud', in L. Clark, ed, *The Fifteenth Century, III: Subversion and Authority* (Woodbridge, 2003), pp. 95–116.

6   S. James, 'Sir Thomas Parr', *TCWAAS*, lxxxi (1981), p. 22; 'Private Indentures for Life Service in Peace and in War, 1278–1476', ed. Michael Jones and Simon Walker, *Camden Miscellany xxxii* (Camden, 5th series, iii, 1994), pp. 150, 157–9; J. Nicholson and R. Burn, *The Histories and Antiquities of the counties of Westmorland and Cumberland* (1777), i, pp. 96–8; *CPR, 1452–61*, pp. 435, 651; History of Parliament Trust, London, unpublished article on Roland Vaux for the 1422–61 section by Charles Moreton.

7   Jones and Walker, 'Private Indentures', pp. 162–3; Either Richard the elder, or his younger son Richard, uncle of the retainer, was the receiver of the south parts for Salisbury in 1451–2 (Hicks, *Warwick*, p. 82). Thomas Musgrave, the father of Sir Richard the younger, does not seem to have been retained by Neville. His virtual absence from public record suggests that he was disabled in some manner. Stapleton died a year later in 1457; the elder Musgrave survived until 1464.

8   P. W. Booth, 'Landed Society in Cumberland and Westmorland, c. 1440–1485: the Politics of the wars of the Roses (Leicester University PhD thesis, 1997), pp. 87–9, 107–8; Summerson, *Medieval Carlisle*, ii, pp. 462, 448–9; Jones and Walker, 'Private Indentures', pp. 165–8, 169–71, 174; F. W. Ragg, 'Helton, Flechan, Askham and Sandford of Askham', *TCWAAS*, xxi (1921), p. 186; *CPR, 1461–7*, 143.

9   Summerson, *Medieval Carlisle*, ii, pp. 406–7.

10 Jones and Walker, 'Private Indentures', p. 168. One does not know whether this meant only two artillery men, or only two of them being granted board.

11 Ibid, p. 163.

12 *CPR, 1461–7*, p. 132.

13 *CPR, 1467–77*, p. 106; S. James, 'Sir William Parr of Kendal: Part I (1434–1471)', *TCWAAS*, xciii (1993), pp. 101–3,105–6; Hicks, *Warwick*, p. 246. Dr James interprets the bond of 1466 as being in respect of a personal debt (p. 106).

14 *CPR, 1467–77*, p. 177. The Richmondshire men were John Catterick, Robert Wycliffe, Miles Metcalfe and James Danby.

15 Booth, 'Cumberland and Westmorland', pp. 92–7; Pollard, *North-Eastern England*, pp. 130, 289: *CPR, 1461–7*, pp. 62, 87, 151, 154.

16 Summerson, *Medieval Carlisle*, ii, p. 462, Booth, 'Cumberland and Westmorland', p. 86; Pollard, *North-Eastern England*, p. 303.

17 Jones and Walker, 'Private Indentures', pp. 173–4. I am grateful to Janette Garrett for making available to me the work she has undertaken on the Sandford family.

18 Storey, *End of the House of Lancaster*, pp. 118–21; J. S. Roskell, *et al, The History of Parliament: The House of Commons, 1386–1421* (Stroud, 1992) ii, pp. 685–6; iii, pp. 546–8; James, 'Thomas Parr', pp. 19–20; 'William Parr, Part I', p. 103.

19 Ragg, 'Sandford of Askham', pp. 187–91.

20 See for instance *History of Parliament*, i, pp. 322, 676.

21 Ragg, 'Sandford', pp. 187–8.

22 A. J. Pollard, 'The Northern Retainers of Richard Neville, Earl of Salisbury', *NH*, xi (1976), 52–69; SC6/1085/20.

23 M. K. Jones, 'Richard III and the Stanleys', in R. E. Horrox, ed., *Richard III and the North* (Hull, 1986), pp. 37–8.

24 Jones and Walker, 'Private Indentures', pp. 165–71.

25 Pollard, *North-Eastern England*, pp. 128–37.

26 *CPR, 1441–6*, p. 429, *1446–52*, p. 281.

27 A. J. Pollard, 'The Richmondshire Community of Gentry during the Wars of the Roses', in Charles Ross, ed, *Patronage, Pedigree and Power* (Gloucester, 1979), pp. 37–59, repr. in *idem, The Worlds of Richard III*, pp. 51–64; *idem*, 'Late Feudalism in England: the case of Richmondshire', in *Courtiers and Warriors: Comparative Historical Perspectives on Ruling Authority and Civilization* (Kyoto, 2003), pp. 469–82; M.J. Devine, 'Richmondshire, 1372–1425' (University of Teesside PhD thesis, 2006), pp. 18–47.

28 A. J. Pollard, 'Richard Clervaux of Croft: A North Riding Squire during the Fifteenth Century', *Yorkshire Archaeological Journal*, l (1978), 162.

29 Ibid, pp. 163–5.

30 Pollard, *North-Eastern England*, pp. 90–1,136–8, 250–3; R. E. Horrox, 'Richard III and the East Riding', in *eadem, Richard III and the North*, pp. 82–5.

31 Pollard, *North-Eastern England*, pp. 286–8.

32 Ibid, pp. 294–8, 300; M. A. Hicks, 'The Forfeiture of the Barnard Castle to the Bishop of Durham, 1459', *NH*, xxxiii (1997), 223–31.

33 Warkworth, *Chronicle*, pp. 25–6.

34 Pollard, *North-Eastern England*, pp. 288–91.

35 Ibid, pp. 293–4; *The Plumpton Letters and Papers*, ed. Joan Kirby (Camden 5th series, 8 (1996), lxvii–iii; *CPR, 1461–7*, p. 177; *CCR, 1461–8*, p. 35; *Three Fifteenth Century Chronicles*, ed. J. R. Gairdner (Camden Soc, 3rd series, xxviii, 1880), p. 161; Storey, *End of the House of Lancaster* p. 194.

36 Kirby, *Plumpton Letters*, 7, pp. 255–6; *The Plumpton Correspondence*, ed. T. Stapleton (Camden, old series, iv, 1839), pp. lxvii–lxx.

37 Kirby, *Plumpton Letters*, p. 37.

38 Ibid, pp. 27–8, 30–2, 257–8.

39 Ibid, pp. 30, 230–4; 260–1.

40 Pollard, *North-Eastern England*, p. 302; Durham University Library, Durh. CC, Miscellanea, 189808. The fee was, however, cancelled a year later. Note also that Christopher Curwen and others associated with the lordship of Cockermouth also came to terms with the new regime.

41 Pollard, *North-Eastern England*, p. 302; Wedgwood, *Biographies*, pp. 882–3.

42 Kirby, *Plumpton Letters*, pp. 40, 45.

43 Pollard, *North-Eastern England*, pp. 304–5.; Waurin, *Recueil des Croniques*, v, p. 579; A. E. Goodman, *The Wars of the Roses: Military Activity and English Society, 1452–97* (1981), p. 69.

44 *CPR, 1467–77*, p. 208; James, 'Sir William Parr', pp. 109–10. Three weeks after Parr was appointed, on 28 May, Gate took out a pardon for all offences before 23 April (*CPR, 1467–77*, p. 209).

45 *Chronicle of the Rebellion in Lincolnshire*, p. 16.

46 Ibid, pp. 12–13, 16–17.

47 Ibid, p. 18.

48   *CPR, 1467–77*, p. 218; William Worcestre in his *Itineraries* listed sons of Lord Latimer, FitzHugh, Dudley and possibly Greystoke as among the dead on the Neville side (J. H. Harvey, *William Worcestre Itineraries* (Oxford, 1969), p. 341.

49   A. J. Pollard, 'Lord FitzHugh's Rising in 1470', *BIHR*, lii (1979), 170–5; *idem, North-Eastern England*, pp. 310–12; *CPR, 1467–77*, pp. 214–6.

50   *CPR, 1467–77*, p. 208.

51   Booth, 'Cumberland and Westmorland', pp. 92–113 Alnwick MSS, CM x.II, 3.a, fo, 1v, 4.

52   *Arivall*, 7. They were described as 'two good knights' and were surely identified because they were such prominent defectors.

53   Jones, 'Richard III and the Stanleys', pp. 35–40; Wedgwood, *Biographies*, p. 611: *PL*, iii, p. 9; P. W. Hammond, *The Battles of Barnet and Tewkesbury* (Gloucester, 1990), p. 76.

54   *CPR, 1467–77*, pp. 277, 288.

55   *Arrivall*, pp. 6–7. Pollard, *North-Eastern England*, pp. 312–14. Thomas Tunstall, who was pardoned on 21 April, was perhaps another in the company of northern men fleeing after the battle (*CPR, 1467–77*, p. 258).

56   *Arrivall*, pp. 312.

57   Warkworth, *Chronicle*, p. 14.

58   See below, pp. 139–40.

Notes to Chapter 8: Calais and the Keeping of the Seas

1   In 1458 an annuity paid from the revenues of Sangatte was granted to Andrew Trollope. J. L. Watts, *Henry VI and the Politics of Kingship* (Cambridge, 1990), p. 345, n. 335, interpreted this as the grant of the custody of the fort. I am grateful to David Grummitt for pointing this out to me.

2   David Grummitt, 'Calais, 1485–1547: A Study in early Tudor Politics and Government' (London University PhD thesis,1997), pp. 112–18.

3   A. Dunlop, *The Life and Times of James Kennedy, Bishop of St Andrews* (1950), pp. 163–4; C. McGladdery, *James II* (Edinburgh, 1990), p. 98; R. A. Griffiths, *The Reign of Henry VI* (1981), pp. 814–15.

4   J. R. Rainey, 'The Defense of Calais' (Rutgers University, PhD thesis, 1987), pp. 115–16.

5   Hicks, *Warwick*, pp. 138–43; David Grummitt, 'Calais 1485–1549', pp. 46–8.

6   Grummitt, *The Calais Garrison: War and Military Service in England 1436–1558* (Woodbridge forthcoming), 'The Organisation of the Garrison' (Ch 3), esp. pp. 2–3, 12.

7   Ibid.

8   *PL*, v, p. 187; A. J. Pollard, *Imagining Robin Hood: the Late-Medieval Stories in Historical Context* (2004), pp. 44–5.

9   Grummitt, 'Calais, 1485–1547', pp. 47–50; Grummitt, *The Calais Garrison*, 'The Nature of Military Service' (Ch. 4), Griffiths, *Henry VI* p. 754).

10   TNA, Prerogative Court of Canterbury, 24–25 Stockton; History of Parliament Trust, London, unpublished article on Sir Edmund Mulsho for the 1422–1461 section by Charles Moreton.

11 *Original Letters Illustrative of English History*, ed. H. Ellis, 2ns series, i (1827), pp. 124–6; History of Parliament Trust, London, unpublished article on Sir Walter Blount for the 1422–61 section by S. J. Payling.

12 G. L. Harriss, 'The Struggle for Calais: An Aspect of the Rivalry between Lancaster and York', *EHR*, lxxv (1960), 43–4.

13 A. J. Pollard, *John Talbot and the War in France, 1427–1453* (1983), p. 81–2; see also Grummitt, *The Calais Garrison*, Ch. 4, 'The Nature of Military Service'.

14 Grummitt, 'Calais, 1485–1547', pp. 32–41; Harriss, 'Struggle for Calais', pp. 30–53.

15 *PL*, iii, p. 118; Hicks, *Warwick*, pp. 144–5.

16 TNA, E101/71/4/938; E404/72/142/3; C. F. Richmond, 'The Earl of Warwick's Domination of the Channel and the Naval Dimension to the Wars of the Roses, 1456–1460', *Southern History*, 20/21 (1997–9), 4; *PL*, iv, p. 35.

17 N. A. M. Rodger, *The Safeguard of the Sea: a Naval History of Britain, Vol 1, 660–1649* (1997), pp. 131–6. Note, however, that both Exeter and Fauconberg, as admirals, commanded fleets at sea in 1460 and 1462 and that in 1458 Exeter was reported as being displeased that Warwick 'occupies his office, and takes the charge of the keeping of the sea upon him', for which he was compensated (*PL*, iii, pp. 125–6). It is not clear whether Warwick did in fact occupy the office of admiral, or whether Exeter considered the keeping of the seas as part of the role of admiral.

18 *CPR, 1461–67*, pp. 195, 197, 214.

19 Hicks, *Warwick*, pp. 144–5, 249–51.

20 C. J. Ford, 'Piracy or Policy? The Crisis in the Channel, 1400–1403', *TRHS*, 5th series, xxix (1979), 63–78; Griffiths, *Henry VI*, pp. 423–33, esp. pp. 30–1 for the 1449 attack on the Hanseatic fleet; J. L. Bolton, 'The City and the Crown, 1456–61', *London Journal*, 12 (1986), 14, 16–17; Hicks, *Warwick*, pp. 146–7. For the high feeling against Italians in 1456–8 see Griffiths, *Henry VI*, pp. 792–5.

21 TNA, E101/71/4/938.

22 C. L. Kingsford, 'The Earl of Warwick at Calais in 1460', *EHR*, xxxvi (1922), 545–6; Richmond, 'Warwick's Domination of the Channel', pp. 1–17: Hicks, *Warwick*, pp. 146–7; Griffiths, *Henry VI*, p. 733.

23 A. F. Sutton, *The Mercery of London: Trade, Goods and People, 1130–1578* (Aldershot, 2005), p. 257; Watts, *Henry VI*, p. 349, n. 371.

24 Gregory's Chronicle, p. 205.

25 Grummit, 'Calais, 1485–1547', p. 49; Harriss, 'Struggle for Calais', p. 46, n. 1.

26 Waurin, *Recueil des Croniques*, v, pp. 280–2; *The Brut or the Chronicles of England*, ed. F. W. D de Brie (EETS, 1908), ii, p. 528.

27 Waurin, *Recueil des Croniques*, v, p. 291; *Annales*, p. 774.

28 On this occasion, it seems, the castle was assaulted (Hicks, *Warwick*, p. 248).

29 Short English Chronicle, p. 73; Waurin, *Recueil des Croniques*, v, pp. 288–9; *Eng. Chron.*, p. 82.

30 Hicks, *Warwick*, p. 174, Griffiths, *Henry VI*, p. 810; Harriss, 'Struggle for Calais', pp. 48–51.

31 Chastellain, *Oeuvres*, iii, pp. 427 also 8; Hicks, *Warwick*, p. 143; Waurin, *Recueil des Croniques*, v, p. 282; Edward L. Meek, 'The Conduct and Practice of English Diplomacy during the Reign of Edward IV' (Cambridge, PhD, 2001), p. 117.

32   Waurin, *Recueil des Croniques*, v, pp. 278 also 91. One should probably read reference to French and Burgundian hostility as referring to a wider context than the current situation, and the importance of Guînes in the long-term defence of Calais.

33   *CPR, 1452–61*, pp. 642, 646; Ibid, *1461–7*, p. 45; TNA, E404/72/1, no. 110; Grummitt, *Calais Garrison*, Ch. 4, 'The Nature of Military Service'.

34   Hicks, *Warwick*, pp. 253, 262.

35   TNA, C76/149 m14; Grummit, *Calais Garrison*, Ch. 4, 'The Nature of Military Service'; Hicks, *Warwick*, p. 249.

36   CSPM, i, p. 47. I overlooked this evidence in my entry on Fauconberg in the *Oxford DNB*.

37   Griffiths, *Henry VI*, p. 816; History of Parliament Trust, London, unpublished article on Sir John Wenlock, Lord Wenlock for the 1422–61 section by Charles Moreton.

38   Grummitt, 'Calais, 1485–1547', pp. 50–1; *idem, Calais Garrison*, Ch. 3, 'The Organisation of the Garrison'; Ch. 4, 'The Nature of Military Service'; Hicks, *Warwick*, p. 248; History of Parliament, 'Sir Walter Blount'.

39   Harriss, 'Struggle for Calais', pp. 50–2; Grummitt, 'Calais, 1485–1547', p. 40; see above pp. 80–1.

40   *PL*, iv, pp. 50, 57; C. D. Ross, *Edward IV* (1974), p. 50.

41   Hicks, *Warwick*, p. 251.

42   Hicks, pp. 144–7, 250–1; 'Arrivall', p. 39; C. F. Richmond, 'Fauconberg's Rising of May 1471', *EHR*, xxxv (1970), 673–92; see also above pp. 70, 74.

43   CSPM, i, p. 83; Meek, 'English Diplomacy', pp. 32–4, 148–9, 158–63.

44   Meek, 'English Diplomacy', pp. 119–29.

45   L. Visser-Fuchs, 'Warwick by Himself: Richard Neville, earl of Warwick, 'The Kingmaker', in the '*Recueil des Croniques D'Engleterre* of Jean de Waurin', *Publication du Centre Europeen D'etudes Bourguignonnes (xive–xvie)*, 41 (2001), 146.

46   Commynes, *Memoirs*, p. 191.

47   Ibid, pp. 181–2, 184–5.

48   Ibid, pp. 191–2.

49   Idid, pp. 185–6.

50   Warkworth, *Chronicle*, pp. 19–20; *Arrivall*, pp. 33, 37.

51   *CPR, 1467–77*, pp. 290–92.

52   *CPR, 1461–7*, p. 294; Grummitt, *Calais Garrison*, Ch. 4, 'The Nature of Military Service'. It would appear that during the sequestration chancery deemed the liberty of Durham to be part of the county of Northumberland. For this constitutional nicety see A. J. Pollard, *North-Eastern England during the Wars of the Roses* (Oxford, 1990), pp. 145–9.

53   CSPM, i, 21, pp. 28–9, 31–4, 41–4, 46–7, 51–3, 69–70, 86, 97, 105–8.

Notes to Chapter 9: The Idol of the Multitude

1   Bale's Chronicle, p. 147.

2   'Short English Chronicle', p. 71.

3   *Historical Poems of the Fourteenth and Fifteenth Centuries*, ed. R. H. Robbins (New York, 1959), pp. 226–7.

4   *Arrivall*, p. 21.

5   *The Crowland Chronicle Continuations: 1459–1486*, ed. Nicholas Pronay and John Cox (Yorkist and Richard III History Trust, 1986) p. 147.

6   Hicks, *Warwick*, pp. 182–3, 191, 210.

7   Ibid., pp. 275, 313.

8   *Great Chronicle*, p. 207.

9   Morice, *Memoirs*, iii, pp. 159–60; Gregory's Chronicle, p. 206.

10 *Eng. Chron.*, p. 86.

11 'Short English Chronicle', p. 74; Gregory's Chronicle, p. 207.

12 Waurin, *Recueil des Croniques*, v, pp. 307–8.

13 Mary-Rose McClaren, *The London Chronicles of the Fifteenth Century* (Cambridge, D.S.Brewer (2002), pp. 51–63.

14 *CSPM*, i, p. 48.

15 Gregory's Chronicle, p. 215. The text is ambiguous. It is not clear whether the report that Warwick told Edward of the favour unto him refers to favour to Edward or to Warwick. If Edward's cause is meant, much of the favour was due to Warwick.

16 Gregory's Chronicle, p. 206.

17 *PL*, iv, p. 207. My italics.

18 C. D. Ross, *Edward IV* (1974), p. 43.

19 *Eng. Chron.*, p. 97.

20 *Arivall*, 6; A. J. Pollard, *North-Eastern England during the Wars of the Roses* (Oxfrod, 1990), pp. 303–4.

21 *CSPM*, i, p. 138.

22 *Great Chronicle*, p. 207.

23 Olivier de la Marche, *Mémoires*, ed. H. Beaune and J. d'Arbaumont, 4 vols (SHF, Paris, 1883–88), iii, p. 69; L. Visser-Fuchs, 'Warwick and Waurin: two case studies on the literary background and propaganda of Anglo-Burgundian Relations in the Yorkist Period' (London University PhD, 2002), p. 69.

24 Bale's Chronicle, 145.

25 J. L. Bolton, 'The City and the Crown, 1456–61', *London Journal*, 12 (1986), 11–24.

26 See above pp. 59–60, 72. I am grateful to Jim Bolton for drawing my attention to these points.

27 J. P. Gilson, 'A Defence of the Proscription of the Yorkists in 1459', *EHR*, xxvi (1911) 521.

28 Gregory's Chronicle, p. 190.

29 Ibid, p. 191.

30 R. H. Britnell, *The Commercialisation of English Society, 1000–1500* (2nd edn, Manchester:, 1996), pp. 1552–37; C. C. Dyer, *Making a Living in the Middle Ages: the People of Britain, 850–1520* (New Haven 2002), pp. 265–365; C. C. Dyer, *An Age of Transition? Economy and Society in England in the Later Middle Ages* (Oxford, 2005); A. J. Pollard, *Late Medieval England, 1399–1509* (Harlow, 2000), pp. 181–6, 188–90.

31 A. J. Pollard, *Imagining Robin Hood: the Late Medieval Stories in Historical Context* (2004), pp. 177–182; *idem, Late-Medieval England*, pp. 253–5; I. M. W. Harvey, 'Was there Popular Politics in Fifteenth-Century England?', in R. H. Britnell and A. J. Pollard, eds, *The McFarlane Legacy* (Stroud, 1995); E. H. Shagan, *Popular Politics and the English Reformation*

(Cambridge, 2003), pp. 1–25; C. C. Dyer, 'The Political Life of the Fifteenth-Century English Village', in L. S. Clark and M. C. Carpenter, eds, *The Fifteenth Century, IV: Political Culture in Late-Medieval Britain* (Woodbridge, 2004), pp. 135–58.

32 See S. Justice, *Writing and Rebellion: England in 1381* (California, 1994) *passim*.

33 J. L. Watts, 'The Pressure of the Public on Later Medieval Politics', in Clark and Carpenter, *Political Culture*, pp. 159–80; G. Dodd, 'A parliament full of rats? *Piers Plowman* and the Good Parliament of 1376', *HR*, lxxix (2006), pp. 41–7.

34 John Hatcher, 'The Great Slump of the mid-fifteenth century', in Richard Britnell and John Hatcher, eds, *Progress and Problems in Medieval England* (Cambridge, 1996), p. 240–5; R. H. Britnell, 'The Economic context', in A. J. Pollard, ed., *Wars of the Roses* (Basingstoke, 1995, pp. 41–64.

35 *Political Poems and Songs relating to English History*, ed. T. Wright (RS, 1861), ii, pp. 282ff.

36 *John Vale's Book*, pp. 204–5. Reference was probably to the July 1449 grant of a half tenth and fifteenth. The last tax before that was a half tenth and fifteenth voted in 1445. The House of Commons was not asked for further supply in the November parliament, because the July subsidy was to be collected over two years. Parliament in the late 1440s had been very reluctant to vote subsidies; other expediencies such as resumption and a tax on aliens were therefore adopted (R. A. Griffiths, *The Reign of Henry VI* (1981), pp. 379–81.

37 I. M. W. Harvey, *Cade's Rebellion of 1450* (Oxford, 1991), p. 189.

38 *Eng. Chron.*, p. 68.

39 Montgomery Bohna, 'Armed Force and Civic Legitimacy in Jack Cade's Revolt, 1450', *EHR*, cxviii (2003), 572–6, 581–2. My gloss is different. A. E. Goodman, *The Wars of the Roses: the Soldier's Experience* (Stroud: Tempus, 2005), pp. 91–2, 115–25; *idem,The Wars of the Roses: Military Activity and English Society, 1452–97* (1981), pp. 143–4. See also P. C. Maddern, *Violence and Social Order: East Anglia, 1422–1442* (Oxford, 1992), pp. 1–74 and the argument of Claire Valente, *The Theory and Practice of revolt in Medieval England* (Aldershot, 2003), *passim*, that armed rebellion by nobles was an integral part of normal political action.

40 Bale's Chronicle, p. 149.

41 *Chronicles of the White Rose of York*, ed. G. A. Giles (1845), p. 24 but see also Waurin, *Receuil des Croniques*, v, 579, on the prominent role of Parr (presumably with men from the west march) alongside Gate (leading the Calais contingent?) above, p. 119.

42 Warkworth, *Chronicle*, p. 42.

43 *Arrivall*, p. 33, which puts the number at 16–17,000 men; *CPR, 167–77*, pp. 299–303; my calculation is different from that made by Richmond, 'Fauconberg's Rising of May 1471', *EHR*, lxxxv (1970), 684–5; Bohna, 'Armed Force', 577–8. Note too that the *Arrivall* represents this host of 'goodmen' in terms similar to Gregory's characterization of the rebels of 1450, as riotous, motivated by 'great rancour and malice', thinking to 'rob and spoil, who 'came for robbing (rather) than for revenging by way of battle', these 'mischievous men' were called 'his soldiers'.

44 *John Vale's Book*, p. 218; *The Anonimalle Chronicle, 1337–1381*, ed. V. H. Galbraith (Manchester, 1927), p. 139. Dodd, 'Parliament full of rats', at p. 45 suggests that the watchword of 1381, 'Wyth kynge Richarde and with the trew communes' was in part a rebuff to the false House of Commons.

45 *John Vale's Book*, p. 214.

46 Harvey, *Cade's Rebellion*, p. 191.

47 M. A. Hicks, *English Political Culture in the Fifteenth Century* (2002), pp. 198–203, has identified this as a 'Reform Movement'.

48 *John Vale's Book*, pp. 208–10.

49 *Eng. Chron.*, pp. 82–5.

50 *John Vale's Book*, p. 209.

51 Gilson, 'Defence', pp. 515, 518–20. It is perhaps with this in mind that we should understand why Edward IV was at pains to have it put in the official account of the earl's treason in March 1470 that obedience to the crown was a better way to ensure the common weal (*Chronicle of the Rebellion in Lincolnshire*, p. 15).

52 J. L. Watts, 'Ideas, Principles and Politics', in A. J. Pollard, ed, *The Wars of the Roses* (1995), pp. 128–9.

53 *John Vale's Book*, pp. 218–19. This was circulated by the earl and Clarence in the summer of 1470 before their triumphant return to England, Hicks suggests possibly *before* Angers (Hicks, *Warwick*, p. 298).

54 *Eng. Chron.*, p. 84.

55 *John Vale's Book*, p. 219. Hicks (*Warwick*, p. 298) sees this as a veiled attack on the Woodvilles. It could have been, but it was open to all readers and auditors to suppose that, on the eve of war against Burgundy, the kingdom was in danger of being placed under the control of Burgundians, or about to be ruled for the benefit of Burgundians.

56 *John Vale's Book*, pp. 220–21.

57 Ibid, pp. 222–3.

58 Ibid, p. 225.

59 J. L. Watts, '"A New Ffundacion of is Crowne": Monarchy in the Age of Henry VII', in Benjamin Thompson, ed. *The Reign of Henry VII* (Stamford, 1995), pp. 319–23.

60 *Chronicle of the Rebellion in Lincolnshire*, p. 15.

61 S. B. Chrimes, *English Constitutional Ideas of the Fifteenth Century* (Cambridge, 1936), p. 172.

62 R. W. Hoyle, 'Petitioning as Popular Politics in Early-sixteenth Century England', *HR*, lxxv (2002), 365–89 *passim*.

63 *The Mirrour for Magistrates*, ed. L. B. Campbell (Cambridge, 1938), pp. 205–11.

64 *John Vale's Book*, p. 212.

65 Ibid, p. 216. See also above, pp. 68–9, below, p. 175.

Notes to Chapter 10: The Flower of Manhood

1 Polydore Vergil, *Three Books of Polydore Vergil's English History*, ed. H. Ellis (Camden Society, 1844), pp. 94–5.

2 *Bale's Chronicle*, pp. 144, 147.

3 *Eng. Chron.* p. 88, ll. 9–10.

4 Waurin, *Recueil des Croniques*, v, p. 277.

5 *Political Poems and Songs relating to English History*, ed. T. Wright, ii (RS, 1861), p. 270.

6 Chastellain, *Oeuvres*, iii, pp. 318–20; v, pp. 223.

7   C. L. Scofield, *The Life and Reign of Edward the Fourth* (1923), i, p. 300; ii, appendix 1.

8   L Visser-Fuchs, 'Warwick and Waurin: two case studies on the literary background and propaganda of Anglo-Burgundian Relations in the Yorkist Period' (London University PhD thesis, 2002), p. 112.

9   Ibid, p. 125; A. Gransden, *Historical Writing in England, II, c.1307 to the Early Sixteenth Century* (1982), pp. 485–7.

10 BL, Harley MS 4224, fo. 255.

11 Chastellain, *Ouevres*, v, p. 495.

12 Visser-Fuchs, 'Warwick and Waurin', pp. 20–1, 42, 51, 55, 57–63; *eadem*, 'Edward IV's *Memoir on Paper* to Charles, Duke of Burgundy: The so-called "Short Version of the Arrivall"', *Nottingham Medieval Studies*, xxxvi (1992), 170. Much of the bitterness may well have stemmed from the duke's personal animosity. He was said to have received the news of Warwick's death with great joy (Visser-Fuchs, 'Warwick and Waurin', p. 70).

13 *Rous Roll*, ed. W. H. Coulthorpe (1859, reissue Gloucester, 1980), nos 56, 57.

14 A. Sinclair, *The Beauchamp Pageant* (Donington, 2003), pp. 13–16, 21–3.

15 *Three Books of English History*, pp. 119–20.

16 Ibid, pp. 145–6; Edward Hall, *The Union of Two Illustrious Houses of Lancaster and York*, fo. xxix r.

17 *The Mirrour for Magistrates*, ed. L. B. Campbell (Cambridge, 1938), pp. 206–8.

18 Ibid, p 208, ll. Pp. 71–7.

19 The Auchinleck Manuscript, eds D. Burley and A Wiggins, http://www.nls.uk/auchinleck/; E. M. D. Legge, *Anglo-Norman Literature and its Background* (Oxford, 1963), pp. 162–71; V. B. Richmond, *The Legend of Guy of Richmond* (New York, 1996); C. Fewster, *Traditionality and Genre in Middle English Romance* (Cambridge, 1987), pp. 104–26; Yin Liu, 'Richard Beauchamp and the Uses of Romance', *Medium Aevium*, lxxiv (2005), 271–3; E. Mason, 'Legends of the Beauchamps' Ancestors', *Journal of Medieval History*, xi (1984), 25–40, esp. 35 for the origin of the badge of the bear and ragged staff. The earl would have known well the four magnificent tapestries hanging in the great chamber of Guy's Tower at Warwick Castle, which depicted the story and which descended to his countess as a family heirloom. Margaret Beauchamp, countess of Shrewsbury, commissioned Lydgate's version of the poem in the mid-1440s (Sinclair, *Beauchamp Pageant*, pp. 14–15).

20 It is owned by the Bibliothèque Publique et Universitaire in Geneva, MS français 166. Identified by his coat of arms encircled by the Garter on fo. 3, it was perhaps made as an intended gift to him in 1464, but was never presented. It is now established that the author was Hue de Lannoy (d. 1456) a frequent ambassador to England in the early years of Henry VI's reign (B Sterchi, 'Hugues de Lannoy, auteur de Lenseignement de Vraie Noblesse', *Le Moyen Age*, cx (2004), 79–117; Visser-Fuchs, 'The Manuscript of the *Enseignement de Vraie Noblesse* made for Richard, Earl of Warwick in 1464', in G.H.M. Claasens and W. Verbeke, eds, *Medieval Manuscripts in Transition* (Leuven, 2006), pp. 337–62.). See also M. H. Keen, *Chivalry* (New Haven, 1984), pp. 15–16.

21 Keen, *Chivalry*, p. 2.

22 John Major, *A History of Greater Britain*, trans and ed. A. Constable (Scottish History Society, 1892), p. 390–1.

23 Commynes, *Memoirs*, 413; Chastellain, *Oeuvres*, iv, p. 159; v, p. 22.

24 Visser-Fuchs, 'Warwick and Waurin', p. 85.

25 *Rous Roll*, no. 57.

26 *Mirrour for Magistrates*, p. 208, ll. pp. 78–84.

27 Waurin, *Recueil des Croniques*, v, p. 579.

28 Gregory's Chronicle, pp. 91–2; Waurin, *Recueil des Croniques*, v, p. 304.

29 Ann Payne, 'The Salisbury Roll of Arms, c. 1463, in D. Williams, ed., *England in the Fifteenth Century* (Woodbridge, 1987), pp. 187–98; Hicks, *Warwick*, pp. 228–30.

30 J. Leland, *Antiquarii de rebus Britannicus Collectanea*, ed. T. Hearne (1770), vi, pp. 2–4; Christopher Woolgar, 'Fast and Feast: Conspicuous Consumption and the Diet of the Nobility in the Fifteenth Century', in M. A. Hicks, ed., *Revolution and Consumption*, pp. 23–5; Hicks, *Warwick*, pp. 230–1. See above, p. 57.

31 Waurin, *Recueil des Croniques*, v, p. 546.

32 *The Chronicle of John Stone*, ed. W. G. Searle (Cambridge Antiquarian Society, 8th series, xxiv (1902), pp. 109–10; Hicks, *Warwick*, p. 232. It is not clear from the Latin whether the existing *Trinity* was refitted (made anew) or whether a new vessel was built.

33 C. F. Richmond and M. C. Kekewich, 'The Search for Stability, 1461–83', *John Vale's Book*, p. 49; C. F. Richmond, 'The earl of Warwick's Domination of the Channel and the Naval Dimension to the Wars of the Roses, 1456–1460', *Southern History*, xx/xxi (1998–9), 18–19.

34 Short English Chronicle, p. 74. They could hardly have been traitors as they were holding the Tower for the king, whose authority Warwick and his fellow lords proclaimed they were upholding.

35 *CSPM*, i, p. 27.

36 Charles Oman, *Warwick the Kingmaker* (1891), p. 241.

37 Short English Chronicle, p. 73; *Eng. Chron.*, p. 98.

38 Warkworth, *Chronicle*, p. 9. This is somewhat puzzling to the modern mind. Was it any more offensive than the customary display of the heads and other parts of the dismembered bodies of traitors in public places? Perhaps the popular displeasure reported by Warkworth was more the expression of anger at the execution of Warwick's men, and thus an expression of sympathy for his cause, than disgust at the particular further brutality.

39 Warwick's summary justice is in fact reminiscent of actions taken by the commons in 1450, not just the murder of the duke of Suffolk but also of Bishop Ayscough and Lord Say, vividly described in *Eng. Chron.*, pp. 67, 69. Brutality and summary execution were taken for granted in the contemporary Robin Hood and other outlaw stories (see A. J. Pollard, *Imagining Robin Hood: the Late-Medieval Stories in Historical Context* (2004), pp. 96–8). If we are to be shocked, we should be shocked by the age, not the man. But who are we, to be shocked?

40 See above, pp. 116–18.

41 Gregory, *Chronicle*, pp. 220–1

42 C. F. Richmond, *The Paston Family in the Fifteenth Century: Fastolf's Will* (Cambridge, 1996), p. 27 and n. 71; and above pp. 97–8, 134.

43 A. J. Pollard, *North-Eastern England during the Wars of the Roses* (Oxford, 1990), pp. 298–300.

44 Waurin, *Recueil des Croniques*, v, p. 307.

45 *John Vale's Book*, p. 216.
46 Vergil, *Three Books of English History*, pp. 119–20.
47 Commynes, *Memoirs*, p. 195. See also Dr Visser-Fuchs conclusion that 'It must have been generally known how 'careful' Warwick was, 'a very reprehensible thing in a knight and a soldier' (Visser-Fuchs, 'Warwick and Waurin', p. 143).
48 Warkworth, *Chronicle*, p. 16.
49 *Arrivall*, p. 20.
50 Wright, *Political Poems*, ii (1861), p. 272.
51 Ibid, p. 276.
52 Gregory's Chronicle, pp. 214, 216. Gregory tells the story of Trollope at St Albans as of a feat of arms in a chivalric romance. Knighted after the battle, he says to the king, 'My lord, I have not deserved it, for I slew but 15 men, for I stood still in one place and they came unto me, but they bode still with me' (ibid, p. 214).
53 Waurin, *Recueil des Croniques*, v, p. 288.
54 *PL*, iii, p. 130; *Six Town Chronicles of England*, ed. R. Flenley (Oxford, 1911), 'Gough 10', p. 160.
55 C. L. Kingsford, 'The Earl of Warwick at Calais in 1460', *EHR*, xxxvii (1922), 545.
56 Bale's Chronicle, p. 147; 'Gough 10', p. 160; *Eng. Chron.*, p. 81; Richmond, 'Domination of the Channel', p. 7.
57 Bale's Chronicle, p. 147; *PL*, iii, p. 130.
58 Visser-Fuchs, 'Warwick and Waurin', pp. 73–5.
59 Waurin, *Recueil des Croniques*, v, p. 300; Scofield, *Edward the Fourth*, i, pp. 162–3.
60 Gregory's Chronicle, pp. 212–14.
61 *Eng. Chron.*, p. 98.
62 *CSPM*, i, p. 49. 'Fortitude' and 'inadequate' are my translations of 'forte' and 'non e stato vero'. I am grateful to Alexandra Elam for her advice.
63 Ibid, p. 54; Gregory's Chronicle, p. 214.
64 Hall, *Chronicle*, fo. xxixr.
65 *PL*, iv, p. 60.
66 *John Vale's Book*, pp. 171–2.
67 Warkworth, *Chronicle*, p. 2.
68 Bale's Chronicle, p. 152; *Eng. Chron.*, p. 98; TNA, SC6/1085/20; Hicks, *Warwick*, pp. 143, 248. See also A. E. Goodman, *The Wars of the Roses, Military Activity and English Society, 1452–97* (1981), pp. 1 70–4 and K. DeVreis, 'The Use of Gunpowder Weapons in the Wars of the Roses', in D. Biggs *et al.*, eds, *Traditions and Transformations in Late Medieval England* (Leiden, 2001, pp. 21–38 for the use of artillery.
69 See David Morgan, 'From a View to a Death: Lous Robessart, Johan Huizinga, and the Political Significance of Chivalry', in S. Anglo, ed., *Chivalry in the Renaissance* (Woodbridge, 1990), pp. 93–106.
70 Sir Thomas Malory, *Morte Darthur: the Winchester Manuscript*, ed. Helen Cooper (Oxford, 1998), pp. vii–xxii; P. J. C. Field, *The Life and Times of Sir Thomas Malory* (Cambridge, 1993), pp. 131–2; A. F. Sutton, 'Malory in Newgate: a New Document', *The Library*, vii (2000), 243–62, for the correct identification of the prison.
71 Field, *Malory*, pp. 128–2; Christine Carpenter, 'Sir Thomas Malory and Fifteenth-Century Local Politics', *BIHR*, 53 (1980), pp. 31–43.

72 C. F. Richmond, 'The Murder of Thomas Dennis', *Common Knowledge*, ii (1993), pp. 85–98.

73 Field, *Malory*, pp. 131–2, 137–47.

74 Sutton, 'Malory in Newgate', pp. 246–8. She also suggests that he died while still in prison, which explains his burial in the nearby Greyfriars, rather than six months after being released at the Readeption, as is usually supposed.

75 Field, *Malory*, p. 143.

76 P. J. C. Field, 'Fifteenth-Century History in Malory's Morte Darthur', in F.H.M Le Saux, ed., *The Formation of Culture in Medieval Britain* (Lampeter, 1995), pp. 31–71).

77 *Morte Darthur*, ed Cooper, p. 507; Sir Thomas Malory, *Works*, ed E. Vinaver (2nd edn 1971), p 708, ll. Pp. 24–41.

78 Ibid., 'new-fangle' is close to other contemporary comment on the fickleness of the people.

79 *Morte Darthur*, pp. 507–27 esp. pp. 511, 514, 521; *Works*, pp. 708–21, esp. 708; ll. 43–5; 709, ll. 1–5; 711, ll. 5–7, 14–18; 712, ll. 25–7; 714, ll. 33–6. The *Eng. Chron.*, p. 97, specifically noted that York should be called Duke of Cornwall as well as Prince of Wales.

80 R. L. Radulescu, *The Gentry Context for Malory's Morte Darthur* (Cambridge, 2003), pp. 136–44.

81 Richard R. Griffith, 'The Political Bias of Malory's 'Morte D'Arthur', *Viator*, 5 (1974), 365–86; Sutton, 'Malory in Newgate', pp. 247–8; Jonathan Hughes, *Arthurian Myths and Alchemy: the Kingship of Edward IV* (Stroud, 2002), pp. 205–10.

82 *Morte Darthur*, p. 507; *Works*, p. 708, ll 35–6.

83 *John Vale's Book*, p. 178; Sutton, 'Malory in Newgate', p. 244. Vale's characterization became the standard Lancastrian/Tudor explanation for the failure of the dynasty; one might note the common use of the phrase 'brought up from nought' in both texts (*Morte Darthur*, p. 507). This is close in spirit to Malory's view of the collapse of Arthur's kingship.

84 Field, *Malory*, pp. 146–7.

85 *Morte Darthur*, p. 517; *Works*, 717, ll 32–4.

86 S. Knight, 'Arthurian Attributes: ideology in the legend of King Arthur', in Knight and S. N. Mukherjee, eds, *Words and Worlds: studies in the social role of verbal culture* (Sydney, 1983), p. 122.

87 E.g., Waurin, *Recueil des Croniques*, v, pp. 271–2, 306–7, 327.

88 See Thomas A. Prendergast, 'The Invisible Spouse: Henry VI, Arthur and the Fifteenth-century Subject', *Journal of Medieval and early Modern Studies*, 32.2 (2002), 306–26.

89 *Morte Darthur*, p. 485; *Works*, pp. 688, ll 27–36.

Notes to Chapter 11: Conclusion

1 *Rous Roll*, no. 57.

2 Hicks, *Warwick*, pp. 232–3.

3 See above pp. 21, 96.

4 L. Monckton, 'Fit for a King? The Architecture of the Beauchamp Chapel', *Architectural History*, 47 (2004), 26–8; A. Payne, 'The Beauchamps and the Nevilles' in R. Marks and P. Williamson, eds, *Gothic: Art for England, 1400–1547* p. 220. M. A. Hicks, 'The Beauchamp

Trust', in *Richard III and his Rivals: Magnates and their Motives during the Wars of the Roses* (1991), pp. 342, 345–8; Hicks, *Warwick*, pp. 56–7.

5   *Rous Roll*, no. 57; Hicks, *Warwick*, 58–9.

6   Hicks, *Warwick*, pp. 237–8. Hicks suggests that he may have been no more than a figurehead. The college was being built in 1465–7. It may well be that Warwick was also responsible for mid-fifteenth century building work at both Middleham and Warwick castles.

7   Ibid, p. 233.

8   C. L. Kingsford, 'Earl of Warwick at Calais in 1460', *EHR*, xxxiv (1922), 545.

9   Alexandra Sinclair, *The Beauchamp Pageant* (Donington: Paul Watkins, 2003), pp. 16–23, and especially 22–3 where it is suggested that the *Pageant* was conceived as an *exemplum* of chivalric conduct for her grandson, Edward of Middleham as Prince of Wales; *Rous Roll*, no. 56.

10 See above, p. 168.

11 W. Shakespeare, *Henry VI, Part Two*, Act 1, Sc. I.

12 Ibid, *Part Three*, Act 2, Sc. VI, end.

13 Ibid, Act 1, Sc. III.

14 Ibid, Act IV, Sc. III.

15 Ibid, Act V, Sc. II.

16 Ibid, Act IV, Sc. III.

17 Hicks, *Warwick*, pp. 1, 4.

18 Thomas Carte, *A General History of England from the Earliest Times* (1750), ii, p. 741.

19 Paul de Rapin de Thoyras, *The History of England*, trans N. Tindal, 3rd edn (1743), vol. 1, p. 596.

20 Ibid, p. 604.

21 Ibid, p. 613.

22 *Oxford DNB*, 46, pp. 68–71.

23 M. H. Keen, *Chivalry* (New Haven, 1984), pp. 249–51.

24 *Oxford DNB*, 28, pp. 751–2.

25 D. Hume, *The History of England* (1871 edn), iii, pp. 160–1.

26 *Oxford DNB*, 28, pp. 751–2.

27 W. Stubbs, *Constitutional History*, iii, p. 212; J. Gairdner, *Houses of Lancaster and York* (1886), p. 186.

28 See above, p. 2.

29 E. Bulwer-Lytton, *The Last of the Barons* (1843), p. 3,

30 Charles Oman, *Warwick the Kingmaker* (1891), pp. 235–43, esp. at p. 243.

31 I. D. Colvin, *The Germans in England, 1066–1598* (National Review, 1915), pp. xi–xii, 94, 103–18, 214. I am grateful to John Ramsden for this reference.

32 P. M. Kendall, *Warwick the Kingmaker* (1957), pp. 8, 271, 281, 324; S. J. Greenblatt, *Renaissance Self-fashion from More to Shakespeare* (Chicago 1982), *passim*. For discussion of a near contemporary example of chivalric self-fashioning see D. A. L. Morgan, 'From a View to a Death: Louis Robessart, Johan Huizinga and the Political Significance of Chivalry', in S. Anglo, ed., *Chivalry in the Renaissance* (Woodbridge, 1990), pp. 93–106.

33 Oman, *Warwick the Kingmaker*, pp. 235–6; Kendall, *Warwick the Kingmaker*, p. 324; Richmond, *John Vale's Book*, p. 49; Hicks, *Warwick*, pp. 6, 313. The italics are mine.

34 Hicks, *Warwick*, p. 275; above pp. 171–2.
35 A. E. Goodman, *The New Monarchy: England, 1471–1534* (Historical Association, Oxford, 1988), *passim*; J. L. Watts, '"A New Ffundacion of is Crowne": Monarchy in the Age of Henry VII', in B. Thompson, ed. *The Reign of Henry VII* (Woodbridge, 1995), pp. 31–53; John Fortescue, *On the Laws and Governance of England*, ed. S. J. Lockwood (Cambridge, 1997).
36 One of the best reiterations of this preconception remains that by S. T. Bindoff: 'A crown which had become a football was ceasing to be a referee, and a game which begins by doing without a referee runs a risk of finishing without a ball. Right was beginning to yield to might at all levels and in all relationships of society, and four centuries of heroic efforts by kings and statesmen to establish the reign of law seemed to be in danger of being brought to nought amid a surfeit of kings and a shortage of statesmen.' (*Tudor England*, Harmondsworth, 1950, p. 8.)
37 Commynes, *Memoirs*, pp. 143–5.
38 L. Visser-Fuchs, 'Warwick and Waurin: two case studies on the literary background and propaganda of Anglo-Burgundian relations in the Yorkist Period' (London University PhD thesis, 2002), p. 85.

Bibliography

Place of publication London unless otherwise stated

The Anonimalle Chronicle, 1337–1381, ed. V. H. Galbraith (Manchester: Manchester University Press, 1927).

Archer, R. E., 'Rich Old Ladies: The Problem of Late Medieval Dowagers', in A. J. Pollard, ed., *Property and Politics: Essays in Later Medieval History* (Gloucester: Sutton Publishing, 1984).

Armstrong, C. A. J., 'Politics and the Battle of St Albans, 1455', *BIHR*, xxxiii (1960).

Arvanigian, M., 'Henry IV, the Northern Nobility and the Consolidation of the Regime', in G. Dodd and D Biggs, eds., *Henry IV: the Establishment of the Regime, 1399–1406* (Woodbridge: The Boydell Press, 2003).

Bean, J. M. W., *The Estates of the Percy Family, 1416–1537* (Oxford: Oxford University Press, 1958).

The Beauchamp Pageant, ed. A. F. J. Sinclair (Donington: Paul Watkins, 2003).

Bindoff, S. T, *Tudor England* (Harmondsworth: Penguin Books 1950).

Bloom, J. H., 'A Letter from the "Kingmaker"' *Notes and Queries*, 12th series, v (1919).

Bohna, M., 'Armed Force and Civic legitimacy in Jack Cade's Revolt, 1450', *EHR*, cxviii (2003).

Bolton, J., 'The City and the Crown, 1456–61', *London Journal*, xii (1986).

Booth, P. L., 'Landed Society in Cumberland and Westmorland, c.1440–1485: the Politics of the Wars of the Roses' (University of Leicester PhD thesis, 1997).

Booth, P. W., 'Men Behaving Badly? The West March towards Scotland and the Percy-Neville Feud', in L. S. Clark, ed., *The Fifteenth Century, III: Subversion and Authority* (Woodbridge: The Boydell Press, 2003).

Britnell, R. H., 'The Economic Context', in A. J. Pollard, ed., *The Wars of the Roses* (Basingstoke: Macmillan, 1995).

The Brut or the Chronicle of England, ed. F. W. D. Brie, 2 vols (EETS, original series, cxxxvi, 1908).

Bulwer-Lytton, E, *The Last of the Barons* (Tauchnitz, 1843).

Calendar of State Papers and Manuscripts … of Milan, vol. 1, ed. A. B. Hinds (1912).

Carpenter, M. C., 'Sir Thomas Malory and Fifteenth-Century Local Politics', *BIHR*, liii (1980).

Carpenter, M. C., *Locality and Polity: a study of Warwickshire Landed Society, 1401–1499* (Cambridge: Cambridge University Press, 1992).

Carpenter, M. C., *The Wars of the Roses: Politics and the Constitution in England, c. 1437–1509* (Cambridge: Cambridge University Press, 1997).

Carte, T., *A General History of England from the Earliest Times* (1750).

Castor, H. R., '"Walter Blount was gone to serve Traitors": The Sack of Elvaston and the Politics of the North Midlands in 1454', *Midland History*, xix (1994).

Castor, H. R., *Blood and Roses; the Paston Family in the Fifteenth Century* (Faber and Faber, 2004).

Chastellain, G. de, *Oeuvres*, ed. K. Letenhove, 6 vols (Bruxelles, 1863–5).

Chatwin, P. B., 'Documents of "Warwick the King-maker" in possession of St Mary's Church, Warwick', *Transactions of the Birmingham Archaeological Society*, lix (1938), 3.

Chrimes, S. B., *English Constitutional Ideas of the Fifteenth Century* (Cambridge: Cambridge University Press, 1936).

A Chronicle of the First Thirteen Years of the Reign of Edward the Fourth, by John Warkworth, ed. J. O. Halliwell (Camden Society, 1839).

Chronicles of the White Rose of York, ed. G. A. Giles (1845).

The Chronicle of John Hardyng, ed. H. Ellis (1802).

The Chronicle of John Stone, ed. W. G. Searle (Cambridge Antiquarian Society: octavo series, xxxiv, 1902).

The Chronicle of the Rebellion in Lincolnshire, 1470, ed. J. G. Nichols (Camden,1847).

The Crowland Chronicle Continuations, 1459–1486, ed. N. Pronay and J. Cox (Gloucester: Richard III and Yorkist History Trust, 1986).

Colvin, I. D., *The Germans in England, 1066–1598* (National Review, 1915).

Devine, M., 'Lancastrian Richmondshire, 1372–1425' (University of Teesside PhD thesis, 2006).

DeVreis, K., 'The Use of Gunpowder Weapons in the Wars of the Roses', in *Traditions and Transformations in Late Medieval England*, eds D. Biggs and others (Leiden: Brill, 2002), pp. 21–38.

Dobson, R. B., *Durham Priory 1400–1450* (Cambridge: Cambridge University Press, 1973).

Dodd, G. A., 'A parliament full of rats? *Piers Plowman* and the Good Parliament of 1376', *HR*, lxxix (2006).

Dunlop, A., *The Life and Times of James Kennedy, Bishop of St Andrews* (Scottish Academic Press, 1950).

Dyer, C. C., *Standards of Living in the Later Middle Ages: Social Change in England, c.1200–1520* (Cambridge: Cambridge University Press, 1989).

Dyer, C. C., 'The Political Life of the Fifteenth-Century English Village', in *The Fifteenth Century, IV, Political Culture in Late-Medieval Britain*, ed. L. S. Clark and M. C. Carpenter (Woodbridge: The Boydell Press, 2004).

Emery, A, *The Greater Medieval Houses of England and Wales, 1, Northern England* (Cambridge: Cambridge University Press, 1996).

An English Chronicle, 1377–1461, ed. W. Marx (Woodbridge: The Boydell Press, 2003).

Field, P. J. C., *The Life and Times of Sir Thomas Malory* (Cambridge: D. S. Brewer, 1993).

Field, P. J. C., 'Fifteenth-Century History in Malory's Morte Darthur', in *The Formation of Culture in Medieval Britain*, ed. F. H. M. Le Saux (Lampeter: Edwin Mellen Press, 1995).

Ford, C. J., 'Piracy or Policy? The Crisis in the Channel, 1400–1403', *TRHS*, 5th series, xxix (1979).

Fortescue, Sir John, *On the Laws and Governance of England*, ed. S. J. Lockwood (Cambridge: Cambridge University Press, 1997).

Gairdner, J, *The Houses of Lancaster and York* (1886).

Gilson, J. P.,'A Defence of the Proscription of the Yorkists in 1459', *EHR*, xxvi (1911).

Goodman, A. E., *The Wars of the Roses: Military Activity and English Society, 1452–97* (Routledge & Kegan Paul, 1981).

Goodman, A. E., *The New Monarchy: England, 1471–1534* (Oxford: Historical Association, 1988).

Goodman, A. E., *John of Gaunt: The Exercise of Princely Power in Fourteenth-Century Europe* (Longman, 1992).

Goodman, A. E., *The Wars of the Roses: the Soldier's Experience* (Stroud: Tempus, 2005).

Gransden, A., *Historical Writing in England, II, c.1307 to the Early Sixteenth Century* (Routledge, 1982).

The Great Chronicle of London, eds A. H. Thomas and I. D. Thornley (Selected from 'printed by George W. Jones at the sign of the Dolphin under the direction of the Library of the Corporation of the City of London' (as given in IHR catalogue, 1938).

Griffith, R. R., 'The Political Bias of Malory's 'Morte Darthur', *Viator*, v (1974).

Griffiths, R. A., 'Local Rivalries and National Politics: the Percies, the Nevilles and the Duke of Exeter, 1452–55', *Speculum*, 43 (1968).

Griffiths, R. A., *The Reign of Henry VI: the Exercise of Royal Authority, 1422–1461* (Ernest Benn, 1981).

Griffiths, R. A., 'The Hazards of Civil War: the Mountford family and the Wars of the Roses', *Midland History*, v (1981), 1–19, reprinted in *King and Country* (Hambledon, 1991).

Griffiths, R. A., 'The King's Council and the First Protectorate of the Duke of York', in *idem*, *King and Country: England and Wales in the Fifteenth Century* (1991).

Gross, A., *The Dissolution of Lancastrian Kingship: Sir John Fortescue and the Crisis of Monarchy in the Fifteenth Century* (Stamford: Paul Watkins, 1996).

Grummitt, D., 'Calais 1485–1547; a study in Early Tudor Politics and Government' (University of London PhD thesis, 1997).

Grummitt, D., '"One of the moost pryncipall treasours belonging to his Realme of England": Calais and the Crown, c.1450–1558', in G. W. Bernard and S. J. Gunn, eds, *The English Experience in France, c. 1450–1558: War, Diplomacy and Cultural Exchange* (Aldershot: Ashgate Publishing, 2002).

Grummitt, D., 'Public Service, Private Interest and Patronage in the Fifteenth-Century Exchequer', in L.S. Clark, ed. *The Fifteenth Century, III: Authority and Subversion* (Woodbridge: The Boydell Press, 2003).

Grummitt, D., *The Calais Garrison: War and Military Service in England, 1436–1558* (Woodbridge: The Boydell Press, 2007).

Hall, E., *The Union of Two Illustrious Houses of Lancaster and York* (facsimile edn, Merston, 1970).

Hammond, P. W., *The Battles of Barnet and Tewkesbury* (Gloucester: Sutton Publishing, 1990).

Hanham, A., *Richard III and his early Historians* (Oxford: Oxford University Press, 1975).

Hare, J., 'Regional Prosperity in Fifteenth-Century England: Some Evidence from Wessex', in M. A. Hicks, ed., *The Fifteenth Century II: Revolution and Consumption in Late Medieval England* (Woodbridge: The Boydell Press, 2001).

Harriss, G. L., 'The Struggle for Calais: An Aspect of the Rivalry between Lancaster and York', *EHR*, lxxv (1960).

Harriss, G. L., *Cardinal Beaufort: A Study of Lancastrian Ascendancy and Decline* (Oxford: Clarendon Press, 1988).

Harriss, G. L., 'The King and His Subjects', in R. E. Horrox, ed., *Fifteenth-Century Attitudes* (Cambridge: Cambridge University Press, 1994).

Harriss, G. L., 'The Dimensions of Politics', in R. H. Britnell and A. J. Pollard, eds, *The McFarlane Legacy: Studies in late-Medieval Politics and Society* (Stroud: Sutton Publishing, 1995).

Harriss, G. L., *Shaping the Nation: England, 1360–1461* (0xford: Oxford University Press, 2005).

Harvey, M., *England, Rome and the Papacy, 1417–1464* (Manchester: Manchester University Press, 1993).

Harvey, I. M. W., *Jack Cade's Rebellion of 1450* (Oxford: Clarendon Press, 1991).

Harvey, I. M. W., 'Was there Popular Politics in Fifteenth-Century England?' in R. H. Britnell and A. J. Pollard, eds, *The McFarlane Legacy* (Stroud: Sutton Publishing, 1995).

Harvey, J. H., *William Worcestre's Itineraries* (Oxford: Clarendon Press, 1969).

Hatcher, J. A., 'The Great Slump of the Mid-Fifteenth Century', in R. H. Britnell and Hatcher, eds, *Progress and Problems in Medieval England* (Cambridge: Cambridge University Press, 1996).

Head, C. 'Pope Pius II and the Wars of the Roses', *Archivum Historiae Pontificiae*, vii (1970).

Hicks, M. A., 'The Changing Role of the Wydevilles in Yorkist Politics to 1483', in C. D. Ross, ed., *Patronage, Pedigree and Power in Later Medieval England* (Gloucester: Sutton Publishing, 1979).

Hicks, M. A., *False, Fleeting, Perjur'd Clarence: George, Duke of Clarence, 1449–78* (Gloucester: Sutton Publishing, 1980).

Hicks, M. A., 'The Case of Sir Thomas Cook', in *idem*, *Richard III and His Rivals: Magnates and their Motives in the Wars of the Roses* (Hambledon, 1991).

Hicks, M. A., 'The Neville Earldom of Salisbury, 1429–71' in *idem, Richard III and His Rivals* (Hambledon, 1991).

Hicks, M. A., *Bastard Feudalism* (Longman, 1995).

Hicks, M. A., 'The Forfeiture of the Barnard Castle to the Bishop of Durham, 1459', *NH*, xxxiii (1997).

Hicks, M. A., *Warwick the Kingmaker* (Oxford: Blackwell Publishers Ltd, 1998)

Hicks, M. A.,'Cement or Solvent? Kinship and Politics in the Fifteenth Century: The Case of the Nevilles', *History*, lxxxiii (1998).

Hicks, M. A., 'Between Majorities: The "Beauchamp Interregnum", 1439–49', *HR*, lxxii (1999).

Hicks, M. A., *English Political Culture in the Fifteenth Century* (Routledge, 2002).

Hicks, M. A., *Anne Neville, Queen to Richard III* (Stroud: Tempus, 2006).

Historical Manuscripts Commission, *Report on the MS of the Duke of Rutland* (1888).

The Historie of the Arrivall of King Edward IV, ed. J. Bruce (Camden Society, 1838).

The Historical Collections of a London Citizen in the Fifteenth Century, ed. J. Gairdner (Camden, new series, xvii, 1876).

Historical Poems of the Fourteenth and Fifteenth Centuries, ed. R. H. Robbins (New York: Columbia University Press, 1959).

Horrox, R. E., 'Richard III and the East Riding', in *eadem, Richard III and the North* (Hull: University of Hull, 1986), pp. 82–5.

Horrox, R. E. 'Service', in *eadem, Fifteenth-Century Attitudes* (Cambridge: Cambridge University Press, 1994).

Horrox, R. E., 'Personalities and Politics' in A. J. Pollard, ed., *The Wars of the Roses* (Basingstoke: Macmillan, 1995).

Hoyle, R. W., 'Petitioning as Popular Politics in Early-sixteenth Century England', *HR*, 75 (2002).

Hughes, J., *Arthurian Myths and Alchemy: the Kingship of Edward IV* (Stroud: Sutton Publishing, 2002).

Hume, D. *The History of England*, 3 vols (Alexander Murray, 1871).

Jack, R. I., 'A Quincentenary; the Battle of Northampton, July 10th, 1460', *Northants. Past and Present*, iii (1960–65), 21–5.

James, S., 'Sir Thomas Parr', *TCWAAS*, lxxxi (1981).

James, S., 'Sir William Parr of Kendal: Part I (1434–1471)', *TCWAAS*, xciii (1993).

'John Benet's Chronicle for the years 1400 to 1462', eds G. L. and M. A. Harriss in *Camden Miscellany*, xxix (Camden 4th series, ix, 1972).

Johnson, P. A., *Duke Richard of York, 1411–1460* (Oxford: Clarendon Press, 1988).

Jones, M. K., 'Richard III and the Stanleys', in R. E. Horrox, ed., *Richard III and the North* (Hull: University of Hull, 1986).

Jones, M. K., 'Edward IV, the Earl of Warwick, and the Yorkist Claim to the Throne', *HR*, lxx (1997), 342–52.

Jones, M. K., *Bosworth 1485: Psychology of a Battle* (Stroud: Tempus, 2002).

Justice, S., *Writing and Rebellion: England in 1381* (California: University of California Press, 1994).

Keen, M. H., *Chivalry* (New Haven: Yale University Press, 1984).

Kendall, P. M., *Warwick the Kingmaker* (Allen & Unwin, 1957),

Kingsford, C. L., *English Historical Literature in the Fifteenth Century* (Oxford: Clarendon Press, 1913).

Kingsford, C. L., 'The Earl of Warwick at Calais in 1460', *EHR*, xxxvi (1922).

Kirby, J., *The Plumpton Letters and Papers* (Camden 5th series, 8, 1996).

Kleineke, H., 'Lady Joan Dinham: A Fifteenth-century West Country Matriarch', in T. Thornton, ed., *Social Attitudes and Political Structures in the Fifteenth Century* (Stroud: Sutton Publishing, 2000).

Knight, S., 'Arthurian Attributes: Ideology in the Legend of King Arthur' in S. Knight and S. N. Mukherjee, eds, *Words and Worlds: Studies in the Social Role of Verbal Culture* (Sydney: Sydney Association for Studies in Society & Culture, 1983).

Lander, J. R, 'Marriage and Politics in the fifteenth century: the Nevilles and Woodvilles, in *idem, Crown and Nobility, 1450–1509* (Edward Arnold, 1976)

Lander, J. R. 'Henry VI and the Duke of York's Second Protectorate, 1455–6', in *idem, Crown and Nobility, 1450–1509* (Edward Arnold, 1976).

Lander, J. R., *Government and Community: England, 1450–1509* (Edward Arnold, 1980).

Laynesmith, L. L., 'Constructing Queenship at Coventry: Pageantry and Politics at Margaret of Anjou's "Secret Harbour", in L. S. Clark, ed., *The Fifteenth Century, III, Authority and Subversion* (Woodbridge: The Boydell Press, 2003).

Leland, J., *Antiquarii de rebus Britannicus Collectanea*, ed. T. Hearne, 6 vols (1770).

Letters and Papers Illustrative of Wars of the English in France. ed. J. Stevenson, 2 vols in 3 (RS, 1864).

Letters of the Fifteenth and Sixteenth Centuries from the Archive of Southampton, ed. R. C. Anderson (Southampton Record Society, xxii,1921).

Liu, Y, 'Richard Beauchamp and the Uses of Literacy', *Medium Aevium*, lxxiv (2005).

Major, J., *A History of Greater Britain*, trans. and ed. A. Constable (Scottish History Society, 1892).

Malory, Sir Thomas, *Morte Darthur: the Winchester Manuscript*, ed. Helen Cooper (Oxford: Oxford University Press, 1998).

Malory, Sir Thomas, *Works*, ed. E. Vinaver, 2nd edn (Oxford: Oxford University Press, 1971).

Marche, O. de la, *Mémoires*, ed. H. Beaune and J. d'Arbaumont, 4 vols (Paris: SHF, 1883–88).

Maurer, H. E., 'Margaret of Anjou and the Loveday of 1458: a Reconsideration' in Douglas Biggs and others, eds, *Traditions and Transformations in Late Medieval England* (Leiden-Boston-Köln: Brill, 2002).

Maurer, H. E., *Margaret of Anjou: Queenship and Power in Late-medieval England* (Woodbridge: The Boydell Press, 2003).

McGladdery, C., *James II* (Edinburgh: John Donald Publishers, 1990).

McLaren, M-R., *The London Chronicles of the Fifteenth Century: a Revolution in English Writing* (Cambridge, Brewer, 2002).

Meek, E. L. 'The Conduct and Practice of English Diplomacy during the Reign of Edward IV (1461–83)' (University of Cambridge PhD thesis, 2001).

Meek, E. L. 'The Practice of English Diplomacy in France, 1461–71', in D. Grummitt, ed., *The English Experience in France, ca. 1450–1558: War, Diplomacy and Cultural Exchange* (Aldershot: Ashgate Publishing, 2002).

The Mirrour for Magistrates, ed. L. B. Campbell (Cambridge: The University Press, 1938).

Monckton, L., 'Fit for a King? The Architecture of the Beauchamp Chapel', *Architectural History*, 47 (2004).

Morgan, D. A. L., 'From a View to a Death: Louis Robessart, Johan Huizinga and the Political Significance of Chivalry', in *Chivalry in the Renaissance*, ed. S. Anglo (Woodbridge: The Boydell Press, 1990).

Munro, J. H., *Wool, Cloth and Gold: the Struggle for Bullion in Anglo-Burgundian Trade* (Toronto: University of Toronto Press, 1972).

Myers, A. R., *The Household of Edward IV* (Manchester: Manchester University Press, 1959).

Nicolson, J. and Burn, R., *The Histories and Antiquities of the Counties of Westmorland and Cumberland* (1777).

Oman, C. W. C., *Warwick the Kingmaker* (London, New York: Macmillan, 1891).

The Oxford Dictionary of National Biography: From the earliest times to the year 2000, eds H. C. G. Matthew and B. Harrison, 61 vols (Oxford: Oxford University Press, 2004)

The Parliament Rolls of Medieval England, ed. C. Given-Wilson, 16 vols (Woodbridge: The Boydell Press, 2005).

The Paston Letters, ed. J. Gairdner, 6 vols (Chatto & Windus, 1904).

Payling, S. J., 'The Ampthill Dispute', *EHR*, civ (1989).

Payne, A., 'The Beauchamps and the Nevilles', in R. Marks and P. Williamson, eds, *Gothic: Art for England, 1400–1547* (V & A Publications, 2003).

The Plumpton Correspondence, ed. T. Stapleton (Camden, old series, iv, 1839).

Political Poems and Songs relating to English History, ed. T. Wright, 2 vols (RS, 1861).

The Politics of Fifteenth Century England: John Vale's Book, eds. M. L. Kekewich and others (Stroud: Sutton for the Richard III and Yorkist History Trust, 1995).

Pollard, A. J., 'The Northern Retainers of Richard Neville, earl of Salisbury', *Northern History*, xi (1976 for 1975).

Pollard, A. J., 'Lord FitzHugh's Rising in 1470', *BIHR*, lii (1979).

Pollard, A. J., 'Richard Clervaux of Croft: A North Riding Squire during the Fifteenth Century', *Yorkshire Archaeological Journal*, l (1978).

Pollard, A. J., 'The North-Eastern Economy and the Agrarian Crisis of 1438–1440', *Northern History*, xxv (1989).

Pollard, A. J., *North-Eastern England during the Wars of the Roses: Lay Society, War and Politics, 1450–1500* (Oxford: Clarendon Press, 1990).

Pollard, A. J., 'The Crown and the County Palatine of Durham, 1437–94', in A. J. Pollard, ed., *The North of England in the Age of Richard III* (Stroud: Sutton Publishing, 1996).

Pollard, A. J., *Late Medieval England, 1399–1509* (Harlow: Longman, 2000).

Pollard, A. J., 'Richard III, Henry VII and Richmond', in *idem, The Worlds of Richard III* (Stroud: Tempus, 2001).

Pollard, A. J., 'The Richmondshire Community of Gentry during the Wars of the Roses', in C. D. Ross, ed., *Patronage, Pedigree and Power* (Gloucester, 1979), pp. 37–59, repr. in *idem, The Worlds of Richard III* (Stroud: Tempus, 2002).

Pollard, A. J. 'Late Feudalism in England: the Case of Richmondshire', in *Courtiers and Warriors: Comparative Historical Perspectives on Ruling Authority and Civilization* (Kyoto: International Research Center for Japanese Studies, 2003).

Pollard, A. J., *Imagining Robin Hood: the Late-Medieval Stories in Historical Context* (Routledge, 2004).

Pollard, A. J., *John Talbot and the War in France, 1427–1453* (Royal Historical Society, 1983 and Pen and Sword Military, Barnsley, 2005).

Prendergast, T. A., 'The Invisible Spouse: Henry VI, Arthur and the Fifteenth-century Subject', *Journal of Medieval and early Modern Studies*, xxxii.2 (2002).

'Private Indentures for Life Service and War, 1278–1476', ed. Michael Jones and Simon Walker, *Camden Miscellany xxxii* (Camden 5th series, 3 (1994).

Pugh, T. B., *The Marcher Lordships of South Wales, 1415–1536* (Cardiff: University of Wales Press, 1963), pp. 145–83.

Pugh, T. B., *Glamorgan County History, iii, The Middle Ages* (Cardiff: University of Wales, 1971).

Pugh, T. B., 'The Estates, Finances and Regal Aspirations of Richard Plantagenet (1411–1460), Duke of York', in M. A. Hicks, ed., *Revolution and Consumption in Late Medieval England* (Woodbridge: The Boydell Press, 2001).

Radulescu, R. L., *The Gentry Context for Malory's Morte Darthur* (Cambridge: D. S. Brewer, 2003).

Ragg, F. W., 'Helton, Flecham, Askham and Sandford of Askham', *TCWAAS*, xxi (1921).

Rainey, J. R., 'The Defense of Calais' (Rutgers University PhD thesis, 1987).

Rapin de Thoyras, P. de, *The History of England*, trans. N. Tindal, 3rd edn (1743).

Rawclife, C. A., *The Staffords, Earls of Stafford and Dukes of Buckingham, 1394–1521* (Cambridge: Cambridge University Press, 1978).

Richmond, C. F., 'Fauconberg's Rising of May 1471', *EHR*, xxxv (1970).

Richmond, C. F., 'The Earl of Warwick's Dominance of Channel and the Naval Dimensions to the Wars of the Roses, 1456–1460', *Southern History*; xx/xxi (1987–9).

Richmond, C. F., *The Paston Family in the Fifteenth Century: The First Phase* (Cambridge: Cambridge University Press, 1990).

Richmond, C. F., 'The Murder of Thomas Dennis', *Common Knowledge*, 2 (1993).

Richmond, C. F., *The Paston Family in the Fifteenth Century: Endings* (Manchester: Manchester University Press, 2000).

Rodger, N. A. M, *The Safeguard of the Sea: a Naval History of Britain, Vol. 1, 660–1649* (Harper Collins, 1997).

Roskell, J. S., 'Sir James Strangeways of West Harlsey and Whorlton', *Yorkshire Archaeological Journal*, xxxiv (1958).

Roskell, J. S., *et al.*, *The History of Parliament: The House of Commons, 1386–1421*, 4 vols (Stroud: Sutton Publishing, 1992).

Ross, C. D., *The Estates and Finances of Richard Beauchamp, Earl of Warwick* (Dugdale Society Occasional Papers, xii (1956).

Ross, C. D., 'Warwick the King-maker', in *History of the English Speaking Peoples: the Wars of the Roses* (Purnell Partworks: BBC Publishing, 1969).

Ross, C. D., *Edward IV* (Eyre Methuen, 1974).

The Rous Roll, ed. W. H. Coulthorpe (1859, reissue Gloucester, 1980).

Scofield, C. L., *The Life and Reign of Edward the Fourth*, vol. 1(1924).

Select Documents of English Constitutional History, 1307–1485, eds S. B. Chrimes and A. L. Brown (A & C Black, 1961).

Shagan, E. H., *Popular Politics and the English Reformation* (Cambridge: Cambridge University Press, 2003).

Shakespeare, W., *Henry VI, Parts Two and Three*.

Sinclair, A. F. J., 'The Beauchamp Earls of Warwick in the Later Middle Ages' (University of London PhD thesis, 1986).

Six Town Chronicle of England, ed. R. Flenley (Oxford: Clarendon Press, 1911).

Sterchi, B., 'Hugues de Lannoy, auteur de Lenseignement de Vraie Noblesse', *Le Moyen Age*, cx (2004).

Storey, R. L., 'The Wardens of the Marches towards Scotland, 1377–1489', *EHR*, lxxii (1957).

Storey, R. L., *The End of the House of Lancaster* (Barrie & Rockliffe, 1966).

Stubbs, W., *The Constitutional History of England*, 5th edn, 3 vols (Oxford: Clarendon Press, 1897).

Summerson, H., *Medieval Carlisle: the City and the Borders from the Late Eleventh Century to the Mid Sixteenth Century* (Cumberland and Westmorland Antiquarian and Archaeological Society, Extra Series xxv, 1993).

Sutton, A. F. and L. Visser Fuchs, 'A Most Benevolent Queen?', *The Ricardian*, 129 (1965).

Sutton, A. F., 'Sir Thomas Cook and his "Troubles": an Investigation', *Guildhall Studies in London History*, iii (1968).

Sutton, A. F., 'Malory in Newgate: a New Document', *The Library*, vii (2000).

Sutton, A. F., *The Mercery of London: Trade, Goods and People, 1130–1578* (Aldershot: Ashgate Publishing, 2005).

Thornton, T., 'The English King's French Islands: Jersey and Guernsey in English Politics and Administration, 1485–1642', in *Authority and Consent in Tudor England*, eds G. W. Bernard and S. J. Gunn (Aldershot: Ashgate Publishing, 2002).

Three Fifteenth Century Chronicles, ed. J. R. Gairdner (Camden Soc, 3rd series, xxviii, 1880).

Valente, C., *The Theory and Practice of Revolt in Medieval England* (Aldershot: Ashgate Publishing, 2003).

Vergil, P., *Three Books of Polydore Vergil's English History*, ed. H. Ellis (Camden Society, 1844).

Visser-Fuchs, L, 'Edward IV's *Memoir on Paper* to Charles, Duke of Burgundy: The So-called "Short Version of The Arrivall"', *Nottingham Medieval Studies*, xxxvi (1992).

Visser-Fuchs, L. '"Warwick by Himself": Richard Neville, earl of Warwick, "the Kingmaker", in the *Recueil des Croniques D'Engleterre* of Jean de Waurin', *Publication du Centre Européen d'études Bourguignonnes* (*XIVe–XVIes.*, 41) (2001).

Visser-Fuchs, L, 'Warwick and Waurin: two case studies on the literary background and propaganda of Anglo-Burgundian Relations in the Yorkist Period' (University of London PhD thesis, 2002).

Visser-Fuchs, L., 'Jean de Waurin and the English Newsletters: the *Chronicle of the Rebellion in Lincolnshire*', *Nottingham Medieval Studies*, xlvii (2003).

Walker, S. J., *The Lancastrian Affinity, 1361–1399* (Oxford: Oxford University Press, 1990).

Watts, J. L., *Henry VI and the Politics of Kingship* (Cambridge: Cambridge University Press, 1966)

Watts, J. L., 'Ideas, Principles and Politics', in A. J. Pollard, ed, *The Wars of the Roses* (Basingstoke: Macmillan, 1995).

Watts, J. L., '"A New Ffundacion of is Crowne": Monarchy in the Age of Henry VII', in Benjamin Thompson, ed. *The Reign of Henry VII* (Stamford: Paul Watkins, 1995).

Watts, J. L., 'The Pressure of the Public on Later Medieval Politics', in *The Fifteenth Century IV: Political Culture in Late-Medieval Britain*, eds L. S. Clark and C. M. Carpenter (Woodbridge: The Boydell Press, 2004).

Waurin, J. de, *Anchiennes Cronicqes d'Engleterre*, ed. E. Dupont (Société de l'Histoire de France, Paris, 1858–63).

Waurin, J. de, *Recueil des Croniques et Anchiennes Istories de la Grant Bretaigne*, ed. W. Hardy, 5 vols (RS, 1864–91).

Wedgwood, J. C., *History of Parliament: Biographies of the Members of the Common House, 1439–1509* (1936).

Whethamstede, J., *Registrum*, ed. H. T. Riley. 2 vols (RS, 1872–3).

Whitaker, T. D. *An History of Richmondshire*, 2 vols (1823).

Wolffe, B. P., *Henry VI* (Eyre Methuen, 1981).

Woolgar, C.M., *The Great Household in Late Medieval England* (New Haven: Yale University Press, 1999).

Woolgar, C. M., 'Fast and Feast: Conspicuous Consumption and the Diet of the Nobility in the Fifteenth Century', in M. A. Hicks, ed., *Revolution and Consumption in Late-medieval England* (Woodbridge: The Boydell Press, 2001).

Wrottesley, G., 'A History of the Family of Wrottesley: Sir Walter Wrottesley, 1464–1473' *Collections for a History of Staffordshire*, vi.ii (1903).

Index

Lightning Source UK Ltd.
Milton Keynes UK
UKHW022318220123
415804UK00004B/66

9 781847 251824